LONELY PLANET'S

1000

ULTIMATE
ADVENTURES

FROM THE WORLD'S LEADING TRAVEL AUTHORITY

CONTENTS

10 ICONS OF TRAVEL

14 BEST SPOTS TO CATCH A BIG WAVE

18 ULTIMATE DESERT DARES

22 MOUNTAIN QUESTS

26 BEST STEEP, DEEP BACK-COUNTRY SKIING

30 WILDEST FLIGHTS

32 GREATEST AIRBORNE ADVENTURES

36 MOST ELECTRIFYING TRIBAL ENCOUNTERS

40 MOST DANGEROUS PLACES TO TRAVEL

42 COLDEST ADVENTURES

46 SCARIEST ANIMAL ENCOUNTERS

50 MOST SPECTACULAR ROCK CLIMBS

54 MOST STELLAR STAR-LIT ADVENTURES

56 MOST THRILLING CANYONING ADVENTURES

60 MOST EXCELLENT EQUINE ESCAPADES

64 ICONIC ASIAN ADVENTURES

68 GOTTA BE IN IT TO WIN IT: BEST RACES

70 BEST TREKS WITH KILLER VIEWS

74 ROCK STARS: WORLD'S BEST BOULDERING

78 BEST OFF-SEASON ADVENTURES

82 MOST SPIRITED HIKING & BIKING

84 HOTTEST VOLCANIC VENTURES

88 FOR PROS ONLY – THE MOST DANGEROUS ADVENTURES

92 BEST HIDDEN HUTS AND SHELTERS

94 ICONIC AMERICAS ADVENTURES

98 ULTIMATE TRAIN RIDES

102 RETRO ACTIVE: OLD-SCHOOL ADVENTURES

104 WILDEST SWIMS IN THE WORLD

108 CRAZIEST CAVES

112 MIND-BLOWING MARATHONS

114 MOST ACTION-PACKED JUNGLES

118 DOWNHILL DASHES

122 BEST ADVENTURE FESTIVALS

124 EPIC RIDES

128 BEST URBAN CLIMBING ADVENTURES

132 HAIR-RAISING ROAD TRIPS

136 SECOND-HIGHEST (NOT SECOND BEST)

138 MOUNTAIN BIKING'S MECCAS

142 GOING TO EXTREMES

146 MONKEY MAGIC: BEST ADVENTURES IN TREES

150 WILD AT HEART: BEST ANIMAL ADVENTURES

152 EPIC SEA-KAYAK PADDLES

156 EYE-CATCHING ATMOSPHERIC EXTRAVAGANZAS

160 BEST CITY HIKES

164 ENDANGERED ENCOUNTERS

166 SAIL OR BUST

170 BEST FOUR-LEGGED ADVENTURES

174 TALL ORDERS! – BEST TOWER-RUNNING RACES

176 CLASSIC RIDES FOR CASUAL CYCLISTS

180 ULTIMATE MOTORBIKE ADVENTURES

184 BEST ADVENTURE FILMS

186 TOP 10 ADVENTURE NATIONS

190 GET ON BOARD!

194 INTREPID TREASURE-HUNTING TRIPS

198 BEST POOCH PURSUITS

200 ICONIC EUROPEAN ADVENTURES

204 BEST WAYS TO BLOW THE KIDS' INHERITANCE

208 BEST ULTRA RUNS

210 ULTIMATE PILGRIMAGES

214 WORLD'S HIGHEST TREKS

218 FAMOUS FOOTSTEPS

220 ZIP IT UP: GREATEST ZIP-LINE EXPERIENCES

224 ICONIC MIDDLE EAST ADVENTURES

228 THE PLANET'S FREAKIEST FOOTRACES

230 TRULY WILD WATERWAYS

234 FAMOUSLY ADVENTUROUS DESTINATIONS

238 GIRLS-ONLY ADVENTURES

240 BEST RAFTING RIVERS

244 MOST MAGNIFICENT COAST-TO-COAST MISSIONS

248 ULTIMATE BORDER CROSSINGS

250 LONGEST TREKS

254 BEST POWDER IN THE WORLD

258 ESSENTIAL AFRICAN ADVENTURES

262 MOST EXCITING MODERN ADVENTURERS

264 BEST BIRDING IN HIGHLANDS AND ISLANDS

268 BEST MARINE ENCOUNTERS

272 SENSATIONAL SNOWSHOE ESCAPADES

274 SPORTIVES FOR SERIOUS CYCLISTS

278 BEST UNDISCOVERED US PARKS

282 BEST ADVENTURES IN THE BUFF

284 SWEETEST SNORKEL SPOTS

288 BEST HUT-TO-HUT TOURS

292 ADVENTURE INSTITUTIONS

294 MOST VERTIGINOUS VENTURES

298 BEST 'PHOENIX' DESTINATIONS

302 TOP ADVENTURE SKILLS

304 BEST BEGINNERS' CLIMBS

308 GET YOUR THRILLS INDOORS

312 ROUSING READS FOR ARMCHAIR ADVENTURERS

314 THE TWO OF US: ADVENTURES IN TANDEM

318 GREAT MOUNTAIN CYCLES

322 BOY'S (AND GIRL'S) OWN ADVENTURES

324 LEGENDARY ODYSSEYS

328 BEST SURF BREAKS FOR BEGINNERS

332 CLASSIC SOLO SORTIES

334 FAMILY-FRIENDLY ADVENTURES

338 TOP DIVING ADVENTURES

342 IN THE FOOTSTEPS OF FILM HEROES

344 MOST SPECTACULAR HONEYMOON ADVENTURES

348 ADVENTURE OFF THE PAGE

350 INDEX

FOREWORD

I sweat in the silence. All around me the sands stretch far away. Nothing moves. The crisp curves and shadows of the dunes cut up into the cloudless sky. There is no sign of life, no sign that anyone has ever been here before.

Despite the heat, despite the struggle, I smile. Perhaps I smile *because* of these things? Because adventures are not supposed to be easy, are they?

I'm walking across the Arabian Peninsula's Empty Quarter desert (p21) – the Rub' al Khali – and the responsibility for my progress and safety is entirely in my hands. It is an exhilarating feeling. But I am not the first person here. My quest is to retrace the great journeys Wilfred Thesiger made here seventy years ago.

Reflecting the very different worlds that Thesiger and I pursue our adventures in, the end of my trek will be the peak of Dubai's Burj Khalifa, currently the world's tallest building. Thesiger would have been horrified. But there's no point living in the past. The world has changed enormously since Thesiger set out across these plains. But the thrill of discovering new places remains. I love going to places I've never been, and seeing glorious sights that I first read about in books such as this one.

We live in fortunate times. The world is more accessible than ever before. These days we have opportunities not only to be armchair adventurers, dipping into the delicious photographs and ideas in this book, but to commit to an adventure of our own. We have the chance to attempt an adventure large or small, and to discover ourselves capable of more than we realised. This book is a brilliant stepping stone to our own adventures either epic or local.

I first began plotting my adventures through stories of the great explorers. They inspired me to dream big. I've been to the beach where Captain Cook was killed and I've followed Marco Polo across the Taklamakan desert (p326). But Burke and Wills' pioneering trek reminds me of a glaring omission on my own travelling CV: I have never adventured in Australia. The world is so big that I will never reach the bottom of my wish list. There's so much to do, as this book makes deliciously plain. All the more reason to get dreaming and planning, and get out there!

My first adventure was cycling the stunning high-altitude Karakoram Highway (p318) from Pakistan to China. I'd been planning on cycling in Tuscany when a friend cajoled me into thinking bigger. Not only was the ride cheaper and more epic than Italy, it was also a catalyst. I was addicted. I haven't looked back.

Don't make the mistake of reading this book without also making the adventures of your choice actually happen. Flicking through these pages I have noted several adventures that fired my imagination, mountain biking the San Juan huts (p291) and paddling the Queen Charlotte Islands (p153) being just two. I'm sure you will do the same. There's a wonderful world out there and this book is a fantastic appetiser. Let's go!

Alastair Humphreys
Scotland, April 2013

The Empty Quarter, a seemingly endless expanse of wind-sculpted dunes – and limitless adventure

ULTIMATE ITINERARIES

ANIMAL ENCOUNTERS

They may not be kings of the jungle, but spying a tiger from the back of an elephant counts as a majestic experience. **p164**

Great white sharks are best viewed from a steel cage in the waters off Port Lincoln, South Australia. **p47**

Sea turtles can live to a ripe old age. Be a witness to their hatching in the Padre Ramos Estuary, Nicaragua. **p54**

It's a dog's life, so why not come along for the ride, racing over an Alaskan glacier on a dog-sled tour. **p172**

How better to experience the vastness of the Mongolian steppes than as Genghis Khan and his horde did: on horseback. **p62**

ARCHETYPAL AFRICA

Zanzibar, mixing spice plantations, pristine beaches and Swahili culture, hovers like an African jewel in the Indian Ocean. **p236**

The rolling dunes of Namibia are perfect slopes for sandboarding... and soft when you crash. **p19**

An epic bike journey from Cape Town to Cairo puts you in touch with the sights, sounds and scents of this mighty continent. **p10**

Migration on an epic scale: 1.5 million wildebeest and zebra move through the Maasai Mara every year. **p260**

In Ghana's Kakum National Park guides lead night safaris through pristine African tropic rainforest. **p55**

MOUNTAIN HIGHS

The W Trek across the Torres del Paine National Park in Chilean Patagonia wows with luminescent glacial lakes and awe-inspiring granite peaks. **p73**

Setting out in Scotland to conquer the Munros take a certain amount of pluck – there are 282 of them, all at above 900m. **p23**

Come at the world's highest mountain, floating face first. You don't necessarily need to climb it, you can skydive over Everest instead. **p296**

Experience the world's most active volcano at close quarters. Lava flows so slowly down Kilauea, in Hawaii's Volcanoes National Park, that it's safe to watch. **p86**

Glacier-topped Mt Kilimanjaro rises majestically out of Tanzania's sun-bleached savannah. It's the highest peak in Africa and siren's call to serious trekkers. **p215**

NO-SWEAT ADVENTURES

After travelling all the way to Iceland, the warm waters of the Blue Lagoon, near Reykjavík, make for a relaxing and rejuvenating dip. **p345**

Glide like a swan or get your groove on along the boardwalk of Venice Beach, California, the self-proclaimed 'roller-skate capital of the world'. **p102**

Start your day by floating silently over other-worldly landscapes and villages of Cappadocia, Turkey, in a hot-air balloon flight. **p32**

Skimming across the Indian Ocean with dolphins swimming in your wake, a schooner trip between the islands of the Seychelles is an idyll come true. **p168**

Cycling in tandem as part of a bike and barge tour of Amsterdam is the ultimate team-building experience. **p315**

ACTIVE AMERICAS

In the vastness of Big Bend, Texas, you can raft down the Rio Grande, or hike or horse-ride into the Chisos Mountains. **p280**

Sentinel over Rio de Janeiro, Mt Sugarloaf offers a climbing challenge that is only rivalled by the views of Guanbara Bay. **p128**

Linking Newfoundland with Vancouver Island, the mighty Trans Canada Trail is the world's longest network of walking trails. **p252**

Dashing horsemen, gauchos are the perfect guides to lead you on a horse trek exploring the rugged mountains and lakes of Chilean Patagonia. **p171**

The sandstone outcrops around Moab, Utah, have a reputation for world-class mountain-bike routes. Come here for pedal-powered thrills and spills. **p96**

INTREPID ANTIPODES

The Blue Mountains are full of geological oddities – waterfalls, gullies, crevices – that can be explored full tilt on a canyoning trip. **p56**

Emerging from the Victorian countryside like a craggy fortress, Mt Arapiles is one of Australia's best rock climbs for beginners . **p306**

The Milford Track is New Zealand's most famous tramping (hiking) route, a four-day odyssey through awesome terrain. **p285**

Surfers and wandering souls make the journey to Byron Bay, in northern New South Wales, for consistent, and consistently great, surf breaks. **p328**

Running 150km near the southern tip of New Zealand, the Central Otago Rail Trail offers spectacular autumn scenery every April. **p176**

VENTURES BY FOOT

Competitors in the Antarctic Ice Marathon take on sub-zero temperatures and freezing winds, but are rewarded by crossing through pristine wilderness. **p113**

A 4300km journey across rugged mountain ranges, the Pacific Crest Trail crosses three US states and seven national parks. **p252**

Pine trees scent the air along the Greenways web of walking trails in the Czech Republic, and at every wayside village pubs serve up home-brewed beers! **p82**

Traversing Spitsbergen from the Barents to the Greenland sea means spending each star-spangled night in a mountain tent on the ice. **p247**

The Camino de Santiago, converging on the reputed remains of St James in Galicia, must be contemporary Christianity's most famous, and popular, modern pilgrimage. **p211**

EXHILARATING EUROPE

With more than 1200 islands in the opalescent Adriatic Sea, Croatia offers idylls and challenges aplenty for sea kayakers. **p153**

Follow in the footsteps of the first great literary traveller, Odysseus, around the ports, bays and islands of the Mediterranean. **p324**

Every morning for a week in June, crowds run frantically down cobbled streets in Pamplona pursued by bulls. What could be more fun than that? **p202**

Cast your gaze skyward in Tromsø, Norway, at the Northern Lights. According to legend, it's the reflected glow of the mythic Valkyries' armour. **p158**

The West Highland Way across Scotland traverses diverse and breathtaking scenery, from desolate moor to mirror-like Loch Lomond. **p70**

AQUATIC ESCAPADES

Floating on your back is never so exciting as it is in the Devil's Pool, on the edge of Victoria Falls. **p107**

Drift languidly amid 10 million jellyfish as the follow the sun as it passes overhead atOngeim'l Tketau, Palau's jellyfish lake. **p271**

Swimming with giant rays in the translucent waters of the Cayman islands is an electrifying experience. **p339**

After plunging over Victoria Falls, the Zambezi River rushes through basalt-lined Batoka Gorge bringing rafters along for the ride. **p241**

Whale sharks, the gentle giants of the sea at up to 10m long, drift through sun-dappled waters in Ningaloo Marine Park in Western Australia. **p269**

AWESOME ASIA

Sprinkled across the lush highlands of northern Vietnam, the villages of the hill tribes feature colourful market days. **p37**

The Annapurna Circuit takes in breathtaking highs and the Kali Gandaki, the deepest gorge in the world. **p318**

China's Great Wall stretches over 8000km, with hikeable sections passing through Hebei Province near Beijing. **p65**

The world's highest motorable road, the Leh–Manali Highway, linking Ladakh with Himachal Pradesh, has an average elevation of over 4000m. **p135**

Get a bird's eye – or monkey's eye – view of the rainforest around Chiang Mai on 5km of zip-lines at Flight of the Gibbons. **p221**

ULTIMATE ITINERARIES

ICONS OF TRAVEL

Think you've got the nerve? Then try one of these beauties – simply the world's ultimate kick-arse adventures.

003 AROUND AUSTRALIA BY COMBIVAN

This isn't a mere holiday, it's practically a rite of passage – the modern-day equivalent of an ancient odyssey. Something about the scale and scope of Australia entices travellers to stock-up their eskies (coolers) and hit the road in classic campervans. Whether you head north from Sydney, west from Adelaide or do a circuit of the whole darn mainland (around 16,000km, in case you're wondering), there are certain givens: you'll have a near-miss with a wallaby, you'll panic about petrol in the back of beyond, you'll develop an obsession with kitsch roadside Big Things, and you'll have the absolute time of your life.

Be prepared: carry spare tyres, plenty of food and water, and a charged phone/ satellite phone. Avoid driving at night.

001 TRACE THE SILK ROAD THROUGH CENTRAL ASIA

There's no sign that says 'Silk Road'; no definitive map or Marco Polo-voiced sat-nav telling you to turn left at the next caravanserai. No, these are the Silk *Roads*, a spidery network of ancient trade routes connecting Mediterranean to Orient in myriad ways across Asia. Start in Istanbul and choose your own path east. Stalwart Silk sites include Uzbekistan's great cities, Kashgar's Sunday market, Pakistan's Karakoram Highway and innumerable offbeat 'Stans spots. Some links of the web – such as those in Iraq and Afghanistan – are best avoided, but no problem, simply take a different strand for an alternative adventure.

Travel west–east: many western Silk Road countries (eg Iran, Turkmenistan) issue visas for specific entry dates so are best visited first.

002 NAVIGATE THE AMAZON, SOUTH AMERICA

'If it wasn't life-threatening, it would be hilarious.' So quipped Ed Stafford who in 2010 became the first person to walk the length of the Amazon – it took him 860 days to cover 6400km from the river's source in the Peruvian Andes to its outpouring into the Atlantic in Brazil. Life-threatening indeed: this gargantuan river, snaking through the world's biggest rainforest, is an intimidating place where snakes, bugs, diseases and potentially unfriendly locals lurk. But it's also where you'll find incalculable biodiversity, fascinating tribes and true Indiana Jones adventure. Simply hop on a boat (ferry, cruiser, dug-out canoe) to speed things up.

Few major towns on the Amazon are accessible by road – travel is by plane or boat. Manaus, Iquitos and Belém are key hubs.

004 CYCLE CAIRO TO CAPE TOWN, AFRICA

Top-to-toeing Africa by truck is an epic undertaking, taking in searing deserts, sweaty jungle and savannah marauded by really big creatures. Now consider doing it by bicycle...12,000km of pedalling, open to the elements and at the mercy of potholed roads, nonexistent roads and roads where elephants have right of way. But while such exposure can make you vulnerable, it also makes you involved; there's no annoying barrier separating you from the people, sights, sounds and smells of the continent so you can really get in amongst it all. Travelling widely, slowly and intensely, this is the way to soak up the real Africa.

The Tour d'Afrique (http://tourdafrique. com) is a supported Cairo–Cape Town cycle; the full journey takes around four months and costs from US$14,000.

UPPA/PHOTOSHOT ©

Reaching Antarctica is adventure enough for some, but how about journeying to the Pole on skis?

005 SKI TO THE SOUTH POLE, ANTARCTICA

Journeying to the mere edges of Antarctica is a bucket-list-ticker. Standing at the Geographic South Pole itself – inaccessibly nestled in the White Continent's forbidding interior – is one even better. But to reach the pole under your own steam – that's a whole different Scott-and-Amundsen-like, icicles-in-the-beard, name-on-a-plaque-somewhere endeavour. Thankfully it's a little easier now, a century after those early pioneers. Today, you can fly by ski plane to 89°S and glide the final 110km to your goal. Or take the longer route: start from Hercules Inlet, at the continent's edge, from where that cheery polar marker is a gruelling 1170km away.

Adventure Network International's 'Ski Last Degree' trip involves five days of skiing to the pole; Hercules Inlet takes 60 days. See www.adventure-network.com.

11

Climbing Mt Everest: enjoy the views from on top of the world – literally

006 DIVE TO THE BOTTOM OF THE SEA

Thousands of climbers have stood atop Mt Everest, the planet's highest extreme. But as of 2012 only three have plunged to its lowest point, Challenger Deep in the Pacific's Mariana Trench. Down here, 320km southwest of Guam and 11km below the surface, life is bleak, black, cold and heavy. Access is via highly specialised submersible and expensive scientific mission.

More expeditions are planned, but perhaps more realistic is a dunk to the *Titanic*, which rests at 3720m beneath the North Atlantic – a few commercial (and costly) trips have taken ordinary travellers down to see the 'unsinkable' at eerily close quarters.

Future dives to the *Titanic*, including two to three hours in the sea bed, are to be confirmed; to follow the progress of the Mariana Trench expedition, see http://deepseachallenge.com.

007 CONTEMPLATE THE IDITAROD, ALASKA, USA

Born of prospector spirit and dying traditions, the Iditarod is known as the Last Great Race. First held in 1973 to help promote Alaska's husky-sledding heritage (and to give the finger to newfangled snowmobiles), this monumental mush from Anchorage to Nome follows the route first taken by gold-rush pioneers. Today it's a 1600km quest of unbelievable harshness.

CHRISTIAN KOBER/AWL IMAGES ©

008 CLIMB MOUNT EVEREST, NEPAL

Well, it's there, right? George Mallory's fabled excuse for tackling the world's highest peak still holds for the ever-growing number of climbers drawn to it each year. Though no other peak can best Everest's 8850m, and despite its treacherous ice fields and sizeable 'death zone' (the realm above 8000m, where the body essentially starts to die), this isn't the hardest summit to master. Obviously it is really, *really* hard, and it's really, *really* expensive (around US$50,000), but with cash, dedication and an awful lot of training, you could actually stand on top of the world.

Everest expeditions start from Lukla (reached via plane from Kathmandu) and take around 70 days. Peak climbing season is March to May.

009 SAIL AROUND THE WORLD

Sailing around the globe like a latter-day Captain Cook or Ferdinand Magellan – though ideally without being bumped off by hostile natives – is one of the most evocative of travel challenges. You can go anywhere and everywhere, guided by the whim of the wind and perhaps safety advice on avoiding pirates...you don't even need a boat. While billionaires might mooch round on their own luxury yachts, there are options for even the most penniless of seafarers – get a sailing qualification and simply sign up to crew on a circumnavigating vessel, then it's Tahiti/the Caribbean/Cape Horn here you come.

Organisations such as Crewseekers match volunteer and experienced sailors with a range of boats looking for crew members; visit www.crewseekers.net.

010 TRAVEL UK TO AUSTRALIA OVERLAND

It's about 17,000km from London to Sydney. In between lie the world's highest mountains, fractious frontiers, tricksy borders, bad roads, good roads and a slither of sea. There's also half a world of humanity, cooped up in buzzing metropolises and sprinkled across the landscape. So it seems a shame to hop on a plane and fly over it all in a day. Take at least six months: you could join an overland tour or seize a heap of maps and the challenge of planning an independent demi-circumnavigation.

Visa regulations vary by country: some need to be arranged before departure, some at borders – check ahead.

Mushers guide their dogs across unforgiving tundra, up mountain passes, and through blizzards and -70°C climes. Leave it to the experts and watch from the sidelines; catch the Ceremonial Start in Anchorage, the Restart in Wasilla (65km north) or rent a snowmobile and try to keep up.

The race (http://iditarod.com) starts in Anchorage on the first Saturday in March; it usually takes competitors nine to 15 days to complete.

ICONS OF TRAVEL

BEST SPOTS TO CATCH A BIG WAVE

Surf the largest and most thrilling breaks in the world for the rush of a lifetime.

Jaws, a thundering wall of water, makes like its namesakes and swallows plenty of wave riders

011 TEAHUPO'O, TAHITI

Catch one of these glassy aqua barrels and successfully shoot out the end without encountering any of the razor-sharp reef in the shallow waters below, and you may find yourself on the cover of a surfing magazine. This is known as the 'heaviest wave in the world' for the massive volume of water that curls over into a thick and perfect barrel, time and time again. Laird Hamilton brought additional fame to the spot when his spectacular wave ride here in August 2000 was captured on video. When you reach the reef, you'll see why even master Hamilton may have been shaking on his board before that ride. Conquer Teahupo'o at your own risk.

The break is reached from 'the end of the road', a literal description of the access point from the village.

012 DUNGEONS, HOUT BAY, SOUTH AFRICA

This ferocious wave near Cape Town has a long-held reputation as a place for wild rides. The Red Bull Big Wave Africa event, held every year in July or August depending on the swell, has helped ramp up Dungeons' notoriety around the globe. As a noncompetitor, you'll enjoy the thrill of dropping into a spectacularly choppy and challenging wave, although multiple reefs and the wide range of weather will ultimately define just what happens for you here. Don't forget your wetsuit; these waves are chilly. Oh yeah, and the sharks like this reef too, but mostly for the fat seals that inhabit the waters.

Fly into Cape Town, rent a car to get to Hout Bay, then catch a boat out of the Hout Bay harbour.

013 PUERTO ESCONDIDO, OAXACA, MEXICO

Join the crowds of surfers who gather in this Mexican paradise to worship one of the best beach breaks in the world. With reliable winds that blow offshore every morning and evening, you can eat fish tacos and take a siesta without missing the deepest tubes, which rip down the bar and thunder as they meet the shore. The waves can be fast and unforgiving, but, hey, the water's warm, and the town is a welcoming and inexpensive hang-out in between sets.

The rainy season, typically lasting from May to October, offers the biggest waves along the entire stretch of beach.

DAVID PU'U/CORBIS ©

014 JAWS, MAUI, HAWAII, USA

While some people flock to Maui for the lei and luau, you've arrived for the ultimate adrenaline rush. Considered by big-wave hunters to be an unparalleled break, Jaws is a thundering deep-water reef break that has become a hot spot for tow-in surfers. On its best days, Jaws is as fast and powerful as it is tall – surfers have been known to navigate a few 18m-plus faces and live to tell the tale. The biggest waves happen between December and February, the season when Australian Mark Visser successfully rode Jaws on one pitch-black night in 2011.

To get a taste of the break without getting wet, park at the top of the Peahi cliffs and join throngs of spectators oohing and ahhing over the best riders.

15

015 SHIPSTERN BLUFF, TASMANIA, AUSTRALIA

Once a well-kept secret known only to the Tasmanian surf community, this bluff, which meets the ocean at the bottom of 200m-high cliffs, has become a destination for the boldest and strongest big-wave riders. Conquer just one of these infamous barrels and join the ranks of a select few with the skills to survive a tremendous booming break. Not only will you paddle against a creeping chill from the bracing Tasmanian waters, you'll be keeping an eye open for great white sharks while navigating plenty of sharp rocks.

Although Shipstern is remote and can only be reached on foot or by boat, nearby Port Arthur is one of the region's most popular travel destinations.

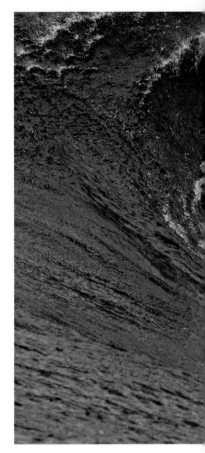

016 MULLAGHMORE HEAD, IRELAND

In-the-know surfers would never scoff at the Irish surf scene, which is epitomised by the roaring reef break on the edge of tiny village Mullaghmore. In late winter and early spring, the storm patterns produce the kind of 15m (49ft) faces you're lucky to ride and grateful to survive. High winds, choppy surfaces and blinding rain can present obstacles, but the heavy, long tubes make up for conditions. Besides, there's always a pint of Guinness waiting at the end of your day on the water.

Give your eyes a rest from eyeing the break by taking in the fairy-tale Classiebawn Castle, which dominates a nearby bluff.

017 BELHARRA, FRANCE

You may have as much chance of winning the lottery as you do of catching a big wave at Belharra, but it doesn't hurt to dream. This rocky reef break 2km (1.25 miles) off mainland Basque Country seethes with surf life just a few days a year, in winter, when swells from Atlantic storms smack into the shallow reef. And, voila, some of Europe's biggest waves are born. Arrive by boat or jet ski and be prepared to hold your own against some of Europe's most daring surfers, not to mention the international big-wave hunters out to catch this roaring beast.

For more mellow, mortal-friendly waves, try La Grande Plage in Biarritz.

018 NELSCOTT REEF, LINCOLN CITY, OREGON, USA

Laugh at whatever rains are pounding this stretch of Pacific Northwest coastline before catching a boat or jet ski to this spectacular break about 800m from shore. Yes, you could paddle out on your board, and many of the world's top big-wave riders have done just that, but you might want to save your energy for the swell, which can deliver some of the largest rideable waves on the planet. While the Oregon coast offers a range of great waves, Nelscott belongs to adrenalin seekers with something to prove.

Top annual surf comp the Nelscott Reef Big Wave Classic is called just 72 hours in advance, when waves are predicted to be at least 9m high.

019 NAZARÉ, PORTUGAL

You – yes, you – can conquer this break. Sure, pro surfer Garrett McNamara rode the largest

SEAN DAVEY/AURORA O/AGEFOTOSTOCK ©

A determined few brave the chilly waters, sharp rocks and occasional passing shark to barrel through Shipstern Bluff

wave in the world here, a terrifying 23m-tall wall of water that garnered him a Guinness World Record. But it's not every day this small fishing town sees those kind of waves, even with the deep underwater canyon that funnels massive quantities of water toward the shore at high speeds. On less epic days, the break at Nazaré is consistent and easy to reach, with nothing but soft sand underneath. Winter's the best time to visit if you crave the big stuff, but even during summer the crowds are small.

Want a refresher before hitting the surf? There are more than a dozen surf schools in Nazaré.

020 ISLA TODOS SANTOS, BAJA, MEXICO

Not to be confused with Todos Santos, the southern Baja tourist town, this Todos Santos doesn't offer surf school or margaritas on the beach. Instead, the craggy desert island, sitting about 19km (12 miles) offshore from Ensenada in northern Baja, boasts a notoriously big break called 'Killers', which builds power in underwater canyons before pounding the nearby reef. If the name doesn't make you contemplate your own mortality, Killers' occasional 15m faces may. Don't worry, you can always ramp it down by heading to one of the

island's smaller breaks, if your ego can handle riding a wave called 'Chickens.'

Catch a boat in the harbour of Ensenada, where fisherfolk are accustomed to charging surfers for a ride.

BEST SPOTS TO CATCH A BIG WAVE

ULTIMATE DESERT DARES

Grit your teeth, shield your eyes and get stuck into this decathlon of desert challenges.

021 BLOKART IN THE MOJAVE DESERT, USA

Dawn yawns over Nevada's Mojave Desert and the lurid glow from the Vegas strip fades to insignificance. Ivanpah Lake, a dusty expanse of pancake flatness 65km from Vegas, looks like a windswept wasteland but it's blokarting heaven. Blokarting involves piloting lightweight, wind-powered, three-wheeled vehicles, and you've come to race some of America's best landsailors. In 2009 Richard Jenkins set a world record here, clocking 202.9km per hour in his land yacht the *Greenbird*. You won't reach such speeds, but the wind is gusting and you're ready to set sail.

Regular regattas are held on Ivanpah Lake. See www.nabsa.org for more info.

022 HORSE TREK ACROSS THE GOBI, MONGOLIA

You'd thought you knew what to expect but the sheer diversity of the Gobi almost knocks you off your horse – the barren terrain is both harsh and beautiful. As you head from Ulaanbaatar out past the rock formations of Baga Zorgol Hairhan Uul and across the Arburd Sands,

you couldn't be happier with your choice of transport. This is where horse riding was born, the stunning steppes of Mongolia once home to the largest herds of horses the planet has ever seen. So how else would you travel across Genghis Khan's old stomping grounds?

Gobi horse treks are offered by several companies; time your visit to coincide with the ancient Naadam festival in July.

023 CANYONING IN THE JUDAEAN DESERT, ISRAEL

Recovering your breath after rappelling down a 100m cliff on the periphery of the Judaean Desert, you wonder how you'd never before heard of Canyon Qumran. You could have gone wet canyoning in the Golan Heights but a desert snapling adventure close to the spot where the Dead Sea Scrolls were discovered was too appealing. Those historic documents lay undisturbed for 2000 years, showing how little human visitation these caves and canyons receive, and therein lies the allure of this semi-subterranean adventure to the lowest place on

earth. Temperature commonly push close to 50°C – lucky the Dead Sea is nearby for a cooling plunge.

Trips can be arranged through Q-Terra (qterra.org). The best time to do activities in the Dead Sea area is October to April.

024 BATTLE THE BLACK SNAKE, AL AIN, ABU DHABI

Outside Al Ain's Green Mubazzarah you clip into your cleats, kick off from the curb and pedal your road bike toward the foothills of Jabal Hafeet, a 1249m-high abrupt interruption to the desert flatness that sprawls over the border of the UAE and Oman. This is the challenge for all visiting roadies: sprint up the 11.7km length of the Jebel Hafeet Mountain Road, around its 21 lung-busting corners and up every centimetre of its 1219m elevation, with an average gradient of eight percent. You've barely begun to climb, but the sweat is flowing and already you're looking forward to the rush of the descent.

Several races use the Jebel Hafeet Mountain Road, including a punishing annual duathlon (cycling and running).

OLIVIER RENCK/GETTY IMAGES ©

No need for a wetsuit while surfing the mighty sandy precipice of Cerro Blanco, but goggles wouldn't go astray

025 CLIMB A MOUNTAIN IN THE WORLD'S OLDEST DESERT, NAMIBIA

Day three of the expedition, and you're camped at Wasserfallflache on the flanks of the Brandberg Massif – Namibia's tallest mountain, close to the coast in the Namib Desert, the oldest on Earth. Yesterday was brutal, with seven hours of scrambling over boulders and up steep inclines, but today is summit day. Another push will bring the group to Königstein (King's Stone) 2573m above sea level. And on the way back down there's the chance to check out Snake Rock Cave, a famous San rock-art site.

The Brandberg Ascent is a guided five-day camping and hiking trip offered by operators out of Windhoek. Winter (April to September) is the best time to climb.

026 SANDBOARD CERRO BLANCO, PERU

Flying over the ancient enigma that is the Nazca Lines is a hard act to follow but this might just top everything else you've done in Peru's Sechura Desert. You're standing on the precipice of nearby Cerro Blanco, steeling your nerves and preparing to launch down its sandy flanks on a sandboard. At 1176m this sand dune in the valley of Las Trancas is the tallest on the planet and there's only one way to see it: through a speed-distorted blur, with your feet strapped to a board and your eyes behind a pair of goggles. This is snowboarding for the cold-adverse.

Cerro Blanco is about a 28km drive and three-hour climb from the city of Nazca. Sandboarding excursions can be arranged through various commercial operators.

19

Running an ultramarathon in the White Desert may conjure up mirages; miraculous scenery is guaranteed

027 RUN THE OCEAN FLOOR, EGYPT

Navigating your way through a surreal forest of wind-carved sand sculptures you wonder whether you're experiencing sleepmonsters – hallucinations suffered by extreme endurance athletes. Maybe you are, because that piece of bedrock over there looks just like a giant ice cream. This terrain was once underwater, but that was 200 million years ago and H_2O is in short supply in the Egypt's Western and White Deserts these days. Shame, since you're in the midst of a four-day, non-stop, 160-mile ultramarathon across this subsection of the Sahara and your mouth is drier than a camel's armpit. Only 60 miles left – got to find the checkpoint and all-important drop-bag soon...must beat that 96-hour cut-off...

The Ocean Floor Race (www.oceanfloorrace.com) is run in February.

028 CYCLE ACROSS THE SIMPSON, AUSTRALIA

You're already awake and fine-tuning your fat-tyred steed as dawn erupts over Purni Bore in outback South Australia. The heat won't arrive until later, but once it does you won't escape its ferocity until the burning ball tips over the horizon. You're about to embark on a 10-stage bike race through the Simpson Desert, a natural arena that's earned the diabolic moniker 'Satan's Velodrome'. The nickname signals a challenge to rough-riding cyclists who contest a brutal 570km course that includes sadistic sand dunes, mirage-producing salt lakes, colossal cattle stations (some the size of small European countries) and the endless puncture-producing rubble of the gibber plains.

The Simpson Dessert Challenge (www.desertchallenge.org) is an annual mountain-bike race held in late September/early October.

029 KITE SKIING IN ANTARCTICA

The corners of your expedition buddy's mouth curl into a grin as their kite catches the katabatic wind. Your kite billows into life too, and the reigns twitch impatiently in your gloved hands. You've broken camp and bundled up, you're clipped into your skis and ready to rock. Wind was once the mortal enemy of travellers to the planet's poles because its chill can send temperatures plunging to lethal levels of -70°C and below. It's now used by modern adventurers to propel themselves across the desert ice fields of Antarctica, the coldest, driest and windiest continent on the planet – an extreme sport in the world's most extreme place.

Though pricey, polar kite-skiing expeditions of various lengths can be arranged through specialist operators such as Weber Arctic (www.weberarctic.com).

030 CAMEL TREK THROUGH ARABIA'S EMPTY QUARTER

Discover your inner Wilfred Thesiger by climbing aboard a camel and exploring the agoraphobia-inducing Rub' al Khali (the Empty Quarter) – the world's largest sandy expanse – which occupies a fifth of the Arabian Peninsula and sprawls across parts of Saudi Arabia, Yemen, the UAE and Oman. This is the home of the Bedouin and over the coming days your Bedu guide will instruct you in the ways of the desert, revealing how his people have survived for millennia in this harshest of environments. At night, once the campfire has dulled to a glow, the sky puts on a kaleidoscopic show performed by a spectacular cast of stars.

Camel safaris into Rub' al Khali are best arranged in Oman or the UAE.

ULTIMATE DESERT DARES

MOUNTAIN QUESTS

Climbing one mountain not enough? Set your alpine sights higher, longer or faster on these extended challenges.

031 100 FAMOUS MOUNTAINS, JAPAN

When noted mountaineer and author Fukada Kyūya put together a list of Japanese mountains in his 1964 book *100 Famous Japanese Mountains*, he was something of an aesthete, choosing peaks not only for their heights but also for their history, shape and character. Nor did he intend the list to be prescriptive. He hoped that others would be inspired to draw up their own lists and set

Striking out to conquer Aconagua, highest peak in South America, and one of the magnificent seven

out to climb them during their lifetimes. Instead, Kyūya's 100 became *the* 100 peaks to climb and the mountain quest of choice for hikers in Japan. In turn, this spawned the 200 Famous Mountains, the 300 Famous Mountains, and even the 100 Famous Flowering Mountains.

Lists of the famous 100 are readily accessible on the internet, but the ultimate resource is still Fukada Kyūya's original book.

KENNETH KOH/ADVENTURE NOMAD/GETTY IMAGES ©

032 8000ERS

Climbing the 8000ers is arguably the pinnacle of mountaineering. The quest: climbers must ascend the 14 highest mountains in the world, all more than 8000m above sea level, from 8848m Mt Everest down to 8027m Shishipangma. All the 8000ers are in the Himalaya and Karakoram ranges, compacted into a tight area through Nepal, Pakistan and China. The group was first conquered by the Tyrolean great Reinhold Messner in 1986, followed a year later by Polish climber Jerzy Kukuczka. By 2012 only 28 more climbers had followed in their crampon marks.

A good reference for the 8000ers is www.8000ers.com.

033 14ERS, USA

Pile a few Munros on top of each other and they will eventually reach a height of 14,000 feet (4267m), which is the point at which a mountain in the USA earns credit as a 14er (though the summit must also be at least 300 feet higher than any connecting ridge or pass). There are 88 14ers across the country, but the genre comes into its own in Colorado, which has 53 of the peaks. A few climbers aspire to bag all 88 of the 14ers, but it's more common to focus on Colorado. People will aim to climb them all in summer, or in winter, and there have even been ski descents of each one.

A handy planning resource is www.14ers.com.

034 SEVEN SUMMITS

Half the number of mountains (and in two cases, almost half the height) as the 8000ers, the Seven Summits involves scaling the highest peak on each of the seven continents. In six out of seven cases, the objective is straightforward: Mt Everest (Asia), Denali (North America), Aconcagua (South America), Kilimanjaro (Africa), Mt Elbrus (Europe) and Vinson Massif (Antarctica). In Australia, however, 2228m Mt Kosciuszko is a simple walk-up, so most mountaineers extend the definition to Australasia, climbing West Papua's Carstensz Pyramid (4884m) instead. If you've worked your way through the Seven Summits (and there are almost 100 people who have) you can always move onto the Second Seven Summits – climbing the second-highest peak on each continent – which some consider a more difficult challenge.

Find full details of mountains and climb information at www.7summits.com.

The Appalachian Trail takes in 14 US states and countless environments from mountains to boulder fields and forests

035 TRIPLE CROWN OF HIKING, USA

Few quests of any sort are going to wear you out quite as much as the Triple Crown of Hiking. To wear this three-pronged achievement you must hike the three longest trails in the country: the Pacific Crest Trail along the Sierra Nevada and Cascade Range in the country's west; the remote and rugged Continental Divide Trail through its guts; and the Appalachian Trail, crossing through 14 eastern states. By the time you're done you'll have racked up almost 13,000km – even if you were to walk at a decent clip of 25km a day, you'd be hiking for almost 18 months.

Seek out Triple Crown info at this triple crown of websites: www.pcta.org; www.cdtsociety.org; www. appalachiantrail.org.

036 MUNROS, SCOTLAND

In 1891 Sir Hugh Munro published a list of Scotland's peaks higher than 3000 feet (914m) above sea level (the height at which they apparently became 'real' mountains) and a national hiking obsession was born. Munro baggers attempt to climb every one of the listed peaks – the list is occasionally revised and currently stands at 282 mountains – whether across their lifetime, or in a single season, or in some self-created timeframe. Reverend AE Robertson was the first to climb them all, in 1901, while the first continuous round was completed in 1974. In 2010 one Munro bagger completed the round in less than 40 days.

A full list of Munros can be found on the Scottish Mountaineering Club website (www.smc.org.uk).

037 ABELS, AUSTRALIA

Inspired by the Munros, a similar list was created for the Australian island state of Tasmania in 1994. Coined as the Abels in honour of Abel Tasman, the first European to sight Tasmania, every mountain on this list is higher than 1100m above sea level, and is separated from other mountains by a drop of at least 150m on all sides. The list runs to 160 summits, including most of Tasmania's most famous mountains: Cradle Mountain, Mt Wellington, Frenchmans Cap and the epic Federation Peak. Some of the mountains are simple strolls (or a drive, in the case of Mt Wellington), while others require days of walking simply to access.

The Abels are covered in a two-volume book series, simply titled The Abels, edited by Bill Wilkinson.

038 NATIONAL THREE PEAKS CHALLENGE, UK

Three countries, three mountains, 24 hours. Hikers who take on the National Three Peaks Challenge – which they often do for charity fundraising – have a single day in which to ascend the highest peaks in Scotland (Ben Nevis, 1344m), England (Scafell Pike, 978m) and Wales (Snowdon, 1085m). It is a day that will see them walk the equivalent of a marathon, and drive around 750km. Typically, hikers begin on Ben Nevis, then move on to Scafell Pike and conclude with Snowdon. Some begin and end at the trailhead car parks, while purists start beside the sea at Fort William and finish back at the sea at Caernarfon.

The official National Three Peaks Challenge website is www. thethreepeakschallenge.co.uk.

039 EVEREST MARATHON, NEPAL

You may have run marathons but have you run the world's highest marathon? Beginning almost 5200m above sea level, in the shadow of Mt Everest, it's no three- or four-hour trot through the streets – just getting to the starting line takes 15 days of trekking, with two mountain ascents for acclimatisation. Then, in the cold of a Himalayan dawn, you begin to run the 42km back to Namche Bazaar. It's a descent of almost 2000m, though it also includes a couple of stiff climbs. Because of the rough nature of the terrain, pure road marathon experience won't gain you entry to the race; you must have experience of major cross-country, mountain running or endurance events.

The marathon is in November; the event website is www.everestmarathon.org.uk.

040 MT KINABALU INTERNATIONAL CLIMBATHON, MALAYSIA

Fancy a run up Southeast Asia's highest mountain? In the Borneo state of Sabah, 4095m Mt Kinabalu is the setting for an annual slog of a run. First held in 1987, it traditionally followed the 21km hikers' trail to the summit, climbing more than 2200m, but has become so popular it moved to a new and longer route in 2012. Competitors now race 23km, though they no longer go to the summit, turning off the trail at Layang-Layang Hut (2700m). The 2012 winning time was just under two hours and 12 minutes. The October event is part of the international Sky Runner World Series, which also includes mountain races in Spain, Italy, Switzerland and the USA.

The Climbathon's official website is www.climbathon.my.

MOUNTAIN QUESTS

BEST STEEP, DEEP BACK-COUNTRY SKIING

Why restrict yourself to the piste when the really good stuff is just over the hill? Strap on your helmet cam and get off the beaten track.

The 'Hole' is not a town but a secluded high mountain valley some 45 miles long and 10 miles wide, bordered by the Gros Ventre range to the east and the Tetons to the west. And the 'hole' truth is that it's stuffed with delicious deep powder all season long and criss-crossed with untracked, unpopulated slopes. There's some mouth-watering back country to be explored here, accessible via the main resort's

Just a short hop from Tokyo, Hakuba offers largely untrammelled, back-country powder on a vast scale

perimeter gates. For the seriously adventurous there are overnight hut-to-hut, or even hut-to-yurt, ski options too. It's easy to see why many die-hard back-country skiers believe this to be the best the US has to offer.

Jackson Hole has its own airport serviced by United Airlines, American Airlines and Delta Air Lines, making it ridiculously accessible and meaning zero transfer time. For more info, see www.jacksonhole.com.

RYAN CREARY/AGEFOTOSTOCK ©

042 LAS LEÑAS, ARGENTINA

No list of back-country beauty would be complete without an Andean entrant and Las Leñas is as good as it gets. Freeskiers from the Northern Hemisphere flock here during their summer months to sate a thirst for the steep and deep in South America's largest total ski area. Las Leñas notched up its 30th anniversary in 2013, having built a reputation for excellent extreme and off-piste skiing. There are easily enough back-country tours to keep you going all week, or operators will help you combine a twin-destination trip with other resorts in Argentina and Chile.

Skiing in South America is considerably less organised and regulated than it is in Europe and North America, so book with a tour operator like www.laslenasski. com, which will arrange everything for you, including your transfer from Buenos Aires.

043 GULMARG, KASHMIR, INDIA

Where better to push your personal boundaries than the mother of all mountain ranges – the Himalaya? After decades as a no-go area due to the border dispute between Pakistan and India, spectacularly beautiful Kashmir is now back on the tourist map. Gulmarg is the region's ski hub and boasts not only the highest gondola in the world (4084m/13,399ft at the summit) but also the heaviest snowfall in the range. The pristine, virtually undiscovered back country here is the stuff of modern legend. And once you've had your fill, you can head back to your chalet for mint tea and a delicious spiced curry. Just watch out for snow leopards...

Ampersand Travel offers an 'Unknown Kashmir' all-inclusive ski package, with optional back-country guidance. For more, see www.ampersandtravel.com.

044 HAKUBA, JAPAN

Lots of people seem to know there's decent back-country skiing in Japan but very few have actually tried it. Which seems like madness, because it's among the best in the world. Who could say no to *apres*-ski sashimi? For the really steep and gnarly stuff – not to mention the 'Ja-Pow' factor when it comes to deep covering – head to Hakuba. This resort, located in the northern Japan Alps only a train ride from Tokyo, was the main venue for the 1998 Winter Olympics. A word of warning though: the powder can get so deep in the back country here that you might want to think about packing your snorkel as well as your goggles.

Inside Japan (www.insidejapantours.com) will organise everything for you except the snow. It comes as standard.

27

045 SAINT ANTON, AUSTRIA

There's an old saying about Austria's Arlberg region: 'You take your spouse to Lech, your lover to Zurs and your skis to Saint Anton.' Internationally renowned for its back-country brilliance, Saint Anton's fame means that you need to be out on the mountain early and know where to go for first (off-the-beaten) tracks. The resort boasts 180km (112 miles) of unpisted 'deep snow runs' to explore, with the infamous Moosewirt and Krazy Kanguruh bars waiting at the finish line for tale telling and helmet-cam playback. With dancing on the tables compulsory at both, you'll be glad you didn't bring your spouse...or lover.

Innsbruck's airport, located 62 miles from the resort, is the nearest. Saint Anton has its own train station just a stone's throw from the village centre. For more, visit www.stantonamarlberg.com.

046 SILVERTON MOUNTAIN, COLORADO, USA

'All thrills, no frills and plenty of spills' is how Silverton markets itself: music to the ears of back-country aficionados. The town has only one ski lift, but this gives you access to seemingly endless miles of back country and more mind-blowing powder than the Spanish Armada. There are no groomed runs, no cut trails and no crowds on Silverton Mountain, which makes for a uniquely pure experience in this Rocky Mountain's uniquely pure snow. With remote landmarks including Hell's Gate, Nightmare and Storm Peak, however, you're strongly advised to hire a guide.

Silverton (www.silvertonmountain.com) is close to the major ski resort of Telluride, which has its own airport, served by six commercial carriers. For more information, see www.tellurideskiresort.com.

047 WHISTLER BLACKCOMB, BRITISH COLUMBIA, CANADA

Constant, reliable snow and a vast lift-accessed back country. How could you possibly improve Whistler Blackcomb? Errr...how about 25,000 new acres open from the 2012–13 season? This is back-country skiing on an almost fathomless scale. Whistler and Blackcomb, the two adjacent mountains that hosted the 2010 Winter Olympics, are like a pair of towering doormen, granting you access to the best club in the world. Let the snow dance begin.

Whistler Blackcomb (www.whistler blackcomb.com) is only 126km (78 miles) and an easy transfer from Vancouver. Take advantage of local knowledge with Extremely Canadian's Backcountry Adventures (www.extremelycanadian .com/backcountry-clinics).

Saint Anton is a popular spot, but its deep snow runs allow plenty of scope for getting seriously off-piste

048 ANDERMATT, SWITZERLAND

One of the snowiest places in the Swiss Alps, Andermatt benefits from its unique geographical location – it's beset by the white stuff from all sides. The precious jewel at the centre of its crown is Gemsstock, a towering peak boasting priceless off-piste options from the summit. A cable car takes you to the top, from where there are myriad back-country routes, including the famous untracked Guspis. A great option for a late-winter European trip, the Gemsstock is north facing, which means you can ski on it until May.

Andermatt is part of Switzerland's Gotthard Oberalp Arena ski area. For accommodation in the village, the River House is highly recommended (www. theriverhouse.ch).

049 CHAMONIX, FRANCE

Genepy, fondue, tartiflette: in the French Alps, some things need little or no introduction. Among them is the town of Chamonix, possibly the most famous ski resort in the world. Basking in the shadow of the monumental Mt Blanc it is also, unsurprisingly, home to some of the best back-country skiing possibilities in Europe. In particular, the Grands Montets and Vallee Blanche are justifiably famous. The multifarious other off-piste options cater for all abilities from cautious to kamikaze.

Chamonix has one of the shortest transfer times from Geneva Airport, the über-hub for multiple resorts in the region. For more, see www.chamonix.com.

050 ALAGNA, ITALY

Situated at the foot of the Mt Rosa glacier, Alagna is one of the last unspoilt splices of white perfection in the European Alps. Plenty of superb back-country skiing makes this a freerider's paradise – its handful of lifts accessing multiple unpisted steep descents. The resort village itself is a beautiful, dark-wooden enclave, equally untouched by Alpine commercialism, that includes some outstanding local restaurants. Get here quickly, before everybody else does.

Alagna is located in Italy's Aosta Valley. The nearest airport is Milan Malpensa, 120km (75 miles) north-east of the resort. See www.alagna.it.

BEST STEEP, DEEP BACK-COUNTRY SKIING

WILDEST FLIGHTS

*A budget flight to Barcelona won't cut it –
aviation addicts demand the most thrilling
landings and teeth-clenching take-offs.*

053 LAND ON THE SAND

A second mention for plucky Scotland, thanks to the tiny airstrip at Barra in the Western Isles. This is perhaps the only airstrip in the world where flight schedules are dictated by the tide. Why? Oh, the runway is the beach. Flights can only land on this tiny Scottish isle at low tide, when the broad shingles at Traigh Mhor become firm enough to function as an improvised runway for daily shuttle flights from neighbouring Benbecula and mainland Glasgow. The chief hazards to landing are errant buckets and spades and absent-minded cockle-pickers.

Check the tide tables on the Barra website (www.isleofbarra.com) before planning your trip. Twin Otter flights to Benbecula and Glasgow are operated by Flybe (www.flybe.com).

051 THE SHORTEST HOP, ORKNEY ISLANDS

Forget long haul – there's more kudos in taking the world's shortest scheduled flight. Clocking in at two minutes in normal conditions, but possible in 47 seconds with a strong tailwind, Loganair Flight 353 nabs the world record. This unlikely commuter hop connects two vital hubs: a field on the Orkney island of Westray and a similar field on the island of Papa Westray, handy if you have an important meeting with a highland cow. Better reasons to visit include spotting rare bird life and exploring the oldest house in northern Europe, hewn from local stone in 3500BC.

Book the world's shortest scheduled flight with Loganair (www.loganair.co.uk). Don't panic if you miss the return flight – ferries shuttle between the islands several times a day.

052 METRES FROM THE BREAKERS, ST MAARTEN

Picture the scene – a tropical beach, the sound of tin drums floating on the breeze. Suddenly, a 747 appears from nowhere, flaps down, engines roaring, so close you can smell the aviation fuel. The airflow sends your cocktail's umbrella spinning across the sand. No, this isn't a scene from *Airport 77-Beach Disaster*. This is the standard approach to Princess Juliana International Airport on the Dutch side of St Maarten. Before touching down on the tarmac, planes skim just metres above the sunbathers on Maho Beach, providing a serious spectacle for plane-spotters from across the globe.

To fully appreciate this adventure, fly long-haul from Paris, Amsterdam or the US and enjoy the landing twice, once from inside the plane and again from Maho Beach.

054 TAKE OFF IN TIBET

Landing on the top of the world requires certain adjustments. Jet engines strain to maintain thrust in the thin air and gaining lift is a constant battle with physics. It's no accident that the runway at Qamdo in Tibet is the longest in the world, as well as the highest. This basic landing strip is perched at 4334m, almost as high as the summit of Mt Blanc, and the shallow trajectory for take-off and landing allows for spectacular views over the Tibetan plateau. The trade-off is a two-hour drive to reach Qamdo town – unfortunately, this was the closest flat ground available!

Air China (www.airchina.com) operates the handful of flights that connect Qamdo to Lhasa and Chendgu but you'll need to arrange a Tibet travel permit as part of an organised tour.

055 LIMITED TARMAC IN LUKLA

How do you land a plane on a mountain? Very carefully is the answer. Perched at over 2800m and hemmed in by 6000m peaks, the tiny airstrip at Lukla in Nepal is wedged between a sheer drop and a vertical mountain wall. Pilots bound for this lofty eyrie must set down their planes on a runway just 460m long, tilted uphill at 12% to help planes achieve the required deceleration for landing and acceleration for take-off. Needless to say, this doesn't deter the thousands of trekkers who fly here every year bound for Everest Base Camp.

Dozens of small aircraft take off daily from Kathmandu bound for Lukla but planes can only land when the airstrip is clear of cloud. Yeti Airlines (www.yetiairlines.com) is the biggest operator.

056 CLOSE ENCOUNTERS WITH VOLCANOES

Plenty of scenic flights take you close to sky-piercing mountains – only a few take you close to mountains that are spitting out fire. Flying over an active volcano might seem like a foolhardy endeavour but Hawaii's Kilauea volcano has been spewing out molten rock continuously since 1983, so local pilots have plenty of practice in these rather unique flying conditions. When the wind is right, helicopters buzz the moving lava flows, offering one of the world's most up-close-and-personal volcano encounters. Some operators even fly with open doors so you can feel the rising heat.

The doors stay on with Blue Hawaiian (www.bluehawaiian.com) but it's consistently voted the top helicopter operator in Hawaii.

057 SLIPPERY LANDINGS IN ANTARCTICA

Landing a plane on a mountain is one thing. How do you land a plane on an ice cube? The entire surface of Antarctica is covered by ice, so even the runways are carved from the stuff. Touching down on the blue-ice airstrips that service the research stations scattered around Antarctica is a slippery business. In the absence of friction, planes have to brake using reverse thrust, requiring runways that run for miles across the empty ice floes. So why do it? Well, you'll be one of just a few hundred people to share the experience every year.

To land here, join a tour to one of Antarctica's permanent research stations; Adventure Network International (www.adventure-network.com) runs trips to the South Pole, landing at Union Glacier Camp.

058 TOUCHING THE HIMALAYA

Sure, there are higher runways in the world, but the allure of flying into Leh is the surreal sensation of soaring above 6000m peaks, then banking and plunging down towards the snow and rock. Your final destination? A narrow valley tucked amongst the desolate peaks. As the engines roar the bare, rocky slopes on either side creep ever closer, then seconds before you run out of sky, the plane executes a giddying slingshot turn and drops you on the tarmac, metres from the waiting porters. Nervous flyers be warned – this acrobatic thrill-ride is the only way in and out of Ladakh October to June.

Demand is high for seats into and out of Leh, particularly once the overland passes close – book well in advance with Jet Airways (www.jetairways.com).

059 IS IT A BOAT, IS IT A PLANE?

Before the boffins invented planes with the range to cross continents, flying boats were the standard way to travel long-haul. Globetrotters would punctuate their journeys with rest stops in harbours and waterways from Cairo to Calcutta. To experience this glorious sky–sea combination, point your compass towards Alaska, where Ketchikan and Juneau are the take-off points for seaplane flights across America's most exhilarating landscape. As well as point-to-point hops, Alaskan airlines offer encounters with wild bears and eye-popping flights over the Misty Fjords.

Many small operators run seaplane flights out of Ketchikan. Alaska Seaplane Service (www.flyalaskaseaplanes.com) runs services out of Juneau, as well as charters.

060 AIRPORT, WHAT AIRPORT?

At less than 2m above sea level, the Maldives have a shortage of land for airports. To build the runway at Male, islanders joined two islands together, pulling sand from the lagoon to create land between. International flights set down on an island only just bigger than the runway: you float over palm-fringed circles of sand, sinking closer to the blue water until the boats are almost level with the windows, before finally touching the tarmac.

When flying to the Maldives, pick a day flight and insist on a window seat!

WILDEST FLIGHTS

GREATEST AIRBORNE ADVENTURES

Take to the skies and adventure into the ether in some of the world's most inspiring locations.

061 PARAGLIDING AT POKHARA, NEPAL

You lift off from Sarangkot Hill, spotting the mammoth peaks of the Annapurna Range as you glide across sky. Sweeping over the lake you have time to contemplate the magical vista of Pokhara Valley, a streak of greenery nestled between the mighty mountains like a hidden Shangri-La. Of course Pokhara's delights are no secret these days. Once you've got your land legs back this Nepalese epicentre of outdoor action is the perfect base from which to take on the world-class trekking of the Annapurna range – those mountains you saw while cruising across the sky are definitely beckoning.

The best season for paragliding in Pokhara is between September and April when near-perfect conditions mean flights take off daily.

063 HOT-AIR BALLOONING IN CAPPADOCIA, TURKEY

The dawn is spreading its buttery light over the rocks just as you gently lift off the ground. The valleys roll out in ruptured waves across the landscape as you rise higher into the sky. Cappadocia is a geological fantasy of rippling rock and the best way to experience the scope of these natural sculptures is on a hot-air balloon ride. Ballooning is an early morning activity, which luckily leaves you with the entire day to explore this fascinating region at ground level. With hiking and horse-riding activities galore, there's plenty of action-packed fun once you've landed back down on earth.

Hot-air balloons flights cost around €140 to €160 per person and take to the Cappadocian skies every morning (weather permitting) throughout the year.

062 HELI-HIKING AT FRANZ JOSEF, NEW ZEALAND

Franz Josef is one of the greatest destinations in the world in which to combine aerial views and adventure activities. From the tiny West Coast settlement of Franz Josef the helicopter takes off giving you supreme views of the surrounding rainforest before it climbs up into the white-topped mountain peaks beyond. Like a massive frozen waterfall the bulk of Franz Josef Glacier comes into view, sliding down the slopes, then you land on the glacier itself and it's time to traverse this icy world by foot. With Franz Josef's deep crevasses and blue-tinged ice needles this is glacier hiking at its best.

Glacier heli-hikes depart up to three times daily (depending on season) and last for about three hours. Get further details at www.franzjosefglacier.com.

By the golden light of dawn, from a gently floating balloon: there's no better way to view Cappadocian terrain

Get a different perspective on the Grand Canyon hovering over the Colorado River in a chopper

MOMATIUK - EASTCOTT/CORBIS ©

064 HANG-GLIDING IN INTERLAKEN, SWITZERLAND

A few running steps along the slope and you're off. With the wind roaring in your ears and the glistening blue of Lake Brienz and Lake Thun below, you glide across the sky with a couple of daredevil dives and spins thrown in for good measure. Interlaken's buildings look like a miniature toy town from this height, surrounded by the towering mountains of the Bernese Alps. This is Switzerland's adventure capital – with rafting, kayaking and mountain biking all on offer when you hit the ground – but the best way to capture the phenomenal beauty of this region is from the air.

Hang Gliding Interlaken (www. hangglidinginterlaken.com) run daily tandem hang-gliding tours costing €195, with the average flight taking around 25 minutes.

065 HOT-AIR BALLOONING OVER WADI RUM, JORDAN

It's the desert, but not as Lawrence of Arabia saw it. In the early morning the subtly changing light washes over the craggy peaks and vast sand seas of Wadi Rum, dappling the rock in shades of soft orange and pink. You gaze out of the balloon basket to see the serrated sandstone mountains thrust dramatically out of the desert and realise why this place is known as the 'Valley of the High Places'. After your flight, opt for a more traditional view of Wadi Rum by exploring the desert TE Lawrence-style with a camel trek through the sands.

Hot-air balloon flights over Wadi Rum usually take one hour and cost about €145 per person. See www.rascj.com for details.

34

066 HELICOPTER RIDE IN THE GRAND CANYON, USA

The rocky jaws of the Grand Canyon rise up as the helicopter angles over the cliffs and dives into the canyon's deep hollow. With the Colorado River snaking through it at the bottom, the Grand Canyon fissures more than a mile into the earth's surface. It's only hovering over the orange-hued rock outcrops with a bird's-eye view that you can properly appreciate the sheer, overwhelming size of this natural phenomenon as it carves across the Arizona countryside. Once you've landed in the dusty rock landscape, continue your adventure with the more down-to-earth activities of hiking or river rafting within the canyon itself.

Helicopter tours of the Grand Canyon cost from about US$300 per person and fly from Boulder or Las Vegas airports.

069 SKYDIVING AT VICTORIA FALLS, ZAMBIA

Is this the ultimate adrenaline rush in Africa? Fly up close to the gushing immensity of Victoria Falls, then jump from the plane to have the mighty Zambezi River rush up to greet you. The town of Livingstone first hit the tourism map because it's close to the falls but its since crowned itself Africa's adventure capital. There's bungee jumping, canoeing, rafting and safaris on offer but for those with a risk-seeking streak nothing can beat the thrilling, immense panoramas of skydiving over the town itself.

Tandem skydive at Livingstone (www. skydivevicfalls.com) from US$230 per person for a 10-second minimum freefall.

067 PARAGLIDING IN ÖLÜDENIZ, TURKEY

You swoop across the clear blue sky, arcing away from the forest-clad coastal cliffs, a tiny presence high above the sparkling blue of the lagoon. The golden sands of Ölüdeniz may be one of Turkey's prime tourist beaches but this resort also lays claim to being one of the best places in the world to paraglide. The jumping-off point is nearby Baba Dağ (Mt Baba) and the treacherous, twisting road up to the summit is a fitting prologue for this dizzying adventure. Powerful thermals allow for near-perfect flying conditions here so there's nowhere better to test out your own wings for the first time with a tandem flight.

Paragliding flights are run daily from April to November in Ölüdeniz and cost between €40 and €60, including transfer to Baba Dağ.

068 SKY DIVING IN KAMCHATKA, RUSSIA

Known as 'the land of fire and ice', this remote territory is an adventure just to get to. You'll need to be a licensed skydiver for the jumps into foreboding volcano calderas – they're not beginners' territory. Soaring above a steaming crater, its jagged pinnacles rushing up to meet you, is the stuff of skydiving heaven. Once you're back on terra firma soak away the aerial rush in the local hot springs, then strike out into this moonscape of active volcanoes, glaciers and geysers which holds enough outdoor activities to satisfy the most serious thrill seeker.

The Kamchatka Travel Group (www. kamchatkatracks.com) organise volcano skydiving tours (for qualified-skydiver groups) in addition to a range of other outdoor pursuits in the region.

070 HOT-AIR BALLOONING IN SERENGETI NATIONAL PARK, TANZANIA

You've ticked off the safari box and viewed the animals close up. Now take to the sky for a different perspective on wilderness watching. As the balloon glides across the acacias you spy herds of zebra grazing and gazelles leaping across the plains. If you're lucky, you may see cheetahs, leopards or lions stalking their prey. As the propane-hiss of the balloon guides you higher, the landscape unfurls and you can appreciate the immensity of this African wilderness.

Hot-air balloon companies operate year-round dawn flights over the Serengeti at an average cost of US$500 per person.

GREATEST AIRBORNE ADVENTURES

MOST ELECTRIFYING TRIBAL ENCOUNTERS

Delve into the world's remotest corners to meet peoples whose cultures and lifestyles have carried across the centuries.

Journey to Ethiopia's remote Omo Valley to discover a panorama of peoples and tribal culltures

WIN-INITIATIVE/GETTY IMAGES ©

071 WATCH THE MASK DANCES OF THE DOGON, MALI

With mud mosques, empty sweeps of the Sahel and legendary caravan hub Timbuktu on its CV, Mali is the very essence of exotic West Africa. And the Dogon villages of the Bandiagara escarpment east of Mopti add another dimension. Take a trek along the well-worn paths linking settlements to find millet-roofed meeting places, ancient cave homes and cemeteries, and the almost-cubist woodcarvings for which this region is famed. But it's the masks and days-long dance ceremonies the Dogon people perform with them that are so memorable – the soaring *sirige*, carved from a single tree branch, is the most potent, binding the people to heaven.

The security situation in Mali has been fraught in recent times; please check travel advisories before planning your trip. November to January is the coolest, most pleasant time to visit.

072 EXPLORE THE AMAZON WITH THE HUAORANI, ECUADOR

It's not much more than half a century since communication was first established with these nomadic hunter-gatherer peoples of Ecuador's Oriente region. Indeed, a couple of groups remain hostile to contact: perhaps not surprising, since their lands are threatened by oil exploitation. Some 2500 Huaoroani, speaking nasal dialects unrelated to any other known language, still hunt with 3m-long blowpipes and preserve the culture that evolved over centuries of isolation. Today, a handful of accommodation options – notably the community-backed Huaorani Ecolodge – offer the chance to stay in the thick of the action, with dazzling birdlife and traditional rituals all around.

Access to the Huaorani heartland is by light aircraft to Quehueri'ono, followed by a paddle downstream along the Shiripuno River in a dugout canoe.

073 LEARN INUIT SURVIVAL SKILLS, NEWFOUNDLAND

Though it seems impossible, there are still areas of true wilderness to be explored – no roads, no phones, no safety net. And when you find one, you'll almost certainly find a native people who have learned to survive. At the far northern tip of Labrador, Torngat Mountains National Park reserve – Canada's newest – is such a land, its craggy mountains riven by glaciers and fjords. Inuit have been hunting and foraging here for thousands of years, and you'll need an Inuit guide not only to explain traditional survival techniques, but also for protection in case of too-close polar-bear encounters.

Torngat is 200km north of the small town of Nain, nudging towards the Arctic Circle; for most visitors, access is only realistic in high summer.

074 MEET THE TRIBES OF ETHIOPIA'S OMO VALLEY

With ornate body decorations and extraordinary rituals, the peoples of the Lower Omo Valley have incredibly rich and vivid tribal cultures. The Mursi are known for stick fights and enormous plates in the lower lips of women; the Karo for spectacular body painting; the Bumi for scarification; and the Hamer for elaborate hairstyles and bull-jumping coming-of-age ceremonies. This remote, often arid region in Ethiopia's far south is a challenging place to eke out a living, and disputes between neighbouring groups are fairly common. It's no easy place to visit. But with the right guide, a journey through Omo can yield unforgettable encounters.

The best time to visit is late June to September, when many ceremonies and rituals take place, but be prepared for heat and rain.

075 BARTER WITH THE HILLTRIBES OF NORTHERN VIETNAM

The verdant highlands of northern Vietnam are pocked with the villages of the various hill-tribe peoples. Probably the most recognisable are the H'mong, their subgroups colloquially named for the hues of their clothes, hence the White, Black, Red and – with rainbow-striped hats and skirts – Flower H'mong. Getting to know the different groups can be as simple as enjoying a spot of bartering at a local market (the hill towns of Sapa and nearby Bac Ha have long been favourite venues) or hiring a responsible guide for a stay in a traditional village.

Bac Ha's market is held on Sunday; Sapa's main market is Saturday, but it's still bustling with traders on other days – best avoid weekends.

37

It's not, stricly speaking, frocking up, but performers at New Guinea's highland cultural shows put on quite a sartorial display

076 SEEK OUT THE ADI AND APATANI OF ARUNACHAL PRADESH

Slung out on a very slender limb, India's far north-east is barely connected with the rest of the country – cartographically, ethnically or spiritually. In the Himalayan foothills and steaming river valleys of Arunachal Pradesh, influences from neighbouring Tibet and Burma are more pronounced than 'mainland' India, though the traditions and religions of tribal groups are different again; many worship (or did, till recently) the sun and moon. Hire a car and guide to visit Adi villages of luxuriantly thatched, stilted homes, or catch a glimpse of Apatani women with tattooed faces and noseplugs.

As well as a tourist visa, most foreign visitors require a Protected Area Permit to visit Arunachal Pradesh.

077 STAY WITH THE MODERN MAYA, BELIZE

The Spanish conquistadors came to the Americas, saw and conquered. Well, mostly. Though Aztec and Inca civilisations were demolished, the Maya had already largely withdrawn into the background – and can still be met in southern Belize, around ancient ruins such as Lubaantun (where one of the mystical 'crystal skulls' was purportedly unearthed). Here, the Kekchi and Mopan Maya have banded together to form the Toledo Ecotourism Association and host visitors in traditional villages. It's no sanitised, Disneyfied experience – no choreographed dances or ceremonies here – but instead a fascinating insight into everyday life, with the odd folk tale or song thrown in.

Five Maya villages near Punta Gorda have simple guesthouses for tourists; simple meals are provided in family homes.

079 VISIT THE SEPIK VALLEY TRIBES, PAPUA NEW GUINEA

The world's second-largest island is also its wildest, with terrain mountainous, jungle-clad or, mostly, both. So it's not too surprising that in such isolation a dizzying diversity of tribes (or, more accurately, language cultures) developed; there's more than 800 of them. If you've seen photos of the highland cultural shows – Mt Hagen hosts the best-known – you'll picture the vividly painted faces and extravagantly feathered headdresses of, in some cases, former headhunters. But take a long, slow boat journey along the Sepik River to experience traditional culture among crocodile-hunting tribes where *tambaran* (spirit houses) are still central to community life.

The coolest, least-humid months in Papua New Guinea are June to September. Mt Hagen Cultural Show is held in August.

078 HUNT WITH THE BUSHMEN OF NAMIBIA

The lifestyle of the Bushmen (or San) of the Kalahari has been romanticised since Laurens van der Post wrote about them in the 1950s, celebrating 'primitive' hunter-gatherers clinging to traditional culture that dates back perhaps 40,000 years. The reality is that Bushman life was (and still is) tough, revolving around hunting for porcupine and antelope with poisoned arrows, eating tubers and wild honey, and sourcing water where it can be found. But visit with an open mind and the experience of sharing daily life with Ju/'hoansi !Kung people, watching their incredible survival skills in action, can be both humbling and uplifting.

Responsible, sensitively organised visits to //Nhoq'ma Bushman village, providing income to the Bushmen, can be made through Nhoma Safari Camp.

080 KEEP YOUR HEAD IN THE KELABIT HIGHLANDS, MALAYSIAN BORNEO

When James Brooke was declared the White Rajah of Sarawak in 1841, he had quite a long to-do list. Near the top, though, was stamping out the bloodthirsty tradition of headhunting that was rife among the tribes of this part of northern Borneo – the Dayaks, the Iban, the Kelabits. It took a while but it got done...or so we hope. Venture into the highlands to stay in imposing riverside Kelabit and Iban longhouses, watch men hunting wild boar or gouging dugout canoes from whole tree trunks, or go the whole hog and trek the five-day Headhunters' Trail from Gunung Mulu to Limbang.

Bario is the hub town for the Kelabit Highlands, accessible by small plane from Miri.

MOST ELECTRIFYING TRIBAL ENCOUNTERS

MOST DANGEROUS PLACES TO TRAVEL

We don't encourage travel here, but if you really must go always check and heed government travel advisories before setting off.

081 PAKISTAN'S NORTHWEST FRONTIER PROVINCE

Steeped in romantic history and ancient lore the mountainous Northwest Frontier Province has always held a wild, intoxicating allure for travellers. The Swat Valley in particular has long been a coveted trekking and climbing region for its raw-edged bucolic beauty but this region's place-apart atmosphere, wild terrain and tribal affiliations have also made it near impossible to control by a centralised Pakistan government. Today this region's name is synonymous with armed insurgency and much of it is considered off-limits with an ever-changing array of travel restrictions put in place to dissuade casual visitors.

Currently foreigners need to apply for a NOC (no-objection certificate) from the Interior Ministry in Islamabad 14 days prior to travelling to the Swat Valley.

082 AFGHANISTAN

When the hippies made their way to India it was Afghanistan that blew their minds, but the small gap in the curtain which opened up this country was closed shortly after the bell-bottomed brigade frolicked through. Wracked by invasion, war, harsh isolationist rule and then war again, this viscerally beautiful country dropped off the tourism radar in 1979 and has stayed that way ever since. You need to realistically weigh up the risk factors before venturing here. Afghanistan's raw landscapes and unique cultural blend may be the ultimate off-the-beaten-path adventure but the current lack of security means that independent travel is officially discouraged.

Despite the fact that the Afghan government is not courting tourism, the application process for tourist visas for the country is fairly straightforward.

083 RIO DE JANEIRO'S FAVELAS

While Rio de Janeiro enjoys fame for its annual Carnival and its glamorous beach life, snaking up the surrounding slopes the city's shanty towns (known as *favelas*) are a reminder that large chunks of the population live a life far removed from this razzamatazz. Controlled by the drug gangs until recently, most of Rio's *favelas* were given a wide berth by all but the most intrepid visitor. A clean-up campaign, permanent police presence and new tourism initiatives are now endeavouring to make the *favelas* an attraction rather than a danger zone and introduce the vibrant culture here to curious travellers.

The best *favela* tour companies are the ones who put money back into the *favela* community by training and utilising tour guides who live there.

084 DEMOCRATIC REPUBLIC OF THE CONGO

The DRC is unlikely to be appearing on any 'top 10 countries to visit' tick-list any time soon. Hugely underdeveloped and decimated by years of conflict by various rebel groups, huge chunks of this massive country are regarded as unsafe. Millions of Congolese have been affected by the wars, fleeing to refugee camps to escape the indiscriminate rapes and killings. At the time of writing the DRC's prime tourist destination Virunga National Park has been closed to tourists and an end to the conflict doesn't seem to be in sight.

Border-crossing points between the DRC and neighbouring Uganda, Rwanda, Burundi and Angola can all close at short notice due to the conflict.

085 SAN PEDRO SULA, HONDURAS

Spare a thought for the tourism minister of Honduras. He's got a tough hill to battle upwards with San Pedro Sula now topping the table for the title of murder capital of the world. Honduras' second city may only have a population of just over 700,000 but a staggering yearly homicide rate of 159 for every 100,000 people sees it easily taking the 'most violent' crown. To be fair, as long as you're not intent on getting yourself involved with the gangland scene, savvy travellers are as safe here as they are elsewhere in Central America and if you pass through you'll likely leave unscathed to continue your Honduran journey.

As home to Honduras' major international airport and an internal transport hub, most visitors to Honduras will at least transit through San Pedro Sula at some point.

086 CHECHNYA

Despite its gorgeous mountain terrain and the end of the bitter civil war, Chechnya has a long way to go before it's considered a safe travel destination. Sporadic bombings, kidnappings and outbreaks of violence are still very real risks. A handful of intrepid travellers though are making their way to this Caucasus republic and discovering the bizarreness of the rebuilt capital Grozny with its flashy shopping malls and high-rises. Don't let the modernity dazzle you, though. Outside of the city, landmines still litter much of the countryside and tourist infrastructure is practically nonexistent.

There are regular flights to Grozny from Moscow and Istanbul or you can travel by train from Moscow.

087 SAHEL REGION OF THE SAHARA

Lawless and remote for most of its course, the Sahel region runs across northern Africa, rolling through some of the world's toughest neighbourhoods and demarcating the Sahara's southern limits. It's the western side of the Sahel which is causing the most strife for travellers these days. Not only are the few roads through the region some of the most lawless and remote in the world, with travellers easy prey for local bandits, but a spate of high-profile kidnappings of foreigners in the Mauritania, Mali, Niger and Algeria Sahel region has made it a no-go zone for all except the most brave and foolhardy.

From west to east, the Sahel region passes through parts of Senegal, Mauritania, Mali, Burkina Faso, Algeria, Niger, Nigeria, Chad, Sudan and Eritrea.

088 IRAQ

This is the Mesopotamian heartland, the cradle of civilisation which gave birth to the first empire builders. Even the names – Nineveh, Ur and Babylon – conjure up an ancient and exotic world. Iraq is a fascinating place of sand-swept ruins and important religious sites but its lustrous past has been overshadowed by a sad modern period of harsh dictatorship and brutal war. The northern province of Iraqi Kurdistan is comparatively safe for travellers (and is actively trying to promote tourism) but with security still shaky throughout the rest of Iraq visiting those ancient Mesopotamian sites may have to wait.

Tourist visas to the Kurdistan region are granted upon arrival. Visas for travelling in the rest of the country must be applied for in advance.

089 DARIÉN GAP, PANAMA/COLOMBIA

The dense jungle and swampland of the Darién Gap is one of the least explored places on the planet. Connecting Panama to Colombia (and Central America to South America) this roadless swath of wilderness is a remote and rough-as-guts jewel in many would-be explorers' eyes. People have got through on foot and by 4WD but most successful attempts were before the narco-traffickers, Colombian paramilitary and rebel groups moved in during the 1990s – so snakes, leeches and malarial mosquitoes are the least of your worries here.

Most travellers either fly or sail around the Darién Gap to avoid it. Sailing from Panama to Cartagena via the San Blas Islands is the most popular alternative.

090 SOMALIA

It has the longest coastline in Africa, several national parks, and its capital was once feted for its beautiful colonial architecture but Somalia is not likely to bounce back to holiday-destination status anytime soon. Having suffered through a long-running civil war, which has left hundreds of thousands dead, destroyed much of the capital's architecture and contributed to woeful famine conditions, casual travel in Somalia is off the cards for the moment. Despite the ongoing security risks, a tiny number of travellers have begun to trickle in, but if Somalia is in your sights you might want to do some serious research first.

Due to the ongoing threat posed by armed militias throughout the country, travellers are advised to hire security before venturing outside of Mogadishu.

COLDEST ADVENTURES

A bit (or a lot) of ice needn't stop you getting out to play.

091 SLEEP IN A SNOW HOLE, SCOTLAND

You're stranded on the side of a snow-covered Scottish mountain and night is closing in, its icy tendrils the harbinger of severe exposure. It's time to start digging! Snow holes are an important survival technique for mountaineers and a surprisingly snug way to spend a night outdoors. You can learn to build one as part of a Scottish winter mountain skills course. It'll take two to three hours to construct your shelter, with ventilation and a raised bed that keeps you closer to the warm air inside. It's a great adventure and you could wake up to the first rays of the dawn glistening on the icy slopes outside.

Stuart Johnson runs courses at www.climbmts.co.uk and you can find more information at the Association of Mountain Instructors website (www.ami.org.uk).

092 POLAR CIRCLE MARATHON, GREENLAND

There should be little chance of overheating during the race billed the 'coolest marathon on earth'. The marathon is held in October (mid-autumn) when the average temperature in Greenland is around -10°C, and you'll crunch along snow-covered gravel roads, past the snout of a glacier and, for 2km to 3km (depending on snow conditions), atop the Greenland ice sheet itself. Don't expect to run your usual marathon time. The course is mostly downhill, though very undulating, and three hours is normally a solid winning time. Conditions have blown at least one race out to four hours.

The marathon is held at Kangerlussuaq in western Greenland. Air Greenland flies here from Copenhagen. The event website is www.polar-circle -marathon.com.

093 AVANTOUINTI, FINLAND

To begin, find a hole in the ice of a lake or sea. Now jump in. It's a simple principle, though *avantouinti* (ice-hole swimming) might not seem so effortless when you're poised at the edge of the hole. And if you're going to do it right, you'll have left the wetsuit at home. Ice-hole swimming isn't unique to Finland, though the Finns do it best and with the most passion – it's so popular, there are waiting lists for *avantouinti* dips at many of the sauna clubs that maintain ice holes. Proponents swear it's good for health, and one of the secrets to a long life. But then, they would, wouldn't they?

Rastila Camping, a campsite in Helsinki's eastern suburbs, offers public *avantouinti*.

094 HIKE ON MORENO GLACIER, ARGENTINA

The world's most picturesque glacier is best experienced as you crunch across it in crampons. From opposite the spaghetti network of viewing trails that keeps most visitors content, guided hikes lead up to and onto the edge of the 23km-long glacier. You'll see the spectrum of glacial features – ice caves, crevasses, fins of blue ice – and probably hear the explosion of ice and water as seracs (ice columns) calve away from the 10-storey-high snout of the glacier into Lago Argentino. Hikes end at a trolley bar on the glacier, drinking whisky with ice chipped direct from the glacier.

Buses run each day to Moreno Glacier from the town of El Calafate, which has direct flights to Buenos Aires. Glacier hikes are operated by Hielo y Aventura (www.hieloyaventura.com).

095 WINTER TREK ON THE ZANSKAR RIVER, INDIA

For local villagers in the chilly Himalayan climes of northwestern India, the Zanskar River has long been a traditional winter pathway. Not by boat, but on foot. When winter blankets Ladakh in snow, the region is all but inaccessible except by plane, and for generations the frozen river was about the only way through the mountains. In recent years this ice route has opened up to visitors, who walk for eight or nine days (return) from the appropriately named Chilling to Lingshed, sleeping in rock shelters or private homes. It's a season of enormous beauty – think frozen waterfalls and a thin skin of blue ice over the river – if rather on the chilly side.

Local company Zanskar Trekking (www.zanskar-trekking.com) operates winter treks on the river.

THOMAS BOEHM ©

Gliding along the Zanskar in winter brings its own chilly delights

096 WATERFALL ICE CLIMB AT BANFF, CANADA

When winter hits and the waterfalls freeze, not everyone in Banff and Canmore is thinking about skiing or boarding. The area around the towns is considered by many to be the premier waterfall-climbing destination on the planet. Routes are plentiful and cater to all abilities, while Canmore is the scene of an annual ice-climbing festival each February. One of Banff's youth hostels even freezes up a wall as an indoor ice-climbing venue. If you're new to front points and ice axes, there are good novice routes at the Junkyards, high above Canmore, and at King Creek in Kananaskis Country, about an hour's drive from Canmore.

Canmore-based Yamnuska Mountain Adventures (www.yamnuska. com) guides ice climbs for all levels of experience: beginner instruction through to five-day multipitch programs.

097 KAYAK TASMAN LAKE, NEW ZEALAND

To paddle among icebergs, you'd surely have to travel to the literal ends of the earth, right? Or you could just travel to New Zealand and the easily accessible Mt Cook Village. A few kilometres from the village, at the snout of the country's longest glacier, is Tasman Lake, which is like a frigid soup filled with croutons of ice. In the grey water float blue icebergs, calved from the glacier (the February 2011 Christchurch earthquake alone is said to have dislodged 30 million tonnes of ice), creating a slalom course of sorts for kayakers who come for the most intimate look possible at the 'bergs.

Glacier Kayaking (www.mtcook.com/glacier-sea-kayaking) operates kayaking trips on Tasman Lake; the season runs from October through April.

098 VISIT OYMYAKON, RUSSIA

It's Siberia, a place with a reputation as frigid as a gulag, so it seems fitting that the small, remote Yakutian town of Oymyakon should have earned itself the title of the coldest permanently inhabited settlement on the planet. The honour befell the town when, in the 1920s, it recorded a brain-numbing minimum temperature of -71.2°C. It remains the lowest temperature ever recorded in a town, as well as the lowest temperature ever recorded in the northern hemisphere. Locally they're pretty proud of their day in the 'sun' – a plaque in the town, which is 350km south of the Arctic Circle, commemorates the occasion.

Expect a long day of rugged driving to reach Oymyakon from Yakutsk, around 800km to the west.

099 SKI TOUR THE HAUTE ROUTE, FRANCE/SWITZERLAND

Arguably the finest and most famous ski-tour route in the world, the Haute Route (High Route) traverses 140km of primo Alpine country between Chamonix, at the foot of Mont Blanc, to Zermatt, at the foot of the Matterhorn – it's a journey from mountain icon to mountain icon. The tour usually takes six or seven days, skiing from hut to hut, crossing more than 20 glaciers

The only way is up when you have a frozen waterfall in Banff to negotiate

and climbing more than 10,000m. The winter views of Mont Blanc, Monte Rosa, Grand Combin and the Matterhorn should be ample reward. The Haute Route has also become a popular summer trek (using a slightly different route).

Chamonix and Zermatt both have good transport links within France and Switzerland. A number of companies offer guided tours, including Chamonix-based Mountain Spirit (www.mountain-spirit-guides.com).

100 ICE DIVING, RUSSIA

Cut into the north coast of Russia, near the border with Finland, the White Sea offers a remarkable winter experience: diving beneath the ice. Water temperatures hover around -1°C, but you'll see sights through your mask that you'll probably see nowhere else on earth – ice hummocks and soft corals growing below ice. Ice-dive training takes place around a pier in 7m to 10m of water, before you head out to visit sites such as Cape Kindo,

the Krestovi Islands and the wreck of a fishing boat. Expect two dives a day, each lasting around 30 minutes. Needless to say, bring a dry suit.

The Arctic Circle Dive Centre (www.ice-diving.ru) operates diving trips in the White Sea.

COLDEST ADVENTURES

SCARIEST ANIMAL ENCOUNTERS

*Animals can be perfect travel companions...
even the ones that bite, scratch and eye you as
though you might be dinner.*

KRUGER WILDERNESS TRAILS, SOUTH AFRICA

If you fancy being even slower prey, there's always an African walking safari. In Kruger National Park there are seven Wilderness Trails, offering two-day walking safaris through one of the world's finest and most wildlife-rich national parks – almost 150 mammal species have been recorded in the park, including the big five. On the Wilderness Trails, which are far from normal tourist activity,

So close you can see the pearly whites of the great whites

walking group sizes are small (maximum eight people). Wildlife count is high; the Napi Trail passes seasonal pans that are good for big-game sightings, while the Sweni Trail heads to Sweni River, where large numbers of animals congregate, attracting predators such as lions.

Trail information can be found at the park website (www.sanparks.org/parks/kruger); follow the 'Travel' link. Book well ahead.

FRANCO BANFI/PHOTOSHOT ©

102 CYCLING SAFARI, BOTSWANA

It's the literal Meals on Wheels. Botswana's Mashatu Game Reserve is home to elephants, giraffes and ostriches, as well as lions and leopards, and for four days you could be mountain biking past the lot of them on a safari with a twist. Cycling trips here start by the Limpopo River on the South Africa border and head across the 25,000-hectare game reserve, bumping through technical terrain and covering around 30km to 40km each day. You'll pass within metres of herds of elephants...and did we mention the lions? If nothing else, when was the last time your cycling partner carried a rifle?

Mountain biking trips through Mashatu are run by Cycle Mashatu (www.mtbsafaris.com). For information on the game reserve, see www.mashatu.com.

103 HAMMERHEAD DIVES, COSTA RICA

You'd have to be a tool to want to swim freely among hammerhead sharks, right? Or you may just have been enticed by the reputation of Isla del Coco (Cocos Island), 600km southwest of the Costa Rican mainland. It's a place Jacques Cousteau described as the most beautiful island in the world, and it may just offer the best and most pure shark diving in the world – no cages here. The quizzically shaped hammerheads are the star feature and the largest schools are found around the submerged mountain at Bajo Alcyone. You can't stay on the island, so your most likely ticket here is on a live-aboard boat.

Okeanos Aggressor (www.aggressor.com) and Undersea Hunter (www.underseahunter.com) run live-aboard diving trips to the island from San José.

104 CAGE DIVE WITH GREAT WHITE SHARKS, AUSTRALIA

The first thing you should know is that some of those really scary scenes from *Jaws* were filmed in the waters near the South Australian town of Port Lincoln. Now, are you ready to be dunked into the Southern Ocean among those very sharks? Cage-diving trips head south from Port Lincoln to the Neptune Islands – home to a large seal colony – where baits are tossed into the sea to attract great whites. You're then lowered into the water inside a metal cage where, for the next 45 minutes or so, you may be circled by one of the world's most terrifying creatures. The largest ones might be about three times your size.

Cage-diving trips are operated by Calypso Star Charters (www.sharkcagediving.com.au).

47

They might look cute and cuddly, but would you want to encounter a polar bear by night?

105 PADDLING WITH ORCAS, CANADA

When you're sitting inside a kayak in Johnstone Strait and a killer whale surfaces just metres away, you can be very thankful you're not a salmon. Each summer, orcas congregate in this narrow strait between Vancouver Island and mainland Canada, feasting on spawning salmon. The fact that the orcas eat only salmon can seem theoretical, however, when a 2m-high dorsal fin suddenly rises beside you. The best paddling trips are those near to Robson Bight, where orcas come to rub skin from their bellies on the pebbly shores – the bight itself is off-limits to kayaks and boats but the waters around its edges are invariably busy with orca traffic.

Natural Focus Safaris (http:// naturalfocussafaris.com) operates kayaking trips in Johnstone Strait.

106 CROCOSAURUS COVE, AUSTRALIA

The waters of Australia's top end are home to great numbers of saltwater crocodiles – prehistoric bits of leather, growing up to 6m in length, that aren't opposed to the idea of giving you a little death roll. Swimming anywhere near them is far from advised. But in the centre of Darwin you can do just that... from the safety of a transparent acrylic cage. At Crocosaurus Cove, visitors are lowered into a crocodile enclosure where they dangle like bait among 5m-long crocs. It doesn't send the crocs into a feeding frenzy but the teeth marks in the cage suggest how close it can occasionally get.

Crocosaurus Cove is on the corner of Mitchell and Peel Sts in the centre of Darwin. For more info, see www. crocosauruscove.com.

107 SLEEP AMONG POLAR BEARS, CANADA

The Manitoba town of Churchill is not a place in which to duck outside for a pee in the middle of the night. The isolated town is on the migration route for polar bears as they head from summers on the tundra to seal-hunting winters on the pack ice of Hudson Bay. Churchill has developed an industry out of bear tourism, and after seeing the mighty snowy beasts throughout the day you can then sleep out amongst them in so-called 'tundra lodges' – rooms on a mobile platform in the tundra. The reality is that you're very safe, but you might start to wonder when you hear things going bump in the middle of the night.

Churchill can be reached by air or rail from Winnipeg. For tundra lodge information, see www.greatwhitebeartours.com.

110 TRACKING MOUNTAIN GORILLAS, UGANDA

An adult male mountain gorilla – a mighty silverback – can weigh up to 160kg. At his chivalrous best he's a gentle fellow, but when he's threatened, or sometimes just when visited by strangers, his reaction is to charge, screaming at the intruder. If that's you, tracking through Bwindi Impenetrable National Park to see some of the park's 400 mountain gorillas, your mission is to hold your nerve. If you stand still and look away from the silverback as he charges, there's little chance he'll hurt you. You just need to remember that over the rising panic.

Tracking permits cost US$500 per day and should be booked through the Uganda Wildlife Authority (www.ugandawildlife.org) months in advance. Travelling with a safari company is a surer bet.

108 SARDINE RUN, SOUTH AFRICA

It sounds harmless – who's afraid of a few sardines? – but when there are millions of sardines massing off the coast of South Africa each June, there are also plenty of bitey things following hard behind. Almost every predator in the sea – game fish, dolphins, seabirds, sharks and orcas – can turn up here to feast on untinned sardines. Boats follow the Run to see the dolphins and whales, but snorkellers get the best of the views, watching the dinner party as it passes beneath them. Diving isn't such a great idea because if you're among the sardines you might also accidentally end up on the menu.

The Wild Coast between Durban and East London makes a good base for getting among the sardines.

109 TIGER TRACKING ON AN ELEPHANT, INDIA

Corbett National Park was India's first tiger reserve and remains one of the country's premier big-cat havens. For visitors, there are two kinds of safaris: jeep and elephant. The latter is by far the most personal and nerve-wracking – riding an animal to see an animal, with all the lack of control that implies. Elephants lope out from the park's main accommodation centre at Dhikala, pushing through the sal forest and the cannabis that grows freely – be grateful because the elephants love to eat it and it may be the very thing that settles them (*'look mon, 'tis a tiger'*) – if they do spot a cat.

The overnight Ranikhet Express train runs from Delhi to Ramnagar, the park entrance.

SCARIEST ANIMAL ENCOUNTERS

MOST SPECTACULAR ROCK CLIMBS

You're crimped to the rock, hanging on for dear life, but there's always time to sneak a peek at the view, right?

AURORA PHOTOS/AWL IMAGES ©

111 KALYMNOS, GREECE

The third-largest island in the Dodecanese was once best known for its sponge diving, but today it's the limestone cliffs that are drawing attention. Despite being undiscovered by climbers until the mid-1990s, Kalymnos (with neighbouring islet Telendos) has become Greece's climbing mecca with 50 different climbing sites. By 2000 it was hosting a climbing festival, and climbers were pouring across the Aegean. New sites and routes continue to open up, and no wonder – you're looking over water so turquoise, it's like climbing into a postcard. Most climbs are around the towns of Masouri and Armeos, from where you can walk to the cliffs or hire a scooter.

Climb Kalymnos (http://climbkalymnos.com) is an excellent resource. The Kalymnos Climbing Festival is held in September.

112 YANGSHUO, CHINA

Is there a rock rat alive who can look at the karst landscape in China's Guangxi province and not want to climb? Staked with limestone peaks, the area resembles a landlocked Halong Bay, and it's the town of Yangshuo, cradled between the spires, that has emerged as one of Asia's climbing heartlands. The rock is scratchy, grippy limestone and it's possible you'll be belaying from beside farmers and buffalo at some walls. Thumb Peak – named for its shape – has good top-roped climbs for starters, while for pure scenic value and novelty it's hard to beat Moon Hill, where you climb on a rock arch, no less.

Yangshuo is about 90 minutes by bus from Guilin. Karst Climber (www.karstclimber.com) is one of Yangshuo's pioneering climbing operators.

113 TOTEM POLE, AUSTRALIA

Much of Australia's island state of Tasmania is composed of columns of dolerite, but nowhere more spectacularly than around the Totem Pole, a slender sea stack standing like an upended cigarette beside the Tasman Peninsula cliffs. More than 60m high, it's just 4m across at its base, which is often lashed by wild seas. Though the classic Free Route is graded at 25 (French 7b; US 5.12b), the challenge is as much mental as physical. Complete this climb and there's always the adjoining Candlestick, somehow less famous but almost twice as tall and requiring a boat, kayak or swim (don't think about the sharks) to access.

The Totem Pole is reached from Fortescue Bay; from here a walking track heads out to Cape Hauy and an abseil point.

Totem poles may well be symbolic but that's no reason not to climb this one

The views from the Trango Towers are as intense as the effort it takes to get to the top

114 TRANGO TOWERS, PAKISTAN

Pressed between the Trango and Dunge Glaciers, the Trango Towers are a line of 6000m-plus granite mountains so ominous it seems almost absurd that anyone could climb them. Nameless Tower and the east face of the Great Trango Tower are two of the highest cliff faces in the world – more than 1300m of near-vertical granite. The Towers are considered among the most difficult ascents in the world. For most, it will be enough to view them from Urdukas, the campsite five or six days' trekking along the Baltoro Glacier – the view from here is one of the finest mountain scenes on the planet.

Access into the Towers and Baltoro Glacier is from the Baltistan town of Skardu; Pakistan International Airlines flies to Skardu from Islamabad.

115 EL CAPITAN, USA

Think climbing, think El Capitan. An imposing monolith that rises 1000m above the Merced River in Yosemite National Park, El Cap is the rock on which big-wall climbing was born. It also happens to be wildly spectacular, looking across at a series of other bald rock domes. The classic climb here is the Nose, first climbed in a 45-day epic in 1958. Today, climbers take about five days to make the 31-pitch ascent (in 2012 Hans Florine and Alex Honnold shot up it in two hours and 23 minutes). It's not regarded as being difficult, but it is long and exposed.

For the true climber experience, base yourself in Camp 4 in Yosemite Valley, with the rock crowd.

116 METEORA, GREECE

The monks knew what they were doing when they began building their monasteries at Meteora in the 14th century. Balancing them atop tall prongs of rock to keep attackers at bay, they are today assaulted by people in harnesses and chalk bags. Rising suddenly from the Thessaly Plain in northern Greece, Meteora is an undeniably spectacular place – probably wasted on ascetic monks anyway – with more than 100 climbing routes on the conglomerate rock. The Holy Ghost (Heiliger Geist) rock tower offers some of the classic climbing; its nine-pitch, 250m Traumpfeiler may be Meteora's signature route.

The town of Kalambaka, at the foot of the Meteora rocks, is the main access point into the area. Vrachos campsite in nearby Kastraki is the climbers' bed of choice.

117 CERRO TORRE, ARGENTINA/CHILE

It seems almost to defy natural laws that such a narrow spire of rock can withstand the fierce weather thrown at it from the Patagonian Ice Cap. Once considered impossible to climb (dispute still surrounds its alleged first ascent in 1959), Cerro Torre rises like a needle from the glaciers below, its climb complicated by a mushroom of ice atop the summit. It's arguably the most difficult bit of rock in one of the most stunning mountain regions in the world, looking across as an equal at the mighty Monte FitzRoy. Only the vastly experienced need apply on this climb.

The nearest airport is at El Calafate, from where it's a 215km bus ride to El Chaltén, the base for climbs in the area.

118 MT THOR, CANADA

Getting to Mt Thor is almost as difficult as climbing it – OK, not true, given that the mountain has the highest purely vertical cliff (1250m) in the world, but it's a heck of a journey nonetheless. The 1675m-high mountain, all but resting against the Arctic Circle, is inside Auyuittuq National Park on Baffin Island. To reach its base requires a flight to the icy hamlet Pangnirtung, then a lengthy boat ride, and finally a 20km river-fording walk. The average gradient on the big wall, which looks like a stone wave about to crash into the valley, is 105 degrees. As this suggests, much of the climb is overhanging – can you sustain that for 1250m of grunt?

The national park website is www.pc.gc.ca; follow the 'National Parks' link to Auyuittuq.

119 AGULHA DO DIABO, BRAZIL

Has ever a summit been better named? Agulha do Diabo – Devil's Needle – spears out of the forest in Nacional Parque Serra dos Órgãos. The park is said to have Brazil's most extensive trail network, which is just as well since it's a walk of several hours in to the Needle. On sight, the 2050m peak – a lone finger of rock pinched between higher summits – is an intimidating prospect. The summit spire is cracked around its base and the rock above is as bent as a broken finger. Also inside the national park, and arguably just as spectacular, is Dedo de Deus (Finger of God), one of Brazil's classic climbs.

Nacional Parque Serra dos Órgãos is about an hour's drive from Rio de Janeiro.

120 CASTLE HILL, NEW ZEALAND

If a god spilled a bag of marbles it would look like Castle Hill. In this basin the grassy fields are strewn with limestone boulders, protruding from the ground like the exposed knuckles of the Earth. Bouldering is the name of the climbing game here, with unroped climbers splayed across the wind- and rain-polished rocks, which rise up to 50 metres in height. Hollywood thought it spectacular enough to film battles scenes for *The Chronicles of Narnia* here and if you don't believe us about the gorgeous setting, perhaps you'll believe the Dalai Lama, who once proclaimed it a 'spiritual centre of the universe'.

Castle Hill is around 100km (90 minutes' drive) from Christchurch, off the road to Arthur's Pass.

MOST SPECTACULAR ROCK CLIMBS

MOST STELLAR STAR-LIT ADVENTURES

Trust more than your eyes and master your fear of the dark on these nocturnal missions.

121 KEEP NIGHT WATCH OVER SEA TURTLES

All seven species of the world's sea turtles are endangered, in part because of illegal trade in turtle meat and eggs. To ensure the security of mothers, eggs and hatchlings, conservation projects worldwide patiently patrol critical turtle-nesting areas, especially at night. One such area is an untrammelled Nicaraguan gem, the Padre Ramos Estuary, which welcomes nearly half the hawksbill nesting in the eastern Pacific. Volunteer activities in Padre Ramos include shadowing experienced project staff on night beach surveys to find, measure and tag nesting mamas or protect their hatchlings. This happens without light, to avoid disorienting the turtles.

Learn about turtle conservation work in Nicaragua (and elsewhere) at www.hawksbill.org and more about sea turtle conservation worldwide at www.seeturtles.org.

122 HUNT FOR TRUFFLES AT TWILIGHT

Most of us have heard of truffles, but few have tasted them fresh (especially not the bank-breakingly dear 'Black Pearl' of the Périgord or 'White Gold' of Alba) and even fewer have seen them whole. Did you know that they're mushrooms that mature underground? And that they're usually harvested at night with specially trained truffle-tracking dogs or pigs? Trowel-toting truffle hunters, called *tartufar* in Croatian, lurk in twilit forests with their four-footed fungus sleuths. Seems somehow Tolkienesque, doesn't it? Join them on an after-dark outing for both the night-lamp-lit quiet of the woods and inspiration to later sample truffle-flavoured treats.

Truffles and truffle tours can also be found in Spain, France and Italy, but for more about the Croatian (Istrian) variety start reading at www.lonelyplanet.com/croatia/travel-tips-and-articles/76139.

123 DIVE IN DARKNESS WITH THE MANTA RAYS

The sensation of night diving is the closest you may ever come to that of soaring through the air. Feelings of weightlessness and invulnerability are enhanced by the absence of near-at-hand visual points of reference. Just as spectacularly, when lights are on, the true colours of the underwater world leap out with a new cast of characters. One place fabled for night-time submarine encounters is Kona, Hawaii, where manta rays plane in from the darkness to feed on light-drawn plankton. Keep to the reef for hunting morays, scampering shrimp, sleeping fish and amazing nudibranchs.

Night diving might sound scary but it's often more relaxing than day diving. Visit www.konahonudivers.com/manta -ray-night-scuba-dive.php.

124 MANOEUVRE MOGULS BY MOONLIGHT

In some ski venues there's no need to hurry one final schuss before the slopes close – the trail lights go on and freestyling continues. It could be the novelty, but there's something gnarly about shredding the slopes at night. There are practical advantages too: no crowds, short lift lines and cheap tickets. Of course, it gets lots colder (bring schnapps!) and sometimes icier. Where to go? Try Bromont, the ski station 85km east of Montreal, Canada. With more than 100 lit trails on seven hillsides, it's the largest night-skiing resort in North America.

Read more about Bromont, both day and night, on www.skibromont.com. For other North American night-skiing locations, see www.winterdirectory.com. Cool tip: use clear goggle lenses.

125 GO ADVENTURE CAVING

Who knew the term 'adventure caving' was coined in Swaziland? It started in 1999, when the country's granite Gobholo cave system opened for more rough-and-tumble guided exploration than normal paved-pathway stalagmite strolling. Today, amateur and professional spelunkers still strap into full-length overalls, helmets, head lamps and safety gear to negotiate 800m of muddy passages, dodge bats and adjust to total blackness. There's no wandering off established routes, since some of Gobholo has not yet been explored. Evening trips emerge into darkness for a 45-minute forest night hike.

Although prior speleological experience isn't necessary, physical effort is required. Check out the details at www.swazitrails.co.sz/adventure-caving.

126 RUN A MOONLIT MARATHON

In daylight, there's something otherworldly about Wadi Rum, an eye-popping landscape of rocky outcrops shipwrecked in the sands of southern Jordan. But when lit by a full moon, it's downright dreamy...as in pinch-yourself-you're-not-imagining dreamy. The annual Full Moon Desert Marathon is your chance to run rampant in the Rum terrain, negotiating gentle sandy inclines and plateaus of hard-packed mud, rock alleys and dunes through 10km, 21km or full-marathon courses lit by all-weather torches.

The run occurs in mid to late May and sets off shortly before sunset. Plan for all desert conditions, even sand storms. Find more information at www.flashback -adventures.com.

127 GOGGLE AT THE NORTHERN LIGHTS

Aurora borealis. While they fluoresce night and day, the Northern Lights are most visible in dark skies (avoid full moons), especially on crisp and cloudless nights. There are many spots to gape at this unforgettable phenomenon, but climate and access are two big considerations that net northern Norway lots of action. One alluring alternative to Tromsø, perhaps the most popular aurora mecca, are the Lofoten Islands, a nature- and (Viking) culture-rich archipelago with great fishing and a comparatively mild climate for somewhere inside the Arctic Circle.

Plan Northern Lights trips to the Earth's 'auroral zone' between October and March. For more about the Lofoten Islands, see www.lofoten.info.

128 HIKE UNDER VERY DARK SKIES

Utah's Natural Bridges National Monument is the world's first International Dark-Sky Park. During the day, its primary attractions are three towering natural bridges. At night, though, the US's only Bortle class-2 skies – the Bortle Scale measures night-sky and star brightness – make the heavens the spectacle, a dazzling density of celestial bodies 300 times greater than that seen by most urban dwellers. On the ground, the nine-mile roadway or canyon-bottom hiking trails, are perfect for peaceful star gazing and nocturnal discovery.

Natural Bridges National Monument is open year-round, day as well as dark-sky night. Visit www.nps.gov/nabr. Other dark-sky destinations are described at www.darksky.org.

129 BRAVE A WALKING NIGHT SAFARI

There's little tropical rainforest left in Africa. In Ghana, though, Kakum National Park is covered with it and accessible. Even on foot and at night. While African night safaris are now common, night *walking* safaris aren't. After all, you're there to see animals you shouldn't meet on foot and in the dark, right? At Kakum, park guides lead two-hour night hikes along forest paths carved by elephants, bongo, duikers and primates. Just don't expect to see much; it's pitch black and you're noisy. Listen instead for the dark-forest sounds and sense the lurking wildlife.

For more about travel in Kakum National Park, see www.touringghana.com/ecotourism/kakum.asp. Also check out its first-in-Africa canopy walkway of vertiginous hanging treetop bridges.

130 CLIMB A MOUNTAIN BEFORE SUNRISE

At 3776m, Mount Fuji is the highest peak in Japan, and a near-perfect inverted cone confectioned in snow most of the year. Four well-signposted hiking routes lead up the mountain's steep, rocky slopes. These are more chilly and challenging at night when most climbers ascend, all aiming to crest in time for the spectacular sunrise. When passable, a 4km path around the crater visits several shrines. The taxing ascent of four to 10 hours can be broken up in mountain huts, the rest also helping with altitude acclimatisation.

Hike Mount Fuji in July and August, except during the Obon holidays, when it's packed (especially the huts). Plan ahead, including for weather extremes, using www.jnto.go.jp/eng/indepth/scenic/mtfuji/fuji_05.html.

MOST THRILLING CANYONING ADVENTURES

Delve under the earth's surface and experience a thrilling nexus of water and stone in these mind-blowing canyons.

BLUE MOUNTAINS, AUSTRALIA

With endless sandstone cliffs, spectacular waterfalls and narrow crevices around 90m (295ft) deep and only a few metres wide, Australia's Blue Mountains are full of geological treasures that can only be accessed during a canyoning expedition. The good news is that a number of these canyons, including Sheep Dip and Fortress Canyon, don't involve abseiling and can be undertaken by adventurers

Exploring the depths of the Massif de Bavella: a whole lot of watery fun

of all ages provided they can swim. Expect lots of slippery dips, exhilarating water jumps, short swims and scrambles in a picturesque setting – it's the perfect recipe for an invigorating day. Other canyons are more physically challenging and involve abseils up to 25m (82ft).

The Blue Mountains are just two hours' drive north of Sydney. Base yourself in Katoomba where you'll find a profusion of operators – do your research and find the best fit for your expectations.

CHARTON FRANCK/GETTY IMAGES ©

132 GRAND STAIRCASE-ESCALANTE NATIONAL MONUMENT, UTAH, USA

One word: heaven. If there's a sport that makes this place special, it's canyoning. Spread out in southern Utah, the Escalante comprises those marvellous, long canyons, known as slots, that make for perfect multiday trips. Rappelling dozens of metres over the lip of a sandstone cliff, wading through icy pools, scrambling over smooth slickrock and scraping your way through a narrow gorge are the best ways to explore this little-known but super-scenic park. It's much less hyped than Zion – all the better for you. At Escalante, you'll really feel like you're exploring the bowels of the earth.

If you want an overview of canyoning options with route descriptions in Utah, check out www.canyoneeringusa.com.

133 ARENAL, COSTA RICA

Adrenalin junkies of the world unite – Costa Rica ain't just about quiet walks in the park. On the contrary, this action-packed country is full of opportunities. Canyoning fiends will make a beeline for the aptly named Lost Canyon in the vicinity of Arenal Volcano. This atmospheric place is full of tropical waterfalls begging to be rappelled down. And what waterfalls! Standing on the edge of a steep cliff and looking over down a 40m (131ft) plunge is sure to make your heart thump. Fear not, your guides will give you a thorough safety briefing and you'll be provided high-quality, easy-to-use climbing gear, making the thrill safe and immensely fun.

Arenal is a good area for those new to canyoning but who have good outdoor experience.

134 MASSIF DE BAVELLA, CORSICA

Picture a series of granite pinnacles resembling a giant shark's jaw, jabbing the skyline at an altitude of more than 1600m (5249ft) in the heart of Corsica, and you have the impressive Massif de Bavella. Once you've had your fill of gorgeous panoramas, you might want to explore in more depth, and there's no better way to do it than canyoning. Of all the stellar spots for this pursuit in Corsica, the Bavella area tops the list with three major canyons: Canyon de la Vacca, Canyon de la Purcaraccia and Canyon de la Pulischella. They're all atmospheric – expect rappelling, various jumps and leaps into crystal-clear natural pools, with the added thrill of fantastic views.

Access to Canyon de la Vacca and Canyon de la Purcaraccia involves a preliminary 30- to 50-minute hike. Canyon de la Pulischella is suitable for families.

Embracing the elements of stone and water: rappeling at Cirque de Salazie

135 PARQUE DE LA SIERRA Y CAÑONES DE GUARA, SPAIN

You're going to get wet! Spain's top *barranquismo* (canyoning) centre is in Aragon's Parque de la Sierra y Cañones de Guara, which is famous for its deep throats, powerful torrents and narrow gorges. You'll follow canyons downstream by whatever means available – walking, sliding, swimming, jumping,

even diving. Base yourself in delightful Alquézar and sign up for a canyoning outing to River Vero Canyon, one of the most attractive of Sierra de Guara's 200 or so canyons. Another plus is that it caters to all levels – bring the kids!

The main season is mid-June to mid-September. A good local agency is Avalancha (www.avalancha.org), which specialises in outdoor activities.

136 SAKLIKENT, TURKEY

The top canyoning spot in Turkey is the spectacular Saklıkent Gorge near Fethiye. What to expect? Jumps, leaps into pools and scrambling over rocks...and serious rappelling. This superb gorge is literally a crack in the mountains – its walls reach a height of 300m (984ft) – and it's too narrow for even sunlight to squeeze through. Luckily you can, but prep yourself

137 CIRQUE DE SALAZIE, RÉUNION

The Washing Machine. The Bath. With designations like these, you know that a visit to the canyon of Trou Blanc won't be just another picnic in central Réunion. Be prepared for some serious action in grandiose scenery – Trou Blanc is said to be the most 'aquatic' canyon in Réunion, with lots of toboggans (plunging water-polished chutes) and leaps. Another iconic canyon in the Cirque de Salazie is Voile de la Mariée (Bride's Veil), a more aerial circuit that includes a 50m (yes!) rappel. A magnificent experience for all the senses.

Most canyons in Réunion are not accessible during the rainiest months (December to March).

for icy water year-round. A wetsuit is a must. Once at the bottom, head downstream for about 18km (11 miles) and jump down a series of waterfalls along the way. Feeling tired? Think about the reward at the end of your trip: a freshly cooked, delectable trout served on wooden platforms suspended over the river. This is the life!

Canyoning in Turkey is excellent value and Saklıkent is a great place for first timers.

138 LAVA TUBES, TAHITI

Why not try canyoning in the dark? On Tahiti's east coast, elongated tunnels have formed via the cooling and rapid hardening of lava. A river runs through the giant, worm-like caves. If the idea of scrambling over slippery wet rocks through tunnels, jumping off ledges and plunging into cold pools puts a knot in your stomach, just wait until you actually try it. You may have to feel your way in the dark to avoid tripping over crevices because you can't see what comes next, but your adrenaline rush will be surging for the entire half-day excursion and maybe even for a while once you're back on dry land.

Canyoning outings can only be attempted when there's little or no chance of rain. The best season runs from May to October.

139 BORDERLANDS, NEPAL

Here's a well-guarded secret: beyond the valley of Kathmandu, near the border with Tibet, there's a quiet and isolated riverside eco-adventure resort that offers an array of outdoor activities, including top-notch canyoning outings. The superb Borderlands Resort runs two-day excursions from Kathmandu. On day one, you'll start with a basic abseiling training session and then practise on nearby cascades. On day two, you'll enjoy a full day of canyoning before returning to the capital. There's no need to be super fit – there are canyons to suit your needs, from 'gentle' to more challenging. One thing is sure: you're going to get wet, so don't even think about this if you have a fear of messing up your hair.

The convivial atmosphere of the Borderlands Resort (www.border landresorts.com) adds to this experience.

140 MORNE TROIS PITONS NATIONAL PARK, DOMINICA

Now's your chance to relive your Indiana Jones fantasies. Covering a big stretch of Dominica's mountainous interior, Morne Trois Pitons National Park has bags of natural panache with soaring peaks, deep gorges, soul-stirring rainforest vistas, volcanic craters, eerie lakes and thundering waterfalls – the perfect geography for canyoning. Put on a wetsuit, helmet, sturdy shoes, grab your climbing gear and a waterproof backpack, and experience the thrill of a lifetime. Most excursions last about four hours, more if you take a picnic, and include sensational abseiling down vertical waterfall-covered rock faces. The best part is, there'll be no crowds to hinder the experience.

Extreme Dominica (www.extreme dominica.com) is a professional adventure centre that runs guided canyoning trips in the park.

MOST THRILLING CANYONING ADVENTURES

MOST EXCELLENT EQUINE ESCAPADES

Saddle a horse and gallop out with cowboys, big-game guides and Mongolian herders in the world's remotest wilderness areas.

141 EXTREME COWBOYING IN THE FAR SOUTH

Riding with local cowboys at the very tip of Patagonia you're closer to Antarctica than to any major city, as snow, rain and katabatic storms will emphasise. Hardy Criollo horses are still used for remote travel and to work cattle on the *estancias* (ranches), but for real thrills join in with a horse drive across the pampas, galloping alongside loose steeds over rough ground. Your companions, flamboyant *baqueanos*, can teach you how to throw a lasso, track

At over 5000km, the Bicentennial National Trail is best tackled on foot – four of them!

pumas who stalk the colts and spot a soaring condor. These guys are as tough as their steeds and you'll need stamina rather than polished riding skills to keep up with them. You'll need energy too, for long nights on remote *estancias* feasting on whole barbecued lamb, downing rough wine and singing *ranchero* songs

BlueGreen Adventures (www.bluegreen adventures.com) runs Patagonian rides, including horse drives, throughout the Southern Hemisphere summer, whilst to see the *baqueanos* demonstrate their skills, try to catch a local rodeo.

142 HERD WILD BULLS HIGH IN THE ANDES

Ride out with *chagras* (cowboys) on the annual round-up of cattle in the Andes. Together you and the other riders form a long line to push the cattle down to the valleys. Consider carefully whether you're going to wear the traditional bright-red poncho, as most of the cattle you're herding are fighting bulls. Down at the corrals there's an opportunity to perfect your lassoing skills catching up steers and unbroken horses destined for branding. And there'll be plenty of feasting on barbecued meat, dancing to strummed guitars and drinking.

The cattle are usually brought down at the end of January. Be prepared for mountain weather and hard riding. See www.rideandes.com.

143 HORSING AROUND THE VIKING WAY

Join bands of Icelandic farmers heading out at summer's end to bring in their horses from the rugged interior. You'll be allotted your own miniherd of three or four riding steeds to change between as you help drive a thousand head of loose animals down from the highlands in a stampede of My Little Ponies. Actually, despite their diminutive size the animals are always referred to as 'horses,' and they are the perfect all-terrain vehicle for fording rivers, *tölting* over rough ground and following tightrope tracks across precipitous slopes. Horse traditions here stretch back a millennia and the village-hall dance on the round-up's last night aspires to Viking-quality hedonism.

In Icelandic weather you don't want fancy riding gear but a trawler-man's boots and oilskins. Check out www.ishestar.is.

144 LONGEST AND REMOTEST TRAIL

Can you get horses for a year or so? Want a life-changing experience? Then how about Australia's 5330km Bicentennial National Trail between Cooktown in Queensland and Melbourne. Be warned: it's long and it's remote. Both. Very. Too much commitment? Then some of Australia's most challenging riding is in the Snowy Mountains where following wild cattle means jumping fallen timber and negotiating steep slopes. For a chance to ride the mountains, drink billy tea and sleep out in swag, sign up with the Rudd family at Reynella, who've been running five- and seven-day horse trips in the Kosciuszko National Park for more than 30 years.

See www.reynellarides.com.au. For inspiration and information about the Bicentennial National Trail and the world's other independent long rides, check out www.thelongridersguild.com.

Originally entertainment for Genghis Khan's hordes, the Mongol Derby lasts a gruelling – and rewarding – two weeks

145 THE WORLD'S TOUGHEST HORSE RACE

The Mongol Derby is the kind of sports day...well, sports fortnight...that Genghis Khan organised for his horde: a 1000km horse race across the Mongolian steppes. The horses are changed at regular intervals and their welfare overseen by vets, but you on the other hand ride the full distance with no comforts provided. And you're limited to carrying just 5kg of emergency kit, which makes you dependent on the local horse-herders for shelter in their gers (huts) and for food. So you'd better like fermented mare's milk, because during the world's longest horse race you'll drink your fill.

If the race is too hardcore for you, Mongolia is still a practical country for the competent to buy or hire horses and head off on an independent trip.

146 AUTHENTIC AMERICAN RANCH EXPERIENCE

The Bitterroot in Wyoming is a working ranch raising Aberdeen Angus beef and providing western-style luxury and food for riding guests. So, in some kind of synchronicity, you can spend the days rounding up cattle and the evenings eating them. Once kitted out in jeans (Wranglers' saddle-friendly, flat inner-leg seam makes them the cowboy's choice), boots and hat, you'll be able to practise cutting steers out of a herd in team-sorting sessions in the arena or ride out into 130 sq km (50 sq miles) of mountains, river valleys and high pastures to bring in strays.

For the greatest fun, go at the end of September when the cattle in the high country are rounded up and brought down. Visit www.bitterrootranch.com.

147 LONGEST JUMP COURSE

Castle Leslie in Ireland's County Monaghan brings together good horses, a historic house and a touch of eccentricity. It's your chance to try out anything and everything horsey, including riding side-saddle, on 20 miles of traffic-free riding trails across the 1000-acre estate or in the heated indoor school. But what's extreme is the cross-country jump course with 300 different fences and obstacles – ranging in size from skip-hops through to Olympic huge – meaning you can pick 'n' mix your route, even changing onto a fresh horse to keep 'lepping'.

Visit www.castleleslie.com for packages for everyone from raw beginners to experienced riders keen to test themselves. As the 'land of the horse' Ireland provides numerous riding options, most listed on www.ehi.ie.

148 AFRICA'S TOUGHEST ENDURANCE RIDE

A 400km stretch in the saddle through Namibia's arid wilderness, the world's oldest desert, is not to be undertaken lightly but the rewards are immense. At trot and canter pace you'll be riding anything up to 70km a day through a world of wind-eroded rocks and sculpted sand dunes. Sand storms and mirages only add to the strangeness of the experience. You'll appreciate the comfort of each night's camp, eating around a campfire and sleeping out under brilliant starscapes. And Windhoek's fairly basic delights at trip's end will also be very welcome.

The incredibly fit horses demand riders who match them in ability for these epic rides which run from March to October. See www.namibiahorsesafari.com.

149 CLOSEST ENCOUNTERS ON A SAFARI RIDE

Ride out on a horse from Macatoo's tented base-camp in Botswana's Okavango Delta and the local fauna will discount you as an odd but harmless centaur-zebra. This means that you'll get thrillingly close to giraffe, buffalo, hippo and a whole Noah's Ark of other big game. Your expert guides have in-depth knowledge, and saddle-slung rifles, to keep things safe, but you'll still need to ride well enough to sit a get-the-hell-out gallop if you end up too close to a lion or irritated elephant.

In the May to July flood season there'll still be fast riding but you'll also be wading, often wither-deep, between the areas of higher ground. Visit www. africanhorseback.com.

150 FURTHEST OFF THE BEATEN TRACK

Sign up for pioneering horse-travel in Canada's Chilcotin mountains and have pack animals carry all the gear needed to 'spike' camp far out in remote mountain country. The riding horses are the hardy Cayuse mountain breed used by generations of cowboys, trail makers, gold miners and outlaws. You'll be expected to help with packing, saddling up and tethering the horses out at night. In exchange you'll reach wild valleys, remote lakes (take a fishing rod), Alpine meadows and high passes, with every chance of riding up on black and grizzly bears, wolves, moose and big-horn sheep.

To get to the remotest regions, you'll need to be on the the Mountain Challenger Horse Pack Trip Level III, which requires previous experience. Chilcotin Holidays (www.chilcotinholidays.com) also runs horse-trip guiding courses.

MOST EXCELLENT EQUINE ESCAPADES

ICONIC ASIAN ADVENTURES

*With surreal landscapes and the world's highest mountains,
Asia beckons to anyone with an adventurous spirit.*

Reputed to be visible from the Moon, the Great Wall offers glimpses of China's history and awesome landscapes

151 OVERLANDING TO SILK ROAD CITIES

Three cities in particular – Samarkand, Bukhara and Kashgar – typify the lingering scent of Silk Road exoticism. These are beacons that for centuries have lured restless souls across the vastness of Central Asia. In Uzbekistan, the breathtaking architecture of Samarkand's Registan Square is probably the Silk Road's most evocative sight. In neighbouring Bukhara the Kalon Minaret impressed a rampaging Genghis Khan and later became a dungeon for officers/spies of the British Empire. The raucous bazaars of Kashgar, in China, still attract travellers and traders who heed the call of one of the great overland routes.

Almost equidistant between Bukhara and Kashgar, Tashkent is the most practical port of arrival.

152 ROCK CLIMBING AT RAILAY, THAILAND

Climb direct from the sands of a tropical beach to the sort of views James Bond swashbuckled through in *The Man with the Golden Gun*. What's not to like? Railay is about as laid back as it gets: huts among the palm trees, bars at the beach edge, and climbing cliffs that look over abrupt headlands, white beaches and longtail boats. There's a great variety of climbing. Beginners will like Diamond Cave North Face and ABC Wall. And there's deep-water soloing, in which you climb a sea cliff unroped and simply drop into the Andaman Sea when you're done or dusted.

The easiest access is by longtail boat from Ao Nang Beach. For instruction, King Climbers (www.railay.com/railay/climbing/climbing_intro.shtml) is the doyen of local operators.

153 HIKING THE GREAT WALL, CHINA

History crunches beneath your feet. The protected lands of China are to the south and the marauding hordes are to the north. At least, that's how it was proposed when the Chinese built this incredible structure. Once stretching more than 8000km, it's now possible to walk around 3000km to 4000km if you follow the Wall's every remain...which isn't as simple as it sounds. The Wall is in disrepair in many areas, and just finding its course can be a challenge. For most who want to hike on it, a week-long commercial trip along the well-preserved section of Wall through Hebei Province near Beijing suffices.

Guided Great Wall treks typically cover the section around Gubeikou, Jinshanling and Simatai. Gubeikou is 140km from Beijing.

65

Paddling amongst the peaks: kayaking at Halong Bay

154 KAYAKING AT HALONG BAY, VIETNAM

Halong Bay is one of Asia's most recognisable landscapes, with its waters pooled around thousands of limestone peaks and islands. For years it was typified by the sight of junks threading between islands but has now become a favourite with kayakers seeking an intimate look at the rock features in this bay. Typical of limestone landscapes, Halong Bay is studded with caves, arches and pillars – whichever way you point the kayak you'll find some new feature. Multiday trips in the bay are usually accompanied by one of those junks – where you'll eat and sleep.

Halong Bay is around three hours by road from Hanoi; commercial paddling trips often depart from Hanoi.

155 RIVER TUBING AT VANG VIENG, LAOS

It sounds sedate enough – floating down the Nam Song River in a tractor tyre tube – but that doesn't account for the party element. River tubing is a pastime so enjoyable and popular, it's become one of the rites of passage of the Southeast Asian backpacking circuit. Limestone cliffs, honeycombed with tunnels and caverns, tower above the river, though for many it's become difficult to see the backdrop for the Beerlao, with bars lining the river's banks, enticing tubers in for a drink or seven. Authorities have closed many of the bars after several tubing deaths, and caution is always advised.

There are bus connections from Vang Vieng to Luang Prabang and Vientiane.

156 CROSS THE BORNEO JUNGLE, INDONESIA

The Borneo rainforest might be one of the most primeval places on earth and a shore-to-shore traverse of the world's third-largest island is one of Asia's ultimate – and least attempted – adventures. Begin in Balikpapan, heading upstream on the Sungai Mahakam in a variety of local boats – the 900-plus kilometres will take around a week. On the other side of the island you descend on the Sungai Kapuas, the world's longest island river, but the traverse's crux is the hike across the Muller Mountains in between – five to seven days of hiking through a range noted for its river fords, leeches and treacherous slopes.

A guide is essential to get you across the Muller Mountains. Recommended are De'Gigant Tours (www.borneotourgigant. com) and Kompakh (www.kompakh.org).

157 CYCLING IN VIETNAM

The bicycle is almost *the* image of Vietnam, whether it be rolling through the colonial streets of Hoi An, or across the elevated banks of rice fields. For visitors, bikes have equally become one of the vehicles of choice. Vietnam offers a variety of cycling experiences. In the south you can cruise across the table-flat Mekong Delta, crossing almost as much water as land – there may be more bridges here than in any other place in the world. In central Vietnam, there's the chance to mix coastal riding around the resorted likes of Danang and Nha Trang with climbs into the highlands, where you'll pedal among rainforests and coffee plantations.

Tour companies around the world offer cycling trips through Vietnam.

158 BUNGEE JUMPING FROM MACAU TOWER

The city of Macau may only be known for two things: the high rollers in its casinos and the high leapers from the world's tallest bungee jump. At 233m, the Macau Tower bungee is the equivalent of leaping from the roof of a 76-storey building – just getting to the deck takes around 60 seconds in an elevator. The good (?) news is that it takes about one-tenth of that time to get down as you plummet at speeds approaching 200km per hour, the city seeming to rise up at you, rather than the other way around. For a unique Macau spin on the bungee genre, try a night jump.

Details about jumping in Macau can be found at http://macau.ajhackett.com.

159 SURFING BALI, INDONESIA

At Bali's southern tip, the Bukit Peninsula is like a breakwater in the sea, snaffling the swells that roll in from the Indian Ocean. All along its east coast are breaks that draw surfers from around the world, and the small peninsula caters to all surfing abilities. On popular Kuta Beach, gentle beach breaks make for an ideal learning environment, while the long, barrelling wave at Padang Padang – aka the Bali Pipeline – is legendary. The most scenic surf spot would arguably be Uluwata, just south of Padang Padang, where surfers paddle out to the five breaks through a cave.

Bali flights land at Denpasar, at the head of the Bukit Peninsula. Surfboards can be hired at busy Kuta. Find surf reports at www.baliwaves.com.

160 TREKKING IN THE HIMALAYA, NEPAL

Nepal only began to develop a trekking industry in the mid-1960s, but quickly it became the planet's most desirable trekking location. Across its length runs the highest band of mountains in the world, veined with valleys that lead trekkers into the orbit of mountains such as Everest, Ama Dablam, Dhaulagiri, Cho Oyu and the Annapurnas. Everest Base Camp is the most popular trek, while the famed Annapurna Circuit has been all but devoured by roads in recent years, dispersing Pokhara-bound trekkers into the Annapurna Sanctuary, or higher up into Mustang. Less mainstream hiking destinations include Dolpo, a region immortalised in Peter Matthiessen's *The Snow Leopard*, and Makalu Base Camp.

Almost all trekking companies have Nepal itineraries, while Thamel, Kathmandu's busy tourist centre, is chock-full of trekking agencies.

ICONIC ASIAN ADVENTURES

GOTTA BE IN IT TO WIN IT: BEST RACES

Buzzing with a competitive instinct and a love of the outdoors? Then adventure racing is for you. Here are 10 events for first timers and old hands.

163 RAID IN FRANCE, FRANCE

The Raid Gauloises was one of the original adventure races, dating back to 1989 when sponsorship of sporting events by cigarette brands wasn't unusual – this is France, after all. Known simply as 'the Raid in France' in its new tobacco-free incarnation, this adventure race has mixed teams of four 'surpassing their limits' (in the words of the organiser) over a week-long odyssey around France. In 2012 organisers revamped the race's recipe, spicing up the basic ingredients of running, mountain biking and kayaking with snow and ice climbing, caving, canyoning and rafting from the Alps to the Cote d'Azur. The winning team that year covered the distance in 125 hours.

Check www.raidinfrance.com for news; the next Raid is in 2014 and its slogan is 'back to nature'.

161 HEBRIDEAN CHALLENGE, SCOTLAND

The sand on the beaches is white, the water is gin-clear, the sky is blue (sometimes). And the temperature? The temperature is *brrr*. The Hebrides, an arc of craggy islands off northwest Scotland, are the venue for what is affectionately known as the Heb. You'll be mountain biking and running (solo or as a team) among the rocks, swimming in the bays and, weather permitting, kayaking between islands with names that roll off the tongue: Eriskay, North Uist, Benbecula. Expect to finish with a warming dram of whisky because this multiday event is famous for its post-race party.

Visit www.theheb.org to enter. The fee includes ferry travel between Oban and the Hebrides, food and camping, and some equipment.

162 MARK WEBBER TASMANIA CHALLENGE, AUSTRALIA

What does a F1 racing driver do in his spare time? A spot of gardening? Painting with watercolours? Or host and compete in a five-day, 350km (217-mile) race across Tasmania? If you're Mark Webber, a man who has broken a leg and fractured a shoulder mountain biking, it's the latter. His Tasmania Challenge speeds across the Australian island by boat, bike and foot before the finale in the state capital of Hobart – if you can leave the map reading to a teammate, it's a great way to appreciate one of the most beautiful corners of the world, including the iconic Bay of Fires.

Keep an eye on www.markwebber tasmaniachallenge.com for news of future events; pairs (Elite or Enthusiast) or teams of three can enter.

164 PATAGONIAN EXPEDITION RACE, CHILE

When the race venue features the Strait of Magellan and the peaks of Torres del Paine, you know you've made it to adventure racing's top league. Racers in this 10-year-old event take on Patagonia's swamps and glaciers, mountains and plains for up to 11 days; wilderness navigation is an essential skill since you'll receive minimal assistance as you cover hundreds of kilometres of wilderness at the tip of the Americas. You'll also need to be proficient in climbing, kayaking and biking – this is probably not the best adventure race for first timers.

Enter the event at www.patagonian expeditionrace.com in mixed teams of four.

165 OPEN5 SERIES, UK

Tuck into a bite-size adventure in some of the UK's most scenic national parks with one of the Open5 series races. With only five hours to reach as many control points as possible on foot or mountain bike, you can spend the rest of the weekend exploring the landscapes of the Lake District, Yorkshire Dales and the South Downs at a more leisurely pace. There's an emphasis on navigation and strategy that will appeal to some, but ultimately Open5 is an affordable and fun introduction to adventure racing.

Visit www.openadventure.com to sign up (solo or in a pair).

166 ADVENTURE RACE SLOVENIA, SLOVENIA

There's no rest for the wicked, they say. A true adventure race must have a minimum of two disciplines (for example, biking and running) and involve navigation and strategy. But the organisers of Adventure Race Slovenia have supersized their event by requiring racers to hike, mountain bike, swim and kayak. Oh, and go caving, canyoning, cross-country skiing and abseiling to cover the 440km from Piran to Velenje in 50 hours. Phew! The event has been held since 2003 in Slovenia, one of Europe's finest adventure playgrounds, giving organisers plenty of time to dream up cruel tricks, such as having to complete a rope traverse of a river while carrying your bike.

See www.adventurerace.si for how to enter; the race is usually staged in June and offers two categories, the two-day Rover and the three-day Explorer.

167 RIVER KWAI TROPHY, THAILAND

You've seen the film, now run the race. Thailand's adventure race series includes events in Koh Samui, Bangkok and this one on the River Kwai at Kanchanaburi in the west of the country, one of Asia's largest adventure races. You'll be kayaking and swimming in the river, then biking and running in the jungle. Bring water, lots of water; the weather is hot and humid in March.

Check www.ama-events.com for registration details. Races take up to eight hours for teams of two in two categories: Adventure (for weekend warriors) and Extreme (for the hardcore racers).

168 XTERRA, USA

How do you make triathlons fun? Take them off-road: competitors in the Xterra race series (founded in 1995) swim in open water, ride a mountain bike instead of a skinny-tyred machine and finish with a trail run. Xterras are staged in some of the most scenic parts of the US, including Utah, California and Hawaii, and although navigation skills are not required, races are usually an adventure – ask former champion Ned Overend, who cycled within swiping distance of a black bear in one event. The annual world championship, like that of Ironman Triathlon, takes place in Hawaii, only in Xterra the running segment is up a volcano. Xterra's world tour makes stops in Spain, Greece, the UK, Australia and New Zealand.

Sign up at www.xterraplanet.com. You can ride, swim and run the course with friends and family before the event.

169 OYSTER ADVENTURE RACING SERIES, USA

Inject a little adrenalin into your visit to Austin, Seattle, Portland, Denver, San Francisco or Nashville by signing up for an urban adventure race in one of each year's host cities. Each race is different: in Portland you might have to kayak the Willamette river, in Nashville pull on your rollerblades for a game of hockey and in Austin you could have the tough task of tasting and ranking four beers. And remember, the organisers 'reserve the right to get you wet'.

Teams of three or more people can enter at www.oysterracingseries.com. The full courses at the 12 cities may cover up to 48km (30 miles) and can take six hours but this is an easy-going, fun and social event rather than a test of endurance.

170 COSTA RICA ADVENTURE RACE, COSTA RICA

Few countries are as tailor made for adventure racing as Costa Rica. Indeed, in 2013, Costa Rica hosted the Adventure Racing World Championship, pitting entrants against tropical beaches, mountain climbs and rainforests as they made their way across the country from the Pacific to Atlantic coast and from the border with Nicaragua to that of Panama in around six days. The temperature range was from 0°C (32°F) in the Cordillera de Talamanca to 35°C (95°F) at the coast. And the distance was 800km, at least some of which was floated via inner tube.

Check www.arcostarica.com for details of the annual race.

BEST TREKS WITH KILLER VIEWS

Trekking may be hard work but it's all worth it to encounter exceptional landscapes, extraordinary mountain peaks and serene snapshots of local colour.

171 PAYS DOGON, MALI

This landscape of rare beauty traverses ancient villages along the Bandiagara escarpment in World Heritage–listed Pays Dogon, with views spanning the vast Sahel Plains. Multiple trails offer a journey into ancient Africa with the sweeping plains from the plateau punctuated by villages built into the towering sandstone cliffs. Tracks wind across along intricately laid stone staircases, up ladders spanning chasms and past adobe homes, which fill the panorama with a rainbow of colours and textures.

Trekking is always warm here but avoid April to June when the temperatures are particularly high.

SKYSCAN/CORBIS ©

172 WEST HIGHLAND WAY, SCOTLAND

Scotland's most famous long-distance walk along the constantly changing highland scenery flaunts an incongruous mix of elegant Munros rising dramatically on every side, hauntingly barren moors stretching to the horizon and back-and-forth switchbacks. Some say the best spot is the top of elongated Conic Hill, where a sparkling Loch Lomond accosts your line of sight. It's spellbinding and mysterious at the same time. It's no wonder they chose to run an entire section of the trail through the National Scenic Area of Ben Nevis and Glencoe, where a narrow, grand glen is shut in by wild and precipitous mountains.

The trek stretches 155km between Fort William and Milngavie. It usually takes five to nine days and is best done between May and October.

173 URAN CHIRRIPO LOOP, COSTA RICA

Situated in Chirripo National Park in the heart of the Talamanca Mountain range, this is trekking at its finest. You'll travel though several ecological zones with scads of biodiversity, from the fantastical old-growth forests with trees towering over a canopy dripping with thick, hanging moss to the bare páramo landscape of scrubby trees, grasslands dominating highland wildlife and the lush cloud forest – looking down at the cotton-ball-like clouds is both awesome and dreamy. And when you summit Mount Chirripo you're rewarded by views of both the Caribbean and Pacific oceans...pretty special.

The trek takes about four days and can be done year-round, but avoid the muddiest months between September and November.

174 THE GRAND CANYON: RIM TO RIM AND BACK, USA

Why not go down first? From one rim across to the other and back again, this trek veers to and fro along different trails each way. As you descend into the depths of the crater, you get up close to the striking rainbows of brick hues filling the strata; the meandering Colorado River beckons and you pass pretty Ribbon Falls, the 30m-high waterfall that resembles ribbons billowing in the breeze. And when you reach the bottom and look up, you feel as tiny as an ant.

Avoid summer when temperatures easily hit 35–40°C (95–104°F) and winter (when parts of the north rim close). The hike takes about four to seven days round-trip.

Loch Lomond beckons like a giant aqua jewel along the West Highland Way

Trekking the Torres has more than its fair share of ups and downs

175 BATHALI VILLAGE TREKS, NEPAL

Paths and options abound here but any Bathali trek takes you through Kathmandu Valley and is ideal for families or people wanting a soft multiday hike with stellar views. You start and end in Kathmandu, meandering past Buddhist temples and rural hamlets, including lovely Bathali village which sits on a plateau amidst terraced rice fields and dusty-red thatched farmhouses. In between, glimpses of the snowy Himalayan peaks and swaths of bright-green forest greet you. Overall this is a relaxing area to trek and remains relatively uncrowded compared to more popular routes in Nepal.

Treks take anywhere between three to six days and can be done year-round, but avoid rainy July and August and hyper-cold in December and January.

176 LAUGARVEGURINN, ICELAND

Glaciers, waterfalls, moss-covered lava plains, volcanic peaks, mirror-like lakes – this hike runs the gamut. The 53km (33-mile) 'Hot Spring Route', named for the plumes of sulphuric steam that rise from the landscape, is Iceland's most popular hiking route and with good reason. The traverse, which winds through the stunning southern highlands, generally takes four days; most people begin at Landmannalaugar and hike south to Þórsmörk, staying at the five huts along the route. If you're up to a challenge, make the most of the midsummer 24-hour daylight and attempt the whole track in one day. Maintain a healthy respect for

177 THE W TREK, TORRES DEL PAINE NATIONAL PARK, CHILEAN PATAGONIA

This up-down-up-down trek (its route forms the letter W) in Torres del Paine National Park is a one of the best ways to embrace Chilean Patagonia and clear the cobwebs out of your brain. Each day brings a new set of wow-inducing vistas, from long stretches along luminescent glacial lakes (look for floating icebergs!), rugged peaks looming above and southern beech trees peppering the vast Magellanic forest. In between, the trail leads you to see the otherworldly Towers – three skyscraping granite spires – and offers a chance to glimpse the onyx-tipped Horns – two spikes topped by metamorphic black rock.

Patagonian weather is unpredictable, but avoid the harshest months between May and September. Dedicate roughly four to five days for the entire stretch.

Iceland's weather gods, though – they can change things up on you in the blink of an eye.

Huts along the route are open from late June to late August; bookings are recommended. Find info at www.fi.is/en/hiking-trails/laugavegurinn. Check volcanic activity in the area when planning your trip.

178 DRUK PATH TREK, BHUTAN

From bucolic blue pine, fir and thick alpine forests and dwarfed rhododendron trees to sparkling lakes and steep valleys nestled beneath Himalayan peaks, the landscape simultaneously feeds the soul and makes the camera happy (this is, after all, the happiest country on earth), yet the subtle beauty of nomadic yak herders you pass while gliding through high-altitude meadows is just as stunning as the dramatic terrain. One of the trek's most extraordinary sights is Bhutan's most sacred Buddhist site perched 3870m high on the precipitous hillside – the 10 temples of the Phajoding monastery, a stunning clutch of white walls and red roofs.

The trek requires five to six days and is best done March to June or September to November.

179 RENNSTEIG, GERMANY

This trek is Germany's best-kept hiking secret: used by traders and messengers since the 14th century, the 168km (104-mile) route winds from the centre of the country along the ridge of the fairy-tale Thuringian Forest, taking in medieval towns, river-filled valleys and mountain peaks, before ending near the Czech Republic border. You can hike the whole path from Hörschel to Blankenstein (which takes around 6 days) or alternatively walk any section in isolation – most of the stages are easily accessible by bus.

Make a detour at Eisenach to take in the stunning World Heritage–listed Wartburg Castle. May to August is the best time to walk the Rennsteig, although sections of it are open in winter for snowshoeing.

180 THE MILFORD TRACK, NEW ZEALAND

With 54km of pristine lakes, abundant birch trees, verdant forests and U-shaped, ice-carved valleys in the wild Fiordland National Park, it's obvious why this is one of New Zealand's most famous walks and considered one of the finest in the world. We're not sure what we love more, the canyons carved out of granite and temperate rain forests, the serene raised platforms extending cross the wetlands, or the zigzag along nine switchbacks to the 1070m MacKinnon Pass summit. And just when you think it can't get any better you'll wander across suspension bridges to find the stunning cascades of Sutherland Falls: at 580m it's the tallest waterfall in the country.

The track takes four days to complete. In high season (October to May) the trail is regulated and must be completed walking north.

BEST TREKS WITH KILLER VIEWS

ROCK STARS: WORLD'S BEST BOULDERING

Bouldering is acrobatic climbing practised close to the ground, without gear; get a grip on the sport in these beautiful settings.

SQUAMISH, CANADA

Sandwiched between Vancouver and Whistler in British Columbia, Squamish is a one-time logging town that is fast becoming an adventure-sport hotspot. And bouldering is one of its irresistible draws. The epicentre of the action is around the forest-fringed Stawamus Chief, a granite peak overlooking the town and Howe Sound. Bouldering locations further south suffer in the sun but summertime under the shade of these Douglas fir trees remains

The spotlight falls on bouldering in the Fontainebleau

comfortable for practising your crimp holds on overhanging rock faces. Squamish is rich in problems for every level and style of climbing but it's also a place to explore beyond the boulders; try kayaking on the Sound or take on the gruelling Test of Metal mountain-bike race.

Visit www.hellobc.com and www. tourismsquamish.com for details. The Squamish Adventure Centre (www.adventurecentre.ca) is the base for all things outdoors.

182 THE GRAMPIANS, AUSTRALIA

Only in Australia can you 'send' – short for 'ascend' in climbing jargon – classic bouldering climbs while being assailed by scents of lemon myrtle and eucalyptus and the sound of screeching cockatoos. The Grampians range in southwest Victoria, around three hours' drive from Melbourne, is Australia's prime climbing corner. Hit the northern Grampians and park at Hollow Mountain for some of the best bouldering in this beautiful region. When you're done conquering the sandstone and feel like a drive south, grab a bite and some top-notch wine at Dunkeld's Royal Mail Hotel.

Book accommodation in Hall's Gap at www.visitvictoria.com. The southern spring and autumn seasons are best for bouldering.

183 TICINO, SWITZERLAND

Cresciano and Chironico are two of Ticino's now not-so-secret bouldering locations. You'd be right in thinking they sound Italian – this southern Swiss canton is bordered by Italy on three sides. Another enchanting (and formerly secret) bouldering spot is Magic Wood to the east. There are problems to suit all levels of climbers – consult the local tourist offices for guides to the boulders on offer. Once a word-of-mouth marvel, the scene in Ticino is now multilingual with climbers setting up here for the whole summer season. As you breathe the fresh Swiss air and look out over crystal-clear lakes, arms tight from a good day's problem-solving, you can understand why.

See www.ticino.ch for transport and accommodation options.

184 FONTAINEBLEAU, FRANCE

What lies in the Forêt de Fontainebleau, 55km (34 miles) south of Paris by car, is every bit as impressive as the grand château that lends its name to the surrounding area of 30,000 sandstone boulders scattered around a sandy forest. There are 10,000 bouldering problems to conquer marked on these rocks, arranged in colour-coded circuits, many at the harder grades of difficulty. Among boulderers worldwide, this forest is a legendary place with a coterie of fans, the bleausards. They focus on the groups of boulders at Bas-Cuvier and Gorges d'Apremont; other hunting grounds include Trois Pignons and Franchard.

From Paris, drive down the A6 or take a train from Gare de Lyon to Bois-le-Roi. Winter, when snow free, offers better grip; spring and autumn are popular times to climb. See www.fontainebleau -tourisme.com.

HENN PHOTOGRAPHY/GETTY IMAGES ©

75

Anything a spider can do... Hampi is a rock climber's paradise

185   HAMPI, SOUTHERN INDIA

In dawn's warm sunshine a monkey leaps left and right up a boulder, making light of the problem before you. To a climber, completing a route up a boulder, without rope and no more than a few metres off the ground, is to solve a 'problem'. And there are plenty of problems in Hampi. Once known as Vijayanagara, the capital city of an all-powerful Indian empire, Hampi is now a vast area of 500-year-old temple ruins punctuated by huge granite boulders – the result not of a cosmic tantrum but three billion years of erosion by wind and water. The best climbing lies on Hampi Island, divided from the travellers' town by the Tungabhadra river.

Fly to Bangalore and take the train to nearby Hospet, then a rickshaw on to Hampi. The best time of year to climb is winter (November to March). Visit www.karnatakatourism.org.

186 ROCKLANDS, SOUTH AFRICA

The problem with bouldering at Rocklands is knowing where to start. The Northern Cederberg climbing mecca, less than three hours' drive north of Cape Town in the Western Cape, has great piles of sandstone boulders. As with all the best bouldering, the 1500 problems here pose a mental as well as a physical challenge – you need to think your way up some of them (especially the Rubik's Cube Wall). Most climbers rent cottages or stay on local farmsteads.

See www.cederberg.com for travel information. The climbing season runs from May to August. Rocklands is accessed via Pakhuis Pass.

187 PEAK DISTRICT, ENGLAND

Pack a crash mat for bouldering in Britain's Peak District – you'll want a soft landing from the very physical challenges the gritstone of central England presents. The region, now a national park, has long been a crucible of hard climbing, and when the weather's too bad to get high up on the crags, local climbers keep their hands (and feet) in with workouts on problems such as Careless Torque. Away from the rock, don't miss seeing the star location of numerous costume dramas, including *Pride and Prejudice*, the stately Chatsworth House.

Read *Peak Performance*, published by the British Mountaineering Council (www.thebmc.co.uk). Learn more about the park at www.peakdistrict.gov.uk and Chatsworth at www.chatsworth.org. The closest city is Sheffield but stay in one of the pretty towns nearby, such as Bakewell.

188 JOE'S VALLEY, USA

There's bouldering and climbing for every taste in the USA, from rhododendron-ringed boulders in the Appalachians to the sandstone Shawangunks of upstate New York. But slap-bang in the boulder-strewn centre of Utah is a place with a simpler name and fewer rules and regulations: Joe's Valley. This is road trip territory. It's a day's drive from Denver and Las Vegas, less from Salt Lake City. Pack a car with provisions, chalk and a lot of water, then pitch your tent at the (very) basic campsite. Like America's best diners, Joe's is a satisfyingly no-frills experience.

See www.utah.com. Peak bouldering seasons are spring and autumn; summer is too hot. The closest town to Joe's Valley is Orangeville.

189 VIRGIN GORDA, BRITISH VIRGIN ISLANDS

Warm water, sunshine and blue skies of the Caribbean, plus bouldering to excite every climber – it all comes together on Virgin Gorda, the third-largest island in the BVI. Granite boulders scatter the white sand beaches of the easternmost island. The difficulty of the routes is mostly moderate, which suits the laid-back vibe of the venue. Your daily rhythm will be to hit the boulders early in the morning, retire for a swim when the sun and rock gets too hot, and finish the day with a sunset session before a cold beer or two.

The British Virgin Islands are a short flight (www.seaborneairlines.com) from San Juan, Puerto Rico; plan your trip at www.bvitourism.com. Stay at Guavaberry Spring Bay resort (www.guavaberryspringbay.com), for boulders on your doorstep.

190 ZILLERTAL, AUSTRIA

Cowbells are clanking all around you and the air has pine-fresh zing...yep, the Austrian Tyrol lives up to your *Sound of Music* fantasies. In the Alpine meadows, forests and mountains of Zillertal, near Mayrhofen and east of Innsbruck, there lies some of Europe's best bouldering. Areas such as Ginzling Wald and Sundergrund, accessed by short hikes, are scattered with fragments of rock offering hundreds of potential problems, such as the lofty Knockin' on Heaven's Door. Some protrude from forest floors dappled in sunlight, others are surrounded by cows in mountain meadows. In winter, the valley becomes a low-key skiing area.

Munich and Salzburg are the closest major cities. Drive or take a train to Innsbruck and transfer to Mayrhofen. Plan your trip at www.austria.info.

ROCK STARS: WORLD'S BEST BOULDERING

BEST OFF-SEASON ADVENTURES

Avoid the crowds and bag a bargain by travelling to the world's best bits when everyone else isn't...

Encounter the mighty blue expanse of Lake Baikal at its frozen best in midwinter

OLIVIER RENCK/GETTY IMAGES ©

191 'GREEN SEASON' SAFARI, BOTSWANA

Botswana is not a cheap safari option – many of its luxury lodges cost up to $1000 per person per night. Gulp. But travellers willing to endure the odd downpour can nab a bargain when the tourist hordes have headed home. November to April is euphemistically dubbed 'green season' – rain is frequent and the resultant thick vegetation can make wildlife harder to spot – but it's also when lodges offer significant discounts and landscapes are lushest, attracting myriad birds. Many animals give birth at this time of year too, and a good guide will point out plenty of healthy young babies, plus the predators inevitably skulking nearby, looking for an easy lunch.

Malaria is present in parts of Botswana, including the Okavango Delta and Moremi and Chobe National Parks – prophylaxis should be taken.

192 WINTER WOLF-TRACKING, YELLOWSTONE NATIONAL PARK, USA

During the summer more than three million people pile into Yellowstone National Park; just 140,000 visit in winter. Sure, some of the roads close from December to March, ranger-led activities fizzle out and temperatures plunge to -20°C. But the pros are manifold: not only are the highlights blissfully tourist-free but the wildlife-watching is superb. Resident species such as elk, bison and bighorn sheep overwinter at lower elevations and stand out a mile against the ice-cloaked land. Plus you can enlist a naturalist guide to tramp through the sparkling landscape, following the footprints of the elusive grey wolf, easily visible in the virgin snow.

Cross-country ski trails are groomed in the Old Faithful, Mammoth, Canyon and Tower areas; half-day ski-touring packages cost $15. See www.nps.gov/yell.

193 MONSOON TREKKING, WESTERN GHATS, INDIA

Mumbai during monsoon? You must be mad! Granted, the Indian metropolis isn't much fun from June to September, when heavy rains flood roads and breed disease. But venture 100km inland to the Sahyadri Mountains and you've got the ideal wet-weather playground. These hills – part of the larger Western Ghats – come to life. Rivers and seasonal waterfalls are in full flow (perfect for rappelling and rafting) while the countryside glows vibrant green. Plus the rains keep temperatures cool for hikes that take in ancient paths, ruined forts and secluded homestays.

Malshej Ghat (154km from Mumbai) is a popular choice for trekkers; migratory flamingos flock here during the monsoon.

194 LAKE BAIKAL, RUSSIA

Lake Baikal is in Siberia – a word to make even the well-fleeced shiver. No surprise, then, that most visitors to this fathomless expanse of blue come in summer. And yet...Baikal in winter, when the mercury plummets to -20°C, is far more fun. The mighty puddle freezes over; you can walk out onto its translucent, creaking surface, the ice 2m thick but so clear you can see kelp forests swaying beneath. Negotiate this crystallised world by husky-sled, skis or snowmobile – or take to an ice-hovercraft, leaping over waves frozen like skate-ramps – then warm up in a *banya* (steam sauna), Russian-style.

Flights connect major Russian hubs to Irkutsk (65km from Baikal) and Ulan-Ude (250km). The Trans-Siberian railway also passes through these cities.

195 RAINY SEASON, IGUAÇU FALLS, BRAZIL/ARGENTINA

'Iguaçu' is a Guaraní Indian word, combining *y* (meaning 'water') and *ûasú* ('big'). Big water – yes. But bigger at some times than at others. Brazil and Argentina share this border-straddling cascade – a 3km-wide, 80m-high spillage of 275 separate falls, gushing through the jungle. At its annual peak, 6500 cubic metres of water a second are tumbling down this cataract. Trouble is, in peak visitor period (the dry months of April to July) this can shrink to a trickle. To see the falls in their full, forceful splendour, come during the December to February wet season. Just bring a waterproof jacket.

The Argentine side offers the most varied close-up views of Iguaçu Falls; the Brazilian side has the best panoramic vantage.

TRAVEL INK/GETTY IMAGES ©

196 WINTER IN VENICE, ITALY

Low mist wisping off the canals, empty alleys of glistening cobbles, St Mark's Square without the tourists: Venice in winter can be cold and damp and even a complete washout (they call this the *acqua alta*, flooding season), but the chance to wander without the crowds is worth donning a pair of wellies for. Wrap up warm and get lost; at some point you'll hopefully find yourself by big-hitters like the Rialto Bridge and awesome Gallerie dell'Accademia but the fun's in the atmospheric back streets – and the warming cafes where, of course, you'll always get a seat.

Alilaguna operates a boat service from Marco Polo Airport to St Mark's Square; journey time is just over an hour.

197 HURRICANE SEASON IN ARUBA, BONAIRE & CURAÇAO

Hurricane season is a serious issue in the otherwise idyllic Caribbean. The warm waters so beloved by tourists can draw in storms from June to November. Though there are no guarantees, it's usual for any given island to experience at least one wild-weather alert a year and take a direct hit every five to 10. But not all outcrops are made equal and those in the southern Caribbean, sitting outside 'hurricane alley', seldom see storms at all. Which makes Aruba, Bonaire and Curaçao – home to colourful colonial architecture, gorgeous sands and great diving – excellent summer choices.

All three islands (formerly the Netherlands Antilles) have international airports; the official languages of the islands are Dutch, English and Papiamento.

198 WINTER BIRDWATCHING, BRIGHTON, ENGLAND

Brighton: the British seaside town of chips-in-newspaper helter-skelter fun, the pebble beach Londoners flock to in good weather, the ideal boutique, boho-chic summer city break. But in December to February? It's low season and things are a bit quieter – unless, that is, you're a bird. As tourists desert Brighton's famous pier in winter, starlings from across the South Downs move in. At dusk they amass in their hundreds of thousands, performing dazzlingly balletic murmurations, rippling like water in the sky, then, as if on unseen cue from Mother Nature, they pour beneath the pier to roost in one great swooshing torrent.

The murmurations (formations of birds in flight) can be viewed from anywhere along the seafront, between the piers or standing on the Palace Pier itself.

199 'LOW SEASON' BARGAIN-HUNTING, HAWAI'I, USA

There are two high seasons on the isles of Hawaii: firstly, deep winter, when travellers want to escape cold weather elsewhere. The second is high summer, when vacationing families descend. Both these periods see price hikes – but neither is actually the best time to visit. In truth, no time is awful here: these volcanic outcrops are balmy year-round, with averages only fluctuating from 25°C to 30°C. But April to June is not only the start of the drier season, it's outside the more hurricane-prone July to November

Cruise canals and cafes without clamorous crowds – winter in Venice

period, plus humpbacks – which amass off Maui from December – stay around until May.

Temperatures drop with elevation – visitors to higher-altitude sites such as Haleakala (Maui) or Kilauea (Big Island) should dress accordingly.

200 WINTER SURFING, PORTUGAL

Mainland Portugal has almost 950km of coast and much of it is ideal for summer holidaying: there's a classy, quiet, golfy or gaudy resort to suit most tastes. But for surfers, winter's the time to be there, when the Atlantic swells are biggest and most consistent, and when beaches are free from other people. And it's not even that cold – though you'll want a decent wetsuit (sea temperatures average 17°C). The southern Algarve is mildest – find laid-back surf spots between Lagos and Sagres. But the gnarliest waves hit further north: brave the breaks around Porto and the Costa Verde if you dare.

Faro is the best access airport for the Algarve. Porto, which has its own airport, is three hours by train from Lisbon.

**BEST
OFF-SEASON
ADVENTURES**

MOST SPIRITED HIKING & BIKING

These trails linking breweries, wineries and distilleries supply liquid refreshment along the way.

201 FOXEN CANYON WINE TRAIL, CALIFORNIA, USA

Even though the Oscar-winning movie *Sideways* made Foxen Canyon famous, the Central Coast grape patch remains unspoiled. Cyclists salivate over the bucolic backroads that gently climb oak-studded hills, passing horse ranches and white clapboard farmhouses, before descending into the Santa Maria Valley awash in strawberry fields. About a dozen or so wineries scatter around the area, meaning you can supplement the gorgeous ride with peppery Syrahs, jammy Pinot Noirs and peachy Chardonnays in tasting rooms. Many places also let you uncork a bottle and picnic among the vines.

The towns of Los Olivos and Santa Maria bookend the trail. Pedalling conditions are finest April to October (though summer gets hot). See www.foxencanyonwinetrail.com and www.bike-santabarbara.org.

202 FRANCONIA TRAILS, GERMANY

More breweries squeeze into Franconia, a rustic region in northern Bavaria, than anywhere else on the planet. Myriad hiking and biking paths connect the sudsmakers, who typically offer beer gardens under the chestnut trees and brews straight from the barrel. From the Aischgrund Beer Road (50km, eight breweries through beech forests) to the Fünf-Seidla-Steig (15km, five breweries by way of apple orchards) and Aufsess Beer Loop (13km, four breweries amid castles), the countryside flows with frothy lagers, caramelly bocks and bacon-tinged smoked ales. Beer halls provide steaming plates of dumplings as needed for additional leg power.

Bamberg and Nuremberg are good base towns. May to October brings the clearest skies. See www.frankentourismus.de and www.franconiabeerguide.com.

203 GREENWAYS, CZECH REPUBLIC

The Greenways are a 402km-long (250-mile) web of trails that weave through the southern Czech Republic's woods and hamlets. Pine trees scent the air along the tracks. Baroque churches chime bells in cobblestone town squares. And no matter what little burg you pull up in – by foot or by bicycle – a pub will be there sloshing beers made by the time-tested local brewery. And we mean *time*-tested, as in castle-crowned Český Krumlov, where Brewery Eggenberg has filled mugs since 1560, and in Třeboň, where Bohemia Regent has hopped suds since 1379.

The Greenways meander between Prague and Vienna; see www.prague viennagreenways.org for maps. Hit the road between May and September for the best weather.

204 CAMINOS DEL VINO, MENDOZA, ARGENTINA

It seems every dusty side-street heads to a vineyard in Mendoza, which explains the 'roads of wine' name. Pedalling in the shadow of the white-frosted Andes shocks and awes (and distracts from the wind), while the colonial-style bodegas and occasional llama nibbling on the plains amp up the atmosphere another notch. When your legs tire of pumping, brake at one of the wineries producing the region's signature Malbec. Spicy? Velvety? Berry-like? Give it another swish before getting back in the saddle and seeking out the next earthy grape juice.

Take a taxi or bus to Maipú; the little town's shops rent bikes. Autumn (March to April) and spring (September to November) are lovely. See www.caminosdelvino.com.

205 ROUTE DES SAVEURS, QUEBEC, CANADA

The 'Flavor Trail' slices for 143km (89 miles) through Charlevoix, the pastoral region that harvests much of Quebec's food. Cycling the rugged, hilly roads isn't easy but it's encouraging to know the lamb farms, tomato vineyards and pear orchards that flash by will provide part of your next meal in true farm-to-table fashion. Village inns and alehouses serve the distinct, locally made wares – say a tomato aperitif with foie gras or pear ice wine with sheep's-milk cheese. Belgian-style microbrewers and baguette bakers provision you further for the Baie-Saint Paul–La Malbaie course.

The route starts northeast of Quebec City. Prime time to cycle and stuff your face is April to mid-October. See www.routedesaveurs.com and www.tourisme-charlevoix.com.

206 BAROSSA TRAIL, SOUTH AUSTRALIA

Cyclists would steer for the Barossa Valley even if it weren't Australia's premier wine region. With its manicured fields, burly red-gum trees and prim, square-spired churches, the landscape is an artist's canvas. Add 60-plus wineries in a compact, flat area, and you see the draw. The car-free Barossa Trail ambles through the valley's core along an old railway corridor, swinging near 10 vineyards in 13km (8 miles). Stop off to sample a fat Shiraz (the local speciality), a fizzy Riesling or tawny port. Or just stop and smell the roses that strew the path.

The valley is an hour north of Adelaide. It's best from November to June, and busiest March to April during the harvest. See www.barossa.com.

207 SPEYSIDE WAY, SCOTLAND

As if heather-purpled moors and fairy-tale castles, medieval kirks and forested glens weren't enough to beguile you along the 104km (65-mile) Speyside Way, several malt-whisky makers cook up their golden elixirs beside the highlands footpath. Follow the peat-sweet air to Macallan, Glenfarclas, Aberlour and Glenfiddich, among others. The distillers invite you in, show off their burbling copper pots and pour a tonsil-singeing dram or three to fuel your hike onward. Come evening in the wee villages, count on a salmon dinner fresh from the River Spey, foot stompin' fiddle music and, of course, more Scotch.

The trail runs between Buckie and Aviemore and takes five to seven days to hike. Apri to October is the best time to go. See www.speysideway.org.

208 URBAN BOURBON TRAIL, KENTUCKY, USA

This is the tenderfoot's hike, requiring that you walk a mere few blocks between bars in downtown Louisville. The city's environs produce most of the world's bourbon and the trail leads to taverns offering at least 50 types. So a 'trek' might go like this: start at stylish Proof on Main for a flight of micro-distilled bourbons. Mosey to Dish on Market for a working-man's shot of Old Grand-Dad and a burger. Onward to the Old Seelbach Bar for a bourbon-and-champagne mix, like patron F Scott Fitzgerald used to sip. After that, just 17 more bars to go…

The bourbon flows year-round but especially when the Kentucky Derby takes over on the first Saturday in May. See www.bourboncountry.com.

209 CAMINO DE SANTIAGO, SPAIN

Christians have been trekking to the town of Santiago de Compostela, where the shrine of Saint James lies, for more than 1000 years. Several pilgrim paths comprise the Camino de Santiago but the most travelled is the 780km (485-mile) Camino Francés. It rambles across northern Spain past Roman aqueducts, Moorish palaces, relic-filled monasteries and – answering the prayers of the thirsty – vineyards. Many of Spain's top winemaking regions splash across the landscape here. So as you're expiating your sins, you're also knocking back glasses of fruity rosés in Navarra, juicy reds in Rioja and zippy whites in Galicia.

It takes four to six weeks to make the pilgrimage on foot. Spring (April to June) and fall (September to October) provide the nicest weather. See www.csj.org.uk.

210 ROUTE DU CIDRE, NORMANDY, FRANCE

You're pedalling the lazy byroad, past fields of Normandy's brown-dappled cows, when the first apple orchard sends out its siren song. You follow the sweet smell and signs marked *cidre* (cider) and *calvados* (apple brandy), and wheel up to a half-timbered farmhouse. The owner invites you in, shows you his barrel-stacked cellar and pours you a tart glass of lip-licking goodness. The scene repeats when you roll by the next grove and the next. About 20 traditional cider makers, plus cheese and honey makers, work their artisan magic along the sleepy lanes.

Cars share the signposted, 40km (25-mile) loop. Peak season is April when the trees blossom but there's good riding until October. See www.larouteducidre.fr.

HOTTEST VOLCANIC VENTURES

Some grumble gases and steam, some belch brimstone and magma – but all of these fire-breathing giants demand awe.

That's one angry volcano! Soufrièr Hills unleashes its fury

DR. RICHARD ROSCOE/VISUALS UNLIMITED/CORBIS

211 KAMCHATKA, RUSSIA

Kamchatka is not a sensible land mass: this remote and inaccessible peninsula in the Russian far east dangles ill-advisedly into the tectonically irritable Pacific Rim of Fire. Which explains why this bear-populated, barely populated place (less than one person per square kilometre) is so especially volatile. There are more than 300 volcanoes here. Some, such as looming 4750m Klyuchevskoy, are huge (and still vigorously active); others, such as Maly Semyachik, hide simmering lakes of startling hues; others are simply acned with belching mud pools, fumaroles and steaming crevices. All, however, are constant reminders of the fire that lies beneath.

The Kamchatkan city of Petropavlovsk is a nine-hour flight from Moscow. Helicopter excursions over the volcanoes and Uzon caldera are available.

212 AVENUE OF THE VOLCANOES, ECUADOR

Christened by explorer Alexander von Humboldt in 1802, the Avenue of the Volcanoes does exactly what it says on the tin: the valley created by the Andes' Eastern and Western Cordilleras is lined with an embarrassment of geothermal giants. Just catch a bus along the main highway south from Quito and you're flanked by an army of them. Snow-sprinkled Cotopaxi is a dangerous beauty – perfectly proportioned but overdue an eruption. Then there's colossal Chimborazo (at 6267m the country's biggest), twin-peaked Pichincha just 10km from Quito and cantankerous Tungurahua (or 'throat of fire') one of Ecuador's most active.

The Avenue of the Volcanoes runs roughly from Cayambe to Tungurahua. Views are best in the drier seasons: June to August and December to January.

213 ISLA DE OMETEPE, NICARAGUA

It's not the snappiest of world records, but Ometepe can lay claim to being the planet's largest volcanic island inside a freshwater lake. Indeed, Ometepe is virtually *all* volcano, consisting of two lofty cones with just a thin strip of land between. Volcán Concepción is the larger and more feisty – this 1610m peak is still active and the strenuous hike to its summit reveals a cloud-swirled caldera prone to burp ash at any moment. Smaller and less tempestuous, Maderas is considered dormant but is still a thrilling expedition; ascend through monkey-laden forests full of orchids to the misty lagoon up top.

Concepción climbs take 10 hours. There are three routes up the volcano; two leave from Moyogalpa, one from Altagracia.

214 MONTSERRAT, LESSER ANTILLES, CARIBBEAN

Two decades ago, 'the Other Emerald Isle' drew discerning tourists who lounged on black-sand beaches, dived fishy waters and hiked verdant hills. Then in 1995 geology struck: having lain dormant for nearly four centuries, the Soufrière Hills volcano released all that pent-up energy. Ash belched, rocks flew. Capital, Plymouth, was buried by mud and debris; the island was evacuated, creating an exclusion zone that remains off-limits. Visit the Montserrat Volcano Observatory to gawp and learn about ongoing activity, or sail round the island's southern tip to see the rooftops of Plymouth, the 'modern-day Pompeii', poking out above a mud-and-lava shell.

Montserrat Volcano Observatory Interpretation Centre opens 10.15am to 3.15pm Monday to Thursday. Up-to-date activity reports on the Soufrière Hills Volcano can be found at www.mvo.ms.

215 THRIHNUKAGIGUR, ICELAND

It's no surprise Jules Verne dispatched the heroes of *Journey to the Centre of the Earth* into the underworld via Iceland – you can hardly move for cones and geysers on this most volcanically active island. But while you're unlikely to encounter dinosaurs or giant mushrooms, except perhaps after a night on the *rúntur* (Reykjavík pub crawl), you can mimic those fictitious Victorian adventurers by plunging 120m into the vast magma chamber of dormant volcano, the unpronounceable Thrihnukagigur. The first descents, via shaky lift, ran in 2012. Future plummets are at the mercy of Mother Nature – and health and safety...

Tours are run by Inside the Volcano and last five to six hours. Details of future trips, if viable, are posted at www. insidethevolcano.com.

216 HAWAI'I VOLCANOES NATIONAL PARK, USA

Usually, volcanic activity is best seen from a distance. But the gloopy lava flows sidling down Kilauea, the world's most active volcano, often move so slowly that it's pretty safe (a relative term) to watch at close range. And combining sizzling heat with glowing pre-pumice means a nocturnal excursion rating *huge* on the adrenalin scale. Though the best locations for lava views vary (it flows, right?), the Pu'u O'o Vent is a hotspot – literally. Or follow Chain of Craters Rd to the coast – you might enjoy an impromptu sauna as steam shoots up where lava plops into the ocean.

Kilauea Visitor Center is open daily from 7.45am to 5pm. The National Park Service website (www.nps.gov/havo) provides regular updates on locations of

217 WHITE ISLAND, NEW ZEALAND

You don't just see the geothermal fury of White Island – you hear and smell it too. This sense-overloading stratovolcano, poking out of New Zealand's Bay of Plenty, is one of the most accessible active craters in the world. Make the 49km trip from mainland North Island by helicopter or boat and you're right there, in the heart of its sulphur-stinking, steam-hissing, vapour-spitting netherworld. No tough hike is required; instead, spend a few hours walking (guided, carefully) around its 2km-diameter mass. Peer into fumaroles, admire acid-yellow crystals and feel the raw, barely contained power of the earth thrumming right beneath your feet.

Boats for White Island leave from Whakatane Wharf; trips last five to six hours, with an hour or two on the island. See

218 MT BROMO, JAVA, INDONESIA

If New Zealand hadn't already snaffled global rights to the adjective 'Tolkienesque', then this almost mystically beautiful volcano would surely trademark the term. Rising from the lunar swathes of the Sand Sea, itself cupped by a vast outer crater, and flanked by two elephant-skin-wrinkled peaks – Kursi (2581m) and Batok (2440m) – Mt Bromo is 2329m of volcanic perfection. The question is how best to appreciate its wonders. Most undertake an hour-long predawn hike from Cemoro Lawang on the rim of the outer crater to climb Bromo for sunrise; alternatively, ascend nearby Mt Penanjakan to take in the whole scene at arm's length.

The nearest large town is Probolinggo, 45km away. The best time to visit Bromo is during the dry season (April

219 OL DOINYO LENGAI, TANZANIA

Kilimanjaro might be Tanzania's most famous volcano. But Ol Doinyo Lengai – or the 'Mountain of God' – is definitely its strangest. That's because this spewing pile in the far north of the country, just south of flamingo-pocked Lake Natron, does a very odd thing: it produces natrocarbonatite lava – that is, lava only half as hot as the norm – which crystallises in midair, only to fracture like glass. The result? A truly surreal summit landscape. Despite its violent personality, the hardy can climb up its 2980m sides for ash piles, molten flows, weird pyroclastics and incredible Rift Valley views.

The tough climb up Ol Doinyo Lengai takes four to six hours; the descent takes two to four hours. Most treks start around midnight to summit for sunrise.

220 SANTORINI, GREECE

In around 1630 BC, a supervolcano destroyed the original island of Santorini. The eruption was so cataclysmic that some historians believe it wiped out the entire Minoan civilisation on nearby Crete. But what a glorious catastrophe: the sunken caldera that remains is an idyllic Greek isle of magical sunsets, whitewash tumbling down cliff-sides – and fascinating diving. There are some 30-odd dive sites in the sea-filled lagoon created by the blast – the resultant gnarly rock walls, lava formations and drop-offs crafted by all that ancient action are now populated by an underwater menagerie of lobster, nudibranch, snapper, barracuda and more.

Santorini's dive sites range from 2m to 30m in depth. There are four wrecks; two are suitable for beginner divers.

HOTTEST VOLCANIC VENTURES

FOR PROS ONLY – THE MOST DANGEROUS ADVENTURES

Let the professionals thrill you with the most death-defying challenges.

There may not be any waves up this high, but who says you can't surf above the Arizona desert?

221 DIVING WITH TIGER SHARKS IN THE BAHAMAS

There's trouble in paradise. The water is incredibly clear and the mood is relaxed as only the mood in sun-blessed spots like the Bahamas can be, but something is in the water at Tiger Beach. Dive in and take a closer look, from the safety of a heavy-duty cage of course – tiger sharks chew, unlike the great whites that might just spit you out. The hookah-style breathing system supplies air from above, not via tanks, so you don't need to be a certified diver and can move around the cage. The sharks are curious and circle with their silent, majestic power, making this a truly awe-inspiring experience.

Eat and drink in West End, the oldest city on Grand Bahama Island, 40km (25 miles) west of Freeport. Dive with www.sharkexpedition.com.

222 BASE JUMPING, KUALA LUMPUR, MALAYSIA

BASE jumping is a little like skydiving but instead of leaping from a plane, jumpers launch themselves from the four fixed locations that spell BASE: buildings, antennas, spans (bridges) and the earth (cliffs). Fatalities happen more easily than in skydiving because there is less time to open the parachute and more to hit, but the high danger factor doesn't seem to deter professional addicts looking for the next daring or famous BASE, such as the Sydney Harbour Bridge or Eiffel Tower. A BASE competition at the KL Tower in Kuala Lumpur, Malaysia, is judged on how accurately jumpers can land on one tiny spot after falling and parachuting a frighteningly low 335m.

For more about how to enter the KL Tower BASE jump competition, visit www.kltowerjump.com.

223 FREESTYLE MOTOCROSS

Don't ask why pros go on these heart-stopping adventures. The answer is because they can. Got a motorcycle? Why not make massive jumps off a ramp while performing stunts mid-air? FMX is a chance for pro riders to perform around the world in competitions such as the Red Bull X-Fighters, which has included sumptuous backdrops in Istanbul, Madrid, Brasilia, Rome and Moscow. The sport is still evolving, with the first back-flip only attempted in 2000 (and even then resulting in a dangerous crash). Thank the motocross gods for protective helmets, boots, gloves, and knee and elbow pads.

You can watch the pros strut their stunts at Supercross and Arenacross freestyle motocross indoor stadium shows. Visit www.motoxaddicts.com for events.

224 SKYSURFING IN ARIZONA

Some see a harsh desert of cacti and intense heat, others see the open spaces of Arizona as skysurfing heaven. After skydiving loses its thrill, the hard-core buzzseekers ask, 'why simply fall from the sky when we could surf it on a board and complete a few creative aerobatic moves into the bargain?' A snowboard-type board is attached your feet to prevent it flying off should you tumble. And you will tumble – keeping balance isn't easy with air ripping against your board. Skysurfing once had sponsor dollars behind it but is now not so lucrative or popular. That won't stop pros from showing off their sky dance.

To make a start or get inspired, you can take lessons through www.skysurfer.com.

225 CANYONING IN INTERLAKEN, SWITZERLAND

Take all the skills from other extreme sports and bring them to the canyoning table. You must have an appetite for adrenalin to leap off a high waterfall into a cold thrashing pool. Why climb down a cliff when you can waterslide on a slippery rockface, be shocked into laughter and thankful for your helmet? You should take a moment to appreciate the jaw-dropping valley views. Now back into the pool to swim around boulders that pierce the water and sometimes have to be clambered over. Battling for survival has never so much fun.

Interlaken is in the Bernese Oberland region of the Swiss Alps and can be reached via the TGV from Paris and the ICE from Frankfurt and Berlin.

89

226 CLIFF DIVING IN LA QUEBRADA, ACAPULCO, MEXICO

No safety equipment, special outfits, shoes or gloves – just a human being leaping off the edge of a cliff into water. It started in Hawaii and grew dangerously infamous in Acapulco, where Mexicans and gringos fell through the air at speed. Today you can watch pros praying before their dives, 10 storeys high up on the La Quebrada cliffs and closer to their god. And no wonder – if their timing is off, soft flesh can smash into the jagged cliff face or they can miss the perfect spot to pierce the battering waves below in the Pacific Ocean. This is not a sport for novices to jump into!

Regular shows occur from 1pm to 10.30pm (once it's dark they bring out flaming torches). Observation decks in the area charge a few dollars, with restaurants charging more than $15.

227 ICE CLIMBING, SCOTLAND

Each winter the Scottish Highlands are encrusted in a thick of layer of snow and ice. The Scots defy hypothermia and climb walls of ice with their crampons, ropes and ice axes. The melting frost on rocks makes for beautiful patterns but also perilous surfaces to grab hold of. In the Cairngorms, even experienced climbers have slipped and dangled by a rope for up to seven hours, or worse, plunged more than 100m. These finger-numbing ranges are where the UK's highest wind speeds (270km per hour) and lowest temperatures (-27°C) have been recorded. Pros learn to love a cold sweat with ever-tougher climbs, such as Centurion on Ben Nevis, which commands a VIII grade, or the Duel in Glencoe, which earns its grade IX badge with serious steepness and mere millimetres of ice to cling to. Heart-warming team work and a whisky will warm the cockles...after you've completed the climb.

If your heart is racing to climb up a Scottish ice face, learn the ropes with experienced, qualified instructors; see www.alpha mountaineering.co.uk/index.html.

228 NAGHOL (LAND DIVING), VANUATU

Bungee jumping is a neat way to get your kicks. *Naghol* (land diving), on the island of Pentecost, is a much more serious business. There are no mod cons here, no modern gadgetry or elastic ropes. Local men take the plunge, attached at the ankle only by liana vines, from 35m-high platforms built of tree trunks and saplings, all to ensure a successful yam harvest. Each diver claps his hands, crosses his arms, and leans forward, describing an arc through the air. If the vines hold – and sometimes they don't – only his hair will touch the soil, and a bounty will ensue.

Land diving happens weekly from April to June on Pentecost; visitor numbers are restricted to 50 for each dive.

229 EATING ONE OF THE WORLD'S HOTTEST CHILLIS IN SRI LANKA

Until recently, the cobra chilli in Sri Lanka was the world's hottest chilli (pipped only by one in Trinidad). If you've gone cold on the ever-popular India, see how much heat

Even if they tell you to go jump off a cliff you should leave it to the pros at La Quebrada

you can take by diving teeth-first into this chilli in culture-packed Sri Lanka. It rates 855,000 heat units on the Scoville scale of spiciness (compared with 2500 for Tabasco sauce) so is definitely only for the brave. You can try the chilli in a mutton curry or on the side with a coconut sambol. Note that a glass of water will not come close to quelling this level of fire.

The best time to visit the ancient cities region of Sri Lanka is in the dry season (April to September).

230 LAND SAILING IN THE BLACK ROCK DESERT IN THE USA

Looking aptly like a sailboat on three wheels, the sand yacht dates back to Ancient Egypt and even then was used for thrills. No wonder, when you can zoom across empty beaches at speeds four times faster than the wind. Wide, open spaces also mean you can hoot with exhilaration as loud as you like. And being air-powered means leaving no pollution. But you'll really need your intrepid boots strapped on tight to take part in a race in the harsh, windy

expanses of the Black Rock Desert, where water, food and medical aid are scarce.

The stunning desert is remote and unforgiving so prep your supplies and go with the pros. More info on land sailing in the USA can be found at www.nalsa.org.

FOR PROS ONLY – THE MOST DANGEROUS ADVENTURES

BEST HIDDEN HUTS AND SHELTERS

As both basecamps and life-saving shelters, mountain huts, remote refugios and basic bothies often become iconic for wild wanderers.

231 VILCABAMBA, ECUADOR

It's years since you last sat astride a horse. Gavin, the overnight expedition's charismatic Kiwi leader, says it's like riding a bike, but you're not sure that you'd even cycle along the narrow, winding trails that hug the mountainside above the Andean village of Vilcabamba. Fortunately your surefooted steed picks her way carefully through a snowmelt river, along dramatic drop-offs and up steep ribbon-like tracks into the cloudforest – she's done it all before. Later, over aji-enhanced stew and wine, you'll hear the story of this hut and alpine wonderland on the periphery of Podocarpus National Park. It's a bluebird day and the peak-framed view soars over fields of orchids and bromeliads back down the valley.

Two-day horseback treks to this private mountain refugio can be arranged through Caballos Gavilan (gavilanhorse@yahoo.com).

232 BLACK SAIL HUT, CUMBRIA, ENGLAND

This is the last place you expected to be face-diving a curry, but how could you fail to be tempted by home-cooked fodder accompanied by fine wine at England's most remote hostel? Black Sail Hut is a former shepherd's bothy sitting under the twin gaze of Pillar and Great Gable Mountains and the chef is caretaker Pete Ellison who takes hut hospitality to a new level – but you've earned it after days spent mountain biking, camping and climbing through The Lakes' valleys and mountains. Lakes Ennerdale, Buttermere and Wastwater (England's deepest, beneath the country's highest peak, Scafell Pike) are nearby, with Black Sail situated conveniently right in the middle of the three.

Black Sail (http://www.yha.org.uk/hostel/black-sail) sleeps 16 people. It's a 2-mile walk from the nearest road.

233 MUNGO HUT, SOUTHERN ALPS, NEW ZEALAND

According to the logbook, only two groups have overnighted at Mungo Hut in the last 12 months. Gazing at the peaks of the Toaroha Range towering majestically above, it feels surreal to be a member of such an exclusive group but then the bushwhack in along the Mungo River is not for the whimsical weekend tramper. It's a relief to reach the turn and take the 15-minute climb up to the hut, set in a tussocky clearing surrounded by montane forest. If there's light enough after you arrive, it's worth taking a half-hour stroll downriver to find the two hot springs that bubble by the Brunswick Stream amid mountain cedar and pink pinewoods.

Mungo Hut has four bunks; see www.remotehuts.co.nz/huts/mungo.

234 ERZHERZOG JOHANN HÜTTE, AUSTRIA

Forcing down an early breakfast you contemplate the Grossglockner. Outside in the beckoning silence some of Europe's other iconic peaks, from Dachstein to the Dolomites, loom into view as day breaks. Although popular enough to require advance booking, this hut's remoteness is underlined by the adventure everyone has to experience in order to get here. Arrival at Austria's highest hut (3454m) requires a climb of five to six hours from the south (Kals) or the east (Heiligenblut), involving glacier crossings and/or fixed-rope assisted ascents. Once there, however, the summit of Austria's highest peak is within a two-hour climb of the door.

Open June to September, but the Winterraum (4 bunks) can be used during the rest of the year.

235 GARBH CHOIRE REFUGE, CAIRNGORMS, SCOTLAND

The roof is creaking and leaking, and dry floor space is at a premium when the bothy's door bursts open to let in the wild Scottish elements as well as couple of bedraggled hikers. You give them a Cairngorms welcome – a steaming cuppa. Since the '60s this basic, busted-up bothy has provided refuge for intrepid hill walkers and climbers brave enough to take on routes between Cairn Toul and Braeriach (Britain's third highest mountain). As the wind howls, conversation turns to the Secret Howff of Beinn a'Bhuird – an elusive shelter rumoured to be nearby, with a stove, floorboards and glass windows. Its location, a fiercely guarded secret, is known by a select few.

Garbh Choire Refuge is a small structure in the Garbh Choire; see www.mountainbothies.org.uk.

236 BURON REFUGE D'EYLAC, AUVERGNE, FRANCE

With Puy Mary as a backdrop, you nibble a chunk of Cantal cheese and sip a glass of red while reflecting on the 2.5km cross-country snowshoe traverse that brought you from Col de Serre to the door of Buron Refuge d'Eylac. This *gîte d'étape* (walkers' guesthouse) is more basic than most in the Parc des Volcans d'Auvergne: no meals are served here and there's no running water or electricity from 16 September to 14 June. The refuge, near the Pas de Peyrol, has 14 beds and a common room but you're not expecting company – the Auvergne is one of Europe's least-peopled regions and humans are outnumbered five-to-one by cows in the Cantal.

Operated by the Régional Nature Park of the Auvergne.

237 SUPPER COVE HUT, DUSKY SOUND, NEW ZEALAND

Paddling onto Supper Cove you dangle a line. This is the first hut you've stayed in that comes with a dinghy and you're looking forward to fish, but also keep an eye on conditions. The sea can turn in an instant, and it's claimed bigger ships in the past. This historic hut sits in an ultraremote corner of New Zealand's World Heritage–listed Fiordland National Park. Dusky Sound is so undisturbed that axe marks left in the trees by Cook's crew when they felled forest to create Astronomy Point are still visible. Supper Cove is midway along the challenging Dusky Track, a 10-day tramp between Lake Hauroko and Lake Manapouri.

To stay at Supper Cove Hut tickets must be purchased from the Department of Conservation (www.doc.govt.nz).

238 ILLAWONG HUT, NSW, AUSTRALIA

Two hours after leaving Guthega, your ski buddy points his pole at a dot on the range and identifies it as Illawong. This alpine refuge sits at 1600 metres in the heart of Kosciuszko National Park, the roof of Australia, and has been at the heart of Australian back-country skiing since the '20s. Surrounded by an undisturbed white meadow on an August morning, this snowy scene – far removed from most people's idea of Australia – bears little resemblance to the shimmering vista that greets summer bushwalkers to this historic hut. Further along the track, across the swing bridge over the Snowy River, myriad trails spider off under the bows of the snowgums.

Illawong Lodge (www.illawong.asn.au) is 2.5km south of Guthega.

239 REFUGIO FREY, PATAGONIA, ARGENTINA

A condor soars above the two-storey hut, silhouetted against the granite walls of Cerro Catedral. Perched high above the chocolate-paved streets of Bariloche in the lake district of Argentina, Refugio Frey is an Andean eyrie for trail walkers, cross-country skiers and mountaineers, and provides a beautiful basecamp for people exploring one of the best rock-climbing areas in South America. While preparing for your attempt to mount the massif and touch the void on the flanks of Torre Principal, glance around the 360-degree vista: the spire-punctured Patagonian skyline and the reflections in the calm green waters at the bottom of the basin.

Refugio Frey is in Nahuel Huapi Park, Patagonia, Argentina. It's reached via various trails.

240 CHUBETSU-DAKE HINAN-GOYA, JAPAN

The whisky washes away the taste of fish sausage. Both have come from the generous hand of your new friend. Conversation's been challenging but you're getting on like a hut on fire, your presence in this alpine refuge proof of a shared passion for the mountains. You're on a week-long trekking traverse along the spine of Daisetsuzan National Park. There's a range of shelters here, from basic lean-tos (be alert for brown bears) to two-storey huts like this one. Some even boast tatami-mat floors and hot springs.

Around a dozen shelters are scattered through Daisetsuzan National Park, a large wilderness area in central Hokkaido. Take a four-season tent just in case.

ICONIC AMERICAS ADVENTURES

From Arctic Canada to sub-Antarctic Patagonia, the Americas is a big place with equally big opportunities for adventure.

OVERSNAP/GETTY IMAGES ©

Leg it up to the lofty eyrie of the Inca emperors, way up in the clouds – Machu Picchu

241 WILDLIFE WATCHING ON THE GALÁPAGOS ISLANDS, ECUADOR

Almost a byword for exotic and diverse wildlife, the Galápagos Islands shot to fauna fame through Charles Darwin's visit in 1835 – his *Origin of Species* turned the archipelago into one of the world's premier wildlife-watching destinations. Cut by the equator, these volcanic islands sit like floating menageries almost 1000km off the South American coast. Most visitors skim between the islands on tour boats, travelling from animal species to animal species – Galápagos' pin-up critters include the land iguana, giant tortoises, Sally Lightfoot crab, Galápagos sea lion and fur seal, the striking blue-footed booby and the endearing Galápagos penguin.

The islands have two airports, on Isla Baltra and Isla San Cristóbal. There are public ferries for interisland transport, though some uninhabited islands can only be visited on tours.

242 DIVING IN THE CARIBBEAN

The Caribbean Sea is peppered with thousands of islands and just as many fantastic dive sites. The island of Bonaire is probably the world's top shore-diving destination, with the island wrapped in coral reefs that bustle with marine life. One of the finest diving and snorkelling sites on the island is 1000 Steps Beach, where the 72 steps to the beach (yes, the name is an exaggeration) keep crowds to a minimum. On the Cayman Islands, Bloody Bay Wall drops away 300m into crystal-clear waters, and you can mix this with a wreck dive on the purpose-sunk submarine rescue vessel, *Kittiwake*. For big things with teeth, the Bahamas form the Caribbean's finest shark hangout.

For information on Bonaire, see www.tourismbonaire.com. For the Cayman Islands, see www.caymanislands.ky. For the Bahamas, www.bahamas.com.

243 SURFING AT PIPELINE, USA

Surfing's most famous waves roll onto the north shore of the Hawaiian island of O'ahu. Here, the glassy tubes of Banzai Pipeline – aka Pipeline, aka Pipe – have become both a boarding nirvana and part of the surfing lexicon. Winter swells can generate waves that tower up to 10m, slamming offshore onto a dangerously shallow reef. Pipeline is no surfing picnic – these waves have real intent, as do some of the local surfers – and it isn't the place to first pick up a board. If the sea is pumping, you can expect to share space among the waves with a few visiting pro surfers.

To find Banzai Pipeline, head for Ehukai Beach Park and, facing the ocean, walk about 100m to the left.

245 HIKING TO MONTE FITZROY, ARGENTINA

With needle-tip Cerro Torre on one side and the Torres del Paine just across the Chilean border on the other, Monte FitzRoy would need to be something special to attract attention. And it is. Stand beneath its enormous summit rock – the rock alone is more than 1km high – and you begin to appreciate why it's considered one of the world's most challenging climbs. Most people come simply to hike, aiming for Laguna de los Tres pooled at its base. Sunrise here is spectacular, if the weather plays its part. A hardier few circuit the mountain, crossing Paso Marconi to traverse the extremely wild Patagonian Ice Cap.

Flights into the region land at El Calafate, from where it's a 215km drive to El Chaltén, the starting point for treks.

244 HIKING THE INCA TRAIL, PERU

High on any list of the world's most famous treks, the 38km-long Inca Trail is *de rigueur* for almost any visitor to Peru. Climbing from the Urubamba River – a tributary of the Amazon – it passes through cloud forests, bare *puna* grasslands, Incan ruins and mountain passes as high as 4200m. The trail ends at the once-lost city of Machu Picchu, South America's most famous archaeological site, which spills down a slope below the peak of Wayna Picchu. The Classic Trail takes trekkers four days, and savvy hikers stick around for a night at Machu Picchu for a dawn look at the place without the crowds.

Permits are required to hike the Inca Trail, and numbers are limited to 500 hikers a day.

246 MOUNTAIN BIKING AT MOAB, USA

This experience all comes down to a single word: slickrock. It's on this sandstone that the Utah town of Moab has built its world-class mountain-biking reputation. Above the town, the 21km Slickrock Trail is arguably the world's most famous mountain-bike route, winding across sandstone ridges, with climbs as steep as the pyramids matched by sudden plunges into pits of sand. Other famed rides here include the technical Porcupine Rim, a playground of cycling rock at Bartlett Wash and the butt-clenching fear factor on the Portal Trail – think 50cm-wide trail above a 100m drop...there's a reason for the warning signs.

Moab has an abundance of cycle shops offering bike rental – try Poison Spider Bicycles (www.poisonspiderbicycles.com) or Chile Pepper (http://chilebikes.com); book ahead to be sure of wheels.

247 SKIING AT WHISTLER-BLACKCOMB, CANADA

Framed around the twin peaks of Whistler and Blackcomb, North America's top ski resort has around 30 sq km of play area and almost 200 marked trails. One-quarter of the runs are black diamond (advanced) and the resort has the highest vertical drop (1609m) of any North American ski field, but there are also beginner-friendly options. It's not all downhill derring-do, with more than 28km of cross-country trails. For the ultimate Whistler-Blackcomb challenge, head for Ruby Bowl where, after a hike to Spanky's Ladder, you'll find 600m of continuous double-diamond steeps.

Whistler-Blackcomb is around 120km from Vancouver, and may be one of the few ski fields accessible by train (the Sea to Sky Climb train). For ski details, see www.whistlerblackcomb.com.

248 CYCLING IN CUBA

Few islands in the Caribbean warrant the effort of bringing a bicycle, but Cuba most certainly does. The Caribbean's largest island – pedal from one end to the other and you'll cover more than 1300km – has become a honey pot for cyclists. Distances are manageable, there's easy pedalling along the coast, and there seems to be a beach around every bend. Whether you're just cruising along the bike lane on Havana's seafront Malecón, or slogging up the island's most notorious mountain ascent – the 1200m climb to the gigantic La Gran Piedra rock – you'll have experienced Cuba in the finest way possible.

Many international tour companies run cycling trips through Cuba. For local bike rental, try Cubalinda (www.cubalinda. com) or WoWCuba (www.wowcuba. com).

249 HIKE THE WEST COAST TRAIL, CANADA

Vancouver Island's West Coast Trail was originally built as an escape route for shipwreck survivors... need we say any more about the nature of this wild coast? The 75km trail, along the southern edge of the Pacific Rim National Park Reserve, passes through virgin spruce, cedar and hemlock forests, across cliff tops and along stretches of deserted beaches. As well as the primeval beauty that will draw you here, expect deep mud, soup-thick fog and heavy rain. Most people take five to

Pedal power reigns supreme over the slickrock terrain around Moab, deep in the Utah desert

seven days to hike it, and it's one of the most demanding walks you'll ever endure. But at least you aren't shipwrecked...

The trail is open May through September; from 15 May to 15 September, permits are required. See www.pc.gc.ca.

250 RAFTING THE GRAND CANYON, USA

You might have heard of the Grand Canyon. You might even have stood on its rim. But the way to know it best is to pour through it in a raft,

as some 25,000 people do every year. How much you see might be up to your boss – with two to three weeks you can raft the entire 446km section through the canyon, while three shorter sections of 160km or less take four to nine days. Rafts come in three flavours: oar, paddle or motorised. In oar rafts your guide does all the rowing, while in paddle rafts you get to share in the workload.

For independent rafting trips, you must enter a lottery for permits – the main lottery is in February. For details, see www.nps.gov/grca.

ICONIC AMERICAS ADVENTURES

ULTIMATE TRAIN RIDES

Ride rails up mountains, around canyons and through deserts…and see how mankind harnessed wildernesses with the world's most sophisticated mode of travel: the train.

PEP ROIG/ALAMY ©

251 THE JACOBITE, SCOTLAND

This Scottish steam train chugs through a land immortalised by movies *Local Hero* (remember those gorgeous beaches?) and *Harry Potter*…this is the Hogwarts Express depicted in the wizardry franchise. Still more famously, the line follows the much-romanticised footsteps of Bonnie Prince Charlie, Scotland's last hope for a Scottish king, who fled to Mallaig (and then across to the Isle of Skye) after being defeated by government troops in 1745. The Prince never returned to Scottish soil but with Skye's mountainous bounty beckoning across the water from the Mallaig terminus, this route will likely prove prequel to further adventures for you.

The Jacobite runs at least once daily, mid-May to mid-October: book through West Coast Railways (www.westcoastrailways.co.uk).

252 COPPER CANYON RAILWAY, MEXICO

The Mexican rail system's one surviving remnant traverses deserts and teeters along canyon rims – rims, note, of the world's greatest canyon system. Giddying 1000m-plus drops are a mere puff away from the gradient-defying course of El Chepe, a grand old steam locomotive that negotiates 2400m of altitude on its way between Mexico's arid northern interior and the Pacific coast. Oh, and it also takes in 37 bridges, 86 tunnels and a masterful set of canyon-scaling switchbacks. Then there's the canyon-dwelling Tarahumara people. Don't miss sampling their food or handicrafts while alighting at Divisadero, the canyon's key viewpoint.

Incorporate El Chepe into a more intensive Copper Canyon adventure with an off-beat agency like Authentic Copper Canyon (http://authenticcoppercanyon.com)

253 MOUNTAIN RAILWAYS, HIMACHAL PRADESH, INDIA

There's steaming-hot competition for India's top train ride, but two of Himachal Pradesh's sub-Himalayan lines are among those on top (at least geographically). One – from Kalka to Shimla – is a Unesco site, whilst further into India's northern mountain province is the narrow-gauge Pathankot–Jogindernagar rail link, as popular with pilgrims journeying to hillside Hindu temples as with tourists. Both are blessed with phenomenal vistas of mountain villages. Kalka–Shimla edges it for views whilst for the overall 10-hour experience, the pottering Pathankot–Jogindernagar train wins through. Do both!

Crane your necks for the 30km or so before Kangra, considered to be the most ruggedly picturesque stretch.

All aboard for vast sub-Himalayan vistas on the Kalka to Shimla train

At over 9000km, the Trans-Siberian might not really qualify as an 'express', but its surely the mother of all epic train rides

254 TRANS-SIBERIAN EXPRESS, RUSSIA

Embark from the edge of Europe on a 9000km-plus adventure to the Far East: this train trip is the one everyone wants to bag. Starting in Moscow, passengers need eight days to travel 'direct' to Vladivostok and must cross seven time zones. Siberia offers more than the clichés of ice and smoking Communist-era factories: towns with wondrous wooden mansions and striking kremlins, mist-swathed steppes and the transfixing beauty of vast, forest-fringed Lake Baikal. Expect trackside encounters with dog-sleds, dodgy salesmen and tract upon tract of stunning, invariably bone-numbing scenery. Then there are those branch lines to Mongolia and China…

Such undertakings require planning; dedicated train websites like Trainsrussia (www.trainsrussia.com), or Lonely Planet's *Trans-Siberian Railway Travel Guide* can help.

255 MARRAKECH–TANGIER, MOROCCO

Much of Africa's train network is in disrepair or difficult to travel, so why not start with the best? This journey south from the continent's northern tip at the port of Tangier down through classic Moroccan destinations, Fes, Rabat and Casablanca, is actually surprisingly comfortable and doable in 11 hours. But what with those desert views and legendary cities en route, you might want to linger a little along the way… To complete the journey in one hit, book a *couchette* for some added leg room.

Tangier has a sketchy reputation and isn't often on Morocco visitors' to-do lists but it's recently seen regeneration and has a fabulous cultural/nightlife scene.

256 INDIAN PACIFIC, AUSTRALIA

This is the planet's only train trek that truly spans a continent, trundling from Perth in the west to Sydney 4350km away on the east coast. From Perth's verdant valleys and farmlands you'll cruise across the desolate Nullarbor Plain (so-named as it's almost treeless), rock up to mellow Adelaide – renowned for festivals and food – skirt the outback, then hit the Blue Mountains before reaching your destination three days later. Mixing modern metropolises with barren swaths of desert, the Indian Pacific paints a poignant picture of Australia's stark contrasts.

Step off at Adelaide for another Australian end-to-ender: the Ghan Train, heading north to Darwin on the Timor Sea.

257 FERROCARRIL CENTRAL ANDINO, PERU

They rethought the catchphrase to sell this classic train traverse through the Peruvian Andes since the Chinese built a higher line: it's now 'the world's highest historic standard gauge railway'. Still, it's the second-highest and, near chilly Ticlio station, boasts the planet's loftiest railway junction. Travelling from coastal Lima to Peru's mineral-rich mountains, you'll rise 4700m from sea level, crossing desert, lush Andean foothills and mining hub La Oroya, before finally dipping into metropolis Huancayo. The country's biggest city and some of its remotest countryside, all in one overnight odyssey.

Huancayo's most traveller-friendly stop is Casa de la Abuela (www.incasdelperu. com), which is also a great source of up-to-date train info.

258 XINING–LHASA, CHINA/TIBET

The first railway to connect Tibet to the outside world had technical headaches aplenty to overcome. How, for example, do you build tracks over permafrost? Or deal with altitudes of over 5000m? Well, the Chinese finally opened this modern engineering marvel in 2006 and it's the world's highest rail run. Not everyone has the chance to experience the giddy Tanggula Pass, though – to do the full 2000km, day-long mission to Lhasa, you must fill in a health form to prove you've the head and the heart for heights. Personal oxygen supplies and onboard doctor provided.

The official website (www.chinatibettrain. com) has fare, route and accommodation information.

259 CANADIAN PACIFIC, CANADA

This is how the west was won or, at least, settled in Canada. Resourceful 19th-century railway honchos made big bucks by selling relocation packages to immigrants, including the ship fare from Europe and railway-owned land on which to start over. And thousands flocked to the Canadian wilderness. A century later, this journey hasn't lost its appeal. You can hop on in Halifax for a coast-to-coast crawl but Toronto is where the Canadian Pacific officially begins. The three-day epic to the Pacific recently rescheduled to show off the Rocky Mountains in their full, day-lit potential.

The Canadian Pacific Railway sought to attract the wealthy by constructing a country-wide hotel network, of which top dog is surely Quebec City's Château Frontenac (www.fairmont.com/frontenac-quebec).

260 EASTERN & ORIENTAL EXPRESS, THAILAND/MALAYSIA/SINGAPORE

Travelling from the modern city state of Singapore through Kuala Lumpur to the full-on sensory assault that is Bangkok, zooming through a sizzling tropical landscape of paddies and tea plantations, this is the eastern (and infinitely more appealing) cousin of the Venice Simplon–Orient Express. The exotic route has regular departures (several monthly), plus some of the most fascinating onboard cuisine of any train service anywhere (a fusion of regional cuisines). Above all, though, this is about glamour: air-conditioned, ensuite cabins; an onboard boutique; and a teak-wood observation lounge carriage. Three- to seven-day packages are available. A warning to dishevelled backpackers: dress code is smart casual.

Use this as a hop-on, hop-off service to explore Malaysian treasures like the Cameron Highlands. Other less-luxurious trains also ply this route, plus there's a loop into Laos offered.

ULTIMATE TRAIN RIDES

RETRO ACTIVE: OLD-SCHOOL ADVENTURES

Just 'cos it's old-school doesn't mean it's old hat – discover why these classic adventures continue to make the grade.

263 ROLLER SKATING ALONG VENICE BEACH, CALIFORNIA

Think roller disco, think 1970s, but the four-wheeled wonders keep rolling on at the Venice Skate Park, flares optional. DJs keep things booty-shakin' as skilled skaters get down in dance routines for spectators. Skates may not be as fast as rollerblades but they definitely have more groove, style and are easier to ride. Venice Beach has a long history of the sport, with LA's 1978 mayor Tom Bradley declaring Venice Beach 'the roller skating capital of the world'. Rent or buy a pair from shops along the busy sun-drenched boardwalk.

Venice Beach, or simply Venice, is the beachfront section west of downtown Los Angeles, California. A bus from Santa Monica takes 15 minutes.

261 ARCHERY IN SEOUL, SOUTH KOREA

The movies *The Hunger Games* and *Brave* made archery popular again, with lead female characters flexing their strength with a bow and arrow. This isn't the first female resurgence: the end of the 18th century saw archery soar in popularity with young women, who could show off their skills while meeting some eligible gents. Archery has been practised around the world, from America to Turkey, and across civilisations. Today you can take aim with gungdo (traditional Korean archery) in South Korea – a country once famous for its skilled archers of Goguryeo, one of the ancient Three Kingdoms of Korea.

The best time to visit Seoul is in the cherry-blossom-filled spring, from the end of March to early May.

262 ZIPPING DOWNHILL IN A BILLYCART IN COROWA, NEW SOUTH WALES, AUSTRALIA

A billycart is a makeshift box or crate with wheels attached (scrounged from wherever you can get them). They were once pulled by billy goats, hence the name. Hundreds have been made by kids in the backyards of suburban Australia but things get a bit more pro in Corowa at the annual Australian Billycart Championships on Easter Saturday, when the main street turns into a festival of food, music and billycarts racing down the centre. Corowa is a classic Riverina town: laid-back atmosphere, sunshine, endless space and beer, and magpie calls echoing from eucalyptus trees.

Read more information on these DIY rides at www.australianbillycartchampionships. com.au.

264 JOUSTING IN BRISTOL, WISCONSIN, USA

Yes, knights in suits of armour on galloping horses, jabbing each other with metal lances as regal flags flap – that's jousting. These days, learning to joust provides a great insight into life in the Middle Ages...and there's no fight to the death at the end. The armour makes it safe enough for children to compete but having solid horseriding skills are a definite advantage – keeping your balance in the saddle with that long lance ain't easy! Watch a jousting match at the Renaissance Faire, held annually in Bristol, near the border with Illinois.

You will need your own transport to get to the Renaissance Faire, which is a 30-minute drive from Milwaukee (or 50 minutes from Chicago). See www.renfair. com/bristol.

265 WING WALKING IN ENGLAND

You're going to stand atop a plane. No, really. If your heart is already racing at the thought of being in the roaring, rushing air of a moving biplane with your friends looking like tiny specks below, then wait till you are moving at 217km per hour. You'll be strapped on, standing against a pole with harnesses around your shoulders and waist; the pilot can see you at all times but not hear you. Now look out and enjoy that endless view of sky and greenery, keeping your head straight so that the rushing air doesn't catch up your mouth.

Various locations across England offer this experience; Wing Walking in Essex (www. wingwalking.co.uk) is a good option.

266 RIDING A PENNY FARTHING, LONDON

This giant bike with one large shoulder-height wheel and one smaller ankle-height wheel may seem impractical but riding high aloft does have a light-headed appeal. Once only for wealthy gents, restored or new penny farthings can now be ridden by anyone with classes for lads and lasses offered in London – ye olde capital of the penny and farthing coins after which the bicycle is named. Despite the odd altitude they are easier to ride than they look. Some enthusiasts make it their mission to ride around the world on these beautiful beasts.

Check out the penny farthing in action in the film *Around the World in 80 Days*, which opens on a penny farthing rider in London. Visit London in the warmer, longer days of July and August.

267 CARVE SOME TURNS AT TELEMARK, NORWAY

Let's go back to what skiing is about. Forget fancy high-tech equipment or posing in expensive outfits. Skiing is about the freedom on two skis. Telemark skis differ to alpine ones because the heel of your boot is detached from the ski, allowing you to kneel and turn smoothly which is what 'tele' is all about: the rhythmic descent. All the other powder-highs of alpine skiing are present – the whoosh on white snow and the speed down the slope. Let's tele where it started in the 1860s, in southern Norway's Telemark, amongst steep mountains and endless cushy snow.

To find out if it's right for you, attend a demo day, watch a video lesson or browse the forums at www.telemarktips.com.

268 LONGBOARDING IN NEW YORK CITY

Longer, wider and easier to ride than a skateboard, a longboard is made for getting you around town, not for tricks – feel the control that those chunky, soft wheels give you. Making some sharp, deep turns, dodging the pedestrian hordes, you realise you might be hooked on this feeling of freedom as you breeze by the world. Longboarding arose from surfers wanting to ride the sidewalks when the surf wasn't right; born in Hawaii, the sport grew up in the '70s and partied in the '90s in this street-style capital of NYC.

Many longboard classes in New York City (and around the world) are for all ages. There is also an international Longboard Girl's Crew (longboardgirlscrew.com).

269 FENCING IN PARIS, FRANCE

'Touché!' you hear as you tap your opponent's chest with the tip of your foil. Fencing is a complicated sport and was difficult to judge even in the Olympics before the advent of recent electronic scoring weapons and chest wear. Modern fencing started in Spain in the 1400s but was developed by aristocratic gentlemen in schools in France, where nowadays ladies and gents still duel. Don your protective clothing, mask and bib and choose your weapon – foil, sabre or épée... then it's time for some serious swordplay.

Search fencing academies in Paris in the iSport directory (http://fencing.isport. com/fencing-clubs/fr/paris/paris).

270 DRAG RACING IN LOS ANGELES

Remember Danny Zuko burning down the canal in Grease's final scenes? Get your own greased lightning on in Southern California where drag racing started. Cars in candy-colour enamel are matched with drivers with slicked-back hair and retro outfits straight out of a '50s diner. It's a wild scene with noisy burnouts and speeds so high that parachutes are needed to slow down the cars – hence many drag strips in Los Angeles (usually abandoned WWII-era runways) have been closed down.

Look for classes approved or run by the NHRA (National Hot Rod Association) and IHRA (International Hot Rod Association).

WILDEST SWIMS IN THE WORLD

Swimwear: optional. Goggles: handy. Bravado: essential. Get ready to take the plunge at the planet's wildest swim sites.

271 WILD DOLPHINS, NEW ZEALAND

You are skimming along in a boat offshore Kaikoura, South Island. Your guide is looking for wild dolphins. Not one or two but big pods, diving, rising, and leaping out of the sea. He sees them and suddenly you're in, duck-diving, swimming in circles and singing into your snorkel. All weird and wonderful ways to attract them – but they work. One eyeballs you, another flicks his tail. Then they're gone and you're back in the boat, chasing the pod...welcome to swimming with dolphins New Zealand–style. The marine reserves here are committed to not bothering the creatures (boat operators are strictly limited and cannot feed them) which makes the experience truly natural.

The weather in Kaikoura is unpredictable, so allow a three-day window for a swim. Early morning slots are most reliable.

272 THE BEAGLE CHANNEL, PATAGONIA

Swim anywhere in Patagonia and it's almost certain to be wild; this is the land of snowy mountains, polar storms and treacherous seas. With waters typically below 5°C, hypothermia is a reality – seas here belong to orcas, seals, penguins and cormorants, not people. But pure water abounds, offering you magnificently petrifying, frigid swimming in glacial rivers and cobalt lakes. Since 1990, a handful of swimmers have taken the wildness one step further, crossing the Beagle Channel between Argentina and Chile. One of the most demanding straits in the world, this shipping channel is not the cleanest, but the 5km crossing takes place in land unhitched from the world as you know it.

Prepare with some serious cold water acclimatisation.

273 BOSPHORUS, ISTANBUL

You're on a ferry with hundreds of other swimmers wearing swimming costumes and sunscreen-smeared goggles, preparing to swim the Bosphorus, a 800m-wide stretch of sea between Asia and Europe. Generally a major shipping channel, for now the huge lumbering tankers that dominate it are held back at either end of the boiling mass of water for the annual Turkish Bosphorus swimming race. Under huge bridges you feel a sense of scale, with you at the tinier end of the world's proportions. Then the sirens go, and lemming-like you dive in, both swimming and being swept down the 6.5km course. Istanbul is full of thrills but this swim, where encounters with jellyfish and dolphins are common, is definitely one of them.

Take advice from other swimmers about avoiding eddies. Sign up through the Turkish website: www.bosphorus.cc.

Take the plunge and swim the Bosphorus in Istanbul, then you can boast that you – literally – swam between continents

274 ROBBEN ISLAND, SOUTH AFRICA

Between the 17th and 20th centuries Robben Island, 7.5km off the coast of Cape Town, was used as a place to which political prisoners and lepers were banished. The prison boundaries were nothing compared to the natural impediment to escape: the sea. Now the island is the setting for one of the toughest cold-water sea races in the world. From the moment you set off, expect to feel very afraid...of great white sharks and unpredictable weather that changes conditions from calm and sunny to 25-knot winds and 4m swell within a morning. Wetsuit or no wetsuit, the icy cold (10–13°C) will eat its way to your bones.

The Cadiz Freedom Swim generally takes place in April to commemorate the end of apartheid and attracts a few hundred swimmers.

275 WHIRLPOOL, SCOTLAND

The Corryvreckan whirlpool – one of only 10 in the world – exists on the wild west of Scotland. In Scottish mythology it is the washtub of the hag goddess of winter. Catch a boat to it and you may see stags silhouetted on the skyline, sea eagles, and seals lying on bladderrack rocks. It's a wild place frequented by strong eddies, unpredictable currents, a confusion of tides and a whirlpool that can often be heard miles away, sucking and hissing. But for half an hour per tide, the whirlpool calms and swimmers have those few minutes to swim across the 1km strait between Jura and Bute, before it starts up again…

This is a 1km swim in 6–14°C water; do not attempt without experienced local boat cover. Swimtrek (http://www.swimtrek.com/) runs trips across the strait.

276 TSUGARA CHANNEL, JAPAN

You might have heard of the English Channel, the Irish Channel, the Cook Strait and the Catalina Channel – all up there as the world's best long-distance swims. But the deep-water channel between Honshu, Tokyo's island, and Hokkaido, Japan's northernmost island, is a lesser-known swim on the 'Ocean's Seven' list (open-water swimming's Seven Summits). With large swell and extraordinarily strong currents you may be met by occasional patches of cold water screwed up by large oil tankers, and large blooms of squid during the night. The swim is 19km (12 miles) as the crow flies – but currents are likely to extend it.

Any swim in the Oceans Seven requires a tremendous amount of will, training and knowledgeable local support teams.

277 GREAT LAKES, NORTH AMERICA

The Great Lakes are a beautiful and vast collection of freshwater lakes between the US and Canada, some the size of seas. Swim here and you can enjoy dreamy swimming, awe-inspiring sunsets, clean sand, lake houses and popular (as well as remote) inland beaches. The options are so abundant the area is sometimes referred to as the 'third coast'. On the five Great Lakes (Lake Superior, Lake Michigan, Lake Huron, Lake Erie and Lake Ontario) there are hundreds of beaches to choose from. Sleeping Bear Dunes National Lakeshore on Lake Michigan has been voted one of the most beautiful but there are also hundreds of small lakes to explore.

You may be safe from sharks and jellyfish but offshore winds still create dangerous rip tides – beware.

Obstacles during the Freedom Swim from Robben Island include ice-cold water, 4m waves and great-white sharks

278 MEXICO CENOTES, YUCATAN

You're skipping through the Yucatan, high on days drinking tequila and nights in hammocks. You've heard about the swimming holes through your pidgin Spanish. You pick your way through a border of high bush that marks the edge of town and on the other side weave along a path amidst lower prickles, looking for a hole in the ground. 'Jump!' says your companion as you arrive – and you leap from dry earth into your first cenote – a clean, azure-blue underground water world. The Yucatan Peninsula is a porous limestone shelf, with all the rivers flowing underground, creating magical subterranean swimming holes with filtered sunlight, stalactites and freshwater caves.

There are cenotes all over the Yucatan area – ask locally.

279 WADI SWIMMING, OMAN

Think of Oman, and you are more likely to think of drought and desert shrub than swimming – but there is some wonderfully wild and secluded swimming to be had in wadis around the country. Wadis are dried-up river beds in mountain valleys, carved by the flash floods that charge through them. Find one retaining water and you will be met with deep, cool pools of emerald water, overhung with greenery and surrounded by supernaturally smooth boulders – both magical and bizarre.

As wadis are prone to flash floods, don't go near go near them if there has just been rain or there's a hint of rain coming. Being respectful of Muslim culture generally means swimming clothed.

280 DEVIL'S POOL, ZAMBIA

You're at the edge of one of the seven natural wonders: Victoria Falls. It's the largest curtain of water in the world, all thundering over a 350ft cliff. Rainbows dance in the spray. Around you thrill-seekers clamber over rocks and wade through shallows to get a better view but not you – you jump! Right into Devil's Pool where you're carried at speed with the moving water – right up to a submerged rock-lip, which halts you just before it's too late. It's the most exciting swimming hole in the world.

Only attempt in the dry season (April to October) and take advice from local guides.

WILDEST SWIMS IN THE WORLD

CRAZIEST CAVES

Bejewelled by eerie crystals, filled with aquamarine waters, these spelunking fantasies are devastatingly beautiful and breathtakingly bizarre – getting acquainted will quicken your pulse.

MICHAEL NICHOLS/GETTY IMAGES ©

281 PUERTO PRINCESA UNDERGROUND RIVER, PHILIPPINES

Xanadu in China? Nah… If there were a physical embodiment today of poet Samuel Taylor Coleridge's famous poem *Kubla Khan*, in which 'Alph, the sacred river, ran, through caverns measureless to man', this 8km-long subterranean stretch of river would be it. Since getting prestigious Seven Natural Wonders of the World status there's a fair amount of hype around the underground river journey itself, but the formations you see high in the caverns above, resonant with the chatter of bats, more than live up to it.

Tours allow as little as 30 minutes underground. To fully appreciate the area, spend time above ground drinking in the beaches, crags and forests around Sabang village.

282 CANGO CAVES, SOUTH AFRICA

For wannabe cavers who like a subsurface challenge but lack the technical expertise, Africa's only show caves fit the bill. The most adventurous guided tour option encompasses 30cm-high tunnels and chimney squeezes. For those claustrophobia-inducing moments you're rewarded with formations gouged into temple-like vaults and some of the finest flowstone speleothems around (where rock takes the shape of melting, bubbling candle wax). Some of the other most impressive limestone likenesses here include the biblical Lot and family – famously turned into pillars of salt – and the dazzling capillaries of the helectite-studded Crystal Palace.

Consider a head-first, on-your-back approach to the narrowest squeezes to cut back on confined-space panic attacks.

283 CARLSBAD CAVERNS NATIONAL PARK, USA

Eighty-odd caves, including one of the world's longest (Lechuguilla), make up this hypogean wonderland in New Mexico. Several exploration options exist, from a self-guided descent 230m on switchback paths to the Big Room – big enough to hold six American football pitches – to the demanding wriggles and squeezes of Hall of the White Giant. On the Kings Palace route, drop down still further to glimpse the chandelier-like tubular stalactites known as soda straws. There are several kilometres of paths all-told. Many of the geological processes that formed what you see are still in action: this is very much a speleological work in progress.

Ask rangers about hikes to and explorations of the infinitely more remote Slaughter Canyon Cave 37km away.

Survey the subterranean stalactites at Carlsbad Caverns National Park

Majlis al Jinn in Oman attracts serious cavers and perhaps a few genies as well

284 MAJLIS AL JINN, OMAN

Its name means 'meeting place of the genies' and an expedition here will truly feel otherworldly: more like Jules Verne's *Journey to the Centre of the Earth* than anything else you'll encounter. A gaping hole in the desert leads down via a ropes-only descent (two rappels) into one of the largest single cave chambers on the planet, complete with a subterranean lake and abundant stalagmites and stalactites. It's a trip for very experienced cavers only: others can marvel at the precipitous mouth from a helicopter ride or a rough 4WD journey to the edge.

Stay tuned: the Omani government plans to make the cave more tourist friendly, with viewing platforms and a glass elevator to the cave floor.

285 CENOTE DOS OJOS, MEXICO

At first you don't see anything – then the lurid turquoise glow of the water pierces the darkness. This cavernous amphitheatre sets the stage for one of the most extensive submerged cave systems there is. It's a playground for everyone from amateur snorkellers to experienced divers, who take to the transparent, 25°C water-filled nooks, crannies and passageways to explore a watery network extending over 60km. After swimming amongst millennia-old columns and stalagmites, a popular scuba dive is to dip down and resurface in Bat Cave (guess what lives there?).

One (pretty spectacular) sector of the cenote is covered by the M$100 (US$7.75) entrance fee; to explore the deeps you'll need a guide.

286 CUEVA DE LOS CRISTALES, MEXICO

Miners working in Naica must have been wowed when in 1910 they discovered the Cueva de las Espadas (Cave of the Swords), as they named it for the huge dagger-like white selenite crystals inside. Fast-forward 90 years and beneath this already magnificent find, the Cueva de los Cristales was unearthed, where selenite crystals many times bigger again criss-cross a cavity in which temperatures reach 58°C. Kept flood free by the mine's pumps, the cave can be visited only by those with special permission (normally scientists and the like), and only for brief periods, due to the extreme conditions.

Consolation prize: in nearby Hidalgo de Parral, home of famous revolutionary Pancho Villa, tour Mina la Prieta, among the world's oldest mines still in action.

287 WAITOMO GLOWWORM CAVES, NEW ZEALAND

From the country that brought the Mines of Moria to life, we give you… well, Waitomo's caves may seem *Lord of the Rings*-esque but those sparkles on the ceiling aren't special effects: they're *Arachnocampa luminosa*, aka glow-worms. This variety is endemic to New Zealand and Waitomo is where they hang, their myriad blue lights reminiscent of an underground aurora borealis. Don't miss the boat journey through Ruakuri Cave – it's glow-worm central. The labyrinthine passageways are steeped in Maori myth and legend – you'll soon see why this has been a sacred place for many centuries.

Be respectful while looking around: this is a place of spiritual significance for Maori people.

288 SLOVENSKÝ KRAS NATIONAL PARK, SLOVAKIA

It's a little-celebrated fact but southern Slovakia possesses one of Europe's most extensive karst systems. Still, not a country to go for quantity over quality, Slovakia secretes real diamonds in its subterranean stash. Gleaming brightly and in close Unesco-listed proximity are Krásnohorská Cave, custodian of the planet's most colossal stalagmite, and Ochtinská Aragonite Cave, one of only three known aragonite caves worldwide. The highlight here, Milky Way Hall, is daubed in explosions of white aragonite crystals, just like gazing up at a mini-galaxy.

Don't pass over visiting Dobšinská Ice Cave (its internal icy formations don't even melt in summer) in nearby Slovenský Raj National Park.

289 PEAK DISTRICT CAVERNS, UK

Anything nicknamed the Devil's Arse will involve a very dark descent. Beyond the show-cave entrance chambers, the Peak Cavern is your gateway into a wet, muddy world of scrambles and sumps (water-submerged passages). It interlinks with Britain's deepest cave-shaft, Titan, via a dunk in the River Styx. For casual cave-goers, Peak Cavern show-cave tickets offer access to Speedwell Cavern, where you can take a boat along an old mine shaft. In nearby Blue John Cavern, chambers glimmer with semi-precious blue-and-yellow fluorite – absolutely ore-some.

TSG (www.tsgcaving.co.uk) provides info and arranges caving trips in Castleton, a caver's mecca, where all aforementioned adventures unfold.

290 CUEVA DE LOS INDIOS & CUEVA DE LOS MANOS, ARGENTINA

In 1977 the myth was reborn: in Bruce Chatwin's travelogue *In Patagonia*, the possible existence of unicorns eons ago was traced to ancient cave paintings in Cueva de los Indios in remote Santa Cruz province. Unicorns, just maybe, could be real. While the faded paintings here are likely bulls, the landscape – wild lakes, plains, tundra, ice-capped peaks – is appropriately mythical. Just west across Ruta 40 lies Cueva de los Manos, a rocky overhang festooned with prints of *manos* (hands) alongside other paintings thought to originate from the 7th century BC. Do unicorns exist? Don't let us tell you different.

Ruta 40, the legendary road-trip route that bisects Argentina almost north–south, provides the only access: a 5000km-plus, mostly off-road adventure of a lifetime.

CRAZIEST CAVES

MIND-BLOWING MARATHONS

If you must run 42km, why not do it somewhere spectacular? Race across the alps, the outback or a world of ice.

293 LOCH NESS MARATHON, SCOTLAND

You don't get many spectators along this marathon route – the rolling farmland, shimmery lakeshore and gaping glens that provide the race backdrop are too remote, and Nessie herself has yet to put in an appearance. But what you lose in support you gain in scenic splendour – and possibly a few deer, eagle and red squirrel sightings en route. Best of all, despite being set in the Scottish 'Highlands', the race is mostly downhill – though you'll be grateful for the lone, kilt-clad bagpipers who pop up at intervals, just when you most need a musical morale boost.

The marathon (held September) is part of a festival, which includes other races, Highland dancing and a Food & Drink Fayre. See www.lochnessmarathon.com.

291 MIDNIGHT SUN MARATHON, TROMSØ, NORWAY

It's 8.30pm, an hour when most might head to the pub. Not so in Arctic Norway when, on one midsummer eve, 1000 runners head to the start-line. Tromsø teeters up at 70°N; here, from mid-May to mid-July, the sun never sets, bathing the city's Arctic Cathedral, Polar Museum and surrounding fjords in an endless ethereal glow. It also provides ideal illumination for the world's most northerly continental marathon, a late-night loop around Fridtjof Nansen Square, over the 1km-long Tromsø Bridge and beneath peaks still snow-capped in June, before finishing to fervent crowd support in the centre. *Then* you can go to the pub...

Entry to the mid-June race (www.msm. no) opens December of the year before – book entrance and accommodation well in advance.

292 AUSTRALIAN OUTBACK MARATHON, ULURU, AUSTRALIA

The indigenous Anangu people own Uluru-Kata Tjuta National Park, and the whole area – from the iconic red rock inside the park to the surrounding Aboriginal bush – is deemed sacred. Consequently, much is off-limits – which makes the Outback Marathon all the more special. On one day in July, 2000 runners are permitted to tramp through a wild expanse of usually private property, with Uluru and the domed peaks of the Olgas as constant companions. The going is dusty, though (bar a few dunes) flat; the experience is anything but, with the spirituality-suffused ochre earth leaving runners on an almost-holy high.

The race starts at 7.45am; mornings can be chilly but average daytime highs in July reach around 21°C. See www. australianoutbackmarathon.com.

294 THE GREAT WALL MARATHON, CHINA

The Great Wall of China was once around 6000km long. Thankfully, this race only requires conquering a tiny fraction if it – but what a fraction. Much of the marathon route lies in the shadow of the ancient barricade, wending between rice fields and remote villages in the traditional Huangyaguan region. The section run on the Wall itself is only around 3.5km long but – completed twice on this looping course – involves 5164 punishingly steep stone steps, where thighs will scream, heads will spin and views of the formidable fortification snaking across the hills will provide welcome distraction.

The race is held in May; independent entry is not permitted – participation is only possible as park of a tour package. Visit www.great-wall-marathon.com.

295 JUNGFRAU MARATHON, SWITZERLAND

Though not *quite* as frightening as it sounds (you don't actually have to run up the 4158m Jungfrau itself), this is no race for the gentle jogger. A flat first half, up the waterfall-tinkled Lauterbrunnen Valley from Interlaken, rears abruptly at the 25km mark: a series of sharp zigzags rises 500 vertical metres in five crippling kilometres. And there's more – the final 12km keep on climbing, though as the air thins the Bernese Oberland's flagship peaks loom ever closer and more dramatic. Just don't dwell on the fact that there's a perfectly engineered Swiss railway that runs right to the 2000m-high finish...

The race (www.jungfrau-marathon.ch) is held in September; to officially finish, runners must complete the course before the 6.5-hour cut-off time.

296 ANTARCTIC ICE MARATHON, ANTARCTICA

Tough on both legs and wallet, this race across the icy innards of the White Continent costs each participant a cool €10,500. But that's a small price to pay for the privilege of being just one of the 40 souls permitted to enter. Conditions are unforgiving: the snow-slippy route is groomed and given a once-over for crevasses but will still sap your energy. Then there's the 1000m altitude, sub-zero temperatures and katabatic winds. But to run in a land of such pristine wilderness, where the only sound is the crunch of your own footsteps, is breathtaking (in every sense) indeed.

The marathon (www.icemarathon.com) is held November/December; the entrance fee includes flights from Punta Arenas in Chile, plus accommodation and meals.

297 REGGAE MARATHON, JAMAICA

Trust the Jamaicans to turn a long slog into a shindig. This palm-tree-tickled marathon has water stations along its scenic, sea-lapped route, but also Rasta drummers, reggae bands and DJ booths to keep you pounding a decent rhythm. Think racing comp meets Carnival. The party atmosphere is enhanced by the 5.15am kick-off, when flaming bamboo torches and the smells of jerk chicken fill the air, and the mercury reads a manageable 20-25°C. You just need to finish before the sun comes up, the temperature rises and the post-race Beach Bash starts mixing margaritas.

The race is held on the first Saturday in December in Negril, one hour's drive from Montego Bay airport. Enter at www.reggaemarathon.com.

298 LEWA MARATHON, KENYA

If ever you needed motivation to get moving, a rhino charging full-pelt through the long grass in your direction ought to do it. Kenya, famed for its long-distance prowess and safaris, combines both in the annual Safaricom Lewa Marathon, a dirt-track, hill-rippled, high-altitude and animal-infested epic unlike any other. The Lewa Conservancy, a swathe of acacia woodland and sweeping savannah just north of Mount Kenya, is home to more than 100 rhino, plus elephant, zebra, giraffe and buffalo. Luckily it's also patrolled by armed rangers and helicopters on race day to keep dangerous beasties at bay.

The Lewa Marathon (www.safaricom.co.ke/safaricommarathon) is held in late June, when midday temperatures reach 30°C; there are water stations every 2.5km.

299 ATHENS CLASSIC MARATHON, GREECE

The first, the original, the granddaddy of all marathons – the route of this run from Marathónas to Athens retraces the footsteps of Pheidippides. In around 490 BC, this speedy messenger allegedly dashed the distance to announce the Greek army's victory over the Persians – then he promptly collapsed and died. The race feels almost as tough today. It's on tarmac but retains some brutal undulation. Finishing in the capital's Panathenaic Stadium – reconstructed for the 1896 Olympics from the remains of an ancient amphitheatre – will make you feel like a legend yourself.

The race is held in November, with applications opening in the previous January (see www.athensclassicmarathon.gr); up to 12,000 runners can enter.

300 BIG SUR MARATHON, CALIFORNIA, USA

Pacific peasoupers, ocean-brewed storms, hailstones, landslides and tectonic ruptures...none of these curveballs thrown by Mother Nature deter 4500 runners from braving the Big Sur Marathon – probably because it's so drop-dead gorgeous. Indeed, the 26.2 miles from Big Sur Village to Carmel may be dissected by the San Andreas Fault and exposed to the climatic vagaries of the Californian Coast but they also follow Highway 1, the USA's first 'Scenic Highway' and one of the world's most distractingly dramatic drives. Best then to run it, to have more time to take in the giant sequoias, wave-crashed cliffs and precipitous bridges en route.

The race (www.bsim.org) is held in April. Runners must finish in under six hours, before the roads are reopened to traffic.

MOST ACTION-PACKED JUNGLES

Make like Tarzan and take on one of these truly original rainforest adventures.

The Kokoda track has enough mud, heat, humidity and awesome scenery to set pulses racing

301 ZIP-LINING, CAPE TRIBULATION, QUEENSLAND, AUSTRALIA

Ancient rainforests are best viewed from the perspective of a bird soaring through the canopy layer; it's achievable through zip-lining, albeit as a bird travelling at warp speed. While you fly through this dense World Heritage–listed tropical rainforest which borders the Daintree Cape Tribulation National Park, you'll catch glimpses of the ocean and Great Barrier Reef, plus butterflies, birds and insects. To truly get to know the jungle's wildlife, which includes rainforest dragons (yes, dragons!), bats, possums, spiders and snakes, tack a two-hour night walk onto your trip.

Jungle Surfing (www.junglesurfing.com
.au) operates in a private reserve using structures designed to have a negligible effect on the trees. It's a 2½-hour drive from traveller-hub Cairns.

302 MOUNTAIN BIKING, CHI PHAT, CAMBODIA

Touring a jungle by bike doesn't just allow you to cover far more leaf-cushioned ground than you would ordinarily be able to but it also makes the scenery whoosh past in a dreamy kind of way. The Chi Pat eco-tourism site offers a range of rides on rugged rainforest trails to a backdrop of mountains, mangroves, waterfalls and, if you're lucky, grazing elephants. Situated in the Krâvanh Mountains, Southeast Asia's largest remaining tract of rainforest, it was established by the NGO Wildlife Alliance in 2007 with a view to giving local families a sustainable income promoting the region's natural wonders.

The rides vary from an easy 12km to a more serious sweat-inducing 42km. Some include camping in the jungle and cool-offs in the natural waterfall-fed pools. Visit www.ecoadventurecambodia.com.

303 BATTLEFIELD CROSSING, KOKODA TRACK, PAPUA NEW GUINEA

Pacifists shouldn't be put off the Kokoda Track, site of bloody battles in WWII, though those in questionable physical shape who aren't sure they can hack hiking a 96km undulating trail in hot, humid conditions surely should be. The trek is the only route over the Owen Stanley Range, which divides the north and south of the island. Hiking the track usually takes nine days and includes river crossings, knee-deep mud and regular downpours, though the awesome deep valleys and jungle scenery provide a welcome diversion.

The best time to do the trek is from April to November. A faster six-day trek is also available for the ultrahardy. Visit www.kotrek.com.

115

The utlimate reward of the torrid journey into Dzang-Sangha is an encounter with western lowland gorillas

304 TIGER SCOUTING, CHITWAN NATIONAL PARK, NEPAL

If you want to see a tiger that isn't shuffling about in a zoo or on the front of a cereal packet, head for the Chitwan National Park in the Nepalese jungle, where there's a 75 percent likelihood of a sighting. There are also night tours to further help you glimpse this nocturnal beast. But even if you don't, it's still the perfect place to channel your inner Mowgli, with heaps of other wildlife on view, such as leopards, sloth and water buffalo. Travel is via a mixture of elephant back, canoe, jeep and foot.

Responsible Travel Tiger safaris (www. responsibletravel.com) are accompanied by a zoologist and local naturalist guides. Jeep tours and walking tracking tours are available, best taken late November to early May.

305 SURFING, G-LAND, ALAS PURWO, INDONESIA

Surfers are no strangers to blazing a trail through the jungle in search of the best breaks and Java's G-Land, off Indonesia's biggest national park, Alas Purwo, was one such find. The expert-only peeling lefthander was discovered by surfers in the 1970s. The name is from a nearby stretch of rainforest which always looks green, hence the 'G'. Aside from surfers and white sand beaches, the park is also home to Hindu temples, meditation caves, turtles, panthers, wild pigs, leaf monkeys and several unique species of bamboo.

The break is best reached by boat charter from Bali (in around half a day) and best surfed March to November. G-Land Surf Camp (www.surfadventuretours.com/ g-land-surf-camp.php) is located just 100m from the wave.

306 TRIBAL TOURING, FOUTA DJALLON, GUINEA

With its fine-looking waterfalls, lush jungle and rare tropical dry forests, Fouta Djallon offers some of the best, horde-free hiking in West Africa. But it is not for the average ambler – most treks average six hours' walking per day, on terrain ranging from mellow, rolling grasslands to single-track forest trails and vine bridges. There are also maze-like rock gorges, one of which presumably isn't called 'Indiana Jones World' for nothing. Alongside the sublime nature are isolated villages with traditional Fouta huts that are home to the friendly Fulbe people.

Fouta Trekking (www.foutatrekking. org) works with the Fulbe and channels funding back into local projects, such as farming initiatives. The best time to go is January to October.

307 GORILLA TRACKING, DZANGA-SANGHA SPECIAL RESERVE, CENTRAL AFRICAN REPUBLIC

When a trip promises 'long and uncomfortable journeys' by plane, jeep and canoe, there had better be a super-bright light at the end of the tunnel. In the case of the Dzanga-Sangha Special Reserve, there certainly is – it's one of the few places where tourists can track the majestic but critically endangered western lowland gorillas. Fewer than 2000 westerners are thought to have visited this stunning jungle region, which is also home to forest elephants, buffalo, crocodiles and red river hogs, and the local Ba'Aka pygmy tribe, who help with the gorilla tracking.

It can take three to eight hours to track the gorillas, after which you'll move with the group or sit as they groom. See www.worldprimatesafaris.com.

308 VOLCANO HIKING, ARENAL, COSTA RICA

The Mirador El Silencio Reserve is a rich primary rainforest, which includes many old-growth trees such as the Ceiba, trumpet tree and Guarumo. It's also just 5km from Arenal, Costa Rica's youngest and most active volcano, in the high-risk zone where all new construction is banned. Though it's been 'on a break' since 2010, Arenal's looming presence on your eye line as you hike through the thick jungle serves to remind you that it can blow its top at any time, as it did in 1968, obliterating three villages in the process. Unwind in the nearby hot springs post-hike.

Anywhere Costa Rica (www.anywhere costarica.com) runs twice-daily, two-hour tours along the nature reserve's hiking trails with a naturalist guide.

309 WHITEWATER RAFTING, AMAZON BASIN, ECUADOR

No jungle list is complete without the daddy of them all – the Amazon rainforest. And the best way to truly appreciate this vast lushness is to take a boat through its inner core, starting with a white-water raft on the rapids of the upper river and moving onto more mellow motorised dug-out canoes as you get deeper downstream. You can also visit a rehabilitation centre for rainforest animals for close-up views of animals you'll have heard of, such as monkeys and snakes, and ones you won't, such as tapirs and ocelots.

Untamed Path (www.untamedpath. com) runs trips from Quito, Ecuador from January to March and July to December.

310 MAYAN TEMPLE TREKKING, TIKAL, GUATEMALA

The Mayans might have been wrong about the apocalypse but their one-time capital Tikal shows they knew a thing or two about building grand temples that poke above the jungle canopy with views dramatic enough to give you goosebumps. Just ask George Lucas, who chose it as the setting for the rebel base in the original *Star Wars*. Tikal has been a World Heritage–listed site since 1979, and the status protects not just the ruins but the unique flora and fauna which call this tropical rainforest ecosystem home. These include spider monkeys, jaguars, crocodiles, toucans, and parrots.

Martsam Travel (www.jungletours guatemala.com) organises hikes within the archaeological site with an indigenous guide; combine them with a hike to a bat cave at El Zotz.

MOST ACTION-PACKED JUNGLES

DOWNHILL DASHES

You know the saying: what goes up, must come down. Strap yourself in, take a deep breath (or three) and enjoy the plunge.

311 ABSEILING IN LESOTHO

At 186 metres, the Maletsunyane Falls, in the remote village of Semonkong, Lesotho, is one of Africa's highest single-drop waterfalls. In fact, Semonkong, meaning 'Place of Smoke', was named after the haze created by the plummeting water. You can abseil into this famous mist for 204 metres – the longest commercially operated single-drop abseil in the world. If that's doesn't sate the adrenalin junkie in you, head out on a Basotho pony trek or throw yourself down a surrounding hill on a mountain bike.

Semonkong Lodge (www.placeofsmoke. co.ls) arranges abseiling and other activities. December to March (summer and wet season) is when the falls are at their gushing peak.

312 SKYDIVING ON THE EAST COAST OF AUSTRALIA

If you are going to feel the ultimate rush anywhere in the world, skydiving in the east coast of Australia – Mission Beach or Cairns – is the perfect sky-high location.

Think panoramic, bird's-eye views of the Great Barrier Reef, rainforest or golden beaches. Beginners do tandem skydives with an instructor, jumping from around 14,000 feet. That's over 60 seconds of free fall, during which time you reach terminal velocity (a cool 220km per hour). The chute is pulled at around 5000 feet, after which you soar like the proverbial eagle before landing on a designated drop-zone. You'll kiss terra firma and want to do it all over again.

Several skydiving operators offer flights over Australia's east coast. See Skydive Australia (www.australiaskydive.com.au).

313 BUNGEE JUMPING IN NEW ZEALAND

Why do people launch themselves from great heights attached to a giant elastic band? Originally based on a tradition in Vanuatu, bungee jumping was reinvented centuries later as a commercial extreme activity in New Zealand. The Nevis Bungee is 134m above the Nevis River in the remote Nevis Valley. After a half-hour drive up stunning back country, you're transported to a specially constructed highwire cable car. After a run through of the safety procedures, there's nothing left to do. Oh, except launch yourself off a platform. And experience 8½ seconds of ground rush, fear and plenty of exhilaration.

AJ Hackett offers a number of jumps around New Zealand; see www.bungy.co.nz.

DOUG PEARSON / GETTY IMAGES ©

Umm...I've changed my mind! Bungee jumping is the quintessential New Zealand experience

Hitting the slopes in Namibia, but not a snowflake in sight

314 SANDBOARDING IN NAMIBIA

Think snowboard on the sand; it might not be as 'extreme' as on snow or ice, but at least you don't get wet and cold, and you have a softer landing. The perfect country for sandboarding is Namibia, where natural high dunes form perfect slopes. As with snowboarding, your feet are strapped to the board, which is made of formica or laminex with a waxed bottom. You can reach speeds of over 50km per hour (real speed geeks can go headfirst). Dune buggies are often used to take you up the mountain as it's a long trudge otherwise. Remember to keep your eyes open (for the spectacular Namibian dune views) but your mouth closed.

Check out Alter Action (www.alter-action.info/web), the first operator to introduce snowboarding to Namibia.

315 MOUNTAIN BIKING IN BOLIVIA

It's rough, tough and exhilarating. We're talking about descending the 'World's Most Dangerous Road' on two bits of revolving rubber – a mountain bike. The trip starts at an altitude of 4700m on the windswept summit of La Cumbre, 40kms from La Paz. It follows 66km of mud, rock and dust (that Bolivians like to call a road) before plunging to the subtropical township of Coroico. Think sheer precipices with drops of over 1000 metres, hairpin bends and memorial crosses. Yes, tragically, locals and tourists have died after plummeting over the edge, be it on bike, bus or truck.

The safest, most recommended tour company is Gravity Assisted (www.gravitybolivia.com).

316 ZORBING IN DORSET, UK

The world is spinning. Well, of course it is but right now it's spinning a little faster as you're rolling down a grassy hillside... strapped inside a clear plastic ball... and it's marvellous. Welcome to zorbing. This sport was invented in adrenalin hotspot New Zealand but has spread around the globe, finding one happy home in Dorset for the past decade. The countryside here is gorgeous but you'll barely have time to see it as you let gravity bounce you through the bucolic scenery to the cheers of onlookers.

Visit in July or August for the best weather. Zorbing South, located a five-minute taxi ride from Dorchester, has a perfect safety record, and offers both harness and hydro zorbing; see www.zorbsouth.co.uk.

317 TOBOGGANING IN VAL THORENS, FRANCE

The Val Thorens' toboggan run defines the phrase 'slippery slope'. At 6km long, it is the longest commercial run in Europe and drops from an altitude of 3000m to 700m. Remember: the only thing between your butt and packed-down snow are several centimetres of plastic with two levers as brakes – eek. The ride can be hairy, think cliffs, and occasional snow boulders and ice on the run. Not to mention other out-of-control sledders who ricochet pinball-style off the run's sides. Amateurs take up to 45 minutes to reach the bottom, while the pros can do it in 10 minutes.

Trips depart daily in snow season from Funitel de Péclet, the main lift office. A sledge and a helmet are included in the price. Night sledding is available, too.

318 EXTREME SLIDING IN BRAZIL

A slide? Extreme? OK, so there are no crocodiles, hairpin bends or parachute cords to worry about, but the name Insano, Portuguese for 'insane', says it all. This slide set high up within an ocean-side fun park, has a 41m drop and takes a mere five seconds to plunge down. This means that you descend the slide at more than 100km per hour. There's a pool at the end into which, organisers claim, participants take a 'relaxing dive' (or not). Ouch. It's the nearest thing to falling 14 storeys unassisted. Except, whew, there is water at the bottom.

Beach Park is located on the Porto das Dunas beach in Ceará, northeast Brazil. Check out www.beachpark.com.br/site/en/complex/ceara-brazil.asp.

319 DRIVING IN ITALY

What does it take for a road to be on a driver's bucket list? Sixty switchback turns (48 of which are continuous): tick. The second-highest paved road in the Alps (2757m): tick. Steep gradient: tick again. The stunning Stelvio Pass road in Italy's Eastern Alps connects Merano and the upper Adige Valley with Valtellina and is one of the most challenging and exacting in the world. Even legendary racer Stirling Moss once plunged over the side during a classic car race. Guides advise that you should approach the ascent from the northwest side via the stunning alpine forest of the Stelvio National Park and descend (slowly) on the other side.

The road gets busy, especially at the top of the pass, so be patient; it's no quick drive.

320 A ROLLER COASTER OF A RIDE IN ABU DHABI

OK, so this one is a gimmick – but it's up there for speedsters. Reaching a top speed of 240km per hour 'Formula Rossa' holds the current record as the world's fastest roller coaster. Not surprisingly, it's in a Ferrari-themed wonderland called – you guessed it – Ferrari World, one of the largest indoor amusement parks in the world. Stare down that track and prepare to tap into your inner Fernando Alonso, except your feet will be nowhere near a brake. Strap yourself in, say a quick prayer and imagine a chequered flag – it's all over in a minute.

For more information see www.ferrariworldabudhabi.com. For the roller coaster with the steepest drop (121°) head to Japan's Fuji-Q Highland.

DOWNHILL DASHES

BEST ADVENTURE FESTIVALS

Meet your heroes, drink beer and hang out with new friends; adventure sports festivals are great places to encounter like-minded souls.

321 EKSTREMSPORTVEKO, NORWAY

The rocky gorges and waterfalls of Voss in western Norway are the venue for the most adrenalin-charged gathering of all, the Extreme Sports Festival. In this wildly beautiful natural setting, white-water kayakers and rafters mingle with skateboarders and mountain bikers, sky divers compare chutes with BASE jumpers, and everybody looks on in awe at the wing-suit flyers' jaw-dropping exploits. Voss is arguably the Northern Hemisphere's adventure capital, in part because of Norway's litigation-averse society, and a visit to the region is a must for outdoors lovers. Note: you're not obliged to throw yourself off a cliff like a fizzy-drink-crazed lemming.

Ekstremsportveko takes place over one week in June; see www.ekstremsportveko. com. Voss is on the Bergen–Oslo train line and is a stop on the famous Norway in a Nutshell journey; make arrangements at www.visitnorway.com.

322 THE BRITS, FRANCE/SWITZERLAND

Britain's skiers and boarders have something of a reputation for hedonism in Europe's Alpine resorts, not least because their nation has no comparable mountain ski resorts of its own. But Britain does put something back into the winter sports community, with two giant festivals of music, snow and, well, hedonism. First, there's the BRITS, a week-long festival featuring the British Snowboard and Freeski Championships. At its quarter-century mark, it has matured into the longest-running winter festival with music. Snowbombing draws bigger acts and more ridiculous costumes to its party in Mayrhofen, Austria. Both are about as much fun as you can have mixing alcohol, snowsports and live music.

The BRITS (www.the-BRITS.com) takes place in March, usually in a resort in France or Switzerland; Snowbombing is in April (www.snowbombing.com). Both sell accommodation and event packages.

323 BANFF MOUNTAIN FILM AND BOOK FESTIVAL, CANADA

The world's best mountain-film festival is headquartered in Banff, Alberta. Deep within Canada's first national park – a Unesco World Heritage site – and surrounded by the Rockies, whose glacier-hewn peaks circle alpine lakes and forests, it's not hard to follow the organisers' reasoning. The festival showcases the best of the year's adventure films and writing, with talks by stars of the outdoor world's firmament, and workshops, classes and exhibitions covering all forms of mountain culture. Don't worry if you can't make it to Banff – the festival comes to you, making around 240 stops in 36 countries on its annual tour.

The festival takes place annually in autumn; check www.banffcentre.ca/mountainfestival for details.

324 KANDERSTEG ICE CLIMBING FESTIVAL, SWITZERLAND

Pack your crampons and axes for this celebration of all things icy in the quiet Swiss town of Kandersteg. Like the town, this is a low-key occasion, allowing novices to mingle with the pro climbers and brush up their technique in workshops. Away from the frozen rock face created especially for the event, there are many more winter adventures in the Bernese Oberland, including cross-country skiing on more than 50km (30 miles) of prepared trails, snowshoe hikes and tobogganing.

The festival runs over a weekend in January; see www.ready2climb.com/kandersteg. For info on the region, visit www.myswitzerland.com. The closest main airport is Bern.

325 ALBUQUERQUE BALLOON FIESTA, USA

Unless you've gulped a hit of peyote, the only time you'll see a giant inflatable Elvis floating across the New Mexico desert in his rhinestone suit is at the world's largest balloon festival. This happens in Albuquerque, a pleasant place otherwise notable for its lack of distinguishing characteristics. Come October, Albuquerque's cloudless skies are filled with 500 hot-air balloons in one of the world's great helium-based spectacles. The Dawn Patrol sees balloons lift off into the darkness, lighting the sky before sunrise. Other times, Albuquerque is one of the best places for a balloon ride, reassuringly surrounded by lots of open space for landing.

Float on over to www.balloonfiesta.com and www.itsatrip.org.

326 ADVENTURE TRAVEL FILM FESTIVAL, USA, UK AND AUSTRALIA

This is a triple celebration. With an emphasis on travel, rather than extreme sport, founders Austin Vince and Lois Pryce haven't stuck to one location but take their festival to the UK, US and Australia. And they prefer camping (or, in the UK, at a girl's school), so expect a folksier feel than some festivals. Films are similarly wide ranging, in recent years covering paragliding across Canada, kayaking down the Congo and a solo motorcycle adventure around the world...filmed in 1933.

Host towns may vary but have included Flagstaff in the US and the mountain town of Bright in Victoria, Australia. Bookmark www. adventuretravelfilmfestival.com for news.

327 SEA OTTER CLASSIC, USA

For much of the year you can spot otters cracking shellfish on their bellies in the sea off Monterey, California. But for four days in April, attention here shifts to the bike festival named after the otters at Laguna Seca. It's North America's top cycling celebration, with 50,000 fans, 9000 competitors and 400 exhibitors. The festival was founded in 1991 as a mountain-bike race, and racing is still its backbone, with road races for lycra-clad types and dusty tracks for mountain bikers. There are night rides, camps for children and the Sierra Nevada Brewing Company puts on a huge barbecue.

Register at www.seaotterclassic.com. Head south from San Francisco and explore the rest of the central California coast; visit www.seemonterey.com.

328 MOUNTAIN SPORTS FESTIVAL, USA

It's a simple proposition: three days of music, sports and beer in Asheville, North Carolina. The mountains are provided by the Blue Ridge range in the Appalachians. The sports are shuffled each year but will include a combination of triathlon, trail running, climbing, volleyball, yoga, ultimate Frisbee and cyclocross. With 15,000 visitors, the emphasis is on fun, families and participation, to which end the annual dodgeball competition is a highlight. When you're not watching the events, there's live music. And the beer? There's lots of great suds from local outfits such as Pisgah Brewery.

The three-day festival usually takes place in May, when the weather can be hot. Find out more at www.mountainsports festival.com and book accommodation at www.exploreasheville.com.

329 FORT WILLIAM MOUNTAIN FESTIVAL, SCOTLAND

February in Britain has little to recommend it, except its most northerly adventure festival. Fort Bill is the self-styled Outdoor Capital of the UK, with nearby Ben Nevis a hotbed of Scottish winter climbing, so festival goers can take part in winter-skills workshops and go on guided walks when they're not enjoying selected films or listening to speakers at this four-day celebration of mountain culture.

Register at www.mountainfestival.co.uk. Drive or take the train to Fort William via Glasgow or Edinburgh: see www. visitscotland.com

330 BIKE FESTIVAL GARDA, ITALY

Europe's largest mountain-bike festival rolls into Riva del Garda every May. The town at the top of Lake Garda in northern Italy is a long-time favourite of mountain bikers and windsurfers (climbers head a little deeper into the Dolomites) but at festival time the sun-kissed place is overrun by 20,000 bikers, bringing nothing more threatening with them than bright clothing and an appetite for pasta. Riders have been hanging out in Riva del Garda for years thanks to the network of rocky trails entwining the surrounding mountains, including Monte Brione. But once a year they get to take part in mass night-rides and an off-road marathon race in the company of fellow mountain-bike nuts.

Check www.bike-festival.de for updates and plan a trip at www.gardatrentino.it. Milan is the closest airport.

EPIC RIDES

Pack a picnic and a puncture repair kit for these epic bicycle rides that cross continents and countries.

PRISMA BILDAGENTUR AG/ALAMY ©

331 PACIFIC COAST BICYCLE ROUTE, USA

Wine, whales and giant trees – no, these aren't figments of some strange dream but scenes from a cycle ride through Washington, Oregon and California. The Adventure Cycling Association's 3000km Pacific Coast route is what might be known locally as a no-brainer, dude. It starts from one of the world's most appealing cities – Vancouver, passes through another (San Francisco) and takes in the best of the west coast, including the redwoods of northern California, the wineries of Santa Barbara and surf-smashed beaches the whole way down to San Diego. Time your trip for December to March and you may be accompanied along the coast by migrating grey whales.

Maps are available from www. adventurecycling.org. The route can be cycled all year round but pack waterproof gear for the northern half.

332 SOUTHERN TIER BICYCLE ROUTE, USA

At 4900km, the Southern Tier coast-to-coast is the shortest of the Adventure Cycling Association's cycle routes across this vast country so it will either whet your appetite for the 6800km TransAmerica Trail or put you off long-distance cycling forever. Starting in San Diego and ending in the 400-year-old city of St Augustine, Florida, it's a doubly blessed route. The saintly suffering arrives early as the deserts of south California give way to a 2400m pass in New Mexico. You'll skip the monotony of the Midwest Corn Belt but will need to traverse the Bible Belt of Texas. By the time you reach Austin the serious climbing is done. Then it's through French-influenced Louisiana, with its intoxicating Cajun food and music, to the Atlantic coast.

Maps are available from www.adventure cycling.org. Avoid tornado season in spring, and summer in the western deserts.

333 LA CICLOPISTA DEL SOL, ITALY

The Cycleway of the Sun, also known by the less enticing name of Eurovelo 7, runs from Norway to Malta. It's the 1600km Italian stretch, from the Brenner Pass, between Italy and Austria, to Sicily that offers the most sun-seeking potential. Signposting is nonexistent and, given the slow-moving wheels of bureaucracy, don't expect any soon. Instead your swifter-turning wheels should seek out their own route from one medieval walled town to the next. Pack a compass, a map and a smartphone, stick to the back roads and enjoy *la bella vita*.

Spring and autumn have the best weather. The websites www.bicitalia.org and www.eurovelo.org will be a little assistance.

Crusing la Ciclopista del Sol: a blissful life on two wheels in Italy

334 NATIONAL HIGHWAY 1, VIETNAM

National Highway 1 is the backbone of this skinny country. It runs the length of the coast and offers some wonderful views, especially from the 496m Hai Van Pass, but it can also be busy with traffic and monotonous in places. Instead, think of the highway's vertebrae as junctures for adventures in rural Vietnam. Most cyclists ride from north (Hanoi) to south (Ho Chi Minh City) with the prevailing wind. You can ride the distance in two weeks, but take your time to explore the waterways of Ninh Binh and the colonial city of Hoi An.

If you're not a solo self-supporting cyclist, consider an organised tour (Exodus, www.exodus.co.uk) or hire a van with a local English-speaking driver.

336 SOUTH DOWNS WAY, UK

It's a midsummer evening in the English countryside and the sun is casting a hazy light over green fields and the white-chalk track. Birds chatter in the trees, anticipating one of the shortest nights of the year. Similarly, you're debating whether to ride on and catch the sunrise or pull over for some sleep. The 160km South Downs Way runs the undulating length of Britain's newest national park. It starts from Winchester, a one-time Anglo-Saxon capital, and ends in Eastbourne, a seaside resort, passing stone circles and Iron Age forts. Fit cyclists can ride it in two days, but on the summer solstice it's tempting to try it in one go… Yet this time you wake at dawn to skylarks' song and views to the twinkling sea.

See www.nationaltrail.co.uk and www.southdowns.gov.uk for details. Most riders overnight in Alfriston.

335 MT VENTOUX, FRANCE

The Tour de France's most iconic mountain occupies neither the Alps nor the Pyrenees and it's not even France's longest or steepest ascent. This extinct volcano lures cyclists to the lavender fields of Provence, but it's no walk in the park. British cyclist Tom Simpson died climbing its sun-seared limestone slopes in 1967. The 'Giant of Provence' has an altitude of 1912m and its name refers to the powerful winds, the Mistral, that swirl around its summit. The most usual approach is via Bédoin. From here it is just over 21km to the top, the final six being around the edge of the rounded peak and exposed to the elements.

Ventoux is blisteringly hot in midsummer; May, June, September and October are better options. Avignon is the closest city. See www.visitprovence.com and www.etape-ventoux.com.

337 MUNDA BIDDI, AUSTRALIA

Prepare to recalibrate your sense of scale. They do things bigger in Western Australia – a state the size of Western Europe with a population of just two million – and that includes the bike rides. The Munda Biddi trail, meaning 'path through the forest' in the Aboriginal Noongar language, unspools for 1000km through eucalyptus forests, bush and river valleys from Mundaring to Albany on the south coast. The complete trail opened in 2013. There are few places left where such a natural route could be plotted, but this trail isn't challenging in either difficulty or logistics; every 50km it passes by handsome country towns or campsites.

Mundaring is 40km from Perth, the state capital. Plan your trip at www.mundabiddi.org.au and www.westernaustralia.com.

338 LUCHON TO BAYONNE, FRANCE

You've pedalled up your first Pyrenean peak. Now for the treacherous part: the steep descent. Hands numb with cold, wreathed in cloud, you trust in two thumbprint-sized patches of rubber to keep you on the rough, narrow road. The Tour de France featured the Pyrenees for the first time in 1910 with a killer 326km stage from Bagnères-de-Luchon to Bayonne on the Atlantic coast, climbing the Col d'Aspin, the Col du Tourmalet, the Col d'Aubisque and the Peyresourde – the eventual winner Octave Lapize hissed the word 'assassins' at race organiser Henri Desgrange. While the profile looks downhill from halfway, it's actually a series of short, energy-sapping hills, but unlike Lapize, who finished in 14 hours, you'll have the option of splitting the ride over several days.

See www.tourisme.haute-garonne.fr. Toulouse is the closest airport.

BANANA PANCAKE/ALAMY ©

The undulating route of the South Down Way offers a way to experience a "green and pleasant land"

339 CAPE EPIC, SOUTH AFRICA

Competitive types can take on the world's largest mountain-bike stage race, which celebrated its 10th anniversary in 2013. Founder Kevin Vermaak was inspired by another gruelling mountain bike marathon, the Ruta de los Conquistadores across Costa Rica. He allows the 1200 racers eight days to cover 800km around the Western Cape. The route changes annually but a full-service experience is always provided with a travelling tented village. It's a taste of mountain biking in South Africa, from the sublime Stellenbosch to the ridiculous Breakback Mountain in the Chandelier Game Reserve. Epic, indeed.

The race takes place in March or April; enter at www.cape-epic.com.

340 LAND'S END TO JOHN O'GROATS, UK

It's the classic end-to-end ride – from England's Cornish toe at Land's End to the top of Scotland at John O'Groats. The 1300km ride is a week-long commitment but you can cherry-pick some of the tastiest sections, such as the National Route 7 from Glasgow to Inverness, a 344km tour through the Cairngorms and Trossachs that has a certain cinematic grandeur. There isn't a set route for LEJOG, so piece together your own based on how scenic or speedy you want it to be. Tip: main roads go around hills, minor roads (with less traffic) go over them…

Get the lowdown from Sustrans (www. sustrans.org.uk).

EPIC RIDES

BEST URBAN CLIMBING ADVENTURES

Climbing is not just about big walls in the wilderness – grab your gear and climb on some cliffs with urban grit.

341 CHEMIN DE FER, DUMBARTON ROCK, SCOTLAND

Steely grey skies that pour down sheets of freezing rain are what the mind conjures at the mention of Scotland. But when the weather clears around Dumbarton Rock the heart of hard British traditional climbing is revealed. Even if you can't muster the guts to tackle iconic 'death routes' like Requiem or Dave Macleod's Rhapsody, there's still plenty here for the bold soul.

For climbing die hards this is the only way to get to the viewpoint on Sugarloaf, Rio de Janeiro

Splitting the 68m-high reddish-grey cliff, Chermin de Fer is one of Scotland's finest crack climbs. A taxing beast in its own right, the basalt demands technical moves and complex sequences, but offers a prize worthy of journeying to this urban wastescape at the junction of the rivers Clyde and Leven.

Dumbarton Rock is historically significant and protected as a scheduled ancient monument – don't climb into the castle grounds.

CHRISTOPHER PILLITZ/IN PICTURES/CORBIS ©

342 POLISH TRAVERSE, RAT ROCK, CENTRAL PARK, NEW YORK, USA

Perhaps here more than anywhere else on earth, the need to get away from it all can be intense. New York is an overwhelming beast of noise and colour, an all-out assault on the senses, so it's a blessing then that Central Park provides an island of natural respite in the middle of the City that Never Sleeps. For years, climbers have needed nothing more than shoes and a chalkbag as they duck past the joggers on Columbus Circle to grapple with the evocatively named Rat Rock, just one of the gnarly little schist boulders of Central Park where city-locked climbers can get their zen on.

The concrete jungle of NYC can be horrifically humid in summer and brutally cold in winter; for maximum enjoyment make your play in spring or autumn.

343 FESSURA DEL BONJO, MONTE COLODRI, ARCO, ITALY

You scoff the last piece of pizza, quaff your espresso, offer a 'ciao' to the waiter and stride through the centre of Arco, the town in love with climbing. Walk the streets lined with gear shops, as climbing videos play in the bars, and 30 seconds later you're at the base of Monte Colodri, the cliff rising 300m above you into the wispy clouds. As you start out, the caffeine courses through your veins drawing adrenalin along with it. The rock is warm, the path magical and the views unforgettable. As you finish the climb under majestic Arco Castle, sweep your gaze across the surrounding valley to Lake Garda and the Sarca River...and fall in love.

Time your trip to coincide with the Rock Masters Festival and watch the best of the best compete in the world's longest-running climbing competition.

344 VIA DOS ITALIANOS, SUGARLOAF, RIO DE JANEIRO

With throbbing samba rhythms of last night's Carnival partying still pulsating, you push through the jungle to the base of Pão de Açúcar (aka Sugarloaf), the 396m sentinel that rises out of Guanabara Bay to stand guard over Rio de Janeiro. Looking up at the tower you eyeball your route that tackles the nose of the monolith directly under the path of the tourist cable car. On the rock, veins of gneiss swirl through the granite creating holds like you've never experienced, the quality of the climbing only rivalled by the view. At the summit you can order a celebratory beer and chat to the bartender before your seconder has even made it up to join you.

129

As bonus for their efforts, climbers are rewarded with a free ride in the otherwise very expensive cable car back down to the party.

345 PEEL STREET, SOHO CRAG, HONG KONG

There is something surreal about climbing on the crags above the megalopolis of Hong Kong. Perching high up on a cliff, looking down at 60-storey buildings below you is enough to warp anyone's sense of reality. One of the financial capitals of the world hums away down there, but up here the stone is solid, the climbing stellar and the setting unrivalled. After waltzing up Peel Street at Soho Crag you'll still be bathed in the glow of glory as you take the escalators down, squeeze into one of the restaurants in Soho and enjoy the best noodles and dumplings of your life.

Avoid coming between March and August when the wet season guarantees hot and humid weather with a chance of typhoons.

346 L'OLIVIER, LA LOUBIÈRE, LA TURBIE, FRANCE

Monaco is best known for glitz, glamour and gorgeous coastline, but high above the opulent playground of Europe's mega-rich lies a playground of a different sort – vertical seas of limestone screaming out to be climbed. You may not have the dollars to compete with the moneyed hordes that pack Monaco's streets and fill her harbour with yachts, but how fat your wallet is counts for nothing when you're hanging from your fingertips 80m up the classic L'Olivier. Standing on the summit of La Loubière as the buildings of Monaco turn gold in sunset is enough to make anyone feel like a superstar.

Stay in the old town in La Turbie, a medieval village of narrow streets paved with stone and brick.

347 ARROW FINAL, AFRICA LEDGE, TABLE MOUNTAIN, CAPE TOWN

You're in Cape Town and from downtown one sight commands your attention: Table Mountain. The striking, flat-topped mesa exudes a powerful pull, drawing your eyes then your feet. What better place for the wilds of nature to butt up against the civilised city than Africa? Leave the thinning tourist hordes behind as you pull onto the hard sandstone. The only sound competing with the birdsong will be gear clanging on your harness and your heartbeat drumming in your ears. The climbing is easy but engaging, safe but a little scary, and the position... it's priceless.

The security situation in South Africa is ever-changing and muggings do occur around Table Mountain; take particular care when not in large groups.

348 THE BUNKER, BERLIN

Berlin might be one of the world's most vibrant cities but the flat, sprawling urban mass is totally devoid of rock. What it does have is history, and while not all of it is heartwarming, it is powerful. And that's how to best describe climbing at the Humboldthain Flakturm (aka the Bunker). It's the only surviving example of the Nazi-era anti-aircraft towers that were once scattered about the city and formed a critical part of its defences. Today you can climb 70 routes there – some holds have been chipped by climbers while others bear the scars of wartime gunfire. Climbing is about connection to place and the connection you form here will be unlike any other.

Though manufactured, the Bunker's routes are often thin and technical – bring your A-game.

349 THINK PINK, AVON GORGE, BRISTOL, ENGLAND

Urban climbing is all about convenience, epitomised by Avon Gorge, only five minutes' walk from Bristol. Follow British tradition and sip a strong preclimb cup of tea from one of the shops at the base of the cliff, before you tackle central line of weakness that splits the pink-and-white limestone to form Think Pink. Don't be fooled by the convenience: this is a real climb with real consequences, intolerant of the foolhardy. Approach Think Pink via Krapp's Last Tape and you've got some of best, bold urban climbing Ol' Blighty has to offer. Cap the climb with an ice cream at the top – you've earned it.

Avon can be hot in summer but the long days allow for climbing well into the cool of the evening.

TOM MUELLER/IMAGEBROKER ©

Forget the cableway, the views from Table Mountain are even more exhilarating if you've climbed

350 PLUMBER'S MATE, BONDI SEA CLIFFS, SYDNEY

Sydney Sea Cliffs: crumbling heaps of terrible rock littered with Sydney's rubbish and rusting detritus? Don't believe the hype. Hidden amongst the beachfront suburbia is some climbing gold, none better than at Down Under's most famous strip of sand, Bondi. Just north of the beach – past bronzed bikini-clad bodies, burnt Englishmen and waves more crowded than Pitt Street at peak hour – lies a big serious cliff. To get there, cross the golf course, dodging whizzing balls, and negotiate the descent down 'Black Filth Couloir'. Your reward is a great climb across some of the best rock Sin City has to offer. Bonza.

For a better experience, brush the sand off the holds on your abseil down – the sandstone is like a magnet for the stuff.

BEST URBAN CLIMBING ADVENTURES

HAIR-RAISING ROAD TRIPS

Strap on your safety belt and set off on the world's most white-knuckle drives, from icy highways to a grand continental traverse.

351 KARAKORAM HIGHWAY, PAKISTAN

Humans have been inching along the Indus Valley for millennia, using this Silk Road strand to spread goods and ideologies between East and West. Goodness knows why – it's such difficult terrain to traverse. But traverse it they did and, finally, in 1986 some master-engineering saw it modernised: the 1200km Karakoram Highway was unveiled, linking Islamabad to Kashgar in China via the Karakorams, Himalaya and Hindu Kush ranges. It's a flabbergasting drive. There are potholes, landslides and vertical drops; there are old trucks done up like Christmas squeezing and wheezing along; there are roadblocks and bandits. But it'll be the drive of your life.

The drive from Islamabad to Gilgit takes 12 to 18 hours; two flights daily connect Islamabad–Gilgit (weather dependent), taking around 70 minutes.

352 TRANS-SIBERIAN HIGHWAY, RUSSIA

Officially there's still a spat over who has the longest road: the Australians reckon it's their Highway 1, the Canadians vote for their Trans-Canada Highway. But this 11,000km network of routes linking Saint Petersburg on the Baltic to Vladivostok on the Sea of Japan must give the Russians a good claim to the title. Even if it's not the longest, it must be the most daunting. Some dirt-track stretches turn to swamp in summer and deep-freeze in winter; in parts, settlements are few and far, *far* between. But that's what you get in the world's biggest country: majestic cities, then great expanses of mind-blowing nothing in between.

Independent drivers must be well prepared: they should carry a petrol can with extra fuel, a spare tyre, food, water and a tent.

353 DALTON HIGHWAY, ALASKA, USA

The ice-road truckers of north Alaska aren't exactly a wimpy bunch. But even they concede the Dalton Highway is a risky drive. The 665km route runs from north of Fairbanks to the town of Deadhorse, just shy of the Arctic Ocean; without stops, it takes 13 hours each way. It's flanked by wildlife refuges (look for moose, caribou and grizzlies, which far outnumber people) and astonishing viewpoints – try Finger Mountain (mile 98) and Gobbler's Knob (mile 132) – but is remote and inhospitable in the extreme. There are no phones, no hospitals, very few people; what there is, is an epic adventure.

Most rental companies do not allow their vehicles to be driven on the Dalton Highway. For preparation tips, see www.blm.gov/ak/dalton.

133

The icy reaches of the Dalton Highway extend through the wilderness of Alaska from Fairbanks to Deadhorse near the Arctic Ocean

Don't take your eyes off the road. The descent on the Troll's Road requires concentration

354 PAN-AMERICAN HIGHWAY, ALASKA-ARGENTINA

Two continents, 18 countries, around 47,000km – this isn't a road trip, it's a mission of a lifetime. The network of interlinking highways collectively called the Pan Americana stretches from far north Alaska to Ushuaia, Argentina – the southernmost city in the world. En route it dissects a travel hall of fame: Arctic tundra, Rocky Mountains, New Mexican desert, Mayan jungle, the Amazon, the Andes, the peaks of Patagonia. There's one chink in its armour though – the North American section halts at Panama's impenetrable Darién Gap; the South American portion restarts in Colombia, 160km south. But it's just a short blip in a mammoth ride.

Buses run along much of the Pan American Highway. There is currently no ferry service from Panama to Colombia.

355 GIBB RIVER ROAD, WESTERN AUSTRALIA

Cattle stations as big as countries, crocs basking by the billabongs, indigenous communities dotted amid the bush, bone-rattling dirt roads that eat tyres for breakfast – the Gibb River Road is Australian Outback at its most raw and classic. But while care must be taken, this 660km track cutting across the Kimberley from Derby to near Kununurra is a doable drive for the non-idiot 4WD novice. There are river crossings to negotiate and road trains to avoid. But there are also secluded gorges for cooling dips, 'roos and wallabies for roadside companions and welcoming ranches offering much-needed fuel, beds and ice-cold beers.

The road is impassable from November to March. 4WD vehicles are recommended; at least two spare tyres should be carried.

356 TROLLSTIGEN, NORWAY

It's as if you're accelerating right up to Asgard. Such is the drama of the Trollstigen Valley that it could be the automobile approach to the Norse gods' realm. For through this netherworld of rugged granite and fairy-tale waterfalls twists the Troll's Road, a slither of snakelike asphalt with a nine-percent gradient and 11 tight hairpin turns that make it one of the human world's most epic drives. In winter, it's impassable; generally the road is only open to cars from May to October, depending on the snowfall in the mountains and, perhaps, the whim of the gods...

Trollstigen is a six-hour drive from Oslo, four hours from Trondheim. The scenic Rauma Railway runs to the nearby town of Åndalsnes.

357 SANI PASS, SOUTH AFRICA/LESOTHO

This is a truly hair-raising roadtrip, but perhaps an endangered one. Plans are afoot to upgrade the twisty, 27-bend, 9km-long gravel track that leads up from South Africa's Drakensberg Mountains into the tiny kingdom of Lesotho. Good for road quality and ease of border crossing, but potentially bad for the tourism business – will a nice, neat line of boring, old tarmac offer the same adventurous appeal? On the plus side, though, the kerbside drop-offs to the valleys below will be no less impressive and the highest pub in Africa (perched at 2874m) will still be waiting at the top.

The Sani Pass is 80km southeast of Durban Airport. Currently a 4WD vehicle is required to tackle the pass.

358 YUNGAS ROAD, BOLIVIA

The Yungas Road has many monikers, but most chilling among them is El Camino de la Muerte – the Road of Death. Indeed, its dubious claim to fame is being the world's most dangerous highway, thanks to its improbable geography: Yungas links capital La Paz (3660m), via the La Cumbre Pass (4650m), to Coroico (1200m) over just 60km. Worse, this breakneck, white-knuckle descent, hewn into the sides of the mist-prone Cordillera Oriental, is often just 3.5m wide – on one side, sheer rock rises up; on the other, valley plummets down. Tackle it, by bus or most popularly by bicycle, at your peril

Bike trips from La Paz to Coroico/Yolosa include four to five hours of cycling (90 percent downhill); the drive back to La Paz takes three to four hours.

359 GUOLIANG TUNNEL ROAD, HENAN, CHINA

Guoliang Road is a fatal lifeline. In 1972 villagers in isolated Guoliang decided to hack a tunnel into the Taihang Mountains in order to connect with the world; sadly, several lost their lives in the process. But they laboured on and in 1977 this 1.2km-long, 4m-wide, 5m-high passage was opened. It's quite some feat, evidenced by its 30 'windows' which offer vertiginous views of the gaping chasm below. It's worth risking either the drive or walk up, though. The hamlet itself is a comely cluster of stone bridges and alleys, with spectacular walking in those once inaccessible hills.

Guoliang is 120km north of Zhengzhou. The nearest train station is at Xinxiang; from here buses go to Huxian, then Guoliang.

360 LEH–MANALI HIGHWAY, LADAKH, INDIA

Breathtaking in the extreme, the average elevation of the Leh–Manali Highway is more than 4000m; at the Taglang La its tarmac tops out at 5328m. Indeed, this is the world's highest motorable road. And that's because, in order to connect Himachal Pradesh's lush, laidback hill station with the chill Ladakhi desert hub of Leh, it has to battle with the Western Himalaya, wheedling between snow peaks and over high passes in an ever-more forbidding land. It's slow going – reckon on 20 hours non-stop. But take your time; the joy is the views, the stupas, the prayer flags and people you encounter en route.

The Leh–Manali Highway is only open from around May/June to October; buses and jeep taxis serve the route.

HAIR-RAISING ROAD TRIPS

SECOND-HIGHEST (NOT SECOND BEST)

Don't underestimate the planet's understudy mountains – many offer better, less-crowded climbs than their bigger brasher brothers.

363 KITA-DAKE, JAPAN

Mount Fuji is so postcard-ubiquitous that you might assume Japan doesn't even have any other mountains. Not so. While the 3776m superstar is the country's tallest, 3193m Kita-dake – the so-called Leader of the Southern Alps – is a respectable understudy. Doable in a weekend trip from Tokyo, Kita-dake sees few of the crowds that cluster Fuji. Still, there are plenty of built-in ropes and ladders to make any tricky bits easier. Plus, the views are magnificent: the trail is edged with forest lower down, alpine plants higher up and, on a clear day, there are views of iconic Fuji itself.

Trekking from Hirogawara trailhead to the summit takes six to eight hours up, three to five hours down; there are two mountain huts en route.

361 BEN MACDUI, SCOTLAND

On a clear day you can see Ben Nevis – the UK's highest point – from the top of Ben Macdui. But you won't mind that you're not there. Because what the latter lacks in altitude (1309m to Nevis's 1344m) it makes up for in isolation. While the Highlands hubtown of Fort William clogs the base of the biggest Ben, Macdui sits within Cairngorms National Park, making hikes here a wilder affair. There are some lovely, if long, routes up the mountain, crossing heathery glens, pine woods and almost-Arctic tundra; just don't underestimate its modest proportions should the weather decide to roll in.

Buses run from Aviemore to the trailhead at the Cairn Gorm ski centre. In winter, crampons and ice-axes are necessary.

362 MT ELGON, KENYA

Named Ol Doinyo Ilgoon (Breast Mountain) by the Maasai, border-straddling Mt Elgon is Kenya's second-highest summit. Well, actually, the very pinnacle of the peak – 4321m Wagagai – is in Uganda. But it's still a massive Kenyan massif, an extinct volcano with the world's largest intact caldera. Its slopes are draped in teak and cedar trees and moorland of giant lobelia; waterfalls tumble down its sides; hot springs (which you can dip in) burble inside the crater. It's also riddled with lava tubes; one such cave, Kitum, is favoured by elephants who tramp in at night to lick salt from the walls.

The best times to trek are the drier months of mid-December to March and June to July. Climbs take three to five days.

364 CERRO VENTISQUEROS, COSTA RICA

Seven metres – the width of a football goal: that's all that separates Costa Rica's highest peak, 3819m Cerro Chirripó, from its second, 3812m Cerro Ventisqueros. But size matters, drawing the majority of hikers to the former, leaving the latter wonderfully free from the hordes. If you can live with missing out on a few metres, it's worth making the swap. Ventisqueros is a fine two- or three-day climb, the wildlife-rich rainforest of its lower flanks segueing to Andean-style paramó dotted with cobalt lakes and far-reaching views. And, if you must, Cerro Chirripó is just a short detour away.

From San Isidro de El General (3 hours from San José), buses run to San Gerardo de Rivas, with a stop at PN Chirripó ranger station.

365 M'GOUN MASSIF, MOROCCO

At 4167m, Jebel Toubkal is not only Morocco's highest mountain but the loftiest summit in North Africa. Which is grand, because it keeps most of the list-tickers away from M'goun – also in the High Atlas and just 100m lower but no less an experience. Trekkers here don't only benefit from quieter slopes. A five-day walk might involve traversing the fruit orchards of the Ait Bougmez Valley, scouting for griffin vultures in Oulilimt Gorge and camping on the dramatic Tarkeddit Plateau. And while other tourists are scarce, there are always Berber villages to be found, where steaming tagines await hungry hikers.

The M'goun Massif is in Azilal Province, around 250km from Marrakesh. The best time to climb is May to September, for fine weather.

366 DOM, SWITZERLAND

Time to get the crampons out...the Dom is the don of Swiss mountaineering. It's not the country's tallest peak – that honour goes to Monte Rosa (4634m); neither is it necessarily the hardest (north face of the Eiger, anyone?). But it *does* boast the largest vertical height gain in all the Alps. In the absence of the cablecars and cog-railways that so often help climbers up the lower reaches of the mountains, there's no such thing on the Dom, which means from the nearest road-head, there's 3100m of legwork to be done in order to reach the spectacular 4545m summit.

The Dom is best climbed July to September. The normal route up starts from the village of Randa, accessible by train from Zermatt.

367 K2, PAKISTAN

It might be lacking a couple of hundred metres (8611m, compared with Everest's 8850m) and it might not even have a proper name, but K2 must never be underestimated. The world's second-highest peak, standing sentinel over the Pakistan–China border, is treacherous; they call it the Savage Mountain as climbers have around a one-in-four chance of not making it back down alive. As only the most experienced must ever dare to attempt K2, try an alternative adventure. Trek in to Concordia, a glacial confluence surrounded by four of the world's 14 8000m-plus peaks, to admire from a close-yet-safe distance instead.

Treks to Concordia take around 21 days, including transfers from Islamabad to the trailhead near Skardu; trekking season is June to September.

368 MT MERU, TANZANIA

Poor Mt Meru, it doesn't stand a chance. Big brother Kilimanjaro is just 70km east and steals all the headlines, what with being 5895m and Africa's highest peak. But Meru – a none-too-shabby 4565m – has charms of its own. It's in Arusha National Park, so climbs offer good wildlife-spotting of mostly birds and monkeys, but hyena and leopard lurk here too. And the trekking route is varied, crossing crater floor, montane forest and moorland to skirt a dicey ridge with views to the volcanic cone below. And if you *do* insist on climbing Kili too, Meru makes the perfect warm-up.

Meru ascents take three to four days. June to February is the best time to climb; December to February offers the best views of Mount Kilimanjaro.

369 COTOPAXI, ECUADOR

This is a slight anomaly among peak-baggers, who tend to think biggest is best. For although 5897m Cotopaxi is Ecuador's second-highest point (behind 6268m Chimborazo), it's easily the country's most popular climb. That might be because it's perfect: the perfectly symmetrical snow-glazed cone is how a child might draw a volcano. But also it's relatively doable. While you do need some technical gear for the icy terrain and while the altitude is lung-gaspingly high, the ascent route is pretty straightforward. Of course, the fact that Cotopaxi's still active (witness the sulphur-steaming fumaroles up top) just adds an extra dash of adventure.

Cotopaxi is 55km south of Quito. From Jose Ribas refuge (4800m) it takes around seven hours to reach the summit.

370 BLUE MOUNTAIN PEAK, JAMAICA

The rumpled island of Hispaniola – divvied up between Haiti and the Dominican Republic – boasts most of the Caribbean's highest peaks. But the region's second-highest isle is Jamaica. Best known for beaches and chilled-out Bob Marleyism, Jamaica doesn't seem the natural choice for 2256m-high schlepping, but Blue Mountain Peak is worth the effort. Set out early through the dark forest to reach summit for sunrise over the mist-tickled range and sea beyond. Then descend amid tree ferns, eucalypts and azaleas, stopping for Blue Mountain coffee, made from beans grown on these very slopes.

The 22km-long Peak Trail takes around seven hours to complete. The best time to climb is during the December to April dry season.

MOUNTAIN BIKING'S MECCAS

Get down and dirty on a pilgrimage to the world's gnarliest mountain biking hotspots.

371 THE BORDERS, SCOTLAND

The Seven Stanes (Scottish Gaelic for stones) is a necklace of seven mountain biking centres on Forestry Commission land, strung across the Scottish Borders. From Kirroughtree, overlooking the Irish Sea, to Glentress and Innerleithen, south of Edinburgh, via Glentrool, Mabie, Dalbeattie, Ae and Newcastleton, the Seven Stanes have earned a worldwide reputation for high quality, man-made, all-weather trails, graded for difficulty like ski runs, from green to blue to red to black. When you've acclimatised to the weather and the accent, head up to the Highlands to make the most of Scotland's enlightened land access laws.

Glasgow and Edinburgh lie at either end of Border country. Bikes can be rented at most of the trail centres; for details see www.7stanes.gov.uk. Book bike-friendly accommodation at www.visitscotland. com. And watch out for the midges (tiny but ravenous insects) in the summer in some locations.

372 NORTH ISLAND, NEW ZEALAND

Clean, green New Zealand was an early adopter of the mountain bike, as you'd expect from a nation of outdoors fanatics. Mountain bikes are restricted in the prized national parks but on the North Island several bike parks have sprung up to meet demand for challenging trails. Makara Peak, minutes from downtown Wellington, welcomes 100,000 riders a year. Further north, near the hot springs of Rotorua, Whakarewarewa Forest has 70km of trails through pines, eucalypts and ferns. On the South Island, they like to go a little bigger: helicopters drop off bikes and riders at the Coronet Peak ski area in the Remarkables.

Winter (June to August) is cold and snowy at altitude; September to May is prime time. International flights land at Auckland. For accommodation visit www.newzealand.com. See www. riderotorua.com and www.makara peak.org.

373 WHISTLER, BRITISH COLUMBIA, CANADA

The mountain bike season starts at Whistler Bike Park in May, when snowboards are shelved and tyres pumped up. British Columbia's largest ski resort first opened its chairlifts to bikers in 1999 and today there are more than 200km of trails swooping 1500 vertical metres down the mountain. If you get tired of being overtaken by 10-year-olds on tracks like A-line or Freight Train, venture along cross-country routes, such as A River Runs Through It. Sun Peaks, Silver Star and other resorts in British Columbia also welcome mountain bikers.

Whistler is a two-hour drive up the Sea to Sky Highway from Vancouver. Plan a trip at www.bikeparksbc.com.

When the snow subsides and the skis are shelved, the bikes take over at Whistler Bike park

Mountain biking rugged terrain in the thin air of Crested Butte – literally breathtaking

374 THE ROCKIES, COLORADO, USA

Mountain biking in Colorado's share of the Rocky Mountains will take your breath away; it's not for nothing that state capital Denver is nicknamed the Mile-High City. But although it takes a few days for lowland mountain bikers to acclimatise to the thin air, few visitors ever get used to the majestic scenery of the western side of the state. The towns of Durango, Crested Butte, Leadville, Telluride, Fruita and Boulder are where mountain bikers aren't so much outsiders as part of the establishment – Colorado brewer New Belgium even has a Fat Tire Ale. Trails, such as the 401 out of Crested Butte, roll for epic distances through remote alpine meadows and canyons. This is 'Be Prepared' country.

Visit www.colorado.com for accommodation options; the towns mentioned will have maps, guides and rental bikes available. Late spring, snow permitting, to early autumn is peak season.

375 THE HIMALAYA, NEPAL

The trekkers may have got here first but finally mountain biking is a player on the most dramatic mountain stage of all. Rather than trudge up to the big peaks with the yak trains and the Sherpas, jump on a bike and get your tyres dirty in the foothills of Kathmandu Valley and around Pokhara to the northwest of the capital. A mountain bike has always been a passport to adventure but here it's also a time machine. Venture off the beaten path and you'll find pagodas and prayer wheels in hidden villages.

There are still more gods than mountain bike guides in Nepal but you can book one of the best local guides at www. himalayansingletrack.com in central Kathmandu. October and November is the start of the dry season.

376 FINALE LIGURE, ITALY

For mountain bikers, the perfect holiday features sun, sea and dusty singletrack. You can find it all at Finale Ligure, a town midway between Nice and Genoa on the Italian Riviera. The first people to create trails along the contours of the area's hills and headlands were locals collecting chestnuts. Today in-the-know mountain bikers weave their way around the trees on these ribbons of dust and limestone. Your reward for those hours in the saddle: a lunch of mozzarella, fresh tomato and local olive oil overlooking the Mediterranean.

Nice and Genoa airports are around an hour's drive away. Summer is hot; spring and autumn are optimum times and the trails are often open in winter. Book a local guide through Just Ride Finale (www.justridefinale.com).

377 THE ALPS, FRANCE

The hills are alive with the sound of brakes squealing. In summer, the ski resorts of the Haute-Savoie open their chairlifts and gondolas to mountain bikers and the slopes of Europe's largest mountain range become playgrounds for riders in body armour and full-face helmets. This is mountainous terrain where, with judicious use of lifts, descents can last hours not minutes. Resorts in the vast Portes du Soleil region, such as Les Gets, open dedicated bike parks with jumps, drops and wall-rides, while in Verbier riders can explore steep singletrack with local guides.

June to August is the peak season and lifts close to bikers in September. Snow is possible at the highest levels all year round. Geneva and Grenoble are the gateways to the mountains. See www.lesgets.com and www.bikeverbier.com.

378 MARIN COUNTY, CALIFORNIA, USA

Pay your respects at the birthplace of the modern mountain bike. It was in the mid-1970s on the dirt roads of Mt Tamalpais in Marin County that a bunch of long-haired, flannel-shirt-wearing men first raced cruiser bikes fitted with knobbly tyres downhill. Sadly, the authorities weren't as enthusiastic and equipped rangers with speed guns. So once you've had a spin on Mt Tam, cross back over Golden Gate and head for Downieville in California's Gold Country. It's here that those '70s pioneers' invention reaches its full potential.

San Francisco is the gateway. See www.visitcalifornia.com for accommodation. Visit April to October but beware of snow at higher elevations.

379 THE NORTH SHORE, BRITISH COLUMBIA, CANADA

'Follow me', says your guide. 'Are you sure!?' you reply. Yes, the trails of the North Shore of Vancouver are where to explore the limits of your skill and balance. The Coastal Mountains, a few minutes' drive north of downtown Vancouver, are where local riders bridged bogs with logs and timber ladders, and rode over rather than around huge boulders. East to west the key peaks are Mt Seymour, Mt Fromme and Cypress. The trails through the mountain hemlocks and cypresses are short, steep and intense; many require a head for heights but some, such as Pangor on Mt Seymour and Lower Oil Can on Mt Fromme, are suitable for those of average ability.

Base yourself in Vancouver (www.tourismvancouver.com) and buy a map from the North Shore Mountain Bike Association (www.nsmba.ca).

380 HURRICANE, UTAH, USA

The ochre ocean of rock around Moab in the east of Utah might get the crowds and the column inches, but go west to the mesas (plateaus) and sagebrush flats around the towns of Hurricane and Virgin for the state's new mountain-biking frontier. On Gooseberry Mesa the singletrack trails hug cliff edges and thread a route through Mars-like boulder fields (you'll need a map and good directions to find the trailheads). Slightly to the north, the town of Virgin is the jumping-off point for mountain biking's most extreme contest, the Red Bull Rampage.

The closest main airport is St George. See www.visitutah.com for accommodation options. Bike shops around Hurricane can provide maps and rental bikes.

MOUNTAIN BIKING'S MECCAS

GOING TO EXTREMES

Push through your personal limits on these adventures exploring record-breaking destinations around the globe.

381 THE WORLD'S BIGGEST SALT FLAT, BOLIVIA

Bolivia's Salar de Uyuni sprawls across 12,000 sq km to every horizon, the white expanse only disturbed by a few tiny 'islands' studded with ancient cacti up to 1000 years old. In the dry season (May to August) the salt has a soft crust like coconut ice or meringue. Come back in the wet season (December to April) and a shimmering veneer of water turns the salt flats into a natural mirror. And unlike the Great Wall of China, it really can be seen from space.

Book with travel agencies in Uyuni and consider staying in the Palacio de Sal hotel (www.palaciodesal.com.bo/en-us) where the walls, floors and furniture are made of salt.

382 THE WORLD'S DRIEST DESERT, CHILE

Chile's Atacama desert is the driest place on earth – some weather stations in the region have never recorded rain – and with flamingos, shimmering salt lakes and sprawling, steaming fields of geothermal activity, it's also one of most otherworldly places on the planet. Hike at sunset through the Valle de la Luna where snow-like salt dusting the rugged valleys glows luminously in the ethereal Atacama twilight, or jump on a mountain bike and journey to Laguna Cejar, a natural salt lake perfect for mineral-rich bathing.

Visit year-round, basing yourself amid the adobe houses of San Pedro de Atacama. See www.knowchiletour.com for tours of Atacama's lesser-known areas.

383 THE WORLD'S HIGHEST MOUNTAIN, MT EVEREST

Every year an increasing number of alpine adventurers attempt the perilous ascent of the world's highest peak but more realistic (and undoubtedly safer) is a trek to Everest Base Camp. Spying Everest will still be ticked off your bucket list and on the way to a challenging altitude of 5545m, the high mountain scenery also showcases the surrounding peaks of

Ama Dablam, Pumori and Nuptse. Most of the trek traverses the World Heritage–listed Sagarmatha National Park. Sherpa villages and Buddhist monasteries provide a cultural counterbalance to the soaring natural beauty and wildlife. Keep an eye out for musk deer, red pandas and Himalayan tahr.

Plan your assault on Everest Base Camp from October to December, allowing two to three weeks for the entire expedition from Lukla.

384 THE WORLD'S MOST REMOTE CAPITAL CITY, WELLINGTON

Wellington was dubbed the 'coolest little capital in the world' by Lonely Planet in 2011 so it's definitely worth considering a New Zealand southern sojourn. Kick off your exploration of the city at Te Papa. With an absolute waterfront location, New Zealand's national museum is a modern and interactive showcase of all things Kiwi. The museum's own *marae* (meeting place) has an excellent collection of Maori artefacts. If you're a movie fan, visit the Weta Cave in Miramar, a compact museum of the Oscar-winning company behind the special effects magic of films like *The Lord of the Rings* and *Avatar*.

Visit in February to catch the New Zealand International Rugby Sevens (www.sevens. co.nz). Just be aware that fancy dress is virtually mandatory for spectators.

No need to pack your umbrella when leaving for Chile's Atacama desert

A plunge in the Dead Sea is highly therapeutic, well perhaps a float is the correct term

385 THE WORLD'S LOWEST PLACE, THE DEAD SEA

Bordered by three countries – Israel, Jordan and the West Bank – the Dead Sea is steeped in ancient history and has been attracting travellers seeking rest and relaxation for centuries. Legend states it was a place of refuge for Cleopatra, and that Herod the Great established one of the world's first health resorts here. In the 21st century, health tourists still flock to the lake 400m (1312 feet) below sea level, the curative properties of the mineral-saturated water – around 1000 percent saltier than seawater – reputedly including alleviation of rheumatism, respiratory problems and arthritis. Being photographed caked in healing Dead Sea mud is also de rigueur.

Look forward to around 330 sunny days per year here; the most comfortable temperatures are during winter (November to March).

386 THE WORLD'S LARGEST ISLAND, GREENLAND

Yes, we know, Australia is bigger but the land Down Under is generally considered a continent, so Greenland takes the planetary gong for biggest island. Optimistically dubbed Greenland by the Viking explorer Erik the Red – apparently to lure settlers from Iceland – this autonomous region of 2.16 million sq km is now part of the Kingdom of Denmark. During summer, the retreat of sea ice in the fjords makes boat trips with local Inuit fisherman possible. Spring is ideal for dog sledding and in the sunlight-deprived days of winter (November to February) the aurora borealis dances across the night sky.

Summer (May to August) offers trekking and sailing; during spring (March to April) there's Nordic skiing and snowshoeing.

387 THE COLDEST PLACE ON EARTH, ANTARCTICA

Unless you're a gung-ho polar adventurer or working with a government agency in Antarctica, travelling by boat is the only way to explore the planet's largest and southernmost continent. If you've got a sturdy constitution when it comes to motion sickness, sign up for a smaller vessel as access into Antarctica's smaller bays and coves will be easier. Most expeditions begin and end in Ushuaia, Chile, negotiating icebergs in the Drake Passage to reach wildlife around the South Shetland Islands and the Antarctic Peninsula. Regular shore landings get travellers up close to penguins, seals and whales.

For travellers, the world's coldest and driest continent is only accessible when the sea ice melts from November to March.

388 THE WORLD'S HOTTEST PLACE, DALLOL, ETHIOPIA

Don't complain to the residents of Dallol about global warming. Near the border of the Eritrea and adrift in the dangerously rugged landscape of the Danakil Depression – a life-sapping amalgamation of salt flats, active volcanoes and earthquakes – the settlement is officially the planet's hottest inhabited place. The average annual average temperature hovers around 35°C (94°F) but in summer the mercury can soar to 64°C (148°F). Factor in the lingering threat of Afar separatist rebels and it's little wonder the incredibly hardy people of this remote and punishing region dub the town the 'gateway to Hell.'

From Addis Ababa, drive north for five hours and then switch to a camel for the final push through an unforgiving desert.

389 THE WORLD'S SMALLEST COUNTRY, VATICAN CITY

With centuries of history, the soaring architecture of St Peter's Basilica and poignant works of art like Michelangelo's heartbreaking *Pietà*, the Vatican (population 830) is an essential Roman destination even for nonreligious travellers. If you're keen to see the Pope's Wednesday-morning address, download a request for free tickets from the Vatican website (www.vatican.va); dress conservatively. Michelangelo's genius is also showcased at the Vatican Museums, a sprawling 5.5-hectare collection of world-beating art. Visit on the last Sunday of the month and you'll be able to experience the glory of the Sistine Chapel for free.

Pay your papal respects year-round but also consider taking in the Estate Romana cultural festival (June to September).

390 THE WORLD'S LONGEST RIVER, THE NILE

At 6650km (4130 miles), the Nile runs through 10 countries, but bypass ongoing debate over the river's source – Burundi, Rwanda, Uganda, Lake Victoria, anyone? – and travel north to Egypt to understand how the mighty Nile has shaped history and supported empires. Negotiating a spidery fertile path through the entire country, it's best experienced around the Nile Valley from Luxor to Aswan. Most river cruises take four to six days to link the two cities. Around Luxor the fascinating necropolis of Thebes is arrayed on the river's west bank, and south at Aswan white-sailed *feluccas* tack in wafting Egyptian breezes.

Visit during the relatively cool shoulder season from October to March, outside of the tourist peak.

GOING TO EXTREMES

MONKEY MAGIC: BEST ADVENTURES IN TREES

Make like a monkey with these arboreal adventures and get to grips with some of the world's greatest trees.

391 GIBBON EXPERIENCE, LAOS

Zip around the mixed forest of Bokeo Nature Reserve in northern Laos with the Gibbon Experience, a conservation project that protects this threatened ecosystem. You'll be on the trail of black gibbons, travelling through the canopy on zip lines and sleeping at their level in tree houses that are several hours' hike into the forest (if the road is impassable). Although you'll need the eyes of a hawk to spot wildlife, you'll be serenaded by the sounds of the jungle as you drift to sleep 40m up in the trees. Miss out on the gibbons? Another meet-the-monkeys experience is in Gombe Stream National Park in Tanzania, with the chimpanzees studied and protected by Jane Goodall (www. tanzaniaparks.com/gombe).

Huay Xai is the closest town and can be reached by boat or bus. The dry season runs from November to March. See www. gibbonexperience.org for details.

392 CLIMB A TREE, AUSTRALIA

If you're going to build a fire-lookout tower in the Australian bush, you may as well use one provided by nature. That's what they reasoned in the 1940s in Pemberton, in the southwest corner of Western Australia. Pegs were embedded in eight of the local karri trees (the third-tallest species in the world) and three of these lofty, straight trees – the Diamond (51m), the Gloucester (61m) and the Dave Evans Bicentennial (75m) – can be climbed today. Being the tallest, the latter is the most popular so to dodge the larger crowds head for the Diamond, topped with a wooden cabin, or the Gloucester, located within the karri forest of Gloucester National Park. All the trees are within 15 minutes' drive of Pemberton.

Bring a head for heights. Pemberton is 330km south of Perth: see www. pembertonvisitor.com.au.

393 TREEHOUSE, SCANDINAVIA

Sleep with the squirrels at Britta and Kent Lindvall's Treehotel in Swedish Lapland. Suspended in conifers just outside the village of Harads, near the Finnish border, are several architect-designed pods. Forget creaky planks and damp blankets, these are sleek and sophisticated tree houses. The Mirrorcube's reflective walls camouflage it in the canopy – only the rope bridge leading to the door gives it away. The Cabin sleeps two and has a deck from where you can watch the aurora borealis. And the Bird's Nest, which sleeps four, is accessed by an electronic retractable ladder. When you're not in your eyrie, local guides can take you horse-riding or kayaking.

Book at www.treehotel.se and explore northern Sweden's archipelago at www. visitlulea.se.

394 FOREST WALKS, AUSTRALIA

Messing about in trees is fun – and there's scientific proof that it's good for you. Research shows that when surrounded by nature we produce less of the stress hormone cortisol, and less stress can improve our neural nimbleness and lower blood pressure. So, getting out of the city for a walk in the woods is good for our brains and bodies. Melburnians don't need much encouragement to hit the Great Ocean Road; stop in the Otway Ranges, just west of Apollo Bay, for the Otway Fly Treetop Adventure, a 600m canopy walk 30m up in the treetops of this beech myrtle forest. Finish the trip with a zip-line ride back to earth.

The canopy walk (www.otwayfly.com) is around 200km from Melbourne. Stay in Apollo Bay; see www.visitvictoria.com.

Kauri Coast rainforest, realm of Maori legend and timeless stands of sturdy trees

395 LEARN TO BE A LUMBERJACK OR JILL, USA

Pack a flannel shirt for your summer semester at the Adirondack Woodsmen's School. On the curriculum for the two-week introductory course for beginners are log-rolling, fire-building, crosscut sawing, axe-swinging, chainsaw maintenance – oh, and an overnight war canoe expedition. Your classroom is the shore of the Lower St Regis Lake, high up in New York State's Adirondacks. The course is provided by Paul Smith College and though you don't have to be a student there, you do need to be of college age. It's one of the few schools still teaching lumberjack skills.

Enrol at www.adirondackwoodsmens school.com.

396 KAURI COAST, NEW ZEALAND

Who are you calling fat? At 50m high, kauri may not be the world's tallest trees but they are among the most stout. Some 19th century examples exceeded 25m in diameter (that's 16.5 hugs, for maths-phobes). Many giant kauri survive today, including 1200-year-old Tane Mahuta in Northland, about which the Maori wove a creation legend. This ancient evergreen stands in Waipoua Forest, north of Dargaville. At nearby Trounson Kauri Park, take a guided night-time hike through the forest to meet its nocturnal residents, the brown kiwi and the morepork owl.

Trounson Kauri Park and Waipoua Forest lie on State Highway 12, north of Dargaville. Plan a trip along the Kauri Coast at www.newzealand.com and see www.doc.govt.nz for details of Waipoua Forest.

147

Go on, hug a tree to feel the love and the mighty dimensions of the giant redwood

397 RIDE THE REDWOODS, USA

Where fog rolls in off the cool Pacific coast and meets the mountains of northern California, the giant redwood, or sequoia, grows. These trees soar 30 storeys high and grow in great stands. Enter one of these stands – minus sightseers – and you may just experience a spiritual connectedness with the natural world's eternal pulse. Or you might just think, 'Damn, that's a lot of floorboards.' Either way, the best method of exploring the Redwood National Park is to ride it by horse, motorbike or bicycle. Bike trails are restricted to the main routes, quiet roads and vehicle tracks – don't forget to keep an eye out for Bigfoot.

Visit the Redwood National Park pages at www.nps.gov and www. visitcalifornia.com. Summers are dry and winters wet in the forests.

398 HUG A TREE, ENGLAND

Mottisfont Abbey, a former medieval priory in the southern county of Hampshire, is home to one of Britain's largest plane trees – an arboreal giant with a girth of 12m. A hug from an adult reaches around 1.5m, making Mottisfont's plane tree an eight-hug wonder. But don't stop with just one hug (or eight). The Woodland Trust wants people to help find the nation's oldest trees by hugging their way around England's national parks. For reference, ancient oak trees – averaging 400 years of age but some dating back 1000 years to the reign of Aethelred the Unready – take three hugs, a sweet chestnut four hugs and a beech, ash or Scots pinetree two hugs.

See www.nationaltrust.org.uk and www. visit-hampshire.co.uk for details of Mottisfont Abbey and www.ancient-tree-hunt.org.uk for the tree-hugging research.

399 TAKE A TREE-CLIMBING COURSE, USA

Tree climbing has changed since you were a kid. No longer is it about getting winded after falling six feet and dusting yourself down before hightailing it home for tea. These days you'll need ropes, harnesses and a helmet. Taking a basic tree-climbing course with Tim Kovar at Tree Climbing Planet near Portland, Oregon (or at other US locations), can teach you safe techniques for tying knots and hauling yourself up to the canopy. His three-day Beyond the Branches course promotes the use of minimal gear. In Atlanta, Georgia, Tree Climbers International offers a beginner's climb for kids on two Sundays per month all year round.

Book a course at www.treeclimbingplanet. com and www.treeclimbing.com.

400 CANOPY TOUR, COSTA RICA

Beautiful butterflies and birdsong from a thousand feathered throats fills the air. You're in one of the most diverse and densely inhabited ecosystems in the world, the cloud forest reserve of Monteverde in Costa Rica. And you're part of the birds' world on a two-hour canopy tour that includes a short hike, zip lines and a rappel down to the forest floor. Back on the ground, spend as much time as possible on the forest hiking trails, spotting rare amphibians, orchids and bromeliads. You're less likely to see jaguars and tapirs...but they might be watching you.

Santa Elena is the closest town to Monteverde Cloud Forest Reserve. The road up the mountain can be impassable after rain during the wet season (May to mid-November); rent a 4WD vehicle. See http://canopytour.com/monteverde.

MONKEY MAGIC: BEST ADVENTURES IN TREES

WILD AT HEART: BEST ANIMAL ADVENTURES

Set your pulse racing with the wildest animal adventures around the world.

403 CHIMPANZEE TRACKING IN TANZANIA

It was pioneering researcher Jane Goodall who put Gombe Stream National Park on the map, as she captivated the world with her chronicles of the native chimps' behaviour. Sitting here amongst the forest trees, watching as these animals groom each other and use tools to get food, the sense of recognition is astonishing; here are some of the human species' closest relatives. Although your time amongst the animals each day is necessarily short, it's an experience that will resonate for a lifetime.

Various companies offer chimp-tracking safaris in Gombe. June to October is the best (driest) time to visit; see http://tanzaniaparks.com/gombe.html. The park is reached via boat from Kigoma.

401 SWIMMING WITH DOLPHINS AT THE RIVIERA MAYA, MEXICO

Mysterious, intelligent, playful – yes, dolphins are all these things and gentle too, as you find when you're swimming with your arms around one of them. This part of the world is blessed with that magic formula of sunshine + water = happiness. At a dolphin centre in the Mexican Caribbean, you'll meet, play and swim freely with the dolphins under expert guidance and then perform some water acrobatics. The dolphins will let you grab them from their dorsal fin and then push you with their nose until you are lifted into the air and drop with a splash.

Only swim at dolphin centres that are clean, have solid experience and treat their animals well. The best centres, such as Dolphinaris Park (www.dolphinaris.com), stipulate no jewellery or sunscreen in the dolphin pool.

402 GET CLOSE TO GIANT PANDAS NEAR XI'AN, CHINA

These black-and-white beauties are battling extinction but you can help them out – and get close and friendly at the same time – by feeding them and cleaning their habitat every day in Lou Guan Tai village, 1½ hours drive from Xi'an (home of the famous terracotta warrior statues). The cuteness factor of watching a cuddly, docile panda chow down on bamboo will make up for having to clean up after them – keeping them comfy is important as happy pandas are more like to get on with breeding. You'll also get to learn about the local Chinese culture and eat some delicious dumplings along the way.

The Lou Guan Tai Wild Animal Protection Centre does not accept visitors, only volunteers; tours are available through www.realgap.com/china-giant-panda-conservation.

404 FALCONRY IN DARTMOOR NATIONAL PARK, DEVON, ENGLAND, UK

Falcons are the fastest animals on earth, swooping at up to 320km per hour towards their prey. It's humbling, then, to have the majestic bird perched heavily on your arm, looking you in the eye, powerfully linking you to them and to a tradition that dates back over 4000 years. Shakespeare was skilled in falconry and you can make a start too on an experience day in Dartmoor amidst an old-world backdrop of green hills and English manors. To cast the falcon, push back and then forward, and off flies your falcon.

On hunting days (October to January) things get more dramatic as you follow the handlers and witness hawks racing to catch their natural prey, rabbits. See www.dartmoorhawking.co.uk.

405 DOG-SLEDDING IN THE SCANDINAVIAN ARCTIC, SWEDEN

Sitting and standing on a sled pulled by furry Siberian huskies is how the Sami people have traditionally crossed the white flat plains and frozen lakes of the Swedish taiga, where mountains of ice are barely distinguishable from snow-buried pine trees. Jump aboard and feel free in the brisk air. You can stay with the Sami people and witness their traditional reindeer-herding life, while meeting some even fluffier husky puppies in training. If you aim for the longest hours of darkness of December to February, you might even catch the Northern Lights.

Dog sled rides with cabins and Northern Light viewing are available through www.naturetravels.co.uk/category-dog-sledding.htm

406 FEED SHARKS AND STINGRAYS IN AUSTRALIA

Don't get nervous, these aren't *Jaws*-style great whites but much tamer shark species and stingrays. At this aquatic centre you can feed and cuddle up to the critters as they tickle your legs in the water. On the feeding menu is octopus, small fish, molluscs and crustaceans for you to hand over to hungry mouths. It is safe enough even for children to wade into the water waist-deep with a zebra shark, a striking silhouetted black stingray hovering nearby. You can feed the marine life from the pool's edge if you wish, but that's not as fun as getting close enough to slide your hand along shark skin.

There are Australian Shark & Ray Centres in both New South Wales and Victoria; visit www.ozsharkandray.com.au.

407 ELEPHANT CARE IN THAILAND

No, not riding an elephant but nursing one to health after abuse as a circus animal. You have to make house calls every day, trekking into the jungle where it lives alongside monkeys and tropical birds. This is no mere elephant hospital or zoo, it's the natural environment of the regal creature. Looking into an Asian elephant's dark eyes, you can feel the emotional connection, which makes it that much harder to say goodbye when it is reintroduced into the wild. You'll be making a connection with the local community too, learning their language and exchanging yours.

Global Vision International runs volunteer programs for a fee or by scholarship. See www.gviusa.com/programs/volunteer-elephants-thailand.

408 WHALE WATCHING IN KAIKOURA, NEW ZEALAND

You're on a catamaran. On one side watching over you are the snowtipped giants of a mountain range. On the other is the ocean stretching out to the horizon till it meets blue sky. Birds dance above. Then in the distance the water breaks as if the ocean is boiling, as the massive nose of a sperm whale lifts into the air with a spray and splutter then smacks back into the deep, exiting with a wave of its gigantic Y-shaped tail. It repeats the dive in and out of the immense ocean, making you feel deliciously small in comparison.

Kaikoura is 180km north of Christchurch, or 2.5 hours' driving in a car or by coach. There are a number of whale-watching tour providers in the town.

409 RIDE A CAMEL ON THE SILK ROAD IN XINJIANG, CHINA

As your sit confidently on your camel, reins in hands, through the rise and fall of straw-coloured dunes in the Taklimakan desert, the wind dries your perspiration and carries the tinkle of camel bells. This ship of the desert is what connected China, the Arabian Peninsula and Europe for thousands of years – a route known as the Silk Road, transporting not only silk and perfume but technology, religion and the sneaky bubonic plague. Camel tours take you across China's deserts to attractions such as ancient Buddha statues and involve a few hours of riding per day.

Find a camel tour in a Silk Road destination such as Kashgar or Hotan, both in Xinjiang. Six to 24-day tours are available through www.uighurtour.com.

410 SNAKE SAFARI, KENYA

If the idea of travelling the Kenyan wilderness seeking out some of Africa's deadliest snakes sounds like heaven rather than hell, this adventure's for you. Driving through the parks, walking in the jungle, you are hyperaware as your expert guide introduces you to cobras, adders, pythons and more. You'll see many of these incredible creatures but it's impossible to get blasé about them; even on the last day, as you watch the massive Green Mamba slither away up a nearby tree, the hairs on your arms will probably still stand on end.

Bio-Ken Snake Farms operates three- and 12-day snake safaris, which include all transport, food and accommodation; see http://bio-ken.com/index.php/snake-safari. Adventures take place in and around Tsavo East National Park.

EPIC SEA-KAYAK PADDLES

To really see a coastline, you need to paddle it. And to see the finest coastlines, you need to paddle these ones.

GETTING YOUR VIKING ON IN THE BOHUSLÄN ARCHIPELAGO, SWEDEN

Sweden doesn't lack sea-kayaking opportunities – the Stockholm archipelago alone is a paddling playground of 30,000 islands – but it's the Bohuslän archipelago, off the west coast, that's earning a reputation among the world's finest paddling destinations. With more than 5000 granite and gneiss islands, it's a place of high outer cliffs, protected inner waters,

Make like a Dalmatian and be spotted paddling the idyllic Croatian coast

island-circled lagoons, and small fishing villages on islands such as Gullholmen and Käringön, where you can pull ashore for oysters and champagne. Most islands are uninhabited, and it's a simple matter of paddling up and pitching a tent. The archipelago is well suited to novice kayakers.

The archipelago is around 80km north of Gothenburg; Uddevalla and Lysekil are good starting points. For self-guided tours, try Nature Travels (www.naturetravels.co.uk).

STIPE SURAC/4CORNERS ©

412 PADDLING THROUGH PARADISE, YASAWA ISLANDS, FIJI

Like stepping stones through the Pacific Ocean, the Yasawa Islands – an 80km-long chain of islands north of Viti Levu – may have been created by a god who fancied somewhere to kayak. The islands are packed close together, making for short crossings, and coral reefs shield them from swells, creating easy beach landings. Cooling off from the tropical heat is a simple matter of rolling overboard into the gleaming waters. Beaches are plentiful, and the islands offer a mix of desert-island perfection and timeless village life. If you feel like you're paddling through *The Blue Lagoon* film set, you are.

The Yasawa Flyer (www.awesomefiji.com) catamaran ferries passengers to the Yasawa Islands from Denarau. Southern Sea Ventures (www.southernseaventures.com) runs kayaking trips through the islands.

413 THE QUEEN OF PADDLES, QUEEN CHARLOTTE ISLANDS, CANADA

This wedge-shaped archipelago of 154 islands, 80km west of the northern British Columbia coast, is wild, sparsely populated and one of the world's finest paddling destinations. Teeming with bald eagles and other birdlife amid old-growth forest, it's sometimes called the Canadian Galapagos. Paddling trips inevitably focus on the Gwaii Haanas National Park Reserve, at the archipelago's southern end, which is frayed with inlets and 640km of truly wild coastline. You can go for days without seeing another human being, paddling between ancient Haida archaeological sites, hot springs and dozens of islands.

Access to the park is by plane or boat only and requires plenty of advance planning – it's easier to book a guided paddle. Try Queen Charlotte Adventures (www.queencharlotteadventures.com).

414 SUN, SEA, SKY AND SECLUSION, CROATIAN ISLANDS, CROATIA

Drop 1200 islands into the Adriatic Sea – 95 percent of them uninhabited – and you really can't go wrong in a kayak. This is a section of water and land seemingly custom-made for paddling, with the bulk of the islands close to shore, and often in easy paddling reach of each other. Choose an archipelago, such as the northern Kvarner islands, circuit one of the larger islands or simply follow chains of islands in any given direction. And just try to look at a map and not be enticed by the idea of paddling Dalmatia from Split to Dubrovnik, via Brač, Hvar, Korčula and Mljet.

Huck Finn Adventure Travel (www.huckfinncroatia.com) is a long-standing and respected kayak operator.

Postcard-perfect paddling around Abel Tasman National Park

415 PRIMO KIWI KAYAKING, ABEL TASMAN NATIONAL PARK, NEW ZEALAND

It's an age-old debate: is Abel Tasman National Park better seen on foot or from a kayak? The site of New Zealand's most popular tramp, the Abel Tasman Track, it's also the country's premier sea-kayaking destination. Beginning from the tiny village of Marahau, you can expect postcard-ready seas, inviting beaches and the company of dolphins and seals. You won't be alone on the water, but if you paddle past Onetahuti Beach to Totaranui, the fleets of kayaks will thin considerably. At Totaranui, you can weigh into the tramp/kayak debate by walking the three or four days back to Marahau — most kayak hire companies offer kayak–walk options.

Abel Tasman Coachlines (www.abeltasmantravel.co.nz) operates a bus service from Nelson to Marahua, where there are plenty of kayak rental firms.

416 BREAKING THE ICE IN GLACIER BAY, USA

Get among the icebergs in Alaska's well-named Glacier Bay, where 10 glaciers spill down from the mountains to the sea. From Bartlett Cove, a short paddle (three to four days) will take you out to the Beardslee Islands, with their beaches and wildlife, but to noodle around the icebergs, head for the Muir Arm or West Arm (allow about a week of paddling). The West Arm has Glacier Bay's most dramatic ice scenes. You can cut out the long approach from Bartlett Cove by having the day-tour boat drop you and your kayak further up the bay.

The national park website (www.nps .gov/glba) has plenty of kayaking information. Glacier Bay Sea Kayaks (www.glacierbayseakayaks.com) in Bartlett Cove rents out kayaks.

417 AFLOAT IN THE FJORDS, GREENLAND

For those whose religion is kayaking, Greenland is like Genesis. It was here that the kayak, a word taken from the local *qajaq*, is said to have originated. Originally they were used for hunting, but now they are the vehicles of choice for seeing the extraordinary beauty of Greenland's inner fjords. As a general rule, the south of the island offers milder conditions, suited to novice paddlers. Narsaq is a good starting point for exploring iceberg-choked fjords in the south, while on the east coast, Disko Bay is like an iceberg conference facility – Jakobshavn Glacier is said to calve 20 million tonnes of ice into this fjord every day.

For access to Narsaq, fly into Narsarsuaq airport. For Disko Bay, use Kangerlussuaq airport.

418 LOSING THE LAND LUBBERS IN THE LOFOTEN ISLANDS, NORWAY

Mix an Arctic location, the warming Gulf Stream, fishing villages clinging to tendrils of land, drying stockfish clattering in the wind, and mountains that rise more than 1000m direct from the sea, and you have one of Europe's most stunning island locations. Fjord-like inlets provide sheltered kayaking, while those more experienced can test the currents between the islands – one current, the Moskstraumen, is the origin of that scary word, 'maelstrom'. The most spectacular section is around Reine and Moskenes, towards the south.

Ferries run to the Lofotens from Bødo. Lofoten Kajakk (www.lofoten-kajakk.no) in Kabelvåg hires kayaks to experienced paddlers and runs guided trips.

419 TROPICAL TIMES AT HINCHINBROOK ISLAND, AUSTRALIA

Of Queensland's 1900-plus islands, Hinchinbrook stands tall – literally. The largest island national park in Australia, it's a wild yet inviting place. Crocodiles patrol its inside channel, and mountains rise almost sheer 1100m from the Coral Sea. For kayakers, it offers a superb beach hop along the outside coast (mostly away from the crocs), with walks inland to waterfalls and the low summit of Nina Peak with its views across the coast. From the island's northern tip, you can island hop – Goold, Hudson, Coombe, Dunk Islands – to the mainland at Mission Beach. It's the tropical dream packed into a kayak.

Locally based Coral Sea Kayaking (www. coralseakayaking.com) runs trips along Hinchinbrook Island.

420 EXPLORING ANCIENT WILDERNESS IN SOUTHWEST TASMANIA, AUSTRALIA

In paper terms, Bathurst Harbour and Port Davey are little more than 100km from the city of Hobart. Yet you can paddle here for a week along World Heritage–listed shores and conceivably not see another person. Kayaking in this strangely remote area is a tale of two paddles: the protected Bathurst Narrows, enclosed by mountains, and the heaving swells around Port Davey and the Breaksea Islands. In Port Davey, southern Spain Bay offers a beautiful beach and a walk to enormous Aboriginal middens on Stephens Bay, while the northern end of the port leads into the Davey River, from where you can paddle upstream – seemingly off the map – into the narrow Davey Gorge.

Local company Roaring 40°S (www. roaring40skayaking.com.au) runs kayaking trips to Southwest Tasmania.

EPIC SEA-KAYAK PADDLES

EYE-CATCHING ATMOSPHERIC EXTRAVAGANZAS

Get up front with the warm, the cold, the humid, the outrageous and the raging; don't wait for the weather to find you – try chasing it instead!

421 WACKY WEATHER FRONTS, LAKE BAIKAL, RUSSIA

The climatic cauldron of Russia conjures up crazed formations that can radically change in a few blustery breaths. It's no good grabbing your forecast at a city even as close as Irkutsk (70km away) – temperatures there regularly differ from those at the lake by 15–20°C. You can swim in this, the world's largest freshwater body, in summer, and ski across its frozen surface in winter. The lake's big freeze lingers until April, with ice rupturing into brilliant blue-hued shapes, whilst lightning storms, sudden rainbows and the sharp spring or autumn light take turns to dazzle kaleidoscopically overhead.

Like a giant awaking from a long slumber, Lake Baikal is opening up to adventure tourism: a hiking trail right around its roughly 1800km shoreline is being constructed.

422 LIGHTNING, WESTERN PROVINCE, RWANDA

Rwanda is putting a dark past of 1994's Rwandan genocide behind it and these days blossoms with great ecotourism possibilities. But it still sports a stormy present. The country is light years ahead of the rest when it comes to lightning-spotting sights, with more than two and a half times as much as America's lightning capital, Florida. Several communities vie for the overall honour of strike top-spot: in previous years Kamembe in Western Province has scooped the title. Visit during the onset of monsoons (from March to May and from October to November) to catch these intense levels of bolts from the blue.

Africa's best-preserved mountain rainforest, Nyungwe Forest in southwestern Rwanda, remains a last bastion for many monkey species, with whom the climate agrees.

423 CELESTIAL OBSERVATION, ATACAMA DESERT, CHILE

Where the world is at its driest, your view of the heavens will be best… nope, not a riddle but just plain fact – an expansive, desolate plain at that, in the Atacama. This desert's remoteness draws tourists by the drove to gawk at geological phenomena like the Salar de Uyuni salt flats, but fewer are aware of the impressive sights right above their heads at night. Cloudlessness and absence of artificial-light pollution means watching these heavens is an out-of-this-world experience – thus scientists have chosen the Atacama as a base for major observatories and world-leading stargazing apparatus, including the world's most expensive telescope ever.

Near San Pedro de Atacama, a former observatory astronomer offers star-gazing sessions at his house with some super-strong telescopes (www.spaceobs.com).

FRANCES LITMAN/GETTY IMAGES ©

Cookin' up a storm - catastrophic cloud bursts descend on Vancouver Island's west coast every winter

424 RAINING FROGS, ISHIKAWA, JAPAN

Ishikawa Prefecture is one of only two places where it's officially rained frogs. Here in 2009, the falling amphibians were accompanied by tadpoles and fish, all of which dropped out of the sky for several weeks. Nanao and Hakusan were the most tadpole-hit areas, where hundreds poured down. Meteorologists were left flummoxed, as the only plausible explanation – water spouts, which occasionally suck up small fish and dump them on the land – had not been reported anywhere nearby.

Shield yourself from raining wrigglers at Komatsu's Hoshi Ryokan: it's among the world's oldest working hotels (operating since 717AD) and is endowed with all necessary creature comforts.

425 STORM WATCHING, VANCOUVER ISLAND, CANADA

It's not everyone that can turn their atrocious winter weather into an incentive to visit, but some cunning souls on Vancouver Island's west coast have managed precisely that. In recent years, travellers have gravitated to villages like Tofino and Ucluelet to do what locals have been doing since time immemorial: gaze out at the amazing storms which brew from November through to March. Most regional annual rainfall drives into the island at this time – much of it horizontally – and peak season storm-baggers can reckon on an average of spectacularly wild weather every other day.

No need to get wet: storm-watch from cosy ocean-fronting hostelry Wickaninnish Inn (www.wickinn.com) with its wide wave-filled vistas.

157

426 NORTHERN LIGHTS, TROMSØ, NORWAY

There's a privileged band of northern hemisphere locales that are party, each winter, to the globe's greatest light show: the Northern Lights (an eerie multicoloured luminescence caused by charged particles from the sun entering the Earth's magnetic field). But Norway is justifiably the most name-dropped viewing location of the phenomenon that was, according to legend, the reflected glow of the mythic Valkyries' armour. Lights sightings in Tromsø are certainly legendary; you're well within the circle around the Magnetic North Pole in which this ethereal blaze of colour flashes most memorably across the night skies.

Join the electromagnetic party during Tromsø's Northern Lights Festival (http://nordlysfestivalen.no), a January feast of classical and jazz music.

427 HAIL, OKLAHOMA, USA

Google the video clip 'swimming pool vs hailstones' to get a grasp of the outlandish balls of ice that pelt out of Oklahoma's skies on a freakishly consistent basis, or just take our word for it that they are *big*. Oklahoma folk will tell you about how, back before records officially began, the biggest hail ever rained here in 20cm-plus monsters. The balls of ice regularly wreak havoc on the state, especially in spring, and when hail isn't falling, tornadoes are often brewing – the state reports the third-highest rates of occurrence nationwide.

Go storm-chasing with Oklahoma outfit Cloud 9 tours (www.cloud9tours.com) that travel this part of 'Tornado Alley', hunting the very worst weather for your viewing pleasure.

428 MONSOON, SALALAH, OMAN

If you like humid, stormy air laced with the scent of frankincense (which is gathered from the abundant trees around Salalah), imbibe this sweltering desert city during the *khareef*, or monsoon months in June and July, when the arid landscape turns a vivid, luscious green. Locals put on the Salalah Tourism Festival as a *khareef*-inspired celebration – an all-you-can-imagine shopping extravaganza (offering everything from farm animals to fragrances) – while the wet, wild weather attracts those with a meteorological bent from all over the region.

Let those winds blow you to Mughsayl Beach outside Salalah, where monsoon-aggravated waves spurt spectacularly through blowholes in the cliffs.

429 GREEN FLASH, HAWAII, USA

Blink, and you miss it. When the sun rises or falls above/below the horizon, it emits a green light that is all but invisible to the naked eye. But just sometimes conditions – the most crucial of which is an unrestricted horizon view – are ideal for green-flash glimpsing a fraction before sundown. And here Hawaii can help: any west-facing beach on a clear day could yield flashes. That green glow can still prove elusive, but don't despair: temperatures and humidity here as such that you're guaranteed gorgeous displays of Hawaii's diverse palette come sunset anyway.

The Star of Honolulu (www.starof honolulu.com) operates some of Hawaii's best-loved sunset dinner cruises.

430 SANDSTORMS, ERG CHEBBI, MOROCCO

The striking gold-red dunes here were fashioned by wind whipping the sand into shape, and while you're unlikely to see anything on such a scale (at least, if you fancy surviving), winds do pretty erratic things pretty quickly around this erg. December to February brings wild Atlantic gales and June to July also often sees strong winds. Gargantuan sandstorms here are easily sufficient to bury you; however Moroccans seeking cures for various ailments are voluntarily buried to the neck at Erg Chebbi, so if you spy a sand-submerged human, it isn't necessarily a bad thing.

Ensure you're here with an experienced local guide, who can predict sandstorms better than most.

BEST CITY HIKES

Stretch your legs over hours or days, without leaving some of the world's biggest cities.

431 TIJUCA FOREST, RIO DE JANEIRO

Welcome to the jungle. Brazil's first national park, the world's largest urban forest, smack bang in the heart of Rio de Janeiro. Reclaimed and replanted as Atlantic rainforest in the latter half of the 19th century, the forest is a green smear of waterfalls, tall trees and rugged peaks. Winding through it all is a series of hiking trails. The sharply pointed Tijuca Peak (1022m/3353ft) is the highest mountain in the park, with a trail leading to a final ascent on stone steps aided by an iron chain. Or for something truly Rio, hike to the summit of Corcovado – inside the park – and its iconic Christ the Redeemer statue.

A number of Rio tour companies offer guided hikes to Tijuca Peak and Corcovado. The national park website is www.parquedatijuca.com.br.

432 THAMES PATH, LONDON

The Thames Path stretches for 294km along the length of England's most famous river, but you needn't leave London to hike some of its finest sections. Begin in Kingston-on-Thames, and it's two solid days of walking to Tower Bridge or the path's end at the Thames Barrier in Greenwich. The walk is like a London highlights reel, passing Kew Gardens, Battersea Park and power station, Westminster and Big Ben, the Millennium Eye, Shakespeare's Globe and so on.

Expect surprising contrasts: the leafy emptiness of the riverbank through Richmond and Kew against the chaos of South Bank, where the entire world seems to come to meet.

Learn more about the path at www. nationaltrail.co.uk/thamespath. There are easy transport connections from central London to many points along the trail.

433 GREAT COASTAL WALK, SYDNEY

Few would argue that Australia's largest city has one of the world's most spectacular urban coastlines. And it's possible to walk the entire thing – all 94km of it – if you have a week to spare. The walk begins at Barrenjoey, at the tip of Sydney's northern beaches, and plods a sandy course to Manly before heading inland to the Harbour Bridge and southern shores of Sydney Harbour. The walk ends in the southern suburb of Cronulla, though if 94km isn't enough, you can always ferry across to Bundeena and continue another 26km on the popular cliff-top Coast Track through Royal National Park.

There are good accommodation options along the coast, or easy transport links into the city each day. For more details, see www. walkingcoastalsydney.com.au.

Sydney, the Emerald City, the Harbour City: call it what you may there are walking opportunities aplenty

Tackle the 9km seawall pathway around Vancouver's Stanley Park

THYLACINE/ISTOCKPHOTO ©

434 HOERIKWAGGO TRAIL, CAPE TOWN

Beginning at southerly Cape Point, on the Cape of Good Hope, this 75km (47-mile) trail crosses Table Mountain, finishing at the aerial cableway above Cape Town's city centre. It's an intimate look at the mountain that defines Cape Town, while offering views of the city. The trail, which was constructed by unemployed workers from the Cape Peninsula townships, is designed to take five days, with four tented camps positioned along its length. The camps contain kitchens and bathrooms, but you'll need to carry all your food. The trail isn't signposted, so be certain to get hold of decent maps or hire a guide.

Details of the trail, including contact points for booking accommodation and guides, can be accessed through the South African National Parks website (www.sanparks.org).

435 BERLIN WALL TRAIL, BERLIN

Best known to cyclists, this trail follows the course of the Berlin Wall that once separated West Berlin from East Berlin and East Germany. Seventeen years after it was famously breached and pulled down in 1989, it became the Berlin Wall Trail, a 160km (99-mile) hiking and cycling path. The trail is well signposted and has interpretive boards detailing the 28-year story of the wall and Germany's division, including memorials to those who tried to escape over the wall. It's a slice of modern history that'll also keep you fit. The trail is divided into 14 sections, each between 7km and 21km (4 and 13 miles) in length and easily reached on public transport.

For a full overview, see www.berlin.de/mauer/mauerweg/index/index.en.php

436 SEAWALL, VANCOUVER

If you want to see the best of Vancouver, you need barely stray off the 22km seawall. Beginning at the convention centre, it rounds Stanley Park, which was originally a military reserve but is now one of the best positioned urban parks anywhere in the world. Out of the park, the trail continues around False Creek, passing the glass bubble of Science World and über-trendy Granville Island, before ending at Kitsilano Beach – if you time it right you might be here for a perfect sunset. If you need to shorten things, consider the 9km section around Stanley Park – the sunsets are just as good from the logs on Third Beach.

The City of Vancouver website has a seawall map at www.vancouver.ca/parks-recreation-culture/seawall.aspx.

437 SOUTH MOUNTAIN PARK, PHOENIX

It's hardly surprising that the USA's largest municipal park (and some say the world's largest city park), covering almost 66 sq km (41 sq miles), should have plenty of good walking. Don't arrive expecting the typical city park of footpaths and neatly manicured deciduous trees; this is the Sonoran Desert, so expect cactus and creosote bush instead. The park has more than 80km (50 miles) of trails open to hikers, horseback riders and mountain bikers. The most spectacular trail rises up the mountain to Dobbins Lookout. Here, more than 300m above Phoenix, you'll be treated to the finest possible view of the city.

South Mountain Park is 10km (6 miles) from downtown Phoenix. Maps and information can be found at http://phoenix.gov/parks; follow the 'Trails & Desert Preserves' link.

438 COAST TO COAST WALK, AUCKLAND

There are coast-to-coast walks in various places in the world, but perhaps only in Auckland can you walk coast to coast and never leave the city. New Zealand's largest city sprawls across an isthmus – the narrowest part of the country – and the Coast to Coast Walk takes just 16km (10 miles) to get from one bit of salt water to another: the Pacific Ocean to the Tasman Sea. The walk begins in Viaduct Harbour, by the city centre, and passes through the city, suburban streets and parklands, and by five ancient volcanoes, before ending in the suburb of Onehunga, on Manukau Harbour.

Walk information and maps are available on the Auckland Council website (www.aucklandcouncil.govt.nz); follow the 'Parks & Facilities' link.

439 ARTHUR'S SEAT, EDINBURGH

Arthur's Seat can hardly be overlooked. The rough lump of volcanic rock – Edinburgh's highest point – looms above the city like a counterpoint to the crag supporting Edinburgh Castle. Taking time to explore Holyrood Park, the former royal park around Arthur's Seat, you'll walk 8km, which can stretch into hours as there's lots to see. From the lookout, there are views over the Scottish capital and along the Salisbury Crags, a line of cliffs across an adjoining spur.

Begin the walk in the Holyrood car park on Queen's Dr, behind the Scottish Parliament building.

440 HONG KONG TRAIL, HONG KONG

The Hong Kong Trail is one of four long-distance hikes in the city – not bad for one of the most densely populated places on earth. The path snakes around Hong Kong Island, covering 50km from Victoria Peak and its cracking views of Victoria Harbour to Tai Long Wan, a beautiful surf beach on the east coast – effectively you'll be walking from the island's highest point to its lowest. The trail is divided into eight sections, some of which can be combined to turn the trail into a three- or four-day hike.

Take the Peak Tram to reach the starting point on Victoria Peak; the return from Tai Long Wan is by bus and MTR metro.

BEST CITY HIKES

ENDANGERED ENCOUNTERS

'Catch them while you can' is the unfortunate story for some of the world's best-loved creatures – take a safari and provide added incentive for keeping them around.

443 TANGLE WITH TIGERS

Ever fewer tigers are burning bright in the jungles of India, China and Southeast Asia but gazing into the eyes of one of the remaining wild tigers – ideally from the back of a lumbering elephant – is one of the world's most memorable wildlife experiences. The reserves in Madhya Pradesh in India offer your best shot at bumping into a *bagha* (tiger) – head to Bandhavgarh or Kanha National Park from April to May when the jungle is parched and dry and the animals are more likely to come out into the open.

Elephant safaris operate at both Bandhavgarh and Kanha National Park; arrange a trip in early morning or late afternoon for the best chance of seeing stripes.

441 SWIMMING WITH THE BIG FISH

Cage diving with great white sharks probably tops the list of adrenalin-fuelled diving experiences, but we'd happily swap this toothy thrill for the sublime experience of snorkelling with whale sharks. From February to April these threatened giants of the deep surface in surprising numbers at Donsol in the Philippines. To get up close and personal with the world's biggest fish, don a mask and snorkel and jump into the deep blue. For our money, meeting a fish the size of a bus in the open water is every bit as thrilling as viewing its saw-toothed cousins from behind bars.

Jeepneys run regularly to Donsol from the town of Legaspi, which is served by regular flights and buses from Manila. Peak season is February to May, when plankton provides ample food for hungry sharks.

442 KICKING BACK WITH SILVERBACKS

The great Sir David Attenborough ranked meeting mountain gorillas as his number-one wildlife encounter, so you know this is something special. Just 880 of these magnificent apes survive in the forests of Uganda, Rwanda and Democratic Republic of Congo, and guides track the family groups on foot through the bush. You are very much a visitor in the gorilla's world, not the other way round. Once a group is located in the rainforest, everyone stops and the gorillas guide the encounter. You might only catch a glimpse or you might get lucky and have a bona fide close encounter of the furry kind.

Special permits are required to go on gorilla safari but local agencies can make all the arrangements – set your sights on the impenetrable forest in Uganda's Bwindi Impenetrable National Park.

444 SNOW LEOPARDS — WAY BETTER THAN NO LEOPARDS

Even more elusive than giant pandas, snow leopards are rarely spotted even by the people who share their mountain homeland. To the people of the high Himalaya the snow leopard is the 'mountain ghost' – a silent killer who creeps into livestock enclosures, leaving nothing but pawprints in the snow. Your best chance of glimpsing a snow leopard is on an expedition to the remotest parts of Mongolia, Ladakh in India, Tibet and Central Asia. Even if you only spot the animal's tracks, you can enjoy some of the most dramatic landscapes on Earth as a consolation.

Most snow leopard expeditions include an element of conservation or scientific research – Biosphere Expeditions (www.biosphere-expeditions.org) runs trips to the Altai Mountains in June and July.

445 NO FOREST FOR OLD MEN

With a name that translates roughly to 'old man of the forest', the orangutan is perhaps the most charismatic animal to languish on the list of endangered species. Logging, poaching and the illegal pet trade have all played a part in clearing the jungle of these ginger giants. Viewing orangutans in the wild is complicated by their habit of hanging out high in the treetops. Your best chance of a wild encounter is on a safari on the Kinabatangan River in Sabah, Borneo. To see orangutans up close, make a detour to the nearby Sepilok Orang-Utan Rehabilitation Centre.

For wild orangutan encounters, head to Kinabatangan Wildlife Sanctuary in Malaysian Borneo and take a river safari from Uncle Tan's Jungle Camp (www. uncletan.com).

446 A WHALE OF A TIME

Oil and corsets were pretty poor reasons for hunting the world's largest animal to the brink of extinction. Blue whales almost vanished from the world's oceans before a ban on hunting in 1966. Even now, encounters with these supercetaceans are few and far between. Try your luck near the Monterey Submarine Canyon, off the coast of California. When the krill population explodes from August to September, blue whales congregate on the canyon, alongside humpback whales, minke whales, killer whales and a veritable menagerie of dolphins, porpoises and other small cetaceans.

Whale-spotting cruises set off from Monterey Bay and regular trips with well-informed guides are run by Monterey Bay Whale Watch (www. montereybaywhalewatch.com).

447 NOW THAT IS A BIG PARROT...

Like the dodos of Mauritius, the kakapos of New Zealand paid the price for being flightless birds in a country that was discovered by hungry Europeans with ships full of dogs, cats and rats. Meeting one of these 4kg parrots is an encounter both comic and tragic – this was once one of the most common birds in New Zealand but now just 125 survive. To clap eyes on a kakapo, arrange a volunteer placement to assist the wildlife officers who keep Codfish, Anchor and Little Barrier islands safe from unnatural predators.

To see kakapos in the wild, volunteer with the Kakapo Recovery Programme (www. kakaporecovery.org.nz). Vacancies for nest minders, feeders and camp cooks come up from November to March.

448 WRANGLES WITH RHINOS

Seeing a rhino from the safety of a jeep is one thing. Encountering a rhino on foot is another. When confronted by three tonnes of irritable ungulate, the natural human instinct is to run for cover. Fortunately, the walking guides in Nepal's Chitwan National Park are well experienced in avoiding charging rhinos. Finding these one-horned wonders amongst the tall elephant grass requires a combination of skill and luck – to maximise your chances, give yourself several days and venture into the national park on foot, by elephant and by river raft or kayak.

The village of Sauraha is the main base for safaris into Chitwan National Park – the prime time for rhino encounters is October to February.

449 SPOTTING PANDAS

Even if you do everything right, seeing a giant panda in the wild is far from guaranteed. The last 1600 wild pandas are scattered across the mountains of Sichuan and central China in impenetrable bamboo forests that double as dinner for these much-loved monochrome mammals. To meet a giant panda on its home turf, you'll have to join an expedition, with only a remote chance of success. However you might then enjoy a wildlife encounter experienced by just a handful of people on Earth – better in our opinion than visiting the captive bears in one of China's panda parks.

The highest concentration of wild pandas is in Foping Nature Reserve. Great Bear Nature Tours (www.greatbeartours.com) runs an annual expedition with a high success rate for panda sightings.

450 HERE THERE BE DRAGONS

If you want the winged, fire-breathing variety of dragon, you may be disappointed. Instead, nature has provided the Komodo dragon, a 3m monster with possibly the worst-smelling breath in the world – it's the closest thing we have to a living dinosaur. Habitat loss has severely reduced the range of these giant lizards. To spot a Komodo dragon today, pay a visit to Komodo National Park in central Indonesia. As well as Komodo dragons, look out for their favourite menu items – deer, monkeys and exotic birds.

Boats to Komodo National Park (www. komodonationalpark.org) leave from Labuan Bajo and Bima on the island of Bali. Once you're onshore, park guides will keep you on the safe side of the monster lizards.

SAIL OR BUST

To the nautical purist, motorboats are just cars without wheels; canvas is the only way to experience the thrill of the seven seas.

451 LAND-LOCKED LIVEABOARDS

A nation with no sea coast might sound an unlikely destination for a sailing safari but Malawi is full of surprises. With more species of fish than any other body of freshwater, Lake Malawi is a diving Mecca and multiday, live-aboard, sailing dive-safaris embark from Senga Bay, just 125km by road from Lilongwe. Spend your days submerged, tracking down hitherto undiscovered species of cichlids, then sleep beneath star-studded skies. Most safaris tack on guided nature treks and visits to villages, game lodges, beach resorts and historic sights onshore.

Sailing safaris on Lake Malawi last from four days to two weeks, depending on how much you want to explore. The catamaran cruises run by Danforth Yachting (www.danforthyachting.com) have a good reputation.

452 NIGHT-BOAT DOWN THE NILE

Luxury cruises down the Nile have a certain Hercule Poirot appeal but we'd rather spend our pounds drifting down Egypt's great artery in a traditional *felucca* sailboat. Just put any thoughts of amorous shenanigans out of your mind – you'll live alongside the crew and everyone sleeps on mattresses on deck. Cruises typically start from Aswan or Luxor, taking two or three days to drift downriver; meals are cooked on deck and the bathroom is the nearest river bank. The reward is the captivating romance of river travel and the chance to witness everyday life on the Nile.

Boatmen will start offering trips the moment you arrive on the riverbank in Aswan or Luxor; check what is included and how many people are sharing the ride.

453 NO, I SAID THE BOATS ARE JUNKS...

With mist-cloaked outcrops rising from the ocean like mythical monsters, Ha Long Bay is the kind of place you find on pirate treasure maps; travelling by junk is the perfect way to explore this other-worldly maritime landscape. Junk cruises around Ha Long Bay have become big business but you can choose the level of luxury and refinement. There are superjunks with every imaginable indulgence and minijunks with room for just a handful of passengers. When not standing on the prow gazing across the bay, you can snorkel, swim and kayak to sea caves and hidden coves.

Most people arrange junk cruises in Hanoi; be sure to look for a multiday trip allowing you to escape the crowded waters close to Bai Chay wharf and Cat Ba Island.

Junk journeys: a maritime adventure on Ha Long Bay to suit all budgets

Scoot across the seductive seascapes of the Seychelles on the cheap – aboard a cargo schooner

454 SCHOONERING ROUND THE SEYCHELLES

Sailing the Seychelles is the stuff of dreams, typically for people sleeping in silk sheets in gold pyjamas. The good news is you don't have to be a billionaire to skim across the Indian Ocean with dolphins surfing on your bow-wave. A tiny fleet of old-fashioned schooners shuttles back and forth between the islands of Mahé, Praslin and La Digue, transporting piles of cargo, and the odd adventurous island-hopper. So long as you don't mind sharing the deck with stacks of boxes, you can sail in the wake of pirates and spice smugglers.

Weather conditions permitting, schooners sail daily between Mahé, Praslin and La Digue; ask about sailing times at Mahé's interisland quay.

455 BAREBOATING FOR BEACH BUMS

Ever since Captain Cook spotted the sand-sprinkled islands off Airlie Beach on Whitsunday in 1770, sailors have been cruising this little patch of paradise. Today, bareboat trips around the Whitsundays are an essential part of the journey up Australia's east coast, but with 74 islands to choose from it's easy to find a spot to escape the sunbathing crowds. Bareboat cruising is the nautical equivalent of self-drive car hire – officially, no experience is necessary but skippers are on hand if you'd rather have help navigating the reefs and sandbars.

Sailing agencies abound in Airlie Beach; Sunsail (www.sunsail.com.au) is well-established, with a base on swanky Hamilton Island.

456 THE QUEST FOR THE GOLDEN BEACH

The Greek Islands have been calling out to sailors ever since Jason and his plucky Argonauts set off in search of a golden sheep. These days, it's golden sand that most people are after, preferably somewhere far from the madding crowds with not a footprint to mar the postcard perfection. With five millennia of sailing experience, the boat charter industry here is highly developed – you can go fully crewed, super-luxury, bareboat or even bare bones. Just pick a boat and package that matches your nautical experience and need for mod cons.

To sail like Odysseus but with fewer sirens, witches and whirlpools, check out the listings, articles and advice at www.greecetravel.com/sailing and www.sailingissues.com/greek.html.

457 CRUISES WITH ADDED SPICE

Once upon a time *dhows* carried spices and slaves, but these days the graceful sailing ships that ply the water around Zanzibar are more likely to bear travellers looking for a touch of *Arabian Nights* romance. Zanzibar's dhows are still constructed by hand in the village of Nungwi but some vessels are fitted out with creature comforts for week-long beach-hopping cruises in the company of sea turtles and dolphins. Adventurous types can talk to local fisherman about arranging a custom trip, with nights on deck and freshly-caught kingfish on the menu.

The less adventurous option is to arrange a cruise through your hotel or agents in Stone Town; to try your luck at a custom charter, approach the fishing crews directly in Nungwi.

458 GOING BACK TO SKIPPER SCHOOL

Tired of being beholden to more-seaworthy-than-thou skippers every time you charter a boat? Why not train yourself and put the deck shoe on the other foot? There are sailing centres worldwide that can train you up to Day Skipper or all the way to Yachtmaster Ocean – the sailing equivalent of Jedi Master. The best courses combine training close to shore with hands-on practical experience out in the open ocean, ideally somewhere studded with islands and undersea obstacles where you'll have to put your newfound tacking and jibbing skills to good use.

Flying Fish (www.flyingfishonline.com) offers a full range of sailing certification courses, with training on the Isle of Wight, around the Greek Islands and off the coast of Australia.

459 HOW MANY ISLANDS CAN YOU HANDLE?

If drifting from sand-circled island to sand-circled island hoists your mainsail, look no further than the 7107 scattered islands of the Philippines, home to dense jungles, teeming coral reefs, lost shipwrecks and indigenous tribes. However if your idea of sailing is sitting around in the marina in a blazer with anchor buttons, this might not be the destination for you – obstacles to plain sailing include hidden reefs, typhoons and modern-day pirates. Puerto Galera and Boracay are top spots to look for a boat to charter; as well as yachts and catamarans, seek out the traditional *paraw*, complete with bamboo mast and outriggers.

Based out of Boracay, *Misty Morning* (www.boracay-activities.com) is a traditional *paraw*, upgraded with German know-how.

460 FINDING BALI HA'I

You don't have to be a fan of musicals to appreciate the allure of sailing the South Pacific – who wouldn't enjoy lowering the mainsail and looking out over a personal piece of paradise? French Polynesia is the undisputed sailing capital of the South Pacific; charter your own boat – with or without skipper – and drift around the Society Islands atolls, stopping off on sandy beaches and dropping into ports to stock up on rum and pineapple juice for your piña coladas. To take the experience to the next level, look into canoe-sailing using traditional Polynesian outrigger canoes.

Boat-rental companies are concentrated at the main marinas on Raiatea, Tahiti and Moorea. Raiatea to the Leeward Islands is a stunning starter itinerary.

SAIL OR BUST

BEST FOUR-LEGGED ADVENTURES

From mountains to jungle, beach and desert, harness the power, grace and companionship of these four-legged members of the animal world.

BRIDGET BESAW/AURORA PHOTOS/CORBIS ©

461 | REINDEER SLEDDING IN SWEDEN

This far north, the light has a pristine, glowing clarity, illuminating the stark monochrome beauty of the surrounding landscape. The wintery labyrinth of snow-clad fir trees and pine forests speeds by as you're pulled through the northern Swedish landscape by Santa's four-legged helpers. Sledding trips are led by members of the local Saami community, and overnight accommodation includes staying in *lavvu* (Saami-style teepees) and in rustic forest lodges. Most sledding groups are small, comprised of around five people, so after a few days surging purposely across the frozen tundra, strong personal bonds are forged during an intense and exhilarating experience.

Journey with the indigenous Saami people of far northern Scandinavia from January to March and there's a good chance you'll also see the Northern Lights.

462 | WORKING WITH ELEPHANTS IN SRI LANKA

Savour this chance to get close to gentle jumbos at the Millennium Elephant Foundation, where the animals are brought to be rehabilitated after difficult lives working in forestry or being left tied up outside temples. Day visitors can groom and bathe the elephants in river waters but longer-term volunteers are always welcomed by the foundation. Placements range from three to six weeks and each volunteer is partnered with an elephant and their *mahout* (elephant carer). On top of daily care of the easygoing giants, volunteers are also encouraged to spend time tutoring local schoolchildren in English-language skills.

Visit in early August for the annual Esala Perahera festival when many ornately decorated elephants parade through the streets of nearby Kandy. See www.millenniumelephantfoundation.com.

463 HORSE TREKKING WITH GAUCHOS IN PATAGONIA

Somehow pulling off the potential fashion crime of a beret, scarf and leather chaps, a Patagonian gaucho may well be the coolest guy you'll ever meet – think late-1960s Keith Richards on a horse. Laid back and laconic, he's also the perfect guide for a horse trek through the unspoiled lake and alpine scenery of Chile's Torres del Paine National Park. If you're lucky, light snow will be falling as you negotiate a careful path to an *asado* (traditional barbecue). When you see and smell the grilled lamb, you'll understand why gauchos always have a big knife tucked into their waistband.

Head south to Chilean Patagonia from October to April and stay at the spectacular Hotel Chico (www.explora.com), tucked into a compact cove on Lago Pehoé.

Experience the wonders of Patagonia on a gaucho-led horse trek – bring your own beret and leather chaps

Rajasthan sand dunes and sunsets all from the back of a 'ship of the desert'

464 CAMEL TREKKING IN RAJASTHAN, INDIA

Experiencing the Thar Desert by camel safari is a once-in-a-lifetime way to explore the Subcontinent's biggest country. Many safaris begin in cities including Jaisalmer, Bikaner or Jodhpur; for the most authentic experience book with a company heading to the towns of Khuri or Sam near the border with Pakistan. The scenery is more dramatic, with rolling sand dunes and desert sunsets, and once your camel train has moved on from the inevitable scrum of *chai* and souvenir sellers around the towns, sleeping under a Rajasthani moon should fulfil your most romantic notions of desert travel.

Time your trek for November to also take in the Pushkar Camel Fair, held at the occurrence of the Kartik Purnima full moon.

465 DOG MUSHING IN ALASKA

The experience begins with an exciting helicopter ride from Juneau to the icy, mountain-framed expanse of the Mendelhall Glacier. You may catch sight of bears in the meadows and riverbanks before you spy the 400-odd dogs in the glacier's dog camp. A symphony of barking suggests these keen canine workers love their job. On the sleds it's an often wild ride, with the dogs surging expectantly across the glacier. Some of them have raced in the famous annual Iditarod endurance race, so a short spin on the Mendenhall must seem like a breeze – no wonder they're happy.

Time an adventure for March to coincide with the arrival of contestants at the finish line of the famous Iditarod race. See www.alaskaadventures.net and www.akdogtour.com.

466 DRIVING YOUR OWN HORSE-DRAWN SULKY IN NEW ZEALAND

Watching a trotting race as a spectator, the action almost seems genteel with the low-slung sulky, horse and driver prescribing a careful path around the racetrack. When you're strapped into the sulky yourself and dressed nattily in colourful racing silks, travelling at 50m km per hour just a metre off the ground is an exciting thrill ride. This is adventure New Zealand-style after all. Participants are teamed with experienced drivers and real-deal champion horses, and after a session grooming the horse and setting them up for racing, it's time to career around the purpose-built, 800m-long racetrack. And they're off!

See www.horsepower.co.nz. Visit around mid- to late-January and you can also put money in the hat at Christchurch's excellent World Buskers Festival (www. worldbuskersfestival.com).

467 DONKEY TREKKING IN FRANCE

Trekking with donkeys through the alpine splendour of the Mercantour National Park is sublime proof that true wilderness areas still exist in Western Europe. The experience begins in the sleepy hamlets and villages of Provence, before eight days spent ascending through meadows to Europe's largest glacial lake. Accommodation combines Mongolian-style huts, *gîtes* (French-style bed and breakfasts), and mountain refuges, and look forward to the company and occasional guidance of an experienced team of donkeys. Each trekker is assigned a personal donkey to carry their baggage, and each sure-footed

animal comes complete with an often idiosyncratic personality.

Trek from mid-June to September for good weather amid rugged European wilderness. Contact Itinerance (www. itinerance.net), an organisation promoting independent walking tours in the French Alps.

468 WAGON TRAIN ADVENTURE IN WYOMING

For a Wild West adventure you won't soon forget, saddle up with a guide from a local ranch and join a wagon train through stunning scenery on the edges of Yellowstone and Grand Teton National Parks. After nightly meals cooked in a traditional Dutch oven over an open fire and eaten by the glow of the flames, you'll bed down full bellied and happy hearted. Trips are usually conducted over four nights and three days, so there's plenty of time for horse riding, canoeing, hiking and learning how to handle a rope. And who *wouldn't* like to add 'lassoing skills' to their resumé?

Make the most of a Wyoming summer from mid-June to mid-August. Book through Teton Wagon Train and Horse Adventure (www.tetonwagontrain.com).

469 BY DONKEY INTO THE VALLEY OF THE KINGS IN EGYPT

Good luck with your choice of donkey when visiting the Valley of the Kings because Egypt's four-legged finest are an entertaining bunch. Even the most settled can easily get distracted, meaning your procession along the dusty narrow cliffs and paths could be a stop/start affair of investigating shrubs for

food, followed by a hang-on-tight canter as your donkey races to catch up to the main tour group. Reins and saddle are usually regarded as flippant, non-necessary items and you'll need to bargain hard with the wily owners of the donkeys for a good rental price. Bring along your negotiation A-game.

Visit during October or March, outside of the peak tourist season of December to February but when it's still relatively cool.

470 RIDING CAMELS IN WESTERN AUSTRALIA

After a busy day exploring Broome's multicultural history as a centre of the pearling industry, get ready to experience one of Australia's strangest scenes. Camel trains trace a languid trail along the sandy expanse of Broome's Cable Beach as the sun sets above the turquoise waters of the Indian Ocean. From here there's nothing until Madagascar, almost 8000km (5000 miles) to the west. First introduced to Western Australia in the 19th century for transport, it's estimated there are now more than a million camels roaming Australia's red dirt desert. Broome camels like Solomon and Saharna are the laid-back loping descendants of those first animals.

Visit Broome in May during the post-wet season lull before the tourists arrive en masse. Book with Broome Camel Safaris (www.broomecamelsafaris.com.au).

BEST FOUR-LEGGED ADVENTURES

TALL ORDERS! – BEST TOWER-RUNNING RACES

See how high you can really get by tower-running up the world's tallest and most iconic buildings.

471 KUALA LUMPUR TOWER, KUALA LUMPUR, MALAYSIA

The mighty KL Tower, looking like a lit-up sceptre with a 421m antenna sitting atop its main crown, is a communications tower. So it's appropriate, as you power up the stairs in the annual Towerthon challenge, that you get the self-talk happening. Your lungs will be screaming with pain, your thighs burning, your feet groaning at the thump of every one of the tower's 2058 steps. It's a mental game – there'll be a little voice inside your head saying that it's OK to stop, but another one will urge you on to attain the glory of reaching the top. Talk it up – you're almost there!

The KL Tower International Towerthon Challenge runs as both a night- and day-race. Look out for registration in March.

472 TAIPEI 101, TAIPEI, TAIWAN

Looking like a cross between a pagoda and gigantic bamboo, this blue-green glass giant towers 101 floors towards the heavens in Taiwan. You can push towards the sky yourself in the elevator, shooting up at 1010 meters per minute. The annual Run Up may be more challenging and certainly will take you longer: no one has been able to scale the 2046 steps in under 10 minutes. Taipei 101 was designed with eight segments of eight floors each, because eight is a lucky number in Chinese, representing abundance. Participants definitely need an abundance of adrenalin as they speed to the top!

Visit the official Taipei 101 site (www.taipei-101.com.tw) for more design trivia and information on how to enter the Run Up.

473 WILLIS TOWER, CHICAGO, USA

Locals call this by its former name of Sears Tower – whatever the moniker it's still the tallest building in the USA. Willis Tower resembles a bundle of nine tubes, but it's the tallest one of 104 floors that you'll be sprinting up for the SkyRise race, the longest continuous indoor stair-running contest in the world. The reward is the observation-deck view across Lake Michigan to Indiana and Michigan. Running up the 2109 particularly steep steps is much easier than climbing the outside as French climber Alain 'Spiderman' Robert did in 1999, using only his bare hands and feet to reach the very top.

You'll find Willis Tower at 233 South Wacker Drive, Chicago, Illinois.

474 CN TOWER, TORONTO, CANADA

This was the world's tallest free-standing structure for 34 years till 2007 and it still poses a true running challenge. You'll have to train hard to beat the thousands of other runners in the annual Enbridge CN Tower Climb for United Way. All there is between you and glory is a measly 1776 steps – just focus on the satisfaction you'll feel at the top, your head light and glorious. The race has been going for more than 35 years, so you'll join a large club who have shirked the 58-second elevator ride to the top to raise money for local communities.

For more information on the climb, http://www.unitedwaytoronto.com/climbforunitedway/main.php

475 COLPATRIA TOWER, BOGOTA, COLUMBIA

Columbia's tallest building is headquarters for numerous banks. It's a symbol of Columbian prosperity (for some) and is lit up in the colours (red, blue and yellow) of the Columbian flag at night. Large sums of cash flow through the 50 storeys, but on 8 December of every year, so can you by racing up the 980 steps in one of the groups of 10 that make the dash towards the top every 30 seconds. It's a mere 196m high – surely you can bolt to the top and beat the record time of 5 minutes 11 seconds. The view of sprawling Bogota is stunning.

If you miss the race, you can take the lift up on weekends and holidays to the lookout cafe on the 49th floor.

476 THE EMPIRE STATE BUILDING, NEW YORK CITY, USA

More than a skyscraper, this 102-storey art deco icon on Fifth Avenue in Manhattan is New York's tallest celebrity. Enter the annual Run-Up and brace yourself to go full tilt up 1576 steps, an opportunity not open to the public at other times. The fastest runners reach the top in around 10 minutes. At the observation deck, catch your breath and have it taken away again with a King Kong's-eye view of New York City. Seek inspiration beforehand by watching *Sleepless in Seattle* (and loads of other films featuring this towering star) for a sneak peak of the observation deck.

The annual Empire State Building Run-Up opens for registration in December and takes place in February. Entry is through a lottery or is guaranteed via a charity (with fee).

477 TOWER 42, LONDON

Conquer this building for a piece of London history. The first skyscraper in London's City district, it held its position as the tallest building in London for 30 years until 2009. Tower 42 was even bombed by an IRA truck but still stands 47 floors proud. All this history will whiz through your mind as you pound your way up 920 steps in the annual Vertical Rush race. The champagne reception at the top might also hurry you along. Tower 42 may be in the financial district but the entrance fee and money you raise will go to the homeless charity Shelter.

Take a peek at Tower 42's acting skills by watching the BBC TV show *Sherlock*, in which it features as a location.

478 EUREKA TOWER, MELBOURNE, AUSTRALIA

When racing up a city tower perhaps it's better not to ponder each concrete step but to consider the significance of the building that pierces the urban skyline. The Eureka Tower, the shining centrepiece of Melbourne's Southbank district, commemorates an episode of local history. It is named after the Eureka rebellion, a miners' uprising that took place in 1854 during the days of the Victorian gold rushes. The Eureka Tower tells this story with its gold crown and a red stripe of 'blood' to commemorate those who died in the revolt. As you climb its 3680 steps in pursuit of gold, you can remember the legacy of the prospectors of yore.

Visit www.eurekaclimb.com.au for more information on how to participate.

479 IDEAL-HOCHHAUS, BERLIN

Ascend this building and forever brag that you ran up the largest residential building in Germany. Get warmed up with a few laps around the bike-loving German capital, then tackle 465 steps up across 29 floors. The race happens every January when the air in Berlin is cold and crisp, perfect for cooling down after the run or biting into hot fresh pretzels, but you'll have to get really hot-blooded to beat the record which stands at under four minutes. The perfect way to make use of excess adrenalin is to hit one of the many dance floors in this party town.

The race is located in the Gropiusstadt neighbourhood in the German capital and charges an entrance fee of less than €10.

480 BITEXCO FINANCIAL TOWER, HO CHI MINH CITY (SAIGON), VIETNAM

If you've never been to Saigon your jaw might drop when you face the 50-storey tower that you have to run up – in under five minutes, if you want any hope of beating the record. A far cry from a time when Americans were not welcome in Vietnam, the tower is an international effort, designed by a New York City firm in the form of a lotus petal, a symbol of Vietnamese culture. The Bitexco Vertical Run began in 2011 so there is plenty of room to be the new conqueror of the 1002 steps to the observation deck on the 49th floor.

To get there, head to District 1 in Ho Chi Minh City and ask for one of its other names: Tháp Tài Chính or The Financial Tower.

CLASSIC RIDES FOR CASUAL CYCLISTS

You don't need thighs like tree trunks to enjoy a bike ride. Try these easy-going routes for casual cyclists.

481 COVERED BRIDGES SCENIC BIKEWAY, OREGON

With a pleasingly horizontal elevation chart, this is one laid-back bike ride. It lies just south of Eugene, one of the US's alternative-lifestyle centres, in Oregon, perhaps the most bike-friendly of all American states. From its start in Cottage Grove, you'll make a circuit of Dorena Lake, passing over some of the pretty bridges that give the bikeway its name. Following part

Yesterday's train tracks make spectacular cycle paths thanks to the Central Otago Rail Trail

of the Row River Trail on traffic-free bike paths, the 60km route is perfect for families, though carry plenty of water in the hot summer and reward yourselves with an ice cream in Cottage Grove afterwards. While you're in the area, explore the Willamette Valley's wineries.

Download turn-by-turn directions from www.rideoregonride.com, which also has a full list of Oregon's bikeways, and visit the Parks and Recreation Department's pages at www.oregon.gov.

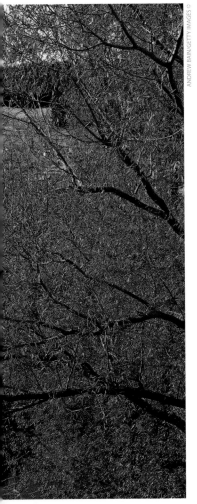

ANDREW BAIN/GETTY IMAGES ©

482 BORNHOLM, DENMARK

Is there a more cycle-friendly place (and people) than this pocket-sized (and flat) portion of Europe? We don't think so. Copenhagen, of course, is the world's most chic cycling capital and from it radiate traffic-free bike routes. But go a little further afield to the tiny Danish island of Bornholm, in the Baltic Sea, and you'll find more than 200km of mostly traffic-free cycle paths, punctuated by white-sand beaches, pine forests, and small, simple churches. A full circuit of Bornholm is 105km; it's Scandinavia in a day.

Visit www.visitdenmark.com. Bornholm can be reached by ferry from Ystad in Sweden or via a 30-minute flight from Copenhagen to Ronne on the west coast. There are bike-hire facilities. Visit in late spring, summer and early autumn.

483 CAMEL TRAIL, ENGLAND

The railway from the Camel Estuary into the green folds of Cornwall transported first clay and slate from Cornish quarries and then fish from Padstow's port to markets. The tracks were torn up in the 1980s and it now carries cyclists along the Camel Valley from Poley's Bridge to Padstow on a traffic-free 25km rail trail through woodland and along waterways rich in wildlife, including otters. The Tarka Trail is another popular rail trail across the border in Devon. The Bodmin and Wenford Railway in Bodmin ensures that steam engine fans aren't disappointed.

The trail is open all year, though the height of summer will see holidaying families flocking to the trail and Padstow's cafes. See www.sustrans.org.uk. Local bike shops rent bikes and buggies or trailers for small children.

484 CENTRAL OTAGO RAIL TRAIL, NEW ZEALAND

Rail trails recycle (get it?) disused railways to provide a relatively flat and traffic-free track for bike enthusiasts. One of the best is the Central Otago Rail Trail at the southern tip of New Zealand. The 150km trail from Clyde to Middlemarch (in this direction the last two-thirds are downhill) is justifiably popular, with 12,000 people pedalling it every year. It's one of New Zealand's 18 Great Rides and part of the NZ$50 million national cycleway project. If you rent a bike you can get a shuttle back to the start, otherwise the historic Taieri Gorge Railway continues to Dunedin, a well-preserved Victorian-era city with a live-and-kicking music scene. Stop for refreshment in the middle at Waipiata, which means 'shining water'.

Check out www.otagocentralrailtrail.co.nz. April is the best (and busiest) time to ride, with autumn colouring the trees' leaves.

177

485 THE ELBE CYCLEWAY, GERMANY

The Rhine and Danube rivers have inspired music, but while there are no symphonies in honour of Germany's second-longest river, the Elbe, it has the distinction of being the most popular riverside cycling route in the country. The cycleway (Elberadweg in German) starts in Prague, crosses the Czech Republic's border with Germany and passes through Dresden and Hamburg before ending where the Elbe flows into the North Sea. No doubt part of its appeal is that, from Dresden, it is largely downhill all the way.

The full route is 840km, but you can ride just a section at a time. Plan your trip at www.germany.travel and www.elbe-cycle-route.com.

486 CLARE VALLEY RIESLING TRAIL, SOUTH AUSTRALIA

Go beyond the Barossa (warm and flat) and explore the greener, eucalypt-shaded Clare Valley wine region by bicycle, 130km north of Adelaide. Your extra motivation: this valley produces some of the best riesling-grape wines in the Southern Hemisphere, with cellar doors such as Skillogalee tempting passing cyclists with tastings and locally sourced lunches. The Riesling Trail runs for 35km but shorter options can be ridden in loops so you can return to the start. The cycleway is a former railway and is free from traffic, so long as you don't count lizards and cockatoos.

Plan your trip at www.southaustralia.com and www.railtrails.org.au. Bikes can be hired in the towns of Auburn and Clare. Autumn, winter and spring (April to November) are the best seasons for cycling; summer is hot.

487 SIGIRIYA TO HAMBANTOTA, SRI LANKA

From viewing the 1000-year-old ruins of Sigiriya and Polonnaruwa in Sri Lanka's cultural heartland to spotting blue whales off the palm-fringed south coast, this is around a 600km bike ride with about 10 days in the saddle. It can be very hot or very wet and it will be hilly – you'll be riding up potholed roads to Kandy and through highland tea plantations – but despite that, this is an easy introduction to this beguiling island thanks to the friendliness and laid-back nature of the locals. On a bicycle, rather than insulated behind the windows of a bus, you're part of daily life, even if it costs you a little sweat.

Sri Lanka has four National Cycle Routes, but casual cyclists will do better to join a supported tour with local guides, such as those run by Exodus (www.exodus.co.uk).

488 LOIRE VALLEY, FRANCE

Saumur, Sancerre and Pouilly are all names that will make wine-loving cyclists fantasise about late-afternoon sunshine, a full glass of fresh, flinty white wine and a slow-swirling river. Work up a thirst on the 800km Loire à Velo bike trail, which was completed in 2012. Two-thirds of it runs beside the Loire River on quiet lanes or cycle paths. And you don't have to do the full 800km; stick to the 100km either side of Tours and you'll enjoy the best of the Loire's châteaux and vineyards. Most major towns have a railway station so it's possible to take a train back to your

RICHARD NEBESKY/GETTY IMAGES ©

The Elbe cycelway may not have inspired any symphonies but it has many cyclists

starting point, unless you make a weekend of it and wobble homeward on two wheels.

Visit www.loireavelo.fr to plan your pedal-powered wine-tasting weekend.

489 PRINCE EDWARD ISLAND, CANADA

Prince Edward Island (PEI for convenience) hovers off New Brunswick's northeast coast. When the island's railway closed in 1989, its route was converted to the 273km east-to-west Confederation Trail from Tignish to Elmira in Ontario. That sounds a lot but divide it into bite-size chunks of 40km and refuel regularly

on peerless seafood – mussels, oysters, clams, lobster or just salty fish-and-chips – and it's much more manageable. In total, 400km of gravel bike paths lace the island.

Peak season is May to October; details at www.tourismpei.com. In the winter, the trails become the domain of snowmobiles.

490 LA VÉLODYSSÉE, FRANCE

The tang of sea air and pine needles fills your nostrils and the only sound is a rhythmic 'ouf' as the Atlantic Ocean pummels the beach. This bike ride is a treat for all the senses. La Vélodyssée, a 1200km route down the French coast (80 percent on

dedicated cycle paths) that opened in 2012, links Brittany with the Basque country. Yes, that's a long way, but follow your nose to the Charente-Maritime region and the beach towns of Royan and La Rochelle, and you can cool off in the surf or even detour to the genteel Île de Ré, a paradise for Parisian families and cyclists.

Research the route at www.lavelodyssee .com and book accommodation at www.france-atlantic.com.

CLASSIC RIDES FOR CASUAL CYCLISTS

ULTIMATE MOTORBIKE ADVENTURES

Luscious contours and curves, bone-breaking trails and breathtaking passes – rev your engine and prepare for the rides of your life.

491 DRIVE THE DENALI HIGHWAY, ALASKA

A ride that puts the 'high' in highway, Alaska Route 8 between Paxson and Cantwell doesn't make the hotlist for its length – a mere 217km. Nor for its surface; there's a bit of paving at the start, and a patch at the end, but everything in between is washboard or squelch, depending when you time your run.

But the payoff comes in the form of the wild vistas – peak after soaring peak, with the 3500m-plus summits of the Wrangell, Chugach and Alaska Ranges breaking the skyline before the finale, 6194m Mt McKinley (the USA's highest) looms into view.

Though in good conditions this route can be tackled on a standard road bike, better to trust an adventure-touring machine.

492 TRAVERSE AFRICA FROM CAIRO TO CAPE TOWN

There's a start and a finish, but everything in between is up for grabs. There will be mountains tempting you to climb (Kilimanjaro and Mount Kenya). You'll get sand in your boots on the Sossusvlei dunes in Namibia and while crossing the Nubian Desert to gawp at Sudan's Meroitic pyramids. You'll have the chance to encounter leopards and hippos in Zambia's South Luangwa, elephants in Botswana's Okavango Delta and mountain gorillas in Uganda. And of course, you'll traverse 12,000-plus kilometres of the most varied, challenging and rewarding biking on the planet.

Riding north to south (Cairo to Cape Town) is easier than vice versa for obtaining visas en route.

493 BITE THE BULLET IN SOUTH INDIA

If there's one contraption that encapsulates the bewitching allure and frustrating contradictions of the Subcontinent, it's the Royal Enfield Bullet. A beauty of a beast, its timeless good looks – setting bikers' hearts throbbing for eight decades – were long accompanied by lumpy handling and technical hiccups. No more. Today's Bullet 500 – its four-stroke, 27bhp engine complementing

TODD LAWSON/GETTY IMAGES ©

classic styling – is the purist's choice for tackling Ladakh's Himalayan highways. But instead, we'd head south from Goa through the Western Ghats, passing hill stations and tea plantations, tiger reserves and teak forests before reaching the sea in Kerala. Karmic bliss.

Bullets can be hired locally or bought from dealers throughout India (http://royalenfield.com). Cool, dry winter (November to March) is the ideal biking season.

494 TACKLE THE TROLL ROAD, NORWAY

Steering the gear-bucklingly steep Troll Road (Trollstigen), if the vistas don't set your head spinning, the 11 hairpin bends certainly will. This landscape of impossibly pristine fjords guarded by 1000m-high cliffs is the stuff of Norse myths – it's easy to imagine giants, dwarves and, yes, trolls battling among the drowned glacial valleys. A bike journey looping north from Bergen makes a

truly epic two- or three-day odyssey: pause at one of the world's longest fjords, 203km-long Sognefjorden; gasp at the dazzling-green Geirangerfjord, fed by ephemeral tumbling waterfalls; and tackle the switchbacks of the Troll and Eagle Roads.

Between mid-April and mid-September Hurtigruten ferries (www.hurtigruten.com) sail between Geiranger and Bergen, offering the option to sail one-way and bike back, or vice versa.

There will be camels crossing and perhaps zebra crossings, too, on the Cairo to Cape Town route

Two wheels, not four legs: scoot around Vietnam on a buffalo

495 RIDE THE ROAD OF BONES, RUSSIA

While you're hauling your bike upright for the umpteenth time, gingerly feeling your own chassis for breaks after yet another tumble, remind yourself of this: the Road of Bones wasn't named for its reputation as a graveyard of motorcycles, but in memory of the countless prisoners of Stalin's gulags who died while building it – and were buried underneath and alongside. This rugged route – officially the M56, or Kolyma Highway – sweeps a 2000km arc through the Siberian Mountains from Yakutsk to Magadan. It

defeated Ewan McGregor on his *Long Way Round* – is it the ultimate biker's challenge?

Don't even think of tackling the Road of Bones outside summer (July and August), and beware of heavy rain washing out stretches.

496 HEAD TO THE END OF THE WORLD ON CHILE'S CARRETERA AUSTRAL

A road, a number, a legend: the road that stretches down from Puerto Montt through some of Patagonia's most remote, dramatic landscapes to the improbably monickered

Villa O'Higgins. Chile's Ruta 7, as it's prosaically named (but better known as the Carretera Austral, literally, the road south), jinks some 1240km past temperate rainforests, Andean peaks, fjords and glaciers. But not bike repair shops...this slender tendril of South America is sparsely populated and the 'road' is rough (rarely tarmac, more often grit). With few facilities of any kind but natural wonders galore, this is a two-wheel adventure of the purist ilk.

Take emergency fuel, plenty of cash, spares and the know-how to repair your bike en route – ATMs and filling stations are sparse.

497 BIKE A BUFFALO AROUND NORTHERN VIETNAM

The remote northern region abutting China is tailor-made for biking, its towering limestone mountains clad with bamboo, cloud forest and rice terraces and dotted with hill-tribe villages of the Hmong, Dao, Tay and Dzao peoples, colourfully clad in various shades of black, red and white. More to the point, countless tracks snake through the hills, luring intrepid bikers. Ride of choice has long been the Belarusian Minsk 125cc, known locally as *con trau gia* ('old buffalo'). With a throaty, smoky engine and little by way of refinement, it's a perfect match for the rough roads around Ha Giang.

Several outfits in Hanoi hire or sell Minsk 125s from about US$10 per day; it's worth learning basic bike repair techniques in case of breakdowns.

500 VESPA ALONG THE AMALFI COAST, ITALY

It's been said that if driving a car is like watching a movie, riding a motorbike is being *in* one. For true film-star quality, the winding corniche that hugs the Mediterranean south of Naples is hard to top. Possibly Europe's most picture-perfect stretch of road, it climbs, snakes and plunges alongside beaches, coves and vertiginous cliffs throughout its 50km length, past chichi Moorish-tinged towns Positano, Praiano and Amalfi. For that Fellini feel, hire a classic Vespa moped and glide along with briny air in your lungs, Dean Martin crooning in your head and Claudia Cardinale in your heart.

The coast road gets clogged with traffic and day trippers in high summer – come out-of-season for a smooth ride.

498 TAKE ON THE ISLE OF MAN TT

It's exactly a century since daring – some might say foolhardy – bikers first tackled the Mountain Circuit, riding the now-legendary 60km loop that swoops and soars around this semiautonomous isle. In 1913, HO Wood clocked 52.12mph (just over 80km per hour), but at that time it was little more than a cart track. Fast forward (very fast) to today, and the speediest riders top 200km per hour during the Isle of Man TT, arguably the world's best-known road race. But you don't have to be Joey Dunlop to caress its curves and corners; for most of the year it's open to all comers.

Come between the end of the TT in June and the Classic TT in August to buzz past the race road markers for that iconic experience.

499 RIDE THE DRAGON'S TAIL, USA

Less a road, more a rite of passage, the 18km section of Route 129 in the Smoky Mountains between Tennessee and North Carolina has become one of the most biked stretches in the USA. We say 'stretches': the Tail of the Dragon, as it's affectionately dubbed, does pretty much the opposite, a convoluted concertina of a road squeezing 318 curves in under 10km as the crow flies. And if the hairpins weren't enough, there are treefalls. And bears, and turkeys. Not to mention trucks and plenty of other daredevil drivers. In short: test your brakes before revving up.

A 190km circuit taking in the Tail of the Dragon but adding the Cherohala Skyway, another biker favourite, makes for a perfect day's drive.

ULTIMATE MOTORBIKE ADVENTURES

BEST ADVENTURE FILMS

These films will inspire armchair adventurers to escape the gravitational pull of their sofas and do more than venture to the refrigerator for another chilled beverage.

501 ENDLESS SUMMER (1966)

Grab some vintage longboard action with Bruce Brown's classic 1960s surf movie, which follows American surfers Robert August and Mike Hynson and their buddies on a quest for the perfect break. The immaculately attired young men chase summer around the world, hitting world-class surf spots – Witches Rock and Ollie's Point on Costa Rica's Pacific coast, Cape St Francis in South Africa and, finally, Waimea in Hawaii. OK, the commentary can be corny if not downright chauvinistic, but the original surfari is a charming trip back to a time of classic cars, tight boardshorts and gloriously empty breaks. Bruce Brown went on to direct *On Any Sunday* (1971), one of the best films about motorcycle racing ever made.

See www.brucebrownfilms.com.

502 KING LINES (2007)

Climbing movies tend to go in two directions; either they're a compilation of climbers and locations (such as the *Masters of Stone* series) or they focus on one climber and their obsession (see *E11* about Dave MacLeod and his Rhapsody route). *King Lines* finds a middle ground. A best-climbing-film prize winner at the Banff Mountain Film Festival with Emmy Award–winning camera work, it follows climber Chris Sharma from Verdon Gorge in France to sea cliffs in Greece via Venezuelan boulders. Memorably he deep-water solos (climbs without rope above water) a sea arch in Mallorca called Es Pontas – look out for the upward, one-handed 2m dyno (leap)… 'I just want to climb the hardest, most beautiful and creative route,' says Sharma.

Buy the DVD at www.senderfilms.com.

503 SIGNATURES (2009)

Since the days of Warren Miller's early ski movies in the 1950s and 1960s – titles such as *Swinging Skis* and *Many Moods of Skiing* – stunts in snowsport films have got bigger, and soundtracks louder. But *Signatures* by Sweetgrass Productions adopts a more meditative approach, taking you to the fluffy back-country powder of Hokkaido, Japan, for a movie that features skiing, boarding, telemark and an indelible sense of place. There are no 50m hucks off cliffs, no big-budget helicopters, just beautiful film-making, some classy moves, and the company of local legend snowboarder and designer Taro Tamai. And importantly, the skiing looks like something the average skier could aspire to pull off in Hokkaido's waist-deep powder.

Buy the DVD at www.sweetgrass -productions.com.

504 TOUCHING THE VOID (2003)

Director Kevin Macdonald specialises in reconstructions. First came *One Day in September*, his reprise of the Munich Olympic's hostage crisis, then his account of a climbing trip gone wrong in *Touching the Void*. Very different topics, similar meticulous approach. You may know the story: British climbers Joe Simpson and Simon Yates attempt to climb Siula Grande in the Peruvian Andes for the first time. Simpson slips, breaks his leg and is left swinging by the rope over a chasm. He can't recover. Yates can't rescue him. Yates, just 21 years old, cuts the rope. What happens next is for you to discover.

505 SEASONS (2008)

If the goal of a mountain-bike movie is to make you want to get out and ride, then *Seasons* succeeds. Made by 'the Collective', Canada-based filmmakers who pioneered zip-line cameras and other innovative techniques, it's an extreme-sports movie with soul, and it suffers slightly less from the hokey, cod-spiritual voice overs that afflict other mountain bike flicks. *Seasons* follows seven mountain bikers, including likeable Vancouver North Shore veteran Andrew Shandro and British champion down-hiller Steve Peat, through a year's riding but the real stars are the Canadian locations seen through the changing seasons. The Whistler Bike Park sequence alone will make you want to jump on a flight to Vancouver.

Buy the DVD at www.thecollectivefilm.com.

506 RIDING GIANTS (2004)

If *Endless Summer* whetted your appetite for surf, you'll be sated by *Riding Giants*. Stacy Peralta, director of classic skateboard movie *Dogtown and Z-Boys*, turns his attention to the cult of big-wave riding, practised by a handful of surfers at the few breaks that can deliver a moving wall of water 12m to 25m (39ft to 82ft) tall. He charts the bullish Greg Noll's 25-year love affair with Waimea, Hawaii, in the 1950s and 1960s. Then Peralta meets Laird Hamilton, the blonde, 6ft 3in ubersurfer who redefined how to surf monster waves when he was exhaled out of super-heavy Teahupo'o on Tahiti in an explosion of spray. Since then, tow-in surfing has gone public but the pleasure of *Riding Giants* lies in hearing the pioneers tell it like it was, back in the day.

507 NORDWAND (2008)

Few mountaineering films – certainly not *The Eiger Sanction*, *Cliffhanger* or *Vertical Limit* – put their viewers as fingernail-shreddingly close to the ice and rock as the German film *Nordwand* (*North Face* in English). It's the fictionalised true story of a 1936 attempt by German climbers Andreas Hinterstoisser and Toni Kurz to scale the North Face of the Eiger, and was mostly shot on location in the Swiss Alps. Racing a pair of Austrian climbers, the German duo are hit by bad weather and rock falls. When they decide to turn back, their life-and-death struggle is watched by journalists and tourists from a luxury hotel, cocktails in hand. Anything in between triumph and disaster is an anti-climax for the spectators. You'll feel frostbitten by the end.

508 A SUNDAY IN HELL (1975)

A Sunday in Hell is to bike racing what *When We Were Kings* is to boxing...a film that just 'gets it'. The mesmerising documentary follows the 1974 Paris–Roubaix, one of the annual Spring Classics that open the cycling season. These brutal races are the domain of gritty Flemish riders and two of the greatest, Roger de Vlaeminck and Eddy Merckx, do battle here. The 250km race, known as the Hell of the North and source of cycling's cult of the 'hard man', crosses northern France, pounding over the narrow cobbled avenues through dark forests and windswept farmland, the riders caked in dust or mud, depending on April's weather. The opening scene of an elegant racing bike being dusted with a brush expresses the obsessiveness to which many cyclists seem to be just a hair's breadth from succumbing.

509 127 HOURS (2010)

Aron Ralston's hike into the slot canyons of Utah's Canyonlands National Park in April 2003 was painfully curtailed when an 800lb (360kg) boulder he was climbing rolled onto his right arm, pinning it against a rock face. Ralston knew two things: first, he couldn't move the rock and, second, nobody would be looking for him, certainly not in that subterranean crevice. This limited his options. Director Danny Boyle's film, *127 Hours,* tells Ralston's story with pace, feeling and drama – quite an achievement for an action film about a guy who can't move. After five days, dehydrated and near death, Ralston breaks the two bones in his forearm. An hour of cutting with a blunt blade later he had freed himself, literally single-handedly. The moral of the true story: always tell somebody where you're going. And carry a good quality multitool. Just in case.

510 PLANET EARTH (2006)

It's not a film but as the first of the BBC's major natural history documentaries to be filmed in high definition, it shares cinema's production values. With David Attenborough at the helm, this is landmark television that required four years of filming in 204 locations across 62 countries. Key scenes? African wild dogs on patrol, filmed from above, and minibus-sized great white sharks hunting Cape fur seals. But the greater question is who will be Attenborough's successor? No other naturalist has reached so many people in so many countries around the world.

TOP 10 ADVENTURE NATIONS

Not all countries are equal when it comes to adventure – a certain few ooze adrenalin.

511 AUSTRALIA

Say the word 'outback' and already it feels like an adventure. You can hike through the outback's desert heart on the 223km Larapinta Trail or find its climatic opposite on Tasmania's famed Overland Track, threading through deep rainforest and between Australia's finest mountain outlines. For rock climbers, Mt Arapiles is a holy grail made of stone – it may look like a small isolated mountain but it has more

Strap yourself in for an exhilarating ride in New Zealand's adventure hotspot of Queenstown

than 2000 climbing routes, from simple to very-not-simple. Get inside the mountains with some canyoning in the Blue Mountains, at Sydney's very edge – slots such as Claustral and Serendipity Canyons mix hidden-from-the-world adventure with enormous beauty. Dive on the Great Barrier Reef, drive on the Canning Stock Route.. the options are endless.

Bone up on adventure possibilities at www.australia.com.

JOHN HAY/GETTY IMAGES ©

512 NORWAY

For raw and rugged beauty, Norway has few peers. Fjords cut deep incisions into the coast and mountains rise on every horizon. But you needn't even leave Oslo to start a Norwegian adventure. In winter, the capital city has a web of more than 2500km of prepared cross-country ski trails, around 100km of which is floodlit at night. Jotunheimen National Park is the country's finest wilderness and hiking destination, containing every Norwegian peak above 2300m (and 275 mountains above 2000m). Above the Arctic Circle you can paddle beneath the inspiring Lofoten Islands skyline, or head to Svalbard where any travel is an adventure: think wandering polar bears, reindeer, walruses and the world's only ice-bound hotel ship.

Go Norge at www.visitnorway.com.

513 SOUTH AFRICA

From lions to great white sharks, there are a few animals that might like to nibble you in South Africa, but don't let that trouble you as you take a walking safari on one of Kruger National Park's Wilderness Trails, or as you're dipped into the sea among sharks in a Gansbaai cage dive. With its summits looking like geometry puzzles, South Africa's highest mountain range, the Drakensberg, offers wonderful hiking. Surfers gravitate to Jeffreys Bay – the famous J-Bay – home to what was once described as 'the most perfect wave in the world'. Discover the bellies of a few gorges and canyons when you go kloofing – canyoning to the rest of the world. Suicide Gorge, on the Western Cape, is a favourite kloof.

Find more details at www.southafrica.net.

514 NEW ZEALAND

In New Zealand, no adventure is content without evolution. Bungee jumping was created here in 1988, on Queenstown's Kawarau Suspension Bridge, and for a time advanced to bungee jumping from a helicopter. The simple act of caving became abseiling and tubing through caves in Waitomo. White-water rafts pitched over a 7m-high waterfall on the Kaituna River, or slimmed down to become white-water sledging – essentially rafting for one, on a glorified boogie board. Zorbing (rolling down a hill inside a large plastic ball) was born here. Thank goodness for an old favourite like tramping: the Milford Track clings to its moniker as the 'finest walk in the world', though many say the nearby Routeburn Track is even better.

There's a full menu of adventure options at www.newzealand.com.

187

515 SLOVENIA

One of Europe's smallest countries is also arguably the one that lives largest. The Slovenian town of Bovec might easily claim to be Europe's adventure hotspot. With the Julian Alps above, the Soča River below and Triglav National Park all around, you could spend a week here hiking, kayaking, mountain biking and, in winter, skiing at Mt Kanin, without ever doing the same thing twice. Away from Bovec, at Postojna, you can delve into the 20km-long cave system that gave the world the word 'karst'. The country's highest mountain, 2864m Triglav, is a beacon for hikers, though with its rocky, knife-edge ridge, it's not a climb for the unfit or faint-hearted.

The Slovenian Tourist Board website is www.slovenia.info.

516 ARGENTINA

From a wildlife-rich coast, to one of the world's most powerful waterfalls, to the highest mountain outside of the Himalaya, Argentina has an impeccable adventure CV. Out of Mendoza, 6960m Aconcagua is not only South America's highest peak, but it's also accessible to determined trekkers. Head south and the ski-bunny town of Bariloche opens out in summer to some of the continent's finest trekking, crossing alpine ridges through the sharply weathered Parque Nacional Nahuel Huapi. Head for the Patagonian coast and you might witness one of nature's most spectacular hunting scenes, as orcas hurl themselves ashore at the Punta Norte beach, on Peninsula Valdes, to snatch sea lion pups.

The private www.welcomeargentina.com has listings of many adventure activities.

517 COSTA RICA

Costa Rica is said to have the greatest concentration of animals per square kilometre of any country on earth. Birds – scarlet macaws, sabrewings – are its prize feature, but people also come here to fly like birds. Ziplining, which involves soaring through the forest canopy as you hang from a cable, has spread across the world, but began in Costa Rica and is now found right across the country. The Río Pacuare is considered one of the world's best rafting rivers, plunging through a series of spectacular canyons clothed in virgin rainforest. Walkers gravitate to wildlife-rich Parque Nacional Corcovado, while hardcore trekkers can attempt a 70km traverse of the country from the Caribbean to the Pacific.

The Costa Rica tourism website (www.visitcostarica.com) has adventure links.

518 CANADA

From shore to shore, Canada offers a plethora of adventure opportunities – you can even hike or cycle from very shore to shore on the emerging 23,000km Trans Canada Trail. As country bookends, hike the brutal West Coast Trail, a former escape route for shipwreck survivors on Vancouver Island, or pedal leisurely across the length of Prince Edward Island on the 470km Confederation Trail. The Rocky Mountains are a smorgasbord of activity, from winter skiing and ice climbing around Banff, to summer mountain biking in world-class Fernie. Head north and there's dog sledding in the Yukon winter, and one of the world's most remote and committing kayak trips down the South Nahanni River – you'll want to portage the 125m-high waterfall.

www.canada.travel is packed with adventure suggestions.

519 NEPAL

Most visitors to Nepal end up on foot somewhere near Everest or the Annapurnas, but there are plenty more adventures here. Cyclists who don't mind a Himalayan climb or three trundle down the Friendship Hwy from Lhasa to Kathmandu, or bump around the Annapurna Circuit on mountain bikes. In Pokhara, birds of prey have been trained to fly among paragliders, guiding them into thermals, creating the unique activity of parahawking. As the rivers tumble out of the Himalaya, they seem to invite rafters to challenge them. Rafting trips can be as short as a couple of turbulent hours, through to days-long journeys through the Kali Gandaki (the world's deepest gorge) and long treks into the wild and remote Tamur River.

For more info, see http://welcome nepal.com.

Rivers and rainforest, walking and wildlife, birds and beaches, Costa Rica beckons to the adventurous traveller

520 FRANCE

France is a country that's all things to all people: foodies, lovers, the glitterati and the adventure-minded. For road cyclists, the Alpine and Pyrenean passes are irresistible, while cycle tourers crisscross the country from *boulangerie* to *boulangerie*. France was paragliding's birthplace and it remains its heartland, being said to have more paragliding sites than any other country. Hikers are spoiled for mountain routes, from the famed Tour du Mont Blanc, to an end-to-end Pyrenean traverse, to the GR20 crossing of Corsica, often said to be the most difficult long-distance hiking route in Europe. The boulders of the Fontainebleau forest have long been a training ground for Alpine climbers, with around 10,000 bouldering (low-level, rope-free climbing) routes across its 30,000 boulders.

France's official tourism website is www.franceguide.com.

TOP 10 ADVENTURE NATIONS

GET ON BOARD!

Strap a board to your feet, add gravity or wind and, hey presto, you've got yourself a new adventure sport.

521 **EXTREME IRONING, WORLDWIDE**

One evening in 1997 Phil Shaw wanted to go rock climbing but had a mountain of ironing to do first. Cleverly, he took the ironing to do while climbing and extreme ironing was born. It combines, says Shaw, the thrills of extreme sport 'with the satisfaction of a well-pressed shirt'. Since then, extreme ironing has been performed on Mt Everest, Mt Rushmore and the M1 motorway in Britain. In 2012 another British extreme ironist, Paul Roberts, ran

Skate state: nowhere else has such a high concentration of skate parks as California

the six-day, 243km Marathon des Sables with his board and iron. Finishing 364th out of 860 runners, he had to time to catch up on his ironing at the finish. The sport borrows from extreme activities, such as climbing, scuba diving and skydiving but you will also need a board that is lightweight and collapsible, but large enough that a pair of trousers or a long-sleeved shirt doesn't pose problems.

Show off your crisp moves at www. facebook.com/ExtremeIroningOfficial.

522 BODYBOARDING, HAWAII

Not everything invented in the 1970s has dated badly: the modern bodyboard – a wide, 1m-long board – was fine-tuned in Hawaii's surf and is more popular now than ever. Unlike a surfboard, you ride a bodyboard flat on your stomach. But what bodyboarders lose in cred to surfers, they gain in manoeuvrability, thanks to the stubby fins their boards sport. Tricks, turns and flips are part of the fun. For the pros, a world-tour competition visits South Africa, Brazil and Australia. But back on O'ahu in Hawaii, Waikiki's 1m to 2m surf is perfect for novices to practise the ancient art.

Honolulu International Airport is 12km from Waikiki. Book accommodation at www.gohawaii.com. Dozens of shops rent bodyboards by the hour or you can buy a cheap board from a grocery store.

523 SANDBOARDING, DUBAI

When bored expats in Dubai were casting around for ways to fill their weekends beyond champagne-fuelled brunches, it seemed a no-brainer to hike to the top of the 200–300m dunes that surround the city, strap a snowboard to their feet and let gravity do its thing. These days you can buy a 'sandboard' and tour operators will take you out to the cinnamon-coloured crests in a 4WD vehicle; Big Red (Al Hamar to locals) is the big name but a guide will take you to less crowded dunes. Of course, cash is almost as abundant as sand in the UAE and so the city bought its own sun-free alternative: an indoor ski slope in a shopping mall – but that's another story.

Local operator Arabian Adventures (www.arabian-adventures.com) offers sandboarding safaris.

524 SKATEBOARDING, CALIFORNIA

There are great cities for skateboarders all around the world but only Tony Hawk's home state has such a high concentration of purpose-built skate parks. With its six concrete bowls and numerous pipes, Lake Cunningham Regional Skate Park in San Jose is one of the largest, and it hosts frequent skate and BMX camps where young skaters can polish their ollies. Most special is the end of the street course that recreates one of the coast's surf breaks in concrete. The park was designed by firm called California Skateparks – another of their constructions graces the backyard of Mr Hawk himself. That one isn't open to the public.

191

Pack up your board and head to the Parks and Recreation sections of www.sanjoseca.gov and www.visitcalifornia.com.

The flat waters of the Great Lakes are the perfect spot to stand up and paddle

525 STAND-UP PADDLEBOARDING, WISCONSIN

What's SUP? It's short for Stand-Up Paddleboarding and it hit the mainstream as an easy-going watersport in the 2000s, having been pioneered by Polynesians and revitalised by surf icons such as Laird Hamilton. So, you need to go to Hawaii or California to practise it, right? Nope, Wisconsin will do just fine. The state that is famous for making cheese and beer is on the doorstep of the Great Lakes, and offers flat water and appealing scenery at lakes such as Monona, near the university town of Madison. Novices will need a long, wide board and a paddle around 20cm (7.8in) taller than their height. Take things further and try the next big thing: SUP yoga. And if that doesn't give you enough of a buzz, finish your day with a few of Milwaukee's craft beers.

Plan your new pastime at www.visitmadison.com, which also lists paddleboard rentals. Spring to autumn is the best time to SUP in Wisconsin.

526 WAKEBOARDING, AUSTRALIA

You'll need not only a wakeboard – about the size of a small ironing board (which is not an acceptable alternative) for this boardsport, but also a friend with a motorboat and a length of cable. You can see where this going. As your friend tows you behind the boat, you can perform tricks in the wake. It helps if you're in a venue designed especially for wakeboarding, which is why you should venture north from Sydney to Stoney Park in sunny New South Wales. Get out there and catch some air!

Tuition and accommodation are available via www.stoneypark.com.au. Having a 'spotter' in the boat is a good idea, so the driver can concentrate on where they're going.

527 WINDSURFING, UK

Britain might not have big surf breaks but stick a sail on your board and there's far more potential for fun. One of the quickest stretches of water for windsurfers is on the south coast at West Wittering, a beach at the mouth of Chichester Harbour that catches wind channelled along the Solent waterway. The gently sloping shingle shore means the water is shallow and flat whatever the weather, attracting wetsuit-clad speedsters from across the country. It's not known whether Rolling Stones guitarist Keith Richards, a long-time resident, has taken to the waves in neoprene – but it seems unlikely.

West Wittering is 12km south of Chichester in West Sussex; find more info at www.visitchichester.org.

528 KITEBOARDING, SPAIN

Kiteboarding (or kitesurfing) is windsurfing's upstart little brother and over the last decade has stolen much of the wind from the latter's sails – not least because you can do more with a kite in less wind. It's not only hipper but harder; launching a kite into a gusty breeze in a choppy sea is not for novices. Most kitesurfers start on terra firma, mastering smaller kites. For a taste of kiting on water, head to Tarifa, a two-hour drive from Málaga in southern Spain. Wind is funnelled through the Straits of Gibraltar where Europe and North Africa pinch together.

Summer is the windiest season but conditions are good all year round. There are several kitesurf schools in the town. Plan a trip at www.spain.info.

529 MOUNTAINBOARDING, UK

Necessity is the mother of invention and, faced with a surplus of rolling hills and green fields and a shortage of snow, thrill seekers in the UK attached rugged wheels to longboards in the early 1990s and invented mountainboarding. The original boards, made by a company called noSno, used snowboard bindings and had a hand-operated brake but these days they're pretty high tech. Boards are around 1m long and have 20cm wheels. Learn how to ride one at one of the 15 mountainboard centres in the UK; one of the best is in rural Herefordshire at Ironsides Court Farm.

Find out more at www.atbauk.org and www.ironsidescourtfarm.co.uk.

530 SPLITBOARDING, JAPAN

As soon as you wake, before you even open the blinds, your senses are telling you that snow has fallen. A lot of snow. From January to March that's business-as-usual for the ski resort of Hakkoda-san at the top of Japan's main island, Honshu. Impatient to get to the powder, you grab your splitboard. Yes, splitboard: a snowboard that separates down the middle so you can use each half as a ski. Attach skins (grippy straps) to these and you're able to shuffle deep into Hakkoda-san's vast back country. Put your board back together and hit the untracked slopes. When you've caught enough pow-pow, finish the day in an onsen with a hot sake.

Beware of big storms in January and February. Aomori is the nearest city. Plan your trip at www.jnto.go.jp and book a guide at www.hakkodapowder.com.

GET ON BOARD!

INTREPID TREASURE-HUNTING TRIPS

It's not just gold in them hills. It's galleons under them waters and opals in them mines. Even if you come away empty-handed, adventure-wise, you'll hit the jackpot.

Seek out the ghosts – and treasures – of mariners lost in the chilly waters of the Scapa Flow

SIMON BROWN/WATERFRAME/AGE FOTOSTOCK ©

531 THE REAL TREASURE ISLAND, NORMAN ISLAND, BRITISH VIRGIN ISLANDS

By all accounts, Norman Island was the blueprint for Treasure Island in Robert Louis Stevenson's classic adventure yarn. Place names like 'Money Bay' and 'Privateer Bay' give buccaneer-ish hints of what happened on this now-uninhabited isle in the BVIs, famed for its snorkelling at the sea caves near the craggy headland of 'The Bight'. Real-life pirates Sir Francis Drake and Sir John Hawkins stopped by at the Bight's sheltered anchorage: time to trawl these shores and prove those rumours of still-sunken treasure true, perhaps.

Recuperate after your adventure with classic West Indian cuisine at island restaurant Pirate's Bight (http://piratesbight.com).

532 BURIED LOOT, ISLA DE LA JUVENTUD, CUBA

Its name might mean 'isle of youth' now but in former times all the pirates anchored here. Sir Francis Drake, Henry Morgan and Edward Tich came a-calling and of course stories abound of how they secreted their stashes of booty in the caves around these cerulean shores. Shiver me timbers, it was even known as Treasure Island in the 16th to 18th centuries. Old coins and other valuables have been unearthed here, and other discoveries have probably only been prevented by the challenges of access, which are considerable despite the lure of La Isla's stupendous dive sites.

Book your flight from Havana weeks in advance, otherwise you're reliant on the far-slower catamaran from the mainland Cuban port of Surgidero de Batabanó.

533 WRECK DIVING, ORKNEY ISLANDS, SCOTLAND

Winds and wet weather frequently rage above surface, but don't be fooled, below, the waters of this archipelago off Scotland's north coast are amazingly clear. That didn't stop them being historically treacherous. Wrecks litter the coast here, not least the blockships sunk in the natural harbour of Scapa Flow as a WWI defence against the Germans and many of the 50+ German fleet that were scuppered by order of German admiral Von Reuter. Whilst some of the latter were subsequently salvaged, many weren't, and what value remains down in the deeps (and shallows) here is anyone's guess. Historic value is certainly huge, and among the motley crew of remains are destroyers, cruisers and torpedo boats.

Get wreck diving with Scapa Scuba (www.scapascuba.co.uk), an outfit based in the picturesque fishing village of Stromness.

195

Gobi Desert, favourite haunt of evolving dinosaurs and modern-day palaeontologists

534 FOSSIL FINDING, GOBI DESERT, MONGOLIA

Palaeontologists whisper that however sparse the Gobi appears, the world's greatest wealth of fossils from Cretaceous creatures lie hidden in these badlands. This boom period in dinosaur evolution some 80 million years ago seemingly had everything converging on this desert from the big boys down to the humbler lizards. Among the stop-press finds has been a potential transitional species between the dinosaurs and modern-day birds, the *Mononykus*. Bear in mind that taking your skeletal spoils home with you is strictly forbidden – the thrill is in the quest.

Hone your hunt at hotspots like Ukhaa Tolgod (the scientists' choice), or the more accessible Flaming Cliffs of Bayanzag.

535 OPAL FORAGING, COOBER PEDY, AUSTRALIA

Don't just ogle the opals: get stooping and scouring yourself! It's a long haul north of Adelaide to the outback's (and the planet's) opal oasis of Coober Pedy, which must possess nearly as many mines in its environs as it does permanent citizens. And whilst these are working mines, many welcome more casual caching. It's often as straightforward as donning a hard hat and joining the pros underground for a session of 'noodling', the local term for ore-boring.

Noodle away at a mine like Tom's Working Opal Mine (www.tomsworkingopalmine.com.au), knowing that an ounce of premium opal could fetch thousands of Aussie dollars.

536 GOLD PANNING, BRITISH COLUMBIA, CANADA

Try your hand at gold panning in the state that became the gateway for the Yukon Gold Rush. Some extremely visitor-friendly panning locales grace this province, allowing easy fossicking without the hardships of the past. The Fraser River (on the course of the historic Gold Rush trail) is a good source for recreational panning but you could prove your weight in gold by entering British Colombia's annual Gold Panning Championships, held in May in Cherryville.

Yukon Dan (www.yukondan.com) is a professional gold-panner who provides great background information and organises family-oriented gold-hunting excursions across BC.

537 RUBIES, MOGOK, BURMA

A bumpy seven-hour road trip northeast of Mandalay (should the authorities permit it) transports you to the heart of rural Burma and the populous mountain valley containing Mogok, the world's principal source of rubies for the better part of a millennium. Gem shops dot the town and most residents have private collections of rubies and the region's other abundant precious stone, sapphires. Purchasing stone-searching gear is possible, but heading up into the nearby mines independently isn't advised. Better are Mogok's gem markets, where locals do their stone- and tale-trading, proving the old adage true: all that glistens isn't gold.

Watch for the local tradition called *kanase*, where locals sort through stones outside the mines for the gems the professional filter systems missed...and often get handsomely rewarded.

538 SILVER MINES, POTOSI, BOLIVIA

In Spain the phrase *valer un Potosi* means 'to be worth a great deal'. That's centuries after the silver mines located near South America's highest city reached their peak in prominence, and had their riches plumbed to gild numerous buildings across Spain's one-time empire. But the silver isn't dried up yet – not quite – although it's now mainly lead and zinc miners are extracting. Mine tours today visit still-active mineshafts, although recent reports warn of tunnel-riddled Cerro Rico (rich hill) being so overmined it's in danger of collapse.

Be sure to bring gifts for the miners you'll encounter on the tour – coca leaves to combat the dizzyingly high altitudes are favoured.

539 GEM MOUNTAIN, PHILIPSBURG, US

'The dirtiest good clean fun you can have', this Montana mine advertises. Fun mostly likely coming with a sheen, as you scrabble through an ample bucket of gravel for the rough sapphires that many find within. All you'll need is a pair of eager hands and some determination – wash screens are supplied and you don't even have to hunt about in a dark shaft for the stones, as they're brought to you by dump truck. Your lust for lustre might be further whetted by Gem Mountain being a shade over an hour by road outside state capital Missoula.

Gem Mountain (www.gemmountainmt.com) is open for plundering mid-May through to mid-October; outside these times, you're limited to Philipsburg's gem stores.

540 DISCOVER EL DORADO, ACRE, BRAZIL

There's no shortage of candidates for the actual location of El Dorado, the legendary Inca city of gold, but this Brazilian state hugging the borders with Peru and Bolivia, in the heart of the Amazon rainforest, has one of the best claims to the honour. The reason? Satellite images have picked up signs of vast earthworks here along the Acre River, pointing to signs of an advanced pre-Columbian culture that could just fit the descriptions conquistadors gave of cities of immense riches secreted within the jungle. No treasure uncovered thus far but, hey, until recently experts dismissed the possibility settlements on such a scale could exist here at all.

The Interoceanic Highway, connecting Brazil's coast to Peru's, should aid explorations hereabouts; tour companies now traversing the road include Oasis Overland (www.oasisoverland.co.uk).

INTREPID TREASURE-HUNTING TRIPS

BEST POOCH PURSUITS

Bow-wow-a-bunga! Fido will have lots to bark about after bounding through these adventures.

543 SKIJORING, YUKON, CANADA

What's skijoring? It's cross-country skiing while attached by tow rope to a leaping dog (or three). Fido runs, you pump your legs and together you glide twice as fast through the firs. The world's longest skijor race is the River Runner 100, held in the Yukon's epic wilderness. For 105 wintry kilometres (65 miles) between Whitehorse and Mendenhall, it's the steady crunch of ski poles and paws hitting the snowpack as you sweep along the Yukon and Takhini rivers. You and Fido will both get icicle face, though if the temperature drops below -30°C they halt the contest.

The River Runner 100 (www.dpsay. wordpress.com) takes place in late February. Tourism Yukon (www. travelyukon.com) lists dog-friendly lodgings.

541 SURFING, HUNTINGTON BEACH, CALIFORNIA, USA

The waves curl with consistent perfection, and well-toned dudes and dudettes paddle out to meet them. If some of the surfers look short and furry, it's not your imagination. Bulldogs, yorkies and pugs have joined the line-up in Surf City USA (as Huntington Beach has trademarked itself). They wear life jackets and Hawaiian-print board shorts, push up on all fours and hang ten. Local surf schools give lessons for pooches and their two-legged pals, and various surf-dog contests take place along the coast to LA. Glory goes to the shih tzu who propels down the face of a 4ft wave, whitewash crumbling in her wake.

April to September sees the most action. SoCal Surf Dogs (www.socalsurfdogs. com) lists events and dog-friendly businesses. It also has tips for teaching Spot to rip.

542 WINERY TOURING, SONOMA COUNTY, CALIFORNIA

With its vineyard-striped hills, atmospheric fog and rustic barn-dotted scenery, Sonoma attracts oenophiles from around the world. Many of the 300-plus wineries welcome four-legged patrons. So while you're swirling, sniffing and discussing the merits of a smoky Merlot with the winemaker, your pooch is sniffing and discussing his jerky treat with the winemaker's hound. In addition to dog-friendly tasting rooms, some winemakers hold special 'yappy hours', others encourage pups to come on vineyard tours, and many places let you and your furry friend uncork a bottle and picnic on the grounds.

Sonoma is an hour's drive north of San Francisco. June to October provides the nicest touring weather. For a list of dog-friendly wineries, see www. sonomacounty.com.

544 SKIING, ASPEN, COLORADO

If Fido whines that skijoring takes too much effort, perhaps he'd prefer being a jet-set pet in Aspen. America's rich and famous schuss the mighty slopes here. While dogs aren't allowed on the ski hills, they can kick up snow on several Nordic trails. The scene rocks hardest during après-ski, when huskies brag about their exploits to tail-wagging schnauzers by the fireplace. Even the glitziest bars, like the Little Nell, welcome pooches. Silver drinking bowls and canine dinner menus are de rigueur. And that cute maltese over there having the grilled salmon? Her surname is Trump.

Aspen's ski season is December to April. For dog-friendly trails, see aspennordic. com; for dog-friendly businesses, see www.aspenchamber.org.

545 HIKING THE PENNINE WAY, ENGLAND

Britain's oldest trail rambles along the mountains that form the backbone of northern England, from the Peak District through the Yorkshire Dales to the Scottish border. With Fido by your side, you'll walk the wild moorlands that inspired the Brontë sisters and along Hadrian's Wall, a stony vestige of Roman times. The route follows country lanes and sheep paths, and drops down into villages. When your boots (and paws) get heavy with mud there's always an old stone inn or pub offering a restorative ale.

The 435km (270-mile) trail runs from Edale, Derbyshire to Kirk Yetholm, Scotland. The best weather is mid-May to September. For planning and accommodation info, see www.nationaltrail.co.uk/pennineway.

546 CANOEING ALGONQUIN PROVINCIAL PARK, ONTARIO, CANADA

When Spot puts his paws in the bow and sniffs the crisp air while you J-stroke from the stern, it gives dog paddling a whole new meaning. Algonquin is Ontario's largest park, a rugged expanse of pine forests, cliffs, mossy bogs and thousands of lakes connected by crystal streams. No one appreciates the fabled back-country canoeing trails more than Spot, swimming at sandy beaches and barking greetings to local moose. The highlight is certain to be when he howls at the moon and his wolf brethren howl back.

May, August and September offer ideal paddling conditions. The website (www.algonquinpark.on.ca) has info. Dog Paddling Adventures (www.dog paddlingadventures.com) organises trips.

547 GOING TO CAMP, ILLINOIS, USA

To canoe or hike? Hang out at the mess hall or by the campfire? Sniff the dachshund or the dane? Camp Dogwood is the quintessential kids' camp made over for Fido (and you). Poodles bunk next to golden retrievers in the cabins. Mutts make plaster paw-prints beside malamutes during activity time. But mostly it's about romping – through sun-dappled fields, along wooded trails, off the end of a dock amid a watery splash. When pooches tire of that, it's on to camp stand bys like movies, cookouts, craft classes and, of course, the talent show.

Camp Dogwood (www.campdogwood.com) is held three times per year in Ingleside, 80km (50 miles) northwest of Chicago. About 100 dogs and their human pals attend.

548 PLAYING AT THE SEASHORE, CANNON BEACH, OREGON

Spot can chase gulls, nose driftwood, paw at crabs and race into sea foam at any old strand of sand. But only at Cannon Beach will he do it against a backdrop of thunderous waves and otherworldly sea stacks rising from the mist. The shore here is awesomely long and wide, prime territory for unadulterated loping. New friendships will be forged while fetching sticks and catching frisbees by day and around the myriad bonfires come nighttime. What's more, the abutting town's cedar-shingled shops and cafes open their doors to dogs.

Cannon Beach is 130km (80 miles) from Portland. July and August offer peak-season sun. Gray whales swim by December to April. See www.cannonbeach.org.

549 HIKING THE VIA ALPINA, ITALY/SWITZERLAND/FRANCE

Cows freckle the green hills, bells clanking. Edelweiss bloom in the meadows. Mountain hamlets proffer cheese and sausages. Spot is already licking his chops and wondering which route to take (five tracks comprise the Via Alpina, through eight countries). Set a course for the Blue Trail. It's the most straightforward, thanks to a group of dog lovers who've compiled routes bypassing the national parks – the rare spots along the way that ban dogs. With that settled, you can focus on your gruyère and pâté.

The Blue Trail runs between Riale, Italy and Sospel, France. It has 61 stages; hikers typically walk one stage per day. June to October is the best time to trek. See www.via-alpina.org for details.

550 BIKEJORING, NAPIER, NEW ZEALAND

It's like skijoring but swap your skis for a bike. Spot wears a harness that links via tow rope to the handlebar. You pedal, he bounds ahead like he's chasing the world's biggest squirrel and you charge over the trails in tandem. Eskdale Mountain Bike Park, in a pine forest on New Zealand's North Island, is one of raddest places to roll. Slog up leg-burning hills for views of Hawkes Bay and its grape-planted environs. Then fly back down, making detours for tree sniffing and stream splashing. Art deco Napier is a wine-enriched, post-ride crash pad.

Hawkes Bay Mountain Bike Club (www.hawkesbaymtb.co.nz) operates the park year-round. Kiwi summer (December to February) has bluebird weather for attacking the trails.

ICONIC EUROPEAN ADVENTURES

With more countries per square kilometre than any other continent, Europe also has arguably more adventure options.

551 CLIMBING AT SNOWDONIA, WALES

Wales' highest mountain region could be said to be the next best thing to climbing Mt Everest. It was here that members of the 1953 British Everest expedition, including Edmund Hillary and Tenzing Norgay, trained for their big moment, as did the climbing team that first summitted Kanchenjunga in 1955. Climbing central is the Pen-y-Gwryd Hotel, in the pass between the climbing cliffs on Snowdon (Wales' highest mountain) and the Glyders. This hotel was the training base for the '53 expedition – it has a collection of memorabilia from the expedition, and the ceiling in the climbers' bar is signed by expedition members.

Snowdonia abounds with climbing guides. Pen-y-Gwryd (www.pyg.co.uk) is on the Sherpa bus network that circuits the foot of Snowdon.

552 TOUR DU MONT BLANC, FRANCE/SWITZERLAND/ITALY

It is arguably Europe's most famous hike, circuiting the highest mountain (4810m) in the Alps and crossing through three countries. The 167km route takes most hikers 10 to 14 days (runners in the Ultra-Trail du Mont Blanc complete it in around a day), and has been popular since the 18th century. The scenery is sublime, taking the eye from lupin-covered streams to the bare rocky heights of the Grandes Jorasses. The trail, known to most who walk it as the TMB, has a number of variations – high or low options – but even the easiest route requires climbs totalling around 8000m.

Most hikers begin in the town of Les Houches, near Chamonix. Walk anticlockwise to get ever-more-dramatic views.

JEAN-LUC ARMAND/GETTY IMAGES ©

553 PARAGLIDE AT CHAMONIX, FRANCE

In the 1970s the sport of paragliding was born in the French village of Mieussy. Four decades on, and its heartland has moved just 50km down the road to Chamonix. Whichever bit of sky you look at in the Chamonix Valley, it's likely there'll be a paraglider in view. Begin with a tandem flight and then stick around to progress through the Chamonix ranks, from the popular launch at Brévent, through to a flight from the 3842m top of the Aiguille du Midi cable car (accessing the site from the cable car requires some mountaineering moves). Flights are even possible from the summit of Mont Blanc, the Alps' highest point.

There's a list of paragliding operators on the Chamonix Tourist Office website (www.chamonix.com).

Paragliders prepare to soar like condors over the Alps, the ultimate way to view Mont Blanc

YOKO AZIZ/AGEFOTOSTOCK ©

Make like 007 and bungee jump at Verzasca Dam – licence to kill not required...

554 VERZASCA DAM BUNGEE JUMP, SWITZERLAND

If it's good enough for 007, surely it's good enough for you. In the movie *GoldenEye*, Bond was neither shaken nor stirred as he plunged from the 220m-high lip of this dam in Ticino, a stunt once voted the greatest in movie history. In turn, the *GoldenEye* moment earned the Verzasca bungee jump – one of the highest in the world – immediate fame, tempting hordes to do what they'd surely never thought to do before: jump from a dam wall into the depths of a rocky gorge. It's eight seconds you'll be boasting about over martinis for years to come.

Verzasca Dam is near the northern end of Lago Maggiore; Locarno makes a good base. Jump information can be found at www.trekking.ch.

555 RUN WITH THE BULLS, SPAIN

Such an icon it's almost a cliché, Pamplona's Sanfermines festival offers the chance to run through the streets being chased by bulls. Each morning from 7 July to 14 July, six bulls are let loose in the city centre, charging 825m over its cobblestones and into the third-largest bullring in the world. Ahead of the bulls sprints a vast crowd of people with the single objective of not being trampled or gored by the stampeding animals in the three minutes from the firing of the rockets that announce the bulls are out and angry.

To run, you must enter the course (from Plaza de Santo Domingo) before 7.30am and take up your position. The bulls are released around 8am.

556 WADLOPEN, NETHERLANDS

They're a filthy mob along the north coast of the Netherlands. When the tide goes out, they head for the exposed mud flats, which can stretch from the coast all the way across the Wadden Sea to the Frisian Islands. It's a unique local activity called *wadlopen* (mud walking), which consists of doing exactly what the name suggests, walking through mud. The walk to the island of Schiermonnikoog is one of the most popular *wadlopen* routes, crossing through the water of several tidal channels along the way. High-top shoes are a must, or they will be sucked from your feet.

The town of Pieterburen, 27km from Groningen, is a major centre for *wadlopen*. Wadloopcentrum Fryslân (www.wadlopen.net) operates *wadlopen* trips.

557 TELEMARK IN TELEMARK, NORWAY

Norway claims itself the birthplace of skiing and, at the very least, it can claim to have revolutionised the sport. In the 19th century Sondre Norheim, from the Telemark town of Morgedal, turned out in skis that were narrow in the middle and had bindings that allowed his heel to move freely. The Telemark ski was born. Today, Telemark, south of Oslo, is the country's largest ski region. Lifjell has great Telemark skiing, while Rauland and Haukeli have around 200km of groomed cross-country trails. Head to Morgedal to pay homage to Norheim at the Ski Adventure Museum, which houses his statue and a replica of his cabin.

Travel and ski information for Telemark is available at www.visittelemark.com.

558 RIVER SURF IN MUNICH, GERMANY

Think of surfing in Europe and places such as Biarritz, Newquay and Mundaka leap to mind. Curiously, so does landlocked Munich. In one of surfing's stranger scenes, a man-made canal through the Englischer Garten is home to a standing wave that's said to lure around 100 surfers a day into the chilly water – the queues of surfers on the riverbank are testament to its popularity. For more than 30 years the wave was surfed illegally, but in 2010 it was legalised. The wave is for experienced surfers only, but novices can console themselves at a gentler standing wave near the Thalkirchen campsite, south of the city centre.

The wave is at the southern end of Englischer Garten, near Prinzregentenstrasse.

559 CYCLE THE HIGH PASSES, FRANCE

Almost every story of legend from the Tour de France comes from the mountains, where the high pass climbs separate the men from the slightly less phenomenal men. They have not only made superstars of cyclists, but also of the mountains themselves. It's on these passes that recreational cyclists come to emulate the Tour riders as they coil up the 21 hairpin bends of 1860m Alpe d'Huez, grunt to the top of the 2115m Col du Tourmalet (the first high climb used in the Tour in 1910), battle the infamous winds of 1912m Mont Ventoux, or scale the 2645m Col du Galibier, the highest-ever stage finish in a Tour.

A peloton of tour companies offer cycling trips over the famed Tour de France passes.

560 CYCLE THE DANUBE PATH, GERMANY/ AUSTRIA/SLOVAKIA

Said to be the most popular cycle touring route on the continent, the Danube Path follows the course of Europe's second-longest river. The river can be followed in its entirety, from its source in Germany's Black Forest, through 10 countries to its end at the Black Sea in Romania, but the main Danube Path begins in Passau and meanders for 365km to Bratislava. There's great infrastructure and the path is mostly flat, making it a good first-time tour – many ride only as far as Vienna, while others stretch the ride out to Budapest. A section of the proposed 3600km EV6 cycling route will follow the Danube from Tuttlingen (Germany) to the Black Sea.

Esterbauer's *Danube Bike Trail* (books two and three) covers the Danube route between Passau and Budapest.

ICONIC EUROPEAN ADVENTURES

BEST WAYS TO BLOW THE KIDS' INHERITANCE

The mortgage is paid and your bank account still looks plump. Can't take it with you, don't want it all squandered by the brood – might as well enjoy some autumn-years adventure action.

MICHAEL NOLAN/CORBIS ©

561 BOOK A FIVE-STAR LIVE-ABOARD DIVING EXPEDITION, QUEENSLAND

The Coral Sea isn't cold but the warm towel waiting on deck is a nice touch. You've just emerged from your third dive of the day. Normally you'd be exhausted but on nitrox-rich air recovery time is quick. Time to laze on the deck, watching for minke whales, before chatting to the onboard marine biologist about what to expect on the night dive. You've dunked your way north from Queensland's Cod Hole to remote and little-visited Tijou, Wishbone and Yule reefs, exploring wrecks and enjoying extraordinary marine life, from tiny nudibranch to big blue sharks and manta rays. And three days still remain before you catch the bug-basher plane from Horn Island back to Cairns across the Great Barrier Reef.

Luxury 10-day, live-aboard expeditions to the far north of Australia's Great Barrier Reef are offered by Mike Ball Expeditions for AU$4745 to $7030.

562 TAKE UP A NEW HOBBY... LIKE CLOUDHOPPING

'Those wing-suit guys are crazy,' you think while ascending gently above the rolling alpine meadows. 'This is a far more civilised way to experience flying.' You'd been looking for a new challenge – it took some training but cloudhopping proved perfect. Like hot-air ballooning, but without the basket, cloudhopping involves solo pilots operating a balloon from a harness equipped with an inflator fan. The entire rig is car-transportable, enabling independent flights of up to 90 minutes to be taken anywhere. Cloudhoppers are responsive and manoeuvrable, can be landed in small areas, and you can walk out of landing spots by keeping the balloon inflated and moon-jumping over hedges and other obstacles.

A cloudhopper rig costs around US$15,000 to US$20,000. Some systems require pilots to obtain a licence from the FAA.

563 DEVELOP A TASTE FOR SEA KAYAKING IN ANTARCTICA

The glassy water is shattered by an eruption of activity somewhere close to your kayak. What the hell was that? You're keen for a whale encounter but maybe not that close. It's OK, just a gang of curious penguins porpoising past. Just penguins (emperor penguins at that): you couldn't have imagined being so blasé a week ago. Now, paddling past icebergs on your way to an Antarctic rookery, you pity the poor fools on those noisy Zodiacs, as only the swish of your blade through the water disturbs the frozen stillness.

Expeditions to Antarctica involving sea kayaking can be arranged through various operators from around £2500 (US$3725) to £13,500 (US$20,120) per 10 to 30 days.

Summertime paddling in the Antarctic is just the thing for your autumn years

With so much scenery to distract, you might not feel the trout at the end of your line in Canada's remote wilderness

564 FOSTER A FLOAT-PLANE FLY-FISHING HABIT IN REMOTE CANADA

The DeHaviland Otter float-plane bounces once and then slows to a gentle stop opposite the fishing lodge. You have the fully equipped wilderness cabin to yourself for a week. Or, if you want to explore another spot, you can get on the radio and summon a bush plane. With more than 70,000 lakes to choose from in northern Ontario's Sunset Country alone, picking a spot to flick your fly can be a daunting decision. You're at least guaranteed some solitude. There's plenty of company in the water anyway, where lake trout, brookies, walleye, bass, northern pike and muskie will keep your rod twitching.

Fly-in fishing trips to Wabakimi Provincial Park and elsewhere in Ontario are available through several operators for around CA$1500 per week.

565 DO THE IDITAROD TRAIL SLED DOG RACE, ALASKA

Ice flicks off the rear husky's paw and into your face. It's cold. Wind chill can go to -73°C but right now you feel truly alive. Some people blow their life savings on a sports car but you wanted to take on the 'Last Great Race', the Iditarod Sled Dog Race. A sports car would have been cheaper, what with the training, the transportation of the dogs and the entry fees. Oh well, it's something to tell the grandkids about. Providing you survive it. The race sees mushers and their dogs compete across 1850km (1150 miles) of punishing, icy wilderness from Anchorage to Nome.

The Iditarod (www.iditarod.com) is run annually in early March. Estimated cost of entry is US$20,000 to US$30,000.

566 CHARTER A ZEPPELIN, GERMANY

You peer over the pilot's shoulder as your friends recline in the spacious gondola. The airship silently sails along at low altitude. Every detail of the terrain 300 metres below is visible, including the envious looks on upturned faces. Zeppelin NTs have been back in the sky above Friedrichshafen for years, and you're considering a pleasure flight when inspiration strikes – why not charter a whole Zeppelin and design your own adventure? The sky isn't the limit here – if you're willing to pay for it, you can take the Zep anywhere you like, from an hour over Lake Constance to a multiday expedition to Cappadocia, Turkey.

Zeppelin charter flights cost €30,000 per day; see www.zeppelinflug.de.

567 BECOME A SUBMARINER AND VISIT THE *TITANIC*

Through the bubble window of *MIR I*, you can clearly see the Marconi Room, where the infamous SOS message was broadcast on that awful night. Further along the flanks of the wreck, the *Titanic*'s gargantuan propellers are visible, while elsewhere smaller, more personal items remind you of the very real human tragedy that played out here before the great ship sank, taking 1500 souls with her. You've sailed 350 nautical miles on the *RV Keldysh* to reach the site, and the dive will take up to 12 hours, but you're profoundly moved by the experience, shared with just 19 other people and your trusty pilot. It's easy to see why James Cameron got so excited.

Titanic dive expeditions can be arranged through Bluefish (www.thebluefish.com/visit-the-titanic) for $59,680 per person.

568 GET HOOKED ON HIGH-END HELI-SKIING IN KANGAAMIUT, GREENLAND

Your legs are screaming, your heart's racing, but you don't want this descent to end. After dropping 2000 metres through deep powder it begins to feel like it won't, but then the ocean comes into view, announcing the end of the run. There are no lifts on Kangaamiut island; the only way back to the top is in a chopper. With hundreds of glacial runs dropping into three fjords, this is summit-to-sea heli-skiing at its steepest and deepest. One guide is looking after your group of four, showing you everything from traversing glaciers to tackling steep couloirs. There's even talk of a first descent.

Heli-skiing trips to Kangaamiut (via Copenhagen) can be arranged for around €8500; see www.bigmountain-trips.com.

569 HIJACK A TRAIN FOR A RAIL-TO-TRAIL ODYSSEY

The waitstaff are more accustomed to dodging golf clubs and guns than they are to manoeuvring around the mountain bikes that lie scattered throughout the carriage, as you riders fine tune your dual-suspension steeds and discuss upcoming trails. Together you've chartered a train from Pretoria to Cape Town in South Africa and instead of steaming between golf courses or going on a bird shoot (as is common), you're linking bike trails. Next stop is Stellenbosch, where you'll hit the dirt on 18km of singletrack that spiders through Delvera.

Rovos Rail's charter trains take tailored tours to wherever there is a railway line in Southern Africa. Prices vary but start from around R380,000 per night for up to 41 passengers in 21 suites. See www.rovos.com.

570 TRAVEL INTO SPACE

The frontier so final there's no Lonely Planet guide to it, is now within your grasp. Providing you're loaded. At the time of writing, Virgin Galactic still had seats left on its Pioneer Astronaut program, guaranteeing a spot on the earliest available space flight. The journey will take you to 350,000 feet (just over 100km) – into the internationally agreed boundary of space, high enough to view the band of atmosphere around Earth and perceive the dark daytime sky of space. You'll travel at 3½ times the speed of sound and experience weightlessness, but won't go into orbit – it's a straight up-and-down deal that lasts around two hours (plus three days' training).

Pioneer Astronaut ticket: US$200,000; Spaceship Charter (exclusive spaceflight for you and five friends) US$1million. Visit www.virgingalactic.com.

BEST WAYS TO BLOW THE KIDS' INHERITANCE

BEST ULTRA RUNS

Lace up for the big, the bad, the beautiful…and the blisters. From alps to deserts, we bring you 10 of the best ultra runs.

573 CANADIAN DEATHRACE

There's nothing like the mention of 'death' to put the wind up a runner, and if the race's name doesn't scare you, some of the places it takes you should, including Hell's Canyon, where you have to ford the aptly named Sulphur and Smoky Rivers. The 125km course through the Canadian Rockies takes in three big summits (which means three big climbs), but the Deathrace is almost more notorious for its descents, which are super steep, super loose and super nasty if you fall over. And if it's a wet year, add in 'super slippery and full of sucking bogs'.

The August race can be undertaken solo or in a relay team of up to five people. It has to be completed in 24 hours.

571 CRADLE RUN, TASMANIA, AUSTRALIA

The cold wind slaps you in the face as you crest the ridge below Cradle Mountain. To the east the sun rises, as cloud inversions fill the valleys. Below you, runners are strung out along the track and below them again, sit the dark, mirrored waters of Dove Lake. One day a year the 82km-long Overland Track, which cuts through some of Tasmania's most spectacular wilderness, becomes a running-race course. The rutted, muddy track takes you below dolerite peaks, past alpine tarns, through ancient Gondwana-like forests and ends on the shore of glassy Lake St Clair. It will hurt, but how you will love it.

The Cradle Run only accepts between 60 to 70 runners who can prove previous endurance-racing form (the run is unsupported). Places fill within minutes.

572 WASATCH 100, UTAH, USA

The Mormon countryside of Utah hosts one of the world's toughest ultras, the Wasatch 100, a race so rugged that one year not a single entrant finished. It's renowned for its steep gradients, a fact your legs will confirm as you climb endlessly through ponderosa pine and trembling aspen, traversing the steep canyons and peaks of the Wasatch Front. And it's not just the ascents that hurt, for what goes up must come down, and with runners accumulating nearly 8000m of ascent, it won't just be your quads that are a smoking pile of pain by time you shuffle into the finish at the Homestead – your knees will be ready to give up the ghost.

The Wasatch 100 is held in early September. Competitors must complete one full day (eight hours) of track work before their entry will be accepted.

574 ULTRAMARATHON CABALLO BLANCO, MEXICO

Traversing the lands of the legendary indigenous people the Rarámuri (literally 'light-footed ones') is the Ultramarathon Caballo Blanco, set in the rugged canyonlands of the Mexican pueblo of Urique. The Rarámuri are famed for their incredible feats of endurance, sometimes running hundreds of kilometres in one session, shod only in sandals made from scraps of rubber and leather. While you may be glad of runners instead of sandals as you finish this tough 50-miler (80km) that takes in nearly 3000m of ascent, you too might have earned the 'light-footed' epithet – although you may not feel it.

The February race was recently renamed after its founder Micah True (Caballo Blanco), who died in 2012 while out running. It used to be called the Copper Canyon Ultramarathon.

575 THE BOB GRAHAM ROUND, UK

The Brits love tradition as much as they love a royal scandal and it doesn't get much more traditional than the Bob Graham Round. This is no race per se; the object here is to climb 42 fells (peaks) in England's Lake District in under 24 hours, a goal first achieved by Bob Graham in 1932. While the distance can vary depending on the order in which the peaks are climbed, the route taken is at least 100km and includes more than 8000m of ascent and descent. Those who achieve this goal become members of the Bob Graham Club.

Bob Graham Rounds are a private matter and can be done anytime. While the standard route includes 42 peaks, the record number climbed in 24 hours is 77 peaks.

577 KEPLER TRACK RUN, NEW ZEALAND

High on an alpine ridge above the cerulean waters of Lake Te Anau on the Kepler Track you may start to have a few *Lord of the Rings* I-am-Aragorn-chasing-the-orcs fantasies. Either that, or you might be wishing you brought your snorkel as the rain comes pelting down. The 60km-long Kepler is in Fiordland on the Southern Island, an area renowned for its six-plus metres of rain annually. But come rain or sun, in the Land of the Long White Cloud it doesn't come much more beautiful than the Kepler.

The Kepler usually takes place in December, with the most elite runners completing the circuit in just over four hours.

579 MANASLU TRAIL RACE, NEPAL

From the shadow of the world's eighth-highest peak springs the Manaslu Trail Race. Climbing from paddy fields to high passes, the course circumnavigates the massive bulk of Manaslu (8156m), following the route of one of the great Himalaya treks. As you imagine the mighty climbs, thin air and 240 unforgiving kilometres, fear not – the run is completed in seven stages over 10 days. Plus, how many runs take you past Buddhist *stupas*, skirt the edge of mighty glaciers or offer sleepovers in ancient monasteries?

The Manaslu Trail Race takes place in November. Organisers suggest that if you're fit enough to run a marathon you're fit enough to do this race.

576 ULTRA-TRAIL DU MONT BLANC (UTMB), FRANCE

Some say life is pain; running up Grand Col Ferret (2500m) – your lungs and quads burning from this and the five earlier big ascents – you may be inclined to agree. But worse than any physical pain will be the knowledge there's still 69km and five big ascents to go. Welcome to the Ultra-Trail du Mont Blanc (UTMB), widely judged to be the world's toughest ultra. The stats bear it out: 168km of trails circling the mountain, 9500m in ascents and less than half the starters making it to the finish. But you will remember, as you stagger across the line at Chamonix, that pain is temporary and finishing the UTMB lasts forever.

Competitors have to qualify to be eligible for the UTMB, then they go into a draw to nab one of the 2000 places.

578 WESTERN STATES 100, USA

While it may seem mad, 100 miles is the gold-ribbon distance of the ultra world – something to which all serious runners aspire – and there is probably no more famous 100-miler (160km) than the Western States 100. Leaving the resort town of Squaw Valley, the race follows a historic route high into California's Sierra Nevada. Half the epic race is run in the dark and temperatures can range from -6°C to the high 30s. At the 78-mile mark runners have to ford the American River, not to mention cope with 5.5km of ascent and 7km of descent.

The race takes place in the last weekend of June. Competition for places is extremely fierce as entries are limited to around 400 competitors.

580 FISH RIVER CANYON ULTRA, NAMIBIA

Located in the southern Namibian desert, the Fish River winds through one of the world's largest canyons. In aerial photos the river looks like a giant serpent splayed across the land, and following its long, meandering bends for 97km is the Fish River Canyon Ultra. The best bit about following a river is you know it's generally going to be downhill. The worst bit about it is you know it's going to be rocky, sandy, or both, and the Fish has boulderfields and sand in abundance. But it isn't all bad – the run finishes at the hot-springs resort of Ai-Ais.

The Fish River Canyon Ultra is run in mid-June and from 2013 also has a shorter 65km option.

ULTIMATE PILGRIMAGES

Get righteous as you join the holy throngs on some of the world's most revered pathways to heavenly blessings.

Take me to the river – the Kumbh Mela is one of the largest gatherings of humanity on Earth

581 CÍRIO DE NAZARÉ, BRAZIL

Second only in scale to Rio's Carnaval, Círio de Nazaré, held on the second weekend of October, has been drawing pilgrims from all over Brazil to the city of Belém for more than two centuries. The pilgrimage focuses on a small statue of *Nossa Senhora de Nazaré* (Our Lady of Nazareth), supposedly sculpted in Nazareth and responsible for miracles in medieval Portugal before it turned up in Brazil. During Círio de Nazaré, the statue is carried to the city along the Amazon from Icoaraci, accompanied by hundreds of boats. The next morning, millions of people fill the streets as the statue is pulled on a carriage to the basilica, surrounded by crowds of barefoot supplicants scrabbling to touch the rope pulling the vehicle.

The Círio de Nazaré's official website is www.ciriodenazare.com.br, in Portuguese.

582 CAMINO DE SANTIAGO, SPAIN

Contemporary Christendom's most famous pilgrimage tracks across northern Spain, angling for the cathedral at Santiago de Compostela, home to the reputed remains of St James, the first apostle martyred (beheaded) in AD 44. Though there are many routes into Santiago, the most popular is the Camino Frances, which begins in Roncesvalles, on the French border in the Pyrenees, and heads through the Rioja wine region, across the dry, dusty *meseta* (high plateau) and over the lush, green hills of Galicia. The Camino Frances is 783km in length and takes most walkers, who traditionally carry a scallop shell (the symbol of St James), around a month. Pilgrims are also permitted to cycle the route, or ride it on horseback.

The Pilgrims' Office official website is http://peregrinossantiago.es.

LUCID IMAGES/AGEFOTOSTOCK ©

583 KUMBH MELA, INDIA

The world's largest religious gathering brings together tens of millions of Hindu pilgrims for a ceremonial dip in the waters of the sacred Ganges, Shipra or Godavari Rivers. The *mela* (festival) is held four times in a 12-year cycle, alternating between the cities of Allahabad, Haridwar, Ujjain and Nasik, where it's said drops of the nectar of immortality were spilled from a *kumbh* (pitcher) during a battle between demigods and demons. Non-Hindus were once banned from bathing in the river during Kumbh Mela, though they're now allowed into the waters. You can also pitch camp in the vast tent city that arises on the riverbank.

The next *mela* will be in Nasik in August/September 2015.

211

Enormous crowds of Muslim pilgrims – almost three million every year – undertake the Hajj to Mecca and Medina

584 HAJJ, SAUDI ARABIA

The world's largest annual pilgrimage draws Muslim pilgrims from around the world to the holy city of Mecca. The *hajj* is centred around the Kaaba – it is to this, Islam's holiest building, that Muslims face when they pray. Of the estimated three million *hajjis* (pilgrims) each year, almost two million come from abroad. For *hajj* visas there's a quota system of one visa for every 1000 Muslims in a country's population. Visas are free, but are valid only for travel to Jeddah, Mecca, Medina and the connecting roads. Non-Muslims are not allowed to enter Mecca.

The *hajj* runs from the 8th to 12th day of the last month of the Islamic calendar; in 2013 and 2014 it will be in October.

585 MT KAILASH, TIBET

Sacred to Buddhists, Hindus, Jains and Bönpos, Mt Kailash is the focus of one of Asia's holiest pilgrimages. Tibetan Buddhists believe that a single *kora* (circuit) of the 6714m mountain cleanses the sins of a lifetime, while 108 circuits brings nirvana in this life. The most pious pilgrims complete the 52km *kora* by prostrating themselves – lying on the ground, standing and walking to the point their hands reached before lying down again – and others complete it in a single day. The circuit crosses a 5630m pass, so trekkers shouldn't rush it and will probably prefer to stretch it out to four days.

Trips to Mt Kailash usually depart from Lhasa or across the border in Nepal at Simlikot.

586 CROAGH PATRICK, IRELAND

Most people know two things about St Patrick: green beer and that trick with the snakes. But there's also Croagh Patrick, a 764m hill in County Mayo, indelibly linked to the saint. Each year, on the final Sunday in July – known as Reek Sunday – thousands of pilgrims ascend to Croagh Patrick's summit to honour the 5th-century saint. It's believed that, Christ-like, St Patrick spent 40 days and 40 nights fasting on this mountain. At the end of the fast, he did Ireland the service of ridding the country of snakes. The hike to the summit takes around two to three hours and finishes at the summit chapel, where Mass is held each Reek Sunday.

The town of Murrisk, at the foot of the hill, is the starting point for the climb.

587 MEDJUGORJE, BOSNIA AND HERCEGOVINA

In late June 1981, on a hill above the town of Medjugorje, 25km from Mostar, six local children claimed to have seen an apparition of the Virgin Mary. The visions continued to appear to the six children for years – and are said to still appear to several of them – and a Catholic pilgrimage was born. Unsurprisingly, late June is the high point for pilgrimages, but people come year-round. On the so-called Hill of Apparitions, there's a pair of crosses marking sites where the figure appeared. The Catholic Church hasn't endorsed the phenomenon, but that hasn't dampened the pilgrim spirit.

There's no lack of Medjugorje websites; the most informative are www. medjugorje.ws and www.medjugorje.net.

588 ADAM'S PEAK, SRI LANKA

A curious quirk of geology – a large 'footprint' in a rock at the summit – has elevated 2243m Adam's Peak, also called Sri Pada, from a simple mountain to a place of reverence. Various religions claim it as part of their mythology. To Christians and Muslims, it's said to be the place where Adam first set foot on earth. For Buddhists, it's the sacred print where Buddha stepped to ascend to paradise. Hindus claim it as the footprint of Shiva. Some think it's St Thomas' imprint. It's little wonder then that it draws so many pilgrims. The pilgrimage season is from December to May, and most climb before dawn – the paths are lit – to see sunrise from the summit.

The most popular pilgrim route begins in Dalhousie, 33km southwest of Hatton.

589 88-TEMPLE CIRCUIT, JAPAN

The best-known pilgrimage in Japan is said to have been mapped out in the 9th century by Kōbō Daishi, the most revered of Japan's saints. To complete the circuit, pilgrims travel between 88 temples – 88 representing the number of evil human passions defined by the Buddhist doctrine – on the island of Shikoku, covering around 1500km. Traditionally, pilgrims have walked between temples (a commitment of around two months), though it's becoming common to travel it by tour bus. Pilgrims wear white clothing and rice-field hats, and around half of the temples have lodging facilities.

The circuit begins in the island's capital of Tokushima and it's customary to walk it clockwise.

590 MT SINAI, EGYPT

There's nothing quite like a burning bush and a few commandments to grab a bit of pilgrim interest. On this desert mountain, at the heart of the Sinai Peninsula, Moses is said to have received the Ten Commandments, the instruction book for life. In his wake today comes an army of pilgrims, climbing the 2285m mountain for a brush with Old Testament immortality, or simply to enjoy an awesome sunrise over the barren, jagged mountains and the dry, colourful desert. There are two approaches: the camel trail or, if you're feeling especially penitent, the 3750 Steps of Repentance.

Trails up Mt Sinai begin at St Katherine's Monastery, which can be reached by bus from around the peninsula and from Cairo.

ULTIMATE PILGRIMAGES

WORLD'S HIGHEST TREKS

Fancy getting high – literally? These treks are among the highest and mightiest in the world.

591 ACONCAGUA, ARGENTINA

Aconcagua is the highest peak in the world's longest mountain range – the Andes – and also the highest mountain outside the Himalaya. And yet the 6960m giant, which rises above the Argentine city of Mendoza, is not the sole preserve of mountaineers. For trekkers it represents the highest point they're ever likely to reach. Acclimatisation requires slow toil, and reaching Aconcagua's summit takes around two weeks. Of the three main routes to the summit, the so-called Normal Route, hiking in across the Horcones Valley, is the one for trekkers – the Polish Glacier and South Face routes require climbing smarts.

Permits are required to climb Aconcagua and are only available in Mendoza. For park information, see www.aconcagua. mendoza.gov.ar (in Spanish).

592 KALA PATTAR, NEPAL

They could be the three most intoxicating words in the trekking lexicon: Everest Base Camp. Words that represent a blurred line between trekking and high-altitude mountaineering, a place rich with the possibility of rubbing shoulders with climbing greats even when you're only trekking. With it comes the chance to ascend 5545m Kala Pattar, a minor (it's all comparative here) peak with views onto nearby Mt Everest. Walk a short way north on the ridge towards Pumori and you'll be granted a view encompassing Everest's summit all the way down to the South Col, as well as a host of peaks that'd be showstoppers in any other land.

Everest Base Camp treks traditionally start in Lukla; it's about 11 days' walking to Kala Pattar.

593 CHIMBORAZO, ECUADOR

At one time, Ecuador's highest mountain was also believed to be the highest mountain in the world. And in one sense, at least, it is. Because of the equatorial bulge in the Earth, the summit of this 6310m mountain, with its five distinct peaks, is the furthest point from the centre of the Earth – more than 2km further from the centre than is the summit of Mt Everest. The most popular route to the top follows the El Castillo Route; the summit day involves around 12 to 14 hours of walking, usually setting out around midnight, and requires mountaineering experience.

Buses from Riobamba can drop you at a turn-off about 8km from Refugio Carrel on the mountain, or taxis to the refuge can be hired in Riobamba.

594 TREKKING PEAKS, NEPAL

In a hazy grey area between trekking and high-altitude mountaineering are Nepal's so-called trekking peaks. These 33 peaks, all between 5500m and 6500m in altitude, come with less of the bureaucracy attached to expedition peaks, but in many cases are also deceptively named. Most of the trekking peaks on the list are serious mountaineering challenges – Kusum Kangru and Cholatse in the Khumbu region, for instance, are very technical climbs. Others that yield more easily and have thus become popular with trekking companies are 6189m Imja Tse (formerly known as Island Peak) and 6476m Mera Peak.

Permits for climbing peaks are issued by the Nepal Mountaineering Association (www.nepalmountaineering.org); fees and climbing rules are on the website.

595 KILIMANJARO, TANZANIA

Another continental apex that yields to trekkers is Africa's 5896m Mt Kilimanjaro. Rising out of the savannah, the glacier-topped mountain has six summit routes. The easiest and most popular is the so-called Coca-Cola Route – the Marangu Route – which takes trekkers to Gilman's Point, on the crater rim at 5685m. Many trekkers stop here, though the true summit, Uhuru Peak, is still two hours away. If you want the mountain at its prettiest, consider hiking the scenic and less-travelled Machame Route. The temptation on Kili is to hurry the trek, but this sort of altitude has a kick, so plan on taking five days to reach the summit.

Independent trekking is not allowed; guides are compulsory and can be arranged in Moshi or Marangu.

215

Setting out to reach a glacier only a short distance from the Equator – one of the thrills of climbing Mt Kilimajaro

596 MT WHITNEY, USA

Crowning the Sierra Nevada range in California, 4417m Mt Whitney is the highest peak in the contiguous USA. Said to be one of the most climbed peaks in the country, the hugely popular trail to its summit begins at Whitney Portal and ascends more than 1800m in around 17km. For most hikers it's a three-day mission, though a number of hardy, hard-headed hikers smash it out in a day. The boulder-studded summit plateau is expansive (just as well given the numbers who come here) and so is the view.

From April to October, Mt Whitney hikers require permits, which are assigned on a predrawn lottery basis, with applications accepted from 1 February to 15 March; see www.fs.usda.gov/inyo.

597 GOKYO RI, NEPAL

Everest Base Camp's little sister, 5350m Gokyo Ri is also its quieter alternative, and arguably comes with better views. Though the mountain is around 200m lower than Kala Pattar, Gokyo Ri has the advantage of distance – being a valley away brings Everest into perspective. The trail to Gokyo Ri branches away from the Everest Base Camp trail just past Namche Bazaar. From the summit, you can see (fickle weather permitting) four of the world's highest six mountains – Everest, Lhotse, Makalu and Cho Oyu – while just below you is the longest glacier in the Himalaya.

Treks to Gokyo Ri usually begin at Lukla, a heart-stopping mountain airstrip with flights from Kathmandu.

598 STOK KANGRI, INDIA

In the Ladakhi city of Leh, it's difficult not to notice Stok Kangri because (a) it rises to a sharp, snowy tip above the city, and (b) every second store seems to advertise Stok Kangri treks. The appeal is obvious – at 6153m, Stok Kangri is considered the highest trekkable peak in India, rising to altitudes usually reserved for mountaineers. Companies offer four- or five-day treks, but you'll have more chance of success if you go for a seven- or nine-day option, allowing for acclimatisation. The climb isn't technical, and you'll be treated to views over the desert landscape below.

Treks usually begin in the village of Stok (home to the Ladakhi royal family), which is around one hour by road from Leh.

GALEN ROWELL/CORBIS

599 MT ELBRUS, RUSSIA

Bulging around 1000m above the main Caucasus Ridge, 5642m Mt Elbrus is Europe's often-overlooked highest point, straddling the geographical border with Asia. Though its upper slopes are covered in glaciers and ice that's said to be up to 200m thick, the climb to its summit isn't technical. Cable cars and a chairlift deposit you at around 3800m. Base camp can be here in the Garabashi Huts, or 90 minutes' walk higher up at Diesel Hut. It's worth spending at least a day at the huts to acclimatise. It's a big trekking day to the top – about eight hours up and eight hours down.

The nearest airport is at Mineralnye Vody; the climb begins at the village of Azau, about four hours' drive away.

600 GONDOGORO LA, PAKISTAN

To even get near to Gondogoro La is to see much of the world's finest scenery. Trekking the Baltoro Glacier, you'll pass the Trango Towers and Gasherbrum before coming to Concordia, the stunning base camp for K2 mountaineers. Most trekking groups then retrace their steps, but it is possible to turn south and cross 5940m Gondogoro La. It's a challenging and technical option with 50-degree slopes, requiring ropes, but the view is incredible, with all of the Karakoram's 8000m peaks at close range.

Treks begin at the town of Thungol. Permits and a licensed mountain guide are required.

WORLD'S HIGHEST TREKS

Crossing the boulder-strewn summit plateau of Mt Whitney is prelude to cresting the highest peak of the contiguous USA

FAMOUS FOOTSTEPS

These days it's hard to be the first person to go anywhere, so why not relive the epic journeys of those who first blazed the trail?

601 LIVINGSTONE, I PRESUME?

You won't be the first traveller to follow in the footsteps of Dr David Livingstone – Henry Stanley tracked the great explorer to the shores of Lake Tanganyika before delivering his famous quip. Travel in this corner of Africa is a little easier than it was in Livingstone's day (you won't need help from slave traders to complete your journey) but you can still take in some of the most spectacular locations in East Africa, from Zanzibar to thundering Victoria Falls. En route, in Mozambique visit the lonely grave of Mary Livingstone who succumbed to malaria after exploring the Zambezi with her husband.

To accurately follow Livingstone's path, start in Quelimane, Mozambique, and continue overland to Luanda, Angola. An easier option is to cherry-pick the highlights – Zanzibar, Lake Tanganyika and Victoria Falls.

602 IN THE DIRT WITH BURKE & WILLS

If you plan to trace the epic journey of Robert Burke and Williams Wills, bring plenty of supplies. The desolate route they followed in their ultimately fatal attempt to cross Australia is only marginally easier today than it was in the 1860s. From Melbourne, beat a passage through the bush, following crude 4WD tracks to Innamincka on the banks of Cooper Creek and on to Birdsville, Cloncurry and finally Normanton on the Gulf of Carpentaria. A stop at the tragic Dig Tree, where Burke succumbed to starvation only metres from the expedition's supply cache, is obviously de rigueur.

Going it alone would be the Burke and Wills way, but it's probably better to play it safe and join a group expedition; look out for notices on 4WD forums or contact Great Divide Tours (www.greatdividetours.com.au).

603 HIKING AFTER HILLARY

Re-creating every step of Edmund Hillary's trip to the top of the world would be a pretty big ask. Among other things, you'd have to climb the world's highest mountain. But the middle stages of the route to Everest are open to anyone with stout walking boots and the endurance of a mountain yak. Start the trek in Lukla and trace the gorge of the Dudh Kosi River and the Khumbu Glacier north towards Everest Base Camp. As a second-best to planting your flag atop Everest, gaze in awe on the southern face from nearby Kala Pattar.

Treks to Everest Base Camp are easy to arrange in Kathmandu, or you can pick up a trekking permit from the Trekking Agencies Association of Nepal (www.taan.org.np) and go it alone.

604 DARWIN & THE GALAPAGOS

Charles Darwin wasn't the first person to visit the Galapagos – Spanish explorers, pirates, whalers and fur traders all stopped here to snack on the abundant wildlife – but it was the naturalist who really put the islands on the map. Thanks to conservation efforts, the plants and animals that inspired Darwin's famous theory can still be seen by visitors. The first step – a flight from Quito or Guayaquil in Ecuador – is fairly conventional; the exciting bit is cruising from island to island and meeting the natives, from giant tortoises to sea iguanas.

Cruises around the Galapagos can easily be arranged in Puerto Ayora or, before you arrive, in Guayaquil or Quito. Make sure the cost includes park entry fee and INGALA Tourist Control Card.

605 IN THE FOOTSTEPS OF INDIANA

OK, so Indiana Jones doesn't really exist and Spielberg took some artistic license with his locations, but with plane tickets in hand it's easy to cover the top Indy destinations. Start your quest in Venice, reliving the conspiracy theory sections of *The Last Crusade*, then follow Spielberg's grail to Petra in Jordan. Make your next stop Tunisia, stand-in for Egypt in *Raiders of the Lost Ark*, then continue to Sri Lanka, the counterfeit India in *The Temple of Doom*. To bring the franchise up to date, finish up on Big Island in Hawaii – it doubled for Peru in *The Crystal Skull*.

The movements of Indiana Jones are a little complicated for a round-the-world plane ticket. It's probably easier to plan the trip step by step, booking the cheapest flights.

606 GOING SOLO WITH POLO

History is still out as to whether Marco Polo really visited everywhere he claimed to on his epic tour across Asia, but most historians agree that he did share a cuppa with Kublai Khan, having completed the arduous overland journey from Venice to Beijing by ship, on foot and by camel, the ship of the desert. These days a few hardy cyclists pit themselves against the rugged Pamir Highway, tracing the northern route followed by Marco Polo from Tajikistan to Kyrgyzstan. Only the brave should consider the onward journey through the Taklamakan and Gobi deserts to Beijing.

Going it alone is rather the point of cycling the Silk Road. Visit www.pamirs.org/cycling.htm for essential tips.

607 LEWIS & CLARK

The maps were mostly blank when Lewis and Clark set off on their pioneering expedition to discover the West. France had sold a vast chunk of America to the new government of the United States without venturing far west of the Mississippi. To pitch camp on the same trails as Lewis, Clark and Sacagawea – who did most of the actual exploring – load your wagon (or RV) in St Louis. Let the Missouri River be your guide to North Dakota's Fort Mandan (near Washburn), then trace the churning Columbia River through the Rocky Mountains to Astoria in the Pacific Northwest.

To cross America like Lewis and Clark, you just need a good road map. Browse www.lewisclark.net and www.lewis-clark.org to find out how the great men (and woman) did it.

608 MEANDER WITH MAYANS

With easy visa rules and an abundance of land borders, Central America is perfectly set up for overland exploring, and history has provided a great explorer to lead the way. When John Lloyd Stephens wrote *Incidents of Travel in Central America, Chiapas and Yucatan* in 1841, he had to dodge warring armies to uncover the ruined cities of the ancient Mayans. These days you can explore the jungle from a ramshackle bus, comparing the magnificent carvings at Copán in Honduras and Uxmal and Palenque in Mexico to the elegant etchings created by Stephens' expedition.

Stephens' *Incidents* is still in print, so arm yourself with a copy then fly into Cancun and pick up the trail.

609 CRUISING WITH CAPTAIN COOK

We don't recommend doing everything like Captain Cook; the man credited with discovering Australia came to a sticky end after a misjudged game of you-steal-my-boat-I-kidnap-your-chief in Hawaii. Much better to follow the route of Cook's more successful first mission along the east coast of Australia. Kick off your journey in Botany Bay, where Cook first made landfall. Essential stops include the Family Islands off Mission Beach, the town of 1770, tropical Cape Tribulation and Cooktown, where the *HMS Endeavour* was repaired after an unfortunate collision with the Great Barrier Reef.

Travel up the east coast of Oz is a breeze – join the dots by local bus or rented camper van. You'll need 4WD to navigate the Bloomfield Track between Cape Tribulation and Cooktown.

610 FOLLOW SCOTT TO THE POLE

Robert Falcon Scott (Scott of the Antarctic) wasn't the first to reach the south pole – Roald Amundsen beat him by five weeks – but it was Scott's ill-fated expedition that captured popular imagination. Even today, travelling to 90° South requires preparation. Expeditions start from Punta Arenas in Chile, continuing to the pole by boat, plane, ski and dog-sled. The reward for all this is the chance to watch your compass spin out of control at the United States Amundsen–Scott South Pole Station.

Various operators run trips to the south pole but Aventuras Patagonicas (www.patagonicas.com) does it the hard way, without food caches or external support. Are you brave enough?

ZIP IT UP: GREATEST ZIP-LINE EXPERIENCES

Make like a bird and soar across the sky on the best zip-line adventures in the world.

611 GRAVITY PLUS SPEED EQUALS FUN, NEW ZEALAND

Trust the Kiwis to come up with the fastest zip-line in the world. It's a dizzying 170m drop down to the Rangitikei River as you step off the launch platform and plunge head first across the canyon soaring at speeds of up to 160km per hour (100 mph) on the one-kilometre, breakneck Mokai Gravity Canyon Flying Fox. Didn't have time to

Gettin' zippy with it – whizzing through the forest in Chaing Mai on a nothing more than a cable

savour the views along the way? After you've sailed across the canyon the first time, you'll be winched all the way back to the launch platform at a more sedate pace so that you can finally check out the dramatic scenery below.

In case you need more scares and thrills, Mokai Gravity Canyon (www. gravitycanyon.co.nz) is also home to New Zealand's highest bridge-bungee and giant swing free-fall.

GREG VAUGHN/ALAMY ©

612 DASH THROUGH THE DOLOMITES, ITALY

What a way to witness this stunning mountain scenery. With the mighty icy peaks of the Dolomites dominating the view, you dive from the highest platform of the San Vigilio Zip-Line and dangle 100m above the dense and verdant conifer forests. A 3km network of zip-lines stretches down the slope, allowing for some of Europe's premier panoramic vistas as you slide on a 400m drop to the valley floor. Some of the longer lines have speeds of up to 80km per hour but others take a much gentler pace allowing you to appreciate those alpine views.

San Vigilio is in Italy's South Tyrol region, easily accessible by car and public transport. Check out www. adrenalineadventures.it for seasonal timings of zip-line tours.

613 GET A ZIP-LINE ALL TO YOURSELF IN COLOMBIA

How about some zip-lining without the screaming crowds? Costa Rica gets the fame when it comes to this activity but plenty of other Latin American countries tout zip-line adventures too. Word has yet to spread about Colombia's so they're refreshingly free of the tourist hordes, meaning you get all the fun without the noise – well, aside from your own screams of delight. Set on a farm not far from Cali, the Finca Mi Universo Zip Line provides a 1.5km ride of full-throttle adventure as you cascade through the sky 200m above a beautiful gorge, reaching speeds of up to 75km per hour.

Finca Mi Universo is a 2km walk from the town of 'Kilometro 18', 18km (not surprisingly) from Cali, on the road to Buenaventura.

614 TACKLE THAILAND'S FLIGHT OF THE GIBBONS

Just outside of Chiang Mai, in Thailand's lushly green north, this adventure combines breathtaking, close-up rainforest views with a web-like extravaganza of zip-lines, meandering for 5km through the jungle canopy. More sightseeing cruise than speedy thrill ride, this course comes complete with guides to offer insight into the explosion of nature surrounding you at the 33 platforms in the treetop network. It's the perfect way to experience Thailand's majestic forest from the perspective of the creatures who make it their home. Flight of the Gibbons even donates 10 percent of their profits to gibbon conservation.

Flight of the Gibbon (www.treetopasia.com) run daily tours from Chiang Mai including transport, lunch, zip-line tour and a short jungle trek for US$105.

221

Hair raising in Hawaii: zipping away over Haleakala volcano, with no hands necessary

615 GET YOUR TARZAN ON IN HAWAII

Stop slothing on the beach. The stark and jagged peak of the Haleakala volcano dominates Hawaii's island of Maui, so what better way is there of sampling the island's inland beauty than launching yourself off the volcano's slope? Putting a distinctly Hawaiian edge into the zip-line experience the Haleakala Skyline Zip has you traversing the towering subtropical forest of the volcano's lower banks in a Tarzan-style treetop spectacular of five interconnecting zip-lines. It's an adventure which shows off the majestic beauty at the heart of Hawaii – and the sand-sea-and sun worshippers usually miss it.

The Haleakala Zip-Line is just one of three that Skyline operates in Hawaii. You can check out all of them at www.zipline.com.

616 ZOOM THROUGH THE NEON BLUR OF VEGAS

Casino took you to the cleaners and there's no money left to splurge on that Vegas show? The Fremont Street Zip-Line may be just the ticket for an evening of cheap thrills in the city of vice and sin that doesn't involve even touching a slot-machine handle. Fly above Fremont Street for an up-close encounter with the famous Viva Vision Canopy, its psychedelic displays burning onto your retinas. Sure, the fastest speed is only 25km per hour but here in the land of over-the-top kitsch it's all about savouring the spectacle of flashing lights and neon-overload. It's definitely Vegas, baby!

The Fremont Street Experience Zip-Line costs US$20 per ride after 6pm. It's open until midnight Sunday to Thursday and until 2am Friday to Saturday.

617 FLY AMONG THE TREETOPS IN COSTA RICA

The lush canopy of the jungle stretches before you. Looking down at your feet, take a deep breath and dive off the platform to rush above the sea of green foliage. It's no wonder Costa Rica is known as the home of zip-lining – its natural beauty is the perfect complement for aerial adventure. With dazzling zip-line heights of up to 200m, Arenal Reserve's Sky Zip Line provides the ultimate in bird's-eye views. The cable car which ferries you to the launch platform provides panoramic vistas as well – great for capturing the sights you see while zipping through the air.

Sky Adventures (www.skyadventures. travel) run zip-line adventures in Arenal and Monteverde. Both cost US$73 for the cable car and zip-line package.

618 FEEL LIKE AN OLYMPIAN, CALGARY

In the seconds before you launch off Calgary's Olympic Park Ski Jump, take a moment to savour those childhood dreams of gold-medal glory. Plummeting from the top of this zip-line is the closest most of us mere mortals will ever get to the thrill of Olympic ski jumping. This is the fastest line in North America – you clock up speeds of 120–140km per hour on the short, sharp, vertical descent of 100m, more than enough to get your inner race-junkie salivating. Bring your own flag-waving crowd for do-it-yourself medal-ceremony pomp afterwards.

Calgary's Olympic Park Zip-Line operates daily during summer and on weekends only during winter months. See www. winsportcanada.ca for details.

619 TAKE ON THE WORLD'S LONGEST ZIP-LINE, SOUTH AFRICA

Is it a bird? Is it a plane? No, it's you doing your very own Superman impression over the South African *veld*. This is going to be the biggest two-minute adrenaline rush of your life. Sun City in South Africa takes this extreme pursuit to its most radical edge with the longest zip-line on earth. You're literally swooping over the sky – face down, caped-hero style – for 2km of pure speed-thrill fun. Sure, the grassland views below aren't gobsmacking but there's no time to notice anyway when you're notching up speeds of 120km/hr.

Five minutes' drive outside Sun City, the Unreal Zip Line 2000 (www.zip2000.co.za) runs tours every two hours from 9am to 3pm Tuesday to Sunday.

620 AN ARBOREAL ISLAND ADVENTURE, VANUATU

Your island idyll just got a bit more zip in it. Just outside of Port Vila, Vanuatu's Jungle Zip-Line flows through jungle and deep canyons for 800m over six sections. Sumptuous island views begin the ride as you skim above the lush canopy, buffeted by the breeze, but you're soon within the trees themselves, enclosed on all sides by dense tropical jungle. The final section, flying over an 80m drop into a canyon, is the real highlight for people who have completed other jungle zip-lines before, providing an exhilarating epilogue to top off the experience.

The Vanuatu Jungle Zip-Line (www. vanuatujunglezipline.com) runs two tours daily; each takes between 40 minutes and 1½ hours to complete.

ZIP IT UP: GREATEST ZIP-LINE EXPERIENCES

ICONIC MIDDLE EAST ADVENTURES

Grab your backpack and head to the Middle East for an adventure away from the crowds.

Traversing the sandy wilderness and rugged mountains of the Sinai there can only be one way to go: by camel of course

PHILLIP HAYSON/GETTY IMAGES ©

621 TREK THE LEBANON MOUNTAIN TRAIL

It may be a mere smidge of a nation but Lebanon is nothing but ambitious when it comes to trekking. The Lebanon Mountain Trail stretches the length of the country for 440km, traversing the tiny villages, stunning national parks and bold mountain scenery that make up the heartland of this country. From high-altitude plateaus, remote mountain slopes covered in pine and fir forests, tumbled ruins of ancient castles and monasteries to deep valleys and historic red-tile-roofed towns, you see it all as you trek along the old agricultural paths that connected this country long before the highways took over.

The Lebanon Mountain Trail is a series of 26 interconnecting hiking trails. Completing the entire trail takes about four weeks. For more information, see www.lebanontrail.org.

622 TREK THE ABRAHAM PATH, ISRAEL AND THE PALESTINIAN TERRITORIES

This is a rarely seen slice of the Holy Land. The Abraham Path is as much a cultural experience as a physical one; use homestay accommodation along the route to enrich your understanding of local life in this contentiously fought-over corner of the world. Through olive groves, over hills and arid plateaus, the back roads bring you to ancient ruins and historic towns but the sights along the way are only part of the route's appeal. It's the opportunity to sample simple village life and talk to locals, experiences that will stay in your memory long after you've trekked to the end.

See www.abrahampath.org for further information on the various trekking trips available through Israel and the Palestinian Territories.

623 CAMEL TREK THE SINAI, EGYPT

Huddling close to the campfire, you watch your Bedouin guide bury the dough under the sand and hot embers as he bakes desert bread. The monstrous silhouettes of Sinai's High Mountains bear down upon the camp, the sky above a glimmering blanket of stars. You hear your camel snort somewhere not far off. This is camping the traditional Bedouin way in the Sinai's sprawling desert wilderness. By day you'll ride through remote sandy stretches, backed by the barren mountain peaks. At night you'll sleep upon the sand with not a wisp of noise or light except from your own camp.

The two best places from which to arrange Bedouin-guided camel treks in the Sinai Peninsula are Dahab and St Katherine.

225

624 CLIMB MT DAMAVAND, IRAN

It's time to take on the Middle East's highest mountain. With its summit at 5671m, Mt Damavand glowers over the surrounding landscape daring climbers to give it a go. The south-face ascent isn't technical although with altitudes of over 4000m to deal with it's a strenuous physical assault that will test your fitness and endurance levels. The views from the dramatic crater summit of this dormant volcano are the prize. Gasping for breath in the thin air, you gaze out over the surrounding peaks of the Alborz Mountain Range and know the effort of the scramble up was all worth it.

Successful summiting attempts on the south face of Mount Damavand are more likely in the summer months of June–August.

625 DIVE SOCOTRA, YEMEN

It's one of the world's least-recognised diving destinations but it's home to an underwater fantasia of pristine corals and fantastic wreck diving. Once below the surface of the sea you will be greeted by schools of colourful fish and mountains of hard and soft coral with rarely another diving group to be seen. Socotra is an ecological anomaly, the very isolation of this tiny Indian Ocean island having given birth to a stunning biodiversity both on land and below the surface. Traveller facilities here are basic, but for divers looking for uncrowded reefs this just adds to Socotra's appeal.

The premium time to take a diving holiday in Socotra is during the months of March and April when underwater visibility is at its best.

626 DUNE DRIVE TO KHOR AL ADAID, QATAR

The driver revs the engine and you grind up the near-vertical sand dune. On the thin crescent at the top he lets the vehicle hang for a second and then you suddenly slip over, speeding down the sand roller-coaster style. These rippling dunes are racer-boy heaven, rolling across the landscape in wave after wave of towering mounds. When you arrive at Khor al Adaid you can stop holding your breath. This huge tidal lake – known as the inland sea – is the perfect place to watch the sunset and let your heartbeat recuperate from the dune-driving buzz.

Dune-driving excursions and overnight camping trips to Khor Al Adaid Reserve can be booked through Qatari tour agents. The reserve is 80km from Doha.

627 CANYONING IN WADI BANI AWF, OMAN

You peer up towards the light and see the sky is reduced to a slither of blue above. Jumping from boulder to boulder, scrambling down the rock, you descend into the suffocating depths of the canyon. The valley of Wadi Bani Awf is home to Oman's most ruggedly beautiful scenery and the country's steepest and scariest roads, but it's the famous fissure of Snake Canyon that adrenalin junkies are seeking out here. Once you get away from the narrow upper canyon corridor, prepare to get wet. You splash through the river to reach the canyon's wide and yawning opening and are once again doused in sunlight.

Snake Canyon tours are offered by nearly all Omani tour operators. The canyon descent takes between one and three hours.

628 DIVE THE FURY SHOALS, EGYPT

Think Egypt's Red Sea dive sites are all over-hyped? Then think again. Down in the blue depths an explosion of colourful hard-coral pinnacles and walls come into view. Darting parrotfish accompany you. A turtle gracefully slides by. Far south of Hurghada, the Fury Shoals is Egypt's great underwater wilderness. Sha'ab Sataya is one of the most famous dive sites here due to the dolphin pods that call it home, but with its atmospheric cavern and cascading boulder corals Sha'ab Claudia has to be the Shoal's most thrilling underwater experience. Once you've dived here, not much else will compare.

The Fury Shoals dive sites are most easily accessed from a live-aboard or by staying at Marsa Alam on the southern Red Sea coast.

JEREME THAXTON/GETTY IMAGES ©

All the thrills and spills of a roller coaster, just with more sand – tackling the dunes of Qatar

629 HIKE DANA BIOSPHERE RESERVE, JORDAN

It's a knee-knocker of a trail all the way to the bottom. From the Great Rift Valley's ridge you hike downhill into Dana. The reserve tumbles in a sprawl of rolling hills, hemmed in by colossal sandstone cliffs, until you reach the desert plateau over 1000m below. Despite Dana Reserve's proximity to touristy Petra, there is a rare, enveloping silence to hiking here with not another soul to be spied most of the way. So when you stumble across a shepherd playing his homemade flute it simply adds to Dana's bewitching arcadian appeal.

The Wadi Dana Trail is a 14km hike from Dana Village to Wadi Feynan and takes four to six hours. See www.rscn.org.jo for further details.

630 RAFT THE ÇORUH RIVER, TURKEY

You are soaked to the bone and that smile can't be wiped off your face. This white-knuckle adventure is one of the world's top 10 white-water rides with grade-five rapids to navigate and a guarantee that you're going to get wet. It also packs a beautiful punch: the Çoruh River cuts through the remote northeast of Turkey amid massive canyons and beside narrow valleys framed by mountain vistas. Don't leave it too long to get here though – the next few years will be your last chance to ride the river as dam construction is closing off this rafting route forever.

Alternatif Outdoor (www.alternatif outdoor.com) runs highly recommended rafting trips on the Çoruh. The best time to raft here is from May to early June.

ICONIC MIDDLE EAST ADVENTURES

THE PLANET'S FREAKIEST FOOTRACES

Bored with marathons? Spice up your running life with these wacky races from around the world.

633 BOOM DAYS PACK BURRO RACE, COLORADO

Despite the fact that you've been paired with a donkey, you're pretty confident that you'll soon be hauling ass along this racecourse. The Boom Days Pack Burro Race in Leadville, a nod to the days when Colorado's miners would walk these hills with their beasts of burden, sees each runner paired up with a burro (donkey). Riding the burro, however, is completely forbidden. Instead, you need to coax the donkey along the technical 35km route through the mountains.

The burro-racing season runs late May to September. There are presently five events in five mountain towns across the region; see www.packburroracing.com.

631 TOWER RUNNING, TAIPEI 101

Reaching the 93rd floor of Taipei's tower, a gasping mess, you wonder if you have a subconscious fear of lifts. Why else would you be doing this? It all started with the Empire State Building Run-Up – an urban race of 1576 steps and 320 metres of ascent to the 86th-floor observation deck. Then you heard about the Bitexco Vertical Run in Ho Chi Minh City – not as big (1002 steps, 178m, 49 floors), but you'd always wanted to visit Vietnam. Next came the Torre Colpatria in Bogotá, Colombia (980 steps, 50 storeys), for the tower-running World Cup. And now Taipei 101, a race up 91 floors with 2046 steps. This was the tallest tower in the world until 2010 when Burj Khalifa opened in Dubai – wonder when they're planning a run up that one…

Tower-running events take place in skyscrapers all around the world; check out www.towerrunning.com.

632 GOING UNDERROUND, LONDON

It's gloriously conspiratorial: you contact a bloke you don't know, who gives you a secret set of directions to complete a mission, should you accept it. The Underround is an 'anytime' metropolitan challenge that sends runners on a clockwise loop of London, directing them to 42 Underground stations where they must descend and ascend station steps and navigate to designated platforms until they've done a full 42km urban marathon. Runners complete the challenge whenever they like, but fastest times are recorded on a database, so an ongoing 'race' is perpetually underway. It's the brainchild of Rory Coleman, an ultra runner who found himself lamenting the lack of fell running in London and decided to do something about it.

Email Rory (rory@rorycoleman.co.uk; www.rorycoleman.co.uk), pay £10.00 and he'll send directions.

634 COOPER'S HILL CHEESE-ROLLING RACE, UK

It's steeper from the top. Peering down Cooper's Hill, the gradient looks like 1-in-1 in places. There's no bottling out now though – you're part of the running, stumbling, tumbling tangle of limbs in comedic pursuit of the cheese as it rolls down the hill at speeds of up to 110km per hour. Every Spring Bank Holiday a wheel of Double Gloucester is chased down Cooper's Hill. The first person to catch it or cross the line after the cheese wins it. Injuries are common, but neither law nor war has been able to stop the custom (although the cheese was replaced by a wooden stunt-double during WWII rationing) and when organisers pulled the pin because of insurance concerns in 2010, locals simply staged the event anyway.

Cooper's Hill is near Gloucester in the Cotswolds. See www.cheese-rolling.co.uk.

635 SANDMINE CHALLENGE, MISSOURI

What do you get if you mix running with spelunking? Sperunking – a noun that describes the high-speed caving involved in the Sandmine Challenge. This race, held annually under Crystal City in Missouri, is a 6.4km (4 mile) underground run through an old sand mine, negotiating obstacles such as low ceilings and quicksand. Organisers recently upped the ante by introducing the 'Extreme Quad', an ultra-sperunking event in which competitors complete four laps of the race circuit (a total of 25.6km). The challenge wraps up a huge post-race party with live music and beer.

Crystal City is around 56km (35 miles) south of St Louis, USA. See www. sandminechallenge.com for event details.

636 THE MARATHON DU MÉDOC, FRANCE

'Allez!' yells someone as you canter past, red faced and sporting a wine-stained top. You're a little light-headed and not entirely sure whether the 'Allez!' was for you or the bloke dressed as an Afghan clown jogging just in front, but you'll take it. This is the final furlong of the Marathon du Médoc in Bordeaux, and that euphoric feeling is either a sense of achievement or the result of the vino you've been supping along the way. Vive la France! What other country would stage a 42km marathon-carnival that passes through the gates of over 30 chateaux, encouraging athletes to tuck into the region's best fare en route?

Swap energy gels for escargot at this brilliantly Bacchanalian race (www. marathondumedoc.com) which starts at Pauillac.

637 SONKAJÄRVI WIFE-CARRYING RACE, FINLAND

Tactics have been agreed, carrying method has been determined (Estonian-style of course) and a strict diet has been planned. Actually, not too strict; the prize for the first person to carry his 'wife' across the line of this obstacle race is her weight in beer, so more wife equals more ale. This sport sees male contestants race a 253.5m track in pairs while carrying a female competitor. Stipulations state that the 'wife' must be over 17 years old and weigh more than 49kg. The sport was pioneered in Finland but has taken off in other countries, including Hong Kong, the US and India.

Sonkajärvi is Eastern Finland. The race (www.eukonkanto.fi) takes place in July.

638 THE GREAT WHEELBARROW RACE, AUSTRALIA

It's day two of the three-day race in Tropical North Queensland. Muscles are screaming, blisters adorn hands and feet, and you may be put off gardening forever. A teammate leaps from a bus driving alongside. She builds pace, taps your shoulder and you pass the wheelbarrow without breaking stride, before jumping on the bus yourself. It's as though you've done it a thousand times before. That's because you have. And you will again, until you reach Chillagoe. This is hard enough with a team and an empty barrow, so imagine the miners who pushed their life possessions along this route to the goldfields in the 1800s.

The 149km Great Wheelbarrow Race (www.greatwheelbarrowrace.com) from Mareeba to Chillagoe is held every May.

639 RUN FOR FUN IN ETHIOPIA

Addis Ababa's altitude is playing hell with your race plan as you pant through Ethiopia's capital. The Great Ethiopian Run mightn't be as big as some races but it's certainly the most anarchic. Officially 35,000 people contest this 10km (6.2 mile) sprint, but plenty are running without numbers and the real size of the field is anyone's guess. Organisers tout this as 'Africa's biggest and noisiest 10km event' – and you'd believe it as you pound the roads amidst the gasping, yelling and laughing. The elbow action at the pointy end is unbelievable, as locals try and establish themselves as the next name in a long list of leggy legends.

The Great Ethiopian Run (http:// ethiopianrun.org) happens annually in November.

640 MAN VS HORSE, WALES

It began with an argument in the pub. When Gordon Green, landlord of the Neuadd Arms in Llanwrtyd Wells, overheard a customer claiming that a good runner could match a horse over a long distance, he promptly set up a 22-mile race across rough terrain to test the theory. It took 25 years for someone to prove the mystery punter right, but in 2004 runner Huw Lobb won the human-versus-horse race in just over two hours to claim a kitty of £25,000, which had been building in increments of £1000 since the first year. Cyclists are also now permitted to compete and the event attracts up to 50 horse riders, which makes it the world's largest horse race.

Llanwrtyd Wells is in Powys, Mid Wales. The race takes place every June; see www.green-events.co.uk.

TRULY WILD WATERWAYS

Navigate these rivers and wetlands for some of nature's best – and most exhilarating – wild aqua encounters.

'What you lookin' at?' One of the locals – best spied from a distance – on Selinda Spillway

641 EVERGLADES, FLORIDA, USA

It's a far cry from Disney World – there are no mouse costumes or saccharine-sweet endings here. This is Florida's wild side, where it's survival of the fittest in an immense damp spread of sawgrass marshes, hardwood hammocks, mangrove forest and cypress swamp. The best way to explore is by boat – hire a canoe or kayak to get closer to the inhabitants. As well as many land mammals, look out for lovably ponderous manatees, prehistoric American crocodiles and alligators (this is the only place they coexist), and a variety of frogs and toads which provide the Everglades with a raucous ribbing chorus.

The Everglades National Park (www. nps.gov/ever) is open year-round. Peak season is the dry winter period; some facilities close during wetter summer months.

642 ZAMBEZI RIVER, ZAMBIA/ZIMBABWE

The Zambezi isn't Africa's longest river. But its 2700km course – which moistens six countries en route from its source to the Indian Ocean – is arguably Africa's wildest. And nowhere is this more true than its run along the Zambia–Zimbabwe border. First it plummets down Victoria Falls, from where multiday rafting trips encounter not just unruly rapids but cantankerous hippos and crocs. Further downstream, the river is flanked by Lower Zambezi (Zam) and Mana Pools (Zim), two of the continent's greatest national parks, and all manner of creatures – from enormous elephants to elegant egrets – come to take a drink here.

Zambezi rafting trips are best August to November, when water is high and more rapids can be run; rapids are mostly Grade IV.

643 MCNEIL RIVER, ALASKA, USA

The world's largest known get-together of hungry brown bears takes place on Alaska's McNeil River from June to August. Up to 70-odd bruins cluster at the rapids and rockpools of this remote water system situated 400km southwest of Anchorage and reached by floatplane. They come for the salmon, which are returning in vast numbers to spawn. As these plucky fish fight the flow, making magnificent leaps to surmount obstacles in their path, the bears wait, open-mouthed, looking for an easy supper. It's not all about the bears though – harbour seals, bald eagles and other birds are also attracted to this fishy frenzy.

Permits, issued by lottery system, are required to visit McNeil River State Game Sanctuary & Refuge; apply at www.adfg. alaska.gov.

644 SELINDA SPILLWAY, BOTSWANA

The Selinda Spillway is a channel linking Botswana's Okavango Delta to the Linyanti and Kwando water systems. Or it is at the moment. Sometimes it's not – that's down to Mother Nature. For three decades this rivulet ran dry; profuse flooding in 2009 saw it flow once more and for now it's possible to canoe part of its 100km length. Seize the opportunity and you won't be disappointed, though you may be scared stiff. Hippos are rampant here, enjoying their newly saturated home and not keen on sharing it with paddlers, but keep a respectful distance, and you'll get on just fine.

The four-day Selinda Canoe Trail begins 45km downstream from Selinda Camp; trips run April to October, depending on water levels. See www. greatplainsconservation.com.

645 SUNDARBANS, BANGLADESH

The Sundarbans is not an easy place to be. This vast delta region – where the Ganges and Brahmaputra rivers discharge into the Bay of Bengal – is a morass of shifting islands, stifling swamp and impregnable mangroves. It's no place for humans. Animals, however, love it. Chital deer and rhesus monkeys hide in the thickets; turtles, fiddler crabs, gharial and crocs patrol the waters; and Bengal tigers – 250 of them – rule the roost. The big cats here are known as two things: great swimmers and maneaters. Boat trips offer the best, and safest, sightings.

231

Bangladesh has three seasons: monsoon (late May to October), cool (November to February) and hot (March to May). Cool season is the driest and best time to visit.

646 CUIABÁ RIVER, PANTANAL, BRAZIL

Stuff the Amazon. If you want to actually see the wildlife of Brazil rather than be stymied by impenetrable jungle, head to the Pantanal. A boat trip on the Cuiabá River – or one of its secretive tributaries – will likely reveal what the Amazon does not: the country's mind-boggling biodiversity. A splash in the water? Could be the wake of a diving kingfisher, the slow skulk of a caiman or the acrobatic antics of a giant otter. Something wallowing? Maybe a capybara cooling off or a thirsty tapir. And that flash of movement along the riverbank? Yep, a jaguar, staring right back.

The best time to visit the Pantanal is May to September, when wildlife is concentrated at shrinking water sources and temperatures are mildest.

647 JACQUES-CARTIER RIVER, QUÉBEC, CANADA

It's estimated that there are between 500,000 and one million moose in Canada. That's a lot of moose. But then there's a lot of Canada. So to make your ungulate-ogling nice and easy, travel just 30 minutes out of Québec City (the country's most historic hub) to Jacques-Cartier National Park. Here a forest-cloaked valley hugs the Jacques-Cartier River, cosy cabins dot the bush, friendly guides staff the visitor centre and moose sightings are virtually guaranteed. Paddle out onto the inky waterway in a traditional *rabaska* canoe to spot the leggy creatures when they come down to the water to feed.

Canoe hire and rafting trips can be arranged from the visitor centre. Fall colours are at their best late September to early October.

648 RIVER STOUR, DORSET, ENGLAND

Around 40 years ago otters were virtually extinct in England. Agricultural pesticides and increased pollution had made the rivers unliveable – things were dire indeed. Fast-forward to 2011, following a concerted effort to clean up the waterways, and the UK Environment Agency happily announced that there were otters present in every county. These sinuous mammals can still be tricky to see – they're shy and most active in the early hours. But the otters of Blandford, a market town on the River Stour, don't seem to have read the rules, unabashedly splashing about in broad daylight to the delight of passers-by.

Blandford Forum is 25km northwest of Poole, 35km southwest of Salisbury, at the junction of the A350 and A354 roads.

649 MEKONG RIVER, KRATIE, CAMBODIA

The Irrawaddy river dolphin is not doing so well. Although considered sacred by many local people, the number of poor *Orcaella brevirostris* in the Mekong River has dwindled to fewer than 100, the species falling victim to pollution, habitat loss and accidental entanglement in fishermen's nets. The World Wildlife Fund is working with both the Cambodian government and Buddhist monks to try to help the dolphins; its outlook is fairly positive. But for now the best chance to see them is from the sleepy town

MORALES/AGEFOTOSTOCK ©

The elusive jaguar is an example of the amazing biodiversity of the Pantanal

of Kratie, where sampan boat trips upriver offer privileged encounters with these gentle, beakless, critically endangered creatures.

Kratie is 350km northeast of Cambodian capital Phnom Penh. The road is surfaced all the way; buses take around five hours.

650 TYSFJORD, NORWAY

The west coast of Norway is notched with thousands of dramatic sea inlets. And, some years ago, a load of herring chose Tysfjord (just north of the Arctic Circle) as the one in which to overwinter. Once the local orca figured this out, they decided this was the place to be in the colder months too. Now, as temperatures drop, hundreds of hefty killer whales cluster here to bait-ball feed, herding the silver fish into a lump, whacking them with their tails and then chomping on the stunned shoal. Sailing out from the village at the base of the fjord, you might get to witness this fish feast in action.

Boat trips run from the Tysfjord Turistsenter at the base of the fjord, Thursday to Saturday, from November to late January; trips usually last 4–6 hours. See www.tysfjord-turistsenter.no.

TRULY WILD WATERWAYS

FAMOUSLY ADVENTUROUS DESTINATIONS

You can feel the aura of adventure glowing from these long-famous names – get ready for the mysterious, the remote and the intrepid.

MASSIMO RIPANI/SIME/4CORNERS ©

Plenty to ponder: no-one is sure what the mighty *moai* of Easter Island represent

651 STEP BACK IN TIME IN SAMARKAND, UZBEKISTAN

Warlords and wanderers, merchants and mendicants have flocked to this oasis city on the Silk Road for hundreds of years. Looming out of the desert, Samarkand exhibits an embarrassment of architectural riches, decorated mosques and *medreses* (seminaries), bristling with blue-tiled domes and lofty minarets that have resonated with poets and playwrights through the ages. The focal point of the city is Registan Square with its three-century-old *medreses*, decorated in majolica and azure mosaics. To get a taste of Silk Road ambience, head to the Samarkand bazaar, where you can imagine yourself as a merchant amongst the crimson tapestries, jewellery and hand-woven carpets.

Visit in spring (May to June) or autumn (September to November) for mild and pleasant weather. Avoid the heat and sandstorms of summer (July to September).

652 SAIL DOWN THE AMAZON RIVER

It's hard not to feel tiny on your small skiff boat as you push along the largest river in the world. Everything is bigger here – lily pads, bird calls, frog croaks, scarlet macaws, the fur of the wonderfully odd monk saki monkey, giant otters, cathedral-like trees and the teeth of the piranha. Along the river is the densest rainforest on earth, where you can meet local tribes who thrive on the richness of the Amazon's waters. The Amazon is fed by the waters of six South American countries: Brazil, Peru, Columbia, Ecuador, Bolivia and Venezuela.

Travel in the dry season from July to December for less rain and mosquitoes, although greater heat.

653 TIMBUKTU

You know of it but where is Timbuktu exactly? The town sits on the edge of the southern Sahara Desert in Mali, its name a kind of shorthand for a distant place. The camel caravans laden with gold, ivory and salt no longer plod across the sands like they did when the Mali Empire was at its peak in the 13th century. The decline in caravan traffic has left Timbuktu remote and mysterious...and now potentially unsafe. For all its allure, Timbuktu is not that spectacular in the flesh, but anyone who makes it this far is guaranteed oodles of traveller kudos.

The political situation in Mali is volatile so travel is not recommended at the moment. Seek current travel advice before considering a trip to such a potentially dangerous country.

654 TIBET

Mention Tibet and instantly conjured up are images of prayer flags and pilgrims on a spiritual quest – with good reason. Buddhist temples such as Tradruk in the Yarlung Valley dominate the mountainscapes. For adventurers seeking an inner journey, hiking up to some of these holy sites can present a real test of faith and leg power. Tibetan monks and nuns are a common sight in their crimson and saffron robes as you make your way to solitary caves where you can feel so wonderfully far from civilisation. The nomadic people here rely on native yaks for survival. They live in tents made from the animal's wool, and use its dung for cooking and heating homes in winter.

To visit Tibet you need a Tibet Tourism Bureau permit, which is only issued if you have booked a guide for your entire trip and prearranged transport for outside Lhasa. Entering from Nepal is possible on a short-term group visa.

655 EASTER ISLAND

Also known as Rapa Nui, this small Pacific island (part of Chile) is famous for its large-headed *moai* statues. Looking up at them, you'll wonder what these long-nosed, wide-browed *moai* were for and what happened to those that carved them. What do the statues represent? Did the craftsmen exhaust their resources on the statues' construction, forcing them to leave the island? The enigmatic faces offer no answers. Locals do live here but it is one of the most isolated islands in the world, making it an out-of-the-ordinary journey.

Get to Easter Island by plane from Santiago in Chile or Lima in Peru. Boat travel is rare, as the island has only a tiny harbour.

656 EXPLORE IDYLLIC ZANZIBAR, TANZANIA

On a balmy evening wandering the alleyways of Stone Town, Zanzibar, you might well imagine yourself inserted into an episode from *The Arabian Nights*. This island, a jewel off the coast of Tanzania in the translucent Indian Ocean, has drawn travellers through the ages, from ancient Greek mariners, to gold and ivory traders, Omani sultans and legendary African explorers Stanley and Livingstone. The air here is scented with cinnamon and cloves, street vendors at the Fordohani Gardens hawk tropical fruits, across the bay *dhows* cut a shark-fin silhouette under a moon. And beyond lies the mighty continent of Africa, beckoning adventurers all.

Zanzibar is blessed with pleasant tropical weather year round, but avoid the short showers of November and December, and the long rains of February to May.

657 SHANGRI-LA, THE HIMALAYA

Is Shangri-La a Himalayan utopia shielded from the outside world with happy inhabitants who stay youthful forever, or is it myth – a mere work of fiction from the novel *Lost Horizon* by James Hilton? Ancient Tibetan scriptures mention locales that could be Shangri-La. Its Tibetan name alludes to a mountain pass – in the Himalaya, that could be anywhere and that is the point. Some also say it could be Zhongdian, across the border in Yunnan province, others say it is in Nepal. Perhaps more than any specific place, Shangri-La describes the heaven on earth, somewhere we all dream of.

Summer in the Himalaya (May to September) sees the greenest grass and mildest weather, but also the most tourists and some rain. For clearer views of Everest, visit during the rest of the year.

658 TIERRA DEL FUEGO, ARGENTINA & CHILE

Any place whose name translates as Land of Fire promises adventure aplenty, and Tierra del Fuego delivers. Ferdinand Magellan fetched up here, as did gold seekers in the 1880s. These days this archipelago, shared between Argentina and Chile, attracts travellers who are drawn not just by end-of-the-world bragging rights but ruggedly diverse natural attractions, from windswept plains to mossy lenga forests and snowy ranges above the Beagle Channel. On the Argentinian side, Ushuaia, the world's southernmost city, is a base for horse riding, hiking and boating. Puerto Williams, in Chile, is gateway to breathtaking scenery and the ragged peaks of Dientes de Navarino.

November to March is ideal for hiking and boating; July to September sees great skiing and snowboarding.

659 MIDDLE EARTH, NEW ZEALAND

Other destinations have built a reputation through stories and whispers over decades and centuries, but New Zealand is a modern celebrity, gaining her fame through the *Lord of the Rings* and *Hobbit* movies. The film adaptations of Tolkien's novels showcase the pristine, natural landscape, perfectly recast as the fictional Middle Earth of Tolkien's novels. Duck your head through the

The evocative, poetic name Zanzibar has been a siren's call to travellers through the ages

circular doorways of Hobbiton and be immersed in the short-of-stature, adventurous-of-heart world of the hobbits. In reality, the Shire is part of the lush dairy farms around the Waikato town of Matamata but close your eyes and you're in Middle Earth.

There are loads of other beautiful locations from Middle Earth to walk through in New Zealand, all listed at www.lonelyplanet.com/campaigns/explore-middle-earth.

660 UNCOVER ANCIENT NATURAL WONDERS IN KAKADU, AUSTRALIA

Cruising along the waterways of Kakadu National Park, you race thousands of years back in time. The eyes peeking from the water belong to a crocodile, an animal that outlived the dinosaurs. A waterfall drenches the air as it cascades into a plunge pool. Plants thrive on the waters, in turn housing colourful birds in their greenery. Around you is the art of indigenous Australians whose galleries were rock faces and caves. Their ancient hand stencils mark a land of 2000-million-year-old rocks.

Visit during the dry season (May to September), preferably from May to mid-June when the falls are still full of water.

FAMOUSLY ADVENTUROUS DESTINATIONS

GIRLS-ONLY ADVENTURES

Thrill seeking in the company of sisters doing it for themselves.

661 SEA KAYAKING IN WASHINGTON STATE, USA

If you want to leave civilisation behind, you can't get much more remote than a boat-paddle around an archipelago that's deserted, save the odd otter, minke whale or bald eagle. Outdoor Odysseys runs Women on the Water sea kayaking trips around the picturesque San Juan Islands in the north-west corner of Washington State. WOW tours are open to novices as well as experienced paddlers but you don't need gladiator-like arms to take part – the kayaks are for two people so you'll get a rest now and then (especially when your partner isn't looking), plus they're very stable. By day you'll paddle and by night you'll camp at waterfront sites and be fed gourmet campfire cuisine. Boats, gear and instruction are supplied.

WOW trips run in June, July and August. Visit www.outdoorodysseys.com/women -on-the-water-wow-kayak-tours/.

662 ICE CLIMBING IN OURAY, COLORADO, USA

Clawing your way up a vertical wall of blue, shiny ice Spiderwoman-style is about as gnarly as it gets. Founded in 1999, Chicks with Picks runs women-only ice climbing courses with all-female guides based out of Ouray, Colorado (the self-coined 'Switzerland of America' due to its striking, steep mountain panorama). Beginners and intermediates can enjoy clinics with a 4:1 student-to-guide ratio at the Ouray Ice Park, which has over 200 climbs on offer, whereas more advanced climbers will take on back-country ice faces in the San Juan mountains with one teacher for every two students.

The ice clinics take place every January and February and cover two to four days of guiding, including lodging in Ouray. The company also donates a share of its profits to local women's shelters. Sign up at www.chickswithpicks.net.

663 HORSE RIDING IN NEW MEXICO, USA

Cowgirls may be thin on the ground in Hollywood folklore but on the dusty plains of Double E Ranch, a working cattle farm with a dramatic canyon backdrop in New Mexico, they are very much in evidence. Open to riders of all ages and abilities, Cowgirl Camps have been running here for almost 12 years with the promise of upping your skill levels and confidence thanks to the ranch's willing and well-behaved horses. Phones are banned and there are no TVs or Jacuzzis; the emphasis is on getting 'your hands dirty and your bottom sore' – this ain't no pampered pony club.

Double E Ranch runs five-day Cowgirl camps throughout the year (except December–January). Visit www. doubleeranch.com/cowgirl_camp.html.

664 TRIATHLON IN NOOSA, AUSTRALIA

However fit you are, taking part in a triathlon requires some serious graft so you'd be wise to do it somewhere warm and ridiculously scenic to distract your body from the pain you're putting it through. Noosa, on Queensland's Sunshine Coast, is one such place, which is perhaps why so many national and international triathletes base themselves here in summer. The All Women's Tri Camp is for beginners and intermediates looking to immerse themselves in the sport and pick up some tips from the coaches who are all hardcore triathlon champions in their respective age groups.

The two-and-a-half-day camps take place in August (the actual Noosa triathlon is in November); sign up at www.mscsport. com.au/women-camp-2013.php.

665 SNOWBOARDING IN AVORIAZ, FRANCE

The first rule of learning to snowboard is not to get taught by a friend or loved one if you want them to remain so. But instead of risking a grumpy ski instructor, at a Rudegirls Snowboard Week you can learn or improve your already budding skills with like-minded girls in a group. You'll likely be taught by friendly, patient Angel (her actual name) who is a former half-pipe World Champion. The Avoriaz ski area has awesome pistes and off-piste for all levels, plus plenty of parks for freestyle fans and tree runs for added atmosphere.

Rudegirls Weeks take place every January and the package includes tuition, half-board chalet accommodation, lift pass, snowboard rental. Visit www.rudechalets. com/winter-holidays/custom-weeks/rudegirls-week/.

666 HELI-SKIING IN REVELSTOKE, CANADA

Perhaps the best-named ski resort in the world, Revelstoke boasts some of the finest helicopter-accessed terrain and juicy above-average snowfall. It gets between 9m and 14m a season, and when it dumps it's mostly fluffy Champagne powder, the stuff ski movies are made of. But charging through chin-deep snow isn't as easy as it looks, so Powder 101 Girls' School from CMH is there to help turn strong resort skiers into proficient powder hounds. By day you'll ski in groups of 10 women and by night you'll watch your best runs on video.

Powder 101 Girls' School usually takes place in Revelstoke in March with trips to Bugaboos in January and Gothics in April; visit www.canadianmountainholidays. com/heli-skiing/trips/women.

667 ROCK CLIMBING IN THE COSTA BLANCA, SPAIN

When it comes to technique, women often climb differently to men, relying less on brute strength – think Sylvester Stallone's quivering biceps in *Cliffhanger* – and more on poise, style and flexibility. Ruth Taylor at Rock & Sun knows how to help women climb as efficiently as possible and at their female-only climbing weeks in the Costa Blanca she promises to share all. The location has perfect and varied rock for scaling, from limestone sea cliffs and mountain ridges to sunny crags and canyon walks, plus around 325 sunny days a year, which kind of helps too.

Rock & Sun runs women's weeks May to September in the Costa Blanca. Included are five days' instructed climbing, equipment, shared accommodation and transport to crags. Visit www.rockandsun.com.

668 SURFING IN NICARAGUA

In the late 1970s and '80s bands of pioneering surfers dodged guerrilla gunfire and trekked through jungle to access Nicaragua's bathwater-like beach breaks. Today there's far less faff involved but a relative lack of development and absence of surf-school hordes mean an original spirit remains. Surf with Amigas, run by US pro surfer Holly Beck, hosts week-long retreats on the northern Pacific coast, where the warm ocean and broad spectrum of waves make it a great place to learn or amp up your surfing.

The camps run year-round except August and September and include surf coaching, boat trips, yoga, and the chance to board down an active volcano. See www.surfwithamigas.com.

669 CYCLING IN THE NEW FOREST, ENGLAND

If you like the idea of riding your bike like a character from an Enid Blyton novel, as in with friends, four abreast, in stunning nature without a snarling motorist in sight, then check out the Cycletta series. First held in 2011 these annual UK-wide women-only rides take place on traffic-free or safely managed, quiet country roads – though they can be lined with enough supporters to make you feel vaguely like an Olympian. Cycletta New Forest is held in and around the grounds of the picturesque Beaulieu castle in the south of England. Just be sure to whoop on the downhills.

The New Forest event normally takes place in October. Novices should opt for the 40km route, while more seasoned or club cyclists can do timed challenges on either the 40km or 80km routes. Enter at www.cycletta.co.uk.

670 MOUNTAIN BIKING AT KIRROUGHTREE, SCOTLAND

The 7stanes mountain biking centres in southern Scotland each have a unique statue reflecting a local myth or legend (stane being a Scots word for stone). At Kirroughtree it's the pink quartz Gem Stane, reflecting the trail's reputation as a hidden gem. It has some of the best technical singletrack in the country along with huge slabs and ridges of exposed granite. It also boasts a range of scenic blue and green-graded trails around the stunning Bargalt Glen and Doon Hill for those seeking a less extreme day of biking.

Bottle Green Biking run women-only coaching days from April to September. Visit www.bottlegreenbiking.co.uk.

BEST RAFTING RIVERS

Zip up your wetsuit, cinch your helmet: we bring you the biggest, baddest and raddest rivers for rafting the world over – and all guided commercially for your convenience.

671 SUN KOSI RIVER, NEPAL

Originating near Mt Shishapangma in Tibet and carving its way through the Himalaya is the mighty Sun Kosi River (literally 'River of Gold'). Draining eastern Nepal, its glacier-fed waters drop for just five months of the year, enough to make it raftable. And what a trip it is! The 273km from the put-in at Dolalghat to the take-out at Chatra Gorge are as exciting as rafting comes – big, bouncy white-water rapids, steep valleys, remote Nepalese mountain villages, superb campsites on white-sand beaches, and hot, sunny days with chilly nights. By the end you'll agree that there's more than one kind of gold.

The Sun Kosi is commercially rafted between September and January, after which the river triples in volume and becomes unrunnable. It takes up to 10 days to run the river.

672 MAGPIE RIVER, ONTARIO, CANADA

As your float plane splashes down in remote Magpie Lake amidst endless pine and spruce forests, you'll know you are at the beginning of something special. What follows is an incredible journey down the Magpie River through granite-lined gorges filled with continuous grade-three and grade-four rapids. Nights are spent on rocky ledges or beaches beneath the spectacular show of the Northern Lights. And as you paddle, watch out for the wildlife: black bears, wolves, osprey and moose. Near the end of the trip you will reach the portage around Magpie Falls, followed by a final sting in the tail – the grade-five rapids just downstream.

August and September are the best months to raft the Magpie River. There is currently a battle to save it from being dammed, so run it while you still can.

673 ZAMBEZI RIVER, ZIMBABWE/ZAMBIA

We hope you like getting wet. Below the mighty cascades of Victoria Falls on the Zambezi River – Africa's fourth-longest river – lie the black-basalt-lined walls of Batoka Gorge, containing what many say is the best single day's white-water rafting anywhere. Right from the get-go at Boiling Point, the treacherous names of the rapids don't provide much comfort: the Washing Machine, the Devil's Toilet Bowl, Oblivion...you're probably catching the drift. More than half the rapids are grade five (grade sixers being impossible to run). Also, did we mention the crocodiles?

The best time to raft the Zambezi is during low water (July to mid-February).

241

The roaring Zambezi River offers supreme white-water rafting beneath the majesty of Victoria Falls

Doing the Franklin frolic – downhill all the way, and very wet

674 ALSEK RIVER, USA/CANADA

Flip your raft on the Alsek and you will redefine your concept of cold. Fed from the largest nonpolar glacier basin in the world, the icy waters of the Alsek average about half a degree Celsius. That's right, dry suits are mandatory. Apart from a unique and incredibly beautiful alpine environment, these mighty glaciers also provide lots and lots of water, and a superfast ride for rafters through 250km of pristine wilderness in the Kluane National Park. Bald eagles and grizzly bears abound – did we mention that the peak grizzly and rafting seasons coincide?

The best time of the year to raft the Alsek is in June. One section of the river is considered so deadly that it is portaged with a helicopter.

675 COLORADO RIVER, ARIZONA, USA

Many would argue it can't get much better than rafting the muddy brown waters of the Colorado. Indeed, what other river carves through the world's most famous hole in the ground, the Grand Canyon? And if numbers are anything to go by, perhaps they are right – 22,000 people run the Grand Canyon section of the Colorado River each year. While you may not find solitude what you will find from the put-in at Lees Ferry is 42 exciting rapids, incredible vistas of geological formations up to half-a-billion years old, plus Native American ruins you can stop off and visit.

The rafting season is May to October and trips can last anywhere from one to 18 days. Private groups may have to wait up to ten years for a permit.

676 MIDDLE FORK OF THE SALMON RIVER, IDAHO, US

After copping a soaking while smashing through grade-three and grade-four rapids, what could be better than relaxing in hot springs at the end of the day? Cutting through the largest wilderness area in the Lower 48 is the Middle Fork of the Salmon River, the longest undammed river in the United States. The Middle Fork is the full package: a multitude of rapids that will keep your pulse racing, amazing wildlife, incredible fly fishing (said to be the best in the US), and, of course, those hot springs – there are six along the river.

The usual Middle Fork season is from May to September. Rafters are required to have a permit (not easy to get) and carry a porta potty.

CATHY FINCH/GETTY IMAGES ©

677 FRANKLIN RIVER, TASMANIA, AUSTRALIA

From the moment you slip into the dark, tannin-stained waters of the Franklin, the river holds you in its thrall, its ceaseless energy an ever-present companion through your days and nights, even your dreams. Moods change with the river; when it's cold and rainy, everything's miserable, when the river rises and the rapids are pumping, so is the adrenalin, and when you drift silently along in the sun beside a platypus, all is at peace. By the time you reach its confluence with the Gordon, it will be with more than a tinge of sadness.

The Franklin is best tackled during summer. Most people end their journey at Sir John Falls, taking a chartered yacht out to avoid the tedious paddle to Strachan.

678 RIO COTAHUASI, PERU

Nowhere is the expression 'mountain high, river low' better expressed than on the Rio Cotahuasi, which carves its way through the Cotahuasi Canyon – the world's deepest canyon (3535m at its lowest point). Just getting to the put-in is epic. It involves a high-altitude 12-hour drive and two-day mule trek. But, as it often is with the hardest things, the reward is prodigious: seven days of grade-four and grade-five rapids that will push you to your limit, beautiful, remote campsites, and unexplored pre-Inca ruins left from the Huari civilisation. Culture and adventure – what more could you want?

This is a trip for experienced rafters only. June and July are considered the best months to tackle the river.

679 RIO FUTALEUFÚ, CHILE

The first thing that strikes you about the Rio Futaleufú is its colour, ranging from an almost unnaturally bright turquoise through to shades of teal, modulated by the minerals in this glacier-fed torrent carving through the Patagonian Andes. And while your days might be spent fighting through big, scary white water (up to grade five), the organisation that guides the Futaleufú, Earth River, has created camps of unprecedented luxury and imagination – with showers, flushing toilets, hot tubs and superb meals – so that you can relax at night in absolute style.

Earth River runs trips on the Rio Futaleufú every summer December–March.

680 NOCE RIVER, ITALY

Smashing through the icy, green waters of the Noce River on big waves, you'll be left in no doubt you're on Europe's best rafting river. Fed by glacial melt, the Noce is in the Dolomites, an Alpine paradise in northern Italy, meandering through the remote and beautiful Val de Sole (Sun Valley). The river caters to all levels, but its most famous rapids are punishing grade-fivers that churn through the gorges of the Mostizzolo. Best of all, you are never too far from civilisation and that perfect short black.

The Noce is best paddled in summer, and is probably the most accessible of all the rivers listed here.

BEST RAFTING RIVERS

MOST MAGNIFICENT COAST-TO-COAST MISSIONS

There are no greater bragging rights than those earned by traversing a region, country or continent from ocean to ocean.

Foot power by day and Guinness by night. Traversing the Emerald Isle in style

GARETH MCCORMACK/GETTY IMAGES ©

681 ACROSS COSTA RICA ON HORSEBACK

Over the last few days you've developed a special bond with your criollo steed. You realise, as you saunter through coffee plantations in the afternoon sun, that this horse – one of a local breed famous for their endurance and temperament – makes a better expedition buddy than some of your amigos. Each day of this sea-to-ocean odyssey you've faced totally new terrain together, from the soft Caribbean sand at the outset to the lushness of the rainforest region. The highlands of this astonishingly diverse country will provide the next challenge, as you cross the back of Central America and descend to Pacific coast.

Activities such as horse riding are best enjoyed during Costa Rica's dry season (December to April). Local operators can help arrange a horse and provide a guide.

682 CONQUER THE COAST-TO-COAST ADVENTURE RACE, NEW ZEALAND

You've spent a year training for this and are as ready as you'll ever be, but tell that to the butterflies having a disco in your stomach as you shuffle on the starting line at Kumara Beach on New Zealand's South Island, the Tasman Sea at your back. What were you thinking, entering the one-day event? They don't call it the 'Longest Day' for nothing. Bang. It's on – self-doubt be silent. Today you will cross the spine of the Southern Alps using sheer muscle power as you run, cycle and paddle a total of 243km before collapsing onto the sand at Sumner Beach on the Pacific Ocean.

A field of around 800 adventurous athletes contest NZ's Coast-to-Coast race (www.coasttocoast.co.nz) each February.

683 ACROSS IRELAND BY FOOT

There are almost 10,000 pubs scattered across Ireland, and by day 23 of your cross-country walk from Dublin to Portmagee on the Atlantic coast it feels as though you've seen the inside of about half of them. Some you prebooked as an accommodation option months ago, while others have provided emergency shelter from the Irish elements. Tomorrow will be your last day on this 387-mile trail and even after three-and-a-half weeks of exposure to wild weather and even wilder hospitality, that still makes you sad. Ireland is a country that refuses to be rushed and this meander has done it justice.

Ireland's coast-to-coast walk stitches together many of the country's most stunning waymarked routes including the Wicklow, South Leinster, East Munster, Blackwater and Kerry Ways.

Tackling glaciers and the icy expanses of Spitsbergen, crossing from the Barents to the Greenland Sea

684 RACE ACROSS AMERICA

The Tour de France, tough? Pffft. Those guys get to stop and sleep at the end of each stage. Try taking on a 4800km (3000-mile) race where the clock never stops ticking, there are no road closures and you have to balance utter exhaustion with the need to bash out up to 800km (500 miles) a day just to stay competitive. Welcome to RAAM, the 'world's hardest bike race', which sends cyclists from Oceanside, California to Annapolis, Maryland. If you're doing this solo you have 12 days to finish but teams only get nine. Some solo racers sleep as little as 90 minutes a day in order to finish before the cut-off.

RAAM (www.raceacrossamerica.org) takes competitors across 12 states and 88 counties en route between the Pacific and the North Atlantic Oceans.

685 PADDLE SCOTLAND'S GREAT GLEN

Portaging your canoe around the locks of Neptune's Staircase in Banavie, you glance at the Scottish sky. The sun is smiling along the length of the Great Glen, which slices the Highlands in two between Fort William on the west coast and Inverness on the east, but conditions can quickly turn feisty. Tonight you'll camp on the beautiful shores of Loch Lochy, tomorrow will take you across Loch Oich, but day three is when you'll face crossing the monstrously deep waters of Loch Ness, an inland sea where waves can easily reach four or five feet in ugly weather.

The Great Glen Canoe Trail (http://greatglencanoetrail.info) was declared Scotland's first official canoe trail in 2012. Wild camping is permitted along the way.

686 RUN ACROSS ITALY

Pasta is perfect for carboloading before an endurance event, right? Brilliant, because there's no shortage of it during the coast-to-coast run across the Apennine Peninsula. In a land of cycling nuts this foot race is both different and special. Four-person relay teams race over four legs as the route traverses a 368km course from the Adriatic to the Tyrrhenian Sea. It takes in the exquisite countryside, hills and small villages of Marche, Umbria and Tuscany and the emphasis is on the quality of the experience rather than the finishing times. Organisers describe the event as a 'slow race' that 'inspires travellers to fall in love.'

Run every year since 2001, the Italian Coast to Coast race goes from Grottammare to Follonica.

687 SKI ACROSS SPITSBERGEN, NORWAY

Those weeks spent running around town dragging a truck tyre – enduring the amused grins of neighbours – seem worth it now as you slip your harness on and set out across the immense white landscape, pulling your *pulka*. How many of those smirkers have done a self-sufficient coast-to-coast traverse of the largest island in the archipelago of Svalbard, skiing across glaciers and spending each star-spangled night in a mountain tent on the ice? You're guessing none. Halfway through the four-day west–east expedition from the Barents Sea to the Greenland Sea, you feel like an Arctic explorer, alone except for the reindeer, walrus and polar bears. Hang on. Polar bears?

Too easy? Adventure tour operators also run 30-day, 550km-long, north–south traverses of Spitsbergen.

690 COAST-TO-COAST MTB ROUTE, ENGLAND

Backpack? Loaded. Pump? Check. Puncture repair kit? Got it. Pebble? Pocketed. The last is a nod to Albert Wainwright – the father of the classic 192-mile coast-to-coast walk across England – who began the tradition of carrying a pebble from St Bees beach to Robin Hood's Bay. You're about to ride roughshod on the rest of Albert's traditions, though, as you clip into your pedals, turn your back on the Irish Sea and begin a mountain-bike journey into the Lakeland Fells, over the Pennine Uplands and the Cleveland Hills, across the Yorkshire Dales and through the North Yorkshire Moors.

Tim Woodcock devised the coast-to-coast MTB ride in 1992. It shares the same trailheads and landscapes as the famous walk but follows a different course.

688 4WD AUSTRALIA'S SAVANNAH WAY

Leaving steamy Cairns and rising through the rainforests to the Tablelands that tower above the Wet Tropics, a long and rough road lies in wait. Driving in the hoofsteps of old drovers, you've got 3700km to negotiate before reaching Broome in the gorgeous Kimberley. And you're committed to taking all the adventurous options, including the Nathan River and Gibb River Roads, both offering incredibly remote driving conditions punctuated by creek crossings, fantastic fishing spots and isolated riverside camping spots. Mind the saltwater crocs.

Dissecting Australia's Top End from east to west, linking the Coral Sea and the Indian Ocean, the Savannah Way (www.savannahway.com.au) traverses Queensland, Northern Territory and Western Australia, passing through 15 national parks and five World Heritage areas.

689 THE AMERICAN DISCOVERY TRAIL

Hike it or bike it? That's the question when considering the American Discovery Trail, an epic series of trails and roads that daisy chain to form one titanic trail across 15 states from the Delmarva Peninsula on the Atlantic Ocean to the northern California coast on the Pacific. There are various route options and the trail forks into two tracks that run parallel from western Ohio to northern Colorado before joining again. If you choose to hike it you'd better have some serious annual leave accrued – it's at least 8000km (5000 miles) and can be almost 11,000km (6875 miles).

The Discovery Trail (www.discoverytrail. org) wends through 14 national parks and 16 national forests. It also traces the course of five national scenic trails, 10 national historic trails and 23 national recreation trails.

MOST MAGNIFICENT COAST-TO-COAST MISSIONS

ULTIMATE BORDER CROSSINGS

Swindlers, sweaty palms, suspect officials and stunning scenery abound as you take a trip across the world's wildest frontiers.

693 DJIBOUTI TO SOMALILAND

A wild and hairy two-day drive across the desert jam-packed into someone else's armpit might not sound like fun but it truly is an adventure. For starters, your own government doesn't even recognise one of these countries. Then there's the amazing hospitality and friendliness of a people striving for their independence, not yet jaded by tourist hordes. That's because there are no hordes, just the odd handful of intrepid souls like yourself putting up with searing days of numb bum to walk that 400m of no-man's land between border posts with a crazy smile on your face.

Streamline customs procedures by applying for a Somaliland visa online. There are no regular buses. Ask around in Djibouti City and Hargeisa for bush taxis making the border run.

691 IBRAHIM KHALIL – TURKEY TO IRAQ (KURDISTAN REGION)

Whose border is this? When you arrive in Turkish Silopi, under no circumstances utter the 'K word'. You might have told your mother you're heading to Kurdistan, but as far as the Turks are concerned, you're going to Iraq, period. If you're not searched by the Turkish border patrol then you'll probably spend the next four hours in the queue, playing backgammon with chain-smoking truck drivers. Once out of Turkey you can sit around drinking *chai* while your passport is lovingly stamped (in Arabic) with a 10-day visa for 'Republic of Iraq – Kurdistan Region'. Don't even think about heading to Baghdad.

Compared to the rest of Iraq, the Kurdish-controlled north is relatively safe. Just avoid remote areas where the PKK (Kurdistan Workers' Party) is still active.

692 AMUR RIVER – CHINA TO RUSSIA

Just getting to this border is an adventure as you ride an ever-diminishing array of transport from Beijing, eventually arriving at the grotty Amur port of Fuyuan. Every day, a set of sleek Soviet-era hydrofoils arrive from Khabarovsk, 25km downstream, primarily bringing Russian shoppers hunting for cheap Chinese consumer goods. Buying a ticket is easy, convincing the Chinese border guards to let you cross is another thing and you might need to wait a day while they get a reply from their Russian comrades. Then it's *zai jian* (good-bye) and 90 minutes and three time-zones later *dobro pozhalovat!* (welcome!) – you're in the Russian Far East and there's not a noodle in sight!

The hydrofoils run May to October. Khabarovsk has excellent transport connections including Kamchatka flights.

694 THE TORUGART PASS – KYRGYZSTAN TO CHINA

Of all China's border crossings, none is more notorious than this Silk Road route from Central Asia to separatist-leaning Kashgar. An ancient bus departs sporadically from Bishkek, climbing high into the Tien Shan where it stops in the dark, chill air, waiting for the border to open. First Kyrgyz then Russian formalities are completed before the final climb over the 3700m pass and the long descent to the Chinese control post. But a Chinese visa isn't enough; to gain entry you need a special permit, a guide and a private vehicle, all of which need to be arranged in advance. Otherwise, you're on the first truck heading back over the pass.

Search online for travel agents in Bishkek, Naryn and Kashgar that can arrange the necessary permits.

695 KAZUNGULA FERRY – BOTSWANA TO ZAMBIA

One of the word's shortest frontiers is the 150m of Zambezi River forming Botswana's border with Zambia. A dilapidated ferry takes roughly 15 minutes to make the 400m crossing. While formalities are reasonable by African standards, things start to get funky the larger your vehicle is, and trucks routinely queue for up to a week. There are plenty of 'agents' looking to help for a fee but the stout-hearted can normally manage fine without them. You could of course detour through nearby Zimbabwe, but if the locals don't want to do this, nor should you.

Get there early, avoid the truck queue on the left, head straight for the water and be prepared for some argy-bargy if you don't have an agent.

696 AMAZONAS – PERU / COLOMBIA / BRAZIL

There's no border paranoia at this junction of three Amazonian countries which includes the towns of Leticia (Colombia), Tabatinga (Brazil) and, on an island, Santa Rosa (Peru). Carved out of the Amazonian rainforest, you're free to cross between the towns as many times as you like because, other than the river, there's nowhere else to go. The only rule is to get one exit stamp from wherever you were before arriving and one entry stamp to wherever you're ultimately heading. Many locals pimp 'eco' tours into the rainforest; chose carefully as horror stories are common. Alternatively just sit back and observe nature at its most sumptuous.

Leticia is the most upmarket of the three towns but consequently also attracts the most touts.

697 EL PASO DE AGUA NEGRA – CHILE TO ARGENTINA

Achingly beautiful and seriously remote, 4765m 'Black Water Pass' is one of the highest border crossings in the Andes. The 505km route linking Chile's La Serena to San Juan in Argentina sees only a handful of cars each year and, while border formalities are straightforward, it's the (mostly) unpaved 177km between the two posts that's the fun bit. A single-vehicle track with blind hairpin-turns, plummeting drops and no crash barriers winds itself to a dizzying height that will push your vehicle and driving skills to the limit. Have we mentioned the snow and ice yet?

The pass is only open December to April. See it while you can, as a tunnel bypass is under construction. There's no public transport.

698 KHUNJERAB PASS – PAKISTAN TO CHINA

Leaving Pakistani immigration at Sust, it's not long before your heart's in your mouth as you slowly climb through countless hairpins to one of the world's highest borders. The Karakorum, Hindu Kush and Pamir mountain ranges collide in a raw, elemental jumble as waterfalls plunge dramatically into deep ravines and avalanche scree litters the road. Your driver keeps glancing up nervously as small pebbles skitter and bounce. Up you go until the needle-sharp peaks close in and your lungs burn trying to find some oxygen. Finally, around 4700m the road levels out and you reach the incongruous Chinese welcome arch. It's all downhill from here.

The border is usually open May to December and can be visited (without crossing) as a day trip from Sust.

699 PANMUNJOM – BETWEEN THE KOREAS

The tension is palpable and your heart is thumping as you enter the pale-blue building. You've sat through the video, signed the waiver that you may be subject to 'injury or death' from 'enemy action' and you're even wearing new runners. There's the microphone cord designating the actual border. There's the 'door of no return' at the other end of the room, leading directly to North Korea. And there, not more than a few feet away, is a DPRK soldier staring directly at you through the window. Unless you have a death wish, this is one border you don't want to cross.

While you can't cross the border between the two Koreas, you can enter the North by train from China and, less commonly, from Russia.

700 NORTHWEST ANGLE – CANADA TO USA

When is the border not a border? Answer: Minnesota's Northwest Angle. Left stranded above the 49th parallel due to dodgy 19th-century map-making, the Angle is cut off from the rest of mainland USA by the Lake of the Woods. The only overland route to the Angle is through Canada's Manitoba province (unless you're happy driving across a frozen lake in the middle of winter). Border control works on an honour system, with a video link in a wooden hut connecting to both US and Canadian Customs. Press the US button on entry, press the Canadian one when you leave.

Bring your angling gear as the fishing is legendary, even more so in winter out on the ice.

LONGEST TREKS

Sometimes a few days of walking isn't nearly enough. How about some trails that can keep you busy for weeks or even months?

Nepal is trekking's heartland, though sometimes it can be difficult to choose between the Everest region, the Annapurnas, Langtang, Kanchenjunga...so why not combine them all into the Great Himalaya Trail. Crossing the length of the country, from near Kanchenjunga in the east to Humla in the west, this is 1700km that'll imprint the Himalayas in your psyche for life. There are two variations: the Lower

This boot – the boot of Italy, that is – was made for walking: striding out on the Sentiero Italia

Route, averaging an altitude of around 2000m, and the at-times-remote Upper Route, crossing passes as high as 6200m and requiring some mountaineering experience and equipment. Expect to be on the trail for five months.

For more information, see http://thegreathimalayatrail.org. World Expeditions (www.worldexpeditions.com) runs an annual 152-day, end-to-end trek along the trail.

GARETH MCCORMACK/GETTY IMAGES ©

702 BICENTENNIAL TRAIL, AUSTRALIA

A big land invites big trails, and the Bicentennial Trail is Australia's longest. Beginning near Melbourne, it takes hikers through temperate Australia and high into the tropics at Cooktown in far north Queensland, a journey on foot, horseback or mountain bike of 5330km – as the kookaburra flies, it's about the equivalent of walking from London to Dubai. Created for Australia's bicentenary in 1988, it effectively follows the line of the Great Dividing Range – Australia's highest line of mountains – just in from the country's east coast. It crosses through 18 national parks, and has been designed, where possible, to follow routes used by early pioneers. Average 30km a day and you'll still be walking for six months.

The Bicentennial Trail website is www.nationaltrail.com.au.

703 E4, EUROPE

Europe is crisscrossed by a series of long-distance hiking trails, classified together as 'E' routes. There are 11 such routes, each one crossing a number of countries, stretching from the likes of Nordkapp to Sicily, and Scotland to Nice. The longest of the routes is the E4, a 10,000km-plus route from Tarifa, Spain's southernmost point, to Cyprus, arching along the way through France, Switzerland, Germany, Austria, Hungary, Romania, Bulgaria, mainland Greece and Crete (the sections through Romania and Bulgaria are incomplete). If 10,000km seems an awful long way, perhaps you could walk the E5 from Brittany to Verona? At 3000km in length, it's a mere dawdle in comparison.

Information about all E routes is available from the European Ramblers' Association (www.era-ewv-ferp.com).

704 SENTIERO ITALIA, ITALY

A country shaped like a leg is surely made for walking, and the longest walk in Italy is the country-long Sentiero Italia. Conceived as an idea in the 1980s, it begins in Trieste, tucked into the country's northeastern corner, and ends more than 6000km later at Santa Teresa Gallura on the northern tip of the island of Sardinia. Along the way it traverses the Alps, bumps south through the Apennines and crosses to Sicily and then Sardinia. Though it's broken into more than 350 distinct sections, it's as much an idea as a reality, still being far from a complete marked trail, but long sections of it do exist and others can be navigated regardless.

The horse's-mouth source is www.sentiero-italia.it; in Italian only.

705 TE ARAROA, NEW ZEALAND

Its name translates as the Long Pathway, and this trail, which was completed only in 2011 after more than 30 years of planning, is certainly that. Reaching from New Zealand's southern point at Bluff to its northern tip at Cape Reinga, Te Araroa covers around 3000km, ranging from the hard-packed Ninety Mile Beach to the Tongariro Crossing, a trail threading between the Central Plateau volcanoes that has been described as the best day walk in the world. The route through the South Island is almost entirely in the mountains, from the Richmond Range in the north to the long line of the Southern Alps through the island's spine.

Further trail details are available through the Te Araroa Trust (www.teararoa.org.nz).

706 PACIFIC CREST TRAIL, USA

One of two hiking trails – along with the Continental Divide Trail – that stretch across the USA from Mexico to Canada, the Pacific Crest Trail is a 4300km journey along the rugged tops of the Sierra Nevada and Cascade mountain ranges, crossing through three states and seven national parks, including Kings Canyon, Sequoia and Yosemite. For most hikers it's a four- to five-month commitment, and as much a challenge of logistics as fitness and endurance – resupply points are often away from the trail. For reward you get incredible mountain variety, from the deserts in the south, to the snowy tips of the Sierra Nevada, to the rainforests of the Pacific Northwest.

The Pacific Crest Trail Association (www.pcta.org) is a good resource.

707 HEYSEN TRAIL, AUSTRALIA

Australia's second great long-distance trail runs from the coast south of Adelaide high into the desert Flinders Ranges. Named after Sir Hans Heysen, a renowned painter of the areas through which the trail journeys, it's 1200km in length and is one of the most daunting walks in the country – most of it is through semiarid country. Sections of the trail are closed from about November through to March because of bushfire risk, but this is a walk you don't want to be doing in summer anyway, with maximum temperatures averaging around 34°C along its northern stretches. Most people take about 60 days to walk the trail.

The Friends of the Heysen Trail website (www.heysentrail.asn.au) has some excellent planning material.

708 TRANS CANADA TRAIL, CANADA

If you're looking for the longest of the long, meet the Trans Canada Trail. Touted as the world's longest network of trails it will eventually cover around 23,000km. By the end of 2012, almost 17,000km of path was open, with plans to complete the trail by 2017, the year of Canada's 150th anniversary of confederation. One end is in Newfoundland, the other on Vancouver Island, but if you need more, there's an offshoot heading north from Alberta into the Yukon and Northwest Territories. You might want to pack some food – the walk could take you two or three years.

The trail's official website is http://tctrail.ca.

Tongariro Crossing: tackling the Long Pathway in the Land of the Long White Cloud

709 SULTAN'S TRAIL, EUROPE

Blend history and hiking as you set out for a 2100km stroll on this new trail from Vienna to Istanbul. Crossing through six countries – Austria, Hungary, Serbia, Croatia, Bulgaria and Turkey – the trail follows (in reverse) the route taken by Ottoman sultan Süleyman the Magnificent when he besieged Vienna in 1529 and again in 1532. It finishes by his tomb in Istanbul, having started at St Stephens Cathedral in Vienna, where the church bell was cast from abandoned Ottoman cannons. The trail is as yet incomplete, but uses sections of the existing Danube Path and the E8 hiking trail.

Contrary to its militaristic raison d'être, the trail is billed as a 'path of peace'.

The trail website is www.sultanstrail.com.

710 LAND'S END TO JOHN O'GROATS, UK

Walking Great Britain from end to end is almost as old as ambition. Unlike other end-to-end country traverses, which have arisen through meticulous planning and construction, this quest has only ever existed in the mind. There is no set trail from Land's End to John O'Groats, and each walker is free to determine their own route. Typically, they will walk around 1900km, linking up existing trails such as the South West Coast Path, Cotswolds Way, Pennine Way, West Highland Way and Great Glen Way. If you like variation, it's been skateboarded, and somebody once walked it hitting a golf ball the entire way.

The Land's End John O'Groats Association (www.landsend-johnogroats-assoc.com) has produced a route information pack, available through the website.

LONGEST TREKS

BEST POWDER IN THE WORLD

Your endless winter is here with snow adventures that take you to the best pow-pow our planet has to offer. Stay frosty.

711 HELI-SKIING, UTAH, USA

While Utah doesn't get the prodigious dumps of the West Coast, the snow here is so light you'll think you are floating on feathers. The resorts – top powder kegs include Snowbird, Alta and Powder Mountain – have tremendous powder skiing. But to sample untracked fluffy bliss, you're best off taking to the air for a 20,000-vertical-foot day with a custom-crafted heli-skiing trip. It'll take you to every type of

Deep and white and pure. Niseko has enough snow to keep even the greediest powder junkies sated

terrain imaginable, from powder-packed glades to steeper bowls and chutes, and you're basically ensured untracked powder all day. The snowpack in Utah is quite unstable, so you won't always get the chance to head up in a helicopter. For more terrestrial adventures, putter out for a snowcat adventure from Powder Mountain.

Visit www.diamondpeaks.com for heli-ski options or www.powdermountain.com for cat tours.

712 ASPEN HIGHLANDS, COLORADO, USA

You can't avoid it. Aspen has been America's top ski destination – attracting the Hollywood glitterati and ski bums alike – for more than half a century. And while most come for the top-notch restaurants, outrageously opulent hotels and hob-knob opportunities, there's skiing here too. Aspen Mountain, Snowmass and Buttermilk offer some fun runs, but the real snow riders all head to Aspen Highlands for the best hardcore terrain in the state on powder troughs like Highland Bowl, Olympic Bowl and Steeplechase. Make sure you leave enough in the tank for après-ski drinks at the Hotel Jerome or Little Nell.

You can fly to Aspen (hopefully on a G6), or you might want to take a shuttle from Denver (2½ hours away). Visit www.aspensnowmass.com for more on skiing, lodging and looking good.

713 HELI-SKIING, VALDEZ, ALASKA, USA

If heli-skiing is bad-ass, than Valdez must be super bad. This once-in-a-lifetime ski adventure takes you to what is perhaps the steepest, deepest, biggest and baddest ski terrain in the world. Over 1000 inches of snow falls on Alaska's Chugach Mountains each year, and there are about 2 million acres of glaciated peaks to explore with your own private guide and helicopter. The operator will tailor a trip to your needs and wants – most deals run for five to seven days – and take you around 20,000 vertical feet over a week. You can go steep with 50-degree white-knuckle couloirs or work on your powder eights on 6000ft top-to-tail cruises. Needless to say, this is an adventure for expert skiers only.

Most operators run trips from February to May. Check out www.valdezheliskiguides.com for more info.

714 NISEKO, JAPAN

There may be better resorts in the world – in fact, there may be plenty of them – but Niseko Ski Resort on Hokkaido has the second-highest average snowfalls of any resort in the world, averaging 595in of the white stuff every year, so it is worth the trip. The five ski areas of the Niseko megaresort, Annupuri, Higashiyama, Hirafu, Hanazono and Moiwa, all offer easy and efficient lift access with 27 chairs and three gondolas. The runs are pretty short, averaging 900m, but there's a sweet hot spring nearby and the steepest run tips the scales at 37 degrees. Plus there's night skiing.

To get here, fly to New Chitose Airport. Skijapan.com provides some basics on the resort.

255

715 LECH, AUSTRIA

Lech and Zürs get more snow than any European ski resort, making this a top Austrian pick. Most people start in the posh village of Lech (using it as a base to explore the Zürs and Arlberg ski areas). Lech is the only resort in Austria to offer heli-skiing so you can almost guarantee fresh tracks. There are also plenty of short hikes to nongroomed off-piste areas that will sate your addiction to the white powdery stuff. The best way to explore Lech's steeps is with a guide. The slopes are avalanche controlled, but not patrolled – watch for hidden obstacles.

This is Austria's most popular resort so check aggregators for deals. More info is available at www.ski-lech.com.

716 WHITEWATER SKI RESORT, NELSON, BRITISH COLUMBIA, CANADA

Whitewater may not be the biggest ski resort in Western Canada (that honour falls on Whistler Blackcomb) but it does get an amazing amount of the white stuff – more than 40ft a year. The resort only has three chairlifts and a tow bar, with a meagre 1184 acres of skiable areas. But good things do come in small packages, and Whitewater's mixed terrain of open glades, chutes and bowls makes it easy to find freshies even a week after a storm. The resort's inland location in the Selkirk Mountains makes for drier snow than the coastal BC offerings.

256

The resort is a long way from everything, so consider a week-long trip. Bring extra ski clothes; you'll be wet by the end of the day. Visit www.skiwhitewater.com.

717 SKI PORTILLO, CHILE

It snows over 8m (27ft) a year at Chile's star resort, known for its dry snow, sunny days, fun nightlife and stellar off-piste terrain. You can hire a guide or go it alone to ski the famous Primavera and Kilometro Lanzado runs on your never-ending winter adventure. While the resort offers 760m (2500ft) of vertical drops and spectacular Andean vistas, you may wish to take to the sky, the way the condors do, and hire a helicopter for a day. While a day of heli-skiing here will cost you a few pesos, it's definitely one for the bucket list.

Ski Portillo (www.skiportillo.com) is an easy two-hour drive from the capital, Santiago.

718 LA GRAVE, FRANCE

France has plenty of great ski areas. The resort-minded head en masse to Chamonix and other Alps hotspots every winter (and sometimes in the summer) but for a big-mountain experience that'll set your mind on fire, La Grave is your spot. You get here from a cozy 12th-century village, heading up at dawn with your guide (de rigueur) by a three-stage gondola. There are only a couple of official runs on the glaciated mountain and where you go is up to your abilities, your imagination and your guide, who will help you stay safe in this crevassed area.

La Grave isn't far from Grenoble, your easy entry point. The resort's website (www.la-grave.com) offers more information.

719 WOLF CREEK SKI AREA, COLORADO, USA

Colorado gets some of the lightest, driest snow in the world and nowhere is the champagne powder better than the small throwback ski area of Wolf Creek. The area opened way back in 1939 and still retains some of that old-time feel, plus its ideal location in the San Juan Mountains gives the resort an average of 465in of natural snow each year – the most of any Colorado resort. The resort has just five chairs, but from the top you can hike into the back country for steep glade and bowl skiing in places like the Bonanza Bowl, Exhibition Ridge and the Peak Chutes.

Get info on Colorado's major resorts at www.coloradoski.com or visit www.wolfcreekski.com.

720 KIRKWOOD, CALIFORNIA, USA

The rugged peaks of California's Sierra Nevada Mountain Range offer some of the steepest ski terrain in the continental US. While there are plenty of resorts in the Lake Tahoe area, Kirkwood is a best bet for ultra-steep terrain and cool couloirs,

GABE ROGEL/GETTY IMAGES ©

Loads of chilly fun! Portillo offers fantastic nightlife, heli-skiing options and Andean vistas where you can soar like a condor

plus a laid-back feel that other resorts in the area lack. After a day or two exploring Wagner Wheel and Sentinel Bowls plus an obligatory huck off the massive Wave cornice, head out with Expedition Kirkwood for a day of snowcat-skiing in the back country. They give you a guide, avalanche gear and take you to some of the gnarliest gnar-gnar Kirkwood has to offer.

Kirkwood is a 30-minute drive from the cheap hotels of South Lake Tahoe. You can stay at the resort, too. Visit www. kirkwood.com for details.

BEST POWDER IN THE WORLD

ESSENTIAL AFRICAN ADVENTURES

Forget the pith helmet but dust off your hiking boots, tap into your inner explorer and head off on these iconic African adventures.

721 'CAPTURING' ANIMALS ON PHOTOGRAPHIC SAFARIS, AFRICA

Capturing and shooting wild animals has never been so fun. Say what? Photographic safaris give snap-happy folk and animal lovers the wonderful opportunity to 'catch' wild animals, from hippos to impala, zebra to leopards, as well as the African wilderness and can't-get-any-redder sunsets. A qualified wildlife photographer-cum-nature-guide gives one-to-one tuition to

Nothing compares to coming face to face with a wild elephant in Tanzania

ARIADNE VAN ZANDBERGEN/GETTY IMAGES ©

help you best capture your subjects, whether you're nestled in a bird hide or perched on a jeep, tracking on foot or pottering around your camp. It's an extraordinary way to experience micro and macro views of the world way beyond the camera.

Expect some early morning starts (dawn is a popular time for birds; dusk for drinking animals). See Botswana-based Pangolin Photo Safaris (www.pangolinphoto.com).

722 TREKKING IN THE SAHARA DESERT, TAMANRASSET, ALGERIA

Calling all desert lovers. This place rocks. Rising out of the sands in Algeria's south, the Hoggar is among the most impressive mountain ranges in the Sahara Desert. Trekking here with local Tuareg guides is like journeying through a magical kingdom from

ancient times. You start at the town of Tamanrasset and head around the Atakor Massif, weaving your way through colourful prehistoric petroglyphs painted onto the rock, *gheltas* (water holes), dunes and 'forests' of basalt pinnacles. You can puff your way to the top of Algeria's highest summit, Jabal Tahat (2908m), and meditate over the sunset on the high plateau of Assekrem.

See www.keadventure.com for info. Many local travel agencies also organise tours. Expect to walk for five hours each day.

724 ELEPHANT SAFARI, BOTSWANA

Hear ye, elephant lovers. There's no better, or quirkier, way to steep yourself in the Botswanan wilderness than atop an African elephant. Not only will you view wildlife from pachyderm heights,

but you'll interact with, swim and walk alongside your elephant and its herd, gaining insight into the behaviour of precocious adolescents and the matriarch. (All this, after a personal introduction to the elephants!). Oh, and did we mention discussing conservation with the local researchers and learning about elephant behaviour? Engaging with these ultraintelligent, extremely sensitive mammals is as close with nature as you'll ever get.

Botswana is one of the few places where you can experience an elephant safari. See www.abucamp.com.

725 4WD THE SKELETON COAST, NAMIBIA

Four-wheel-drive explorers in Namibia make a beeline for the Skeleton Coast, an ultraremote desert coastline with misty beaches strewn with bleached whale bones and rusted shipwrecks, the legacy of a bygone whaling industry. Early Portuguese sailors called it As Areias do Inferno, 'the Sands of Hell'. Fortunately these days it's a slightly different story. Drive through some of world's most hauntingly beautiful landscapes along the beach and the hinterland, between sand dunes, across saltpans, by fossil beds, up mountains and through towering canyons. For an exceptional treat, a trip in a light aircraft gives you a mind-boggling, Dali-esque view of this desolate, magnificent lunarscape.

Tour companies operate out of Windhoek. Cardboard Box Travel Shop (www.namibian.org) is a good place to start. Skeleton Coast Safaris (www.skeletoncoastsafaris.com) run awe-inspiring land and air safaris.

723 WALK ON THE WILD SIDE IN TANZANIA

If you really want to get in touch with nature, slip on your walking shoes and take to the Serengeti, Tanzania's most famous national park. Here, extraordinary wilderness walking safaris take you across the park's savannah and along river courses. Skilled Maasai and other rangers chat about the ecosystem, from zebra stripes to ant mounds, acacia trees to wild grasses. Of course, there's the region's famous wildebeest migration (see below) but there's a lot, lot more. After a day of multisensory stimulation, doze off in your tent to the sounds of distant lion roars and let Africa continue to weave its magic.

Only selected, responsible operators are permitted to take Serengeti walking safaris; walks vary, from hourly hikes to multiday camping trips.

726 WITNESS THE WILDEBEEST MIGRATION FROM HORSEBACK, MAASAI MARA, KENYA

If ever there were a wildlife extravaganza, the wildebeest migration is it. Each year from July to October, more than 1.5 million wildebeest and zebra head off in pursuit of the green pastures of the Maasai Mara. Wildebeest herds storm down river banks into crocodile-infested waters while opportunistic lions lie in wait. The best way to see this spectacle is on horseback. Why? Wild animals are not afraid of horses, giving you the most up-close-and-personal, natural experience possible. You can gallop alongside herds of wildebeest during the migration or literally go wild by getting off the beaten track in places that you can't reach on foot or by jeep.

Some riding experience is recommended; this isn't for the faint-hearted. See www.safarisunlimited.com.

727 DISCOVERING THE OASES OF EGYPT

Get in touch with your nomadic past and head out in a jeep beyond Egypt's ancient pyramids, sphinx and Nile River Valley to the Oases in the Western Desert. These amazing, isolated oases appear – and function – like miraculous kingdoms in the sand. But they are very real. At Siwa Oasis wander through the date plantations and a 13th-century fortress; in Bahariya soak in the hot water springs; at Farafra photograph the incredible formations of the White Desert. Dakhla, too, delivers the archetypal image: lush palm groves, orchards and over 600 hot springs.

It's difficult to cover all oases in one short circuit but you can visit several on a tour; a reliable operator is Desert Eco Tours (www.desertecotours.com/English/western_desert.asp).

728 KAYAKING IN MADAGASCAR

Madagascar's white, sandy beaches are one thing, its wildlife is quite another. Forget the jungle trips – jump in a kayak and start paddling. This not only gives you the opportunity to explore Madagascar's southeast archipelago via waterways, but you'll head through lush mangroves and the secluded lakes of the St Luce Nature Reserve to catch a glimpse of the country's wild lemurs, giant chameleons, rare birds and unique flora. As well as kayaking,

Leap of faith. Wildebeest crossing the Mara River on their mighty annual migration across the grasslands of Kenya

head out on rainforest walks, snorkelling and boat trips (whale season is June to December). That is, if you can pull yourself away from chatting to the welcoming locals.

Madagascar's kayaking safaris are suitable for anyone who is reasonably fit. See www.jenmansafaris.com.

729 CAMEL TREK ACROSS MOROCCO

Saddle up and climb aboard. A camel trek is the most traditional and atmospheric way to experience the unfurling magic of the Sahara Desert. While, for some, riding isn't necessarily easy on the bum, it is a 'must do' for those travellers who want to experience the lifestyle of the region's Berber nomads. This goes way beyond shimmering sand dunes. Think kasbahs, oases, orange sunrises and red sunsets. After a

day loping 'on the hump', you relax at your Bedouin tent and watch the explosion of stars appear. Finally you fall asleep to the distant sound of tribal drumming and dream of your desert ancestors.

The best time of year for camel trekking is September to February. See www.cameltrekking.com.

730 SLAVE HISTORY IN GHANA

Warning: this is a heart-wrenching experience. By the 17th century, Cape Coast and Elmina made up the largest slave-trading centres in West Africa. Hundreds of thousands of Africans were forced through the dungeons of the towns' forts and loaded onto slave ships. These days the forts are beautifully preserved; Elmina Castle is now a Unesco World Heritage site. The forts

reveal this painful history: the cast-iron ball and chain where slaves were shackled; dark, tiny cells; and the grim Door of No Return – the last door through which captives walked to be loaded onto ships before leaving Africa forever.

Local tours can be organised in Cape Coast and Elmina.

ESSENTIAL
AFRICAN
ADVENTURES

MOST EXCITING MODERN ADVENTURERS

The age of exploration is not dead, as proved by this gaggle of young-gun adventurers.

733 DAVID CORNTHWAITE

Not satisfied by taking on one major mission, Cornthwaite has set himself an ongoing challenge to complete 25 expeditions of 1000 miles or more using a variety of nontraditional methods of human- and nature-powered transport. To date his trips have included a 5789km skateboarding journey across the width of Australia from Perth to Brisbane; a record-breaking 3846km (2404-mile) source-to-sea expedition along the Mississippi River on a stand-up paddleboard; a 1602km (1001-mile) 58-day swim along the Lower Missouri River; a 2233km (1396-mile) tandem-bicycle ride from Vancouver to Vegas and a 1600km (1003-mile) bike-car pedal from Memphis to Miami.

www.davecornthwaite.com

731 ED STAFFORD

There have been several source-to-sea paddling descents of the Amazon River since Polish kayaker Piotr Chmielinski and American journalist Joe Kane first nailed their names to the feat in 1985–6, but only one man has walked the entire length of the mighty river: Ed Stafford. English explorer and former British Army captain Stafford began his riverbank stroll with a friend, Luke Collyer, on 2 April 2008 in Peru. Three months later Collyer bailed but Stafford continued with Peruvian forestry worker Gadiel 'Cho' Sanchez Rivera by his side. Some 860 days after setting off – having walked 6000 miles, battled all sorts of exotic beasties and after being accused of murder en route – Stafford popped out on Brazil's Atlantic coast and was promptly named European Adventurer of the Year 2011.

www.edstafford.org

732 JUSTIN JONES & JAMES CASTRISSION

This pair of Australian adventurers hit headlines in 2008 after becoming the first to paddle between Australia and New Zealand, crossing 3318km of the Tasman Sea. Taking place shortly after fellow Australian adventurer Andrew MacAuley was lost while attempting to sea-kayak across the Tasman, the expedition saw them endure 10m swells, savage winds, adverse currents, and severe food and sleep deprivation. They also walked 2275km from the edge of Antarctica to the south pole and back, losing 50kg between them on the 89-day trek. In a stunning display of sportsmanship, Norwegian skier Aleksander Gamme, who was ahead of the pair on his rival solo bid to be the first to complete an unsupported return expedition to the pole, waited so they could walk to Hercules Inlet together and share the honours.

casandjonesy.com.au

734 SÍLVIA VIDAL

One of the world's best big-wall climbers, Barcelona-born Vidal excels at multiday solo ascents and often spends weeks living on a portaledge. She has completed first ascents and repeated super-difficult multibivouac routes all over the planet, including in the Indian Himalaya, Karakorum, Baffin Island, Cordillera Blanca, Patagonia and Main de Fatima. Notable achievements include a first ascent of Brakk Zang and a solo ascent of Shipton Spire (both in Pakistan), the latter involving 21 days on the wall with no communication. She also established a new route on the east face of Huascaran North (Cordillera Blanca, 18 days on the wall) and completed a solo climb of a virgin wall in Kinnaur Valley (Kailash Parbat massif, 25 days on the wall).

www.vidalsilvia.com

735 STEVE FISHER

Fisher started kayaking competitively before moving into adventure- and expedition-based missions. The South African has thrice been voted the world's best all-rounder by his paddling peers and has made around 100 first descents in almost 50 countries. Notable descents include the Irrawaddy in Burma, the Salween in China and the Yarlung Tsangpo in Tibet. The pinnacle of his career came in 2011, with the successful running of the Inga Rapids on the Congo River – a furious section of whitewater that had killed everyone else who'd attempted it, and which forced even the explorer Henry Stanley to concede defeat.

www.stevefisher.com

736 FELIX BAUMGARTNER

In terms of pushing the exploratory envelope, it's hard to go past this Austrian skydiver and BASE jumper. Known as Fearless Felix, Baumgartner set a world record for skydiving in 2012, jumping from a helium balloon 39km up in the stratosphere and plummeting to Earth at an estimated speed of 1342 km per hour (834 mph, Mach 1.24), becoming the first person to break the sound barrier without vehicular power. Baumgartner previously set world records for the highest parachute jump from a building (Petronas Towers, Kuala Lumpur), the lowest recorded BASE jump (29 metres, from the hand of the Christ the Redeemer statue in Rio de Janeiro) and by skydiving across the English Channel using specially made carbon-fibre wings.

www2.felixbaumgartner.com

737 ROZ SAVAGE

At 34, unhappy with life in suburban England, Savage made an abrupt decision – she quit her day job as a management consultant and became an ocean rower. Three oceans, 15,000 miles, over 500 sea days and approximately 5 million oarstrokes later, she's one of the most accomplished rowers in history and holds several world records – including being the first woman to row solo across the Atlantic, Pacific and Indian Oceans. Savage has used her expeditions to highlight plastic pollution of the world's waterways (among other environmental issues) and when not in her 23-foot rowboat she's active on terra firma as a United Nations Climate Hero.

www.rozsavage.com

738 MIKE LIBECKI

The architect and executioner of over 45 eclectic expeditions around the world, Mike Libecki did a first-ascent climb of a 2000-foot tower in Borneo, risked avalanches while completing a series of first descents in Afghanistan's Koh-e Baba mountains by snowboard and then dodged Taliban operatives to kite-ski across remote mountain lakes. He then headed north to Franz Josef Land to stand-up paddleboard around the icy archipelago and knock off a few first ascents, before visiting Greenland to establish a new mountain route, and then the Philippines for jungle climbing in the Cordillera Mountains. It was all capped off with a trip to Antarctica's Queen Maud Land where he joined a team climbing some previously unscaled blades of rock. And this was all in 2012.

mikelibecki.com

739 ALASTAIR HUMPHREYS

Humphreys' major expeditions are impressive but his 'Year of Microadventure' was truly innovative. The project saw him undertake a series of adventures on home soil (in the UK) during 2011, while encouraging others to get outside their comfort zone and similarly explore their backyard. Prior to this, Humphreys' macro adventures included a four-year 73,600km (46,000-mile) round-the-planet bicycle journey, a run across the Sahara desert, a rowing trip across the English Channel, a walking traverse of India, a packrafting expedition across Iceland and a 45-day trans-Atlantic row.

www.alastairhumphreys.com

740 FREYA HOFFMEISTER

In 2009, Freya Hoffmeister completed a 332-day solo circumnavigation of Australia by sea kayak, surviving shark attacks and the threat of saltwater crocodiles to become the first woman and the second person ever to achieve this phenomenal feat. She shaved 28 days off Paul Caffyn's time by cutting across the Gulf of Carpentaria in an eight-day crossing, during which she snatched micromoments of sleep by laying back across her kayak and using paddle floats – one on each blade – to balance. This expedition followed the German's record breaking 70-day solo circumnavigation of New Zealand's South Island in 2008. Next up: a mammoth circumnavigation of South America.

freyahoffmeister.com

BEST BIRDING IN HIGHLANDS AND ISLANDS

Close encounters of the bird kind: a field guide to finding (feathered) friends in far-flung places.

741 LINE ISLANDS WARBLER, KIRITIMATI (CHRISTMAS ISLAND), PACIFIC OCEAN, KIRIBATI

This admittedly undistinguished warbler is the only native land bird on Kiritimati, the world's biggest coral atoll. But it's endemic to only two small islands in the vastness of the Pacific Ocean and is a noteworthy tick off the birding bucket-list. Resident colonies of seabirds – frigate birds, terns and boobies in their thousands – afford plenty of other feathered action. The birds' presence is a victory over isolation and geography, and your presence will feel like a victory too. The flight schedule is whimsical and most locals travel by sea; the occasional yachtie makes landfall.

See Air Pacific (www.airpacific.com) for current flight information. If you're time rich and cash poor, ask about infrequent boat services to and from Tarawa.

742 NOISY SCRUB-BIRD, WA, AUSTRALIA

As you might expect from its name, you're likely to hear this bird before you see it. If you see it, that is.

743 GREATER BIRD OF PARADISE, WEST PAPUA, INDONESIA

Getting to the remote landscapes where these magnificent birds live is almost as exciting as actually finding the bird. The direction is usually up: up-river, uphill and peering upwards in rainforest. Villagers will know of any local dancing trees, the morning and evening venues where groups of preening, prancing males to strut their stuff in front of the females. Birds, that is, though there's probably a spot where local boys and girls do the same. As you'll likely be staying in a village, you may even get a chance to join them.

Wasur National Park near Merauke, the easternmost town in Indonesia, is a good place to start birding. If you don't speak Indonesian, take a point-and-ask picture dictionary.

The call is unmistakable; if you've never heard it before, listen for a beautiful and extraordinarily ear-piercing song emanating from thick heathland scrub and you'll know you're in the right place. But this bird is sneaky and camera-shy. One of the most sought-after endemic birds in Australia, you'll have to be quick to spot it dashing, road-runner style, across gaps between islands of bush along a tiny stretch of Western Australia's isolated south coast.

Cheyne's Beach Caravan Park has info about the most recent sightings; ask at reception for the bird file behind the desk. See www. cheynesbeachcaravanpark.com.au.

MARIA ISMAWI/GETTY IMAGES ©

The trek to spot the greater bird of paradise can be as rewarding as the sighting itself

Quetzal quest: with its shimmering emerald plumage this forest-dwelling bird lives up to its 'resplendent' moniker

744 RESPLENDENT QUETZAL, COSTA RICA

Picture a flamboyant punky hairdo, dyed bright green. Add emerald zigzag epaulettes on a scarlet belly and long tail streamers and, voila, it's a Resplendent Quetzal in breeding plumage. While usually foraging in inconveniently high trees (be prepared for the occupational hazard of birder's stiff neck), these, um, resplendent birds often nest in rather more conveniently placed fence posts and tree stumps; look for the tail feathers poking out. If you're in the right part of the country – cloud forest and its fringes in the highlands – your host is sure to know the nearest likely nesting site.

Breeding season is March to June. Head for rugged Monteverde Cloud Forest Reserve or low-key villages around Cerro de la Muerte. Pack a waterproof poncho.

745 ORANGE DOVE, FIJI

Are those feathers? Or is it wearing a wig made of fluorescent orange hair? This improbably coloured bird blends equally improbably into its forest home on several smaller Fijian islands. Your first indication that it's around may be its call – a repeated click, coughed out by the male. On Taveuni Island, the predatory (introduced) mongoose is absent, so wildlife is less fearful and more abundant than elsewhere. Most visitors hug the coastline, but venture inland and you'll find lush forests and well-maintained bush-walking tracks that make birding here a calm, quiet pleasure, albeit a sweaty one.

Head to Taveuni's Bouma National Heritage Park to try birdwatching on rugged Des Voeux Peak or on the Vidawa Rainforest Trail. More at www.bnhp.org.

746 PEL'S FISHING OWL, BOTSWANA

There's an extra frisson of anticipation when watching birds around water in Africa. Are those ripples on the surface of the river from a heron spearing fish on the shoreline or is a hippo about to surface next to your canoe? If the waterway's lined with trees and you're beside it with a spotlight after nightfall, you can double the anticipation factor, especially if a wailing scream, followed by a series of booms, emerges from the dark. The former is a young (and hungry) Pel's Fishing Owl, the latter is the parent birds' reply.

Seasonal islands in the meandering Okavango Delta are the place to look for this species (and the delta's 400 or so others). Visit www.botswanatourism.co.bw.

747 PINK FLAMINGO, FRANCE

Immortalised as the Queen of Hearts' croquet mallet in *Alice in Wonderland*, the pink flamingo remains something of an eccentric oddity. Revisit the book's illustrations before you visit the real thing on the briny lagoons of the world's largest river delta in the Camargue. Rather than whacking croquet balls, their flattened, upside-down bill is handy for filtering small critters from shallow swamps. They're here all year in small numbers and up to 10,000 gather during peak breeding season to parachute in and cosy up in photogenic silhouettes against the sunset.

Parc Ornithologique de Pont de Gau is 40km drive from Arles, Provence. Breeding season is November to March. Take a serious mosquito repellent.

748 RED-BREASTED MERGANSER, CHRISTMAS ISLAND, CANADA

Widespread in the northern hemisphere, this duck is one of few that stays around when most water bodies in north-east Canada freeze over. Their red breasts offer a welcome flash of colour on the sheltered winter waters of Bras d'Or lake. Join the (very) few hardy human visitors that brave the chilly weather and you'll soon spot the few hardy waterbirds that do too. Not much else will be moving out in the open except you and them, bound by a sense of both solitude and solidarity in the wild snowscape.

Dreaming of a white Christmas on this Christmas Island? Stay at Hector's Arm B&B (www.bbcanada.com/hectorsarm). The nearest airport and car hire is in Sydney, Nova Scotia.

749 GOLDEN BOSUNBIRD, CHRISTMAS ISLAND, INDIAN OCEAN, AUSTRALIA

The stunning plumage of this unique tropicbird gives it its local name, the golden bosun. Endemic to this isolated island, it's a beautiful exhibitionist and its tail-streaming, low-flying aerial displays are in your face. Sometimes literally; bike riders beware. It nests at a low level, mostly on sea cliffs and in tree hollows but occasionally on public paths (handy for photographers). And there's nothing quite like floating on your back in limpid water, looking at golden bosuns and black frigate birds – also endemic – outlined against turquoise sky.

Birding's less fun during the December to April heavy wet season. Most flights leave from Perth, Western Australia. More information is at www.christmas.net.au.

750 WESTERN TRAGOPAN, INDIA

This rarest of all pheasants has a mix-and-match design with a patchworked red and orange head above a black and white polka-dot body. Hiking high into the forests of the Great Himalayan National Park and Kullu Valley, you can give your neck a rest and look down into the understorey where the birds feed. And look outwards too, to saw-toothed, snow-capped mountains.

The park is closed in winter. For fees, access details and dates, see www.greathimalayannationalpark.com.

BEST BIRDING IN HIGHLANDS AND ISLANDS

BEST MARINE ENCOUNTERS

Dive in and get up close and personal with the planet's fascinating array of marine creatures.

751 FLOATING FLY-BYS WITH MANTA RAYS, FIJI

The Pacific nation of Fiji is exceedingly laid back, but after swimming with manta rays with wingspans of up to five metres it's quite OK for visitors to the Yasawa islands to be more than a little excited. Nature's largest rays – reputedly the inspiration for the iconic shape of the stealth bomber – move with surprising speed through the tropical waters. Their underwater action is almost bird-like, with wingtips propelling them gracefully and purposefully. Keeping up with them isn't easy so boat trips deliver swimmers in front of where the rays are heading. Time it right and you can get very close.

From April to October, manta rays congregate in the feeding channels around Naviti Island and Drawaqa Island in Fiji's Yasawa group. Contact www. barefootislandfiji.com.

752 COMMUNING WITH TUNA, SOUTH AUSTRALIA

How do like your tuna? Lightly seared with a soy, ginger and lime sauce or plated gracefully as gossamer-thin layers of sashimi? How about speeding past your face underwater at 70 km per hour? Swimming with fish in Port Lincoln's tuna farms is akin to crossing a busy street in a big Asian city. Like traffic in Hanoi or Bangkok, the fishy commotion effortlessly parts and the sleek beasties divert carefully around swimmers without actually touching. Some tuna weigh up to 150 kg and a steady supply of pilchards keeps them eating and moving so the water is almost white-water, roiling with a restless energy from their smoky-black piscine muscularity.

See www.swimwiththetuna.com.au. Go tuna crazy at Port Lincoln's annual Tunarama Festival (www.tunarama.net) around Australia Day weekend every January.

753 SWIMMING WITH DOLPHINS, NEW ZEALAND

Yes, it can be a long journey to New Zealand but when the reward is swimming with the world's smallest and rarest dolphin, it's a trip worth taking. The Hector's dolphin is only found in New Zealand waters and stunning Akaroa harbour is the location for regular tours. The harbour is the flooded crater of an extinct volcano, so the dolphin experience often takes place in sheltered waters framed by spectacular volcanic cliffs. If you're keen to experience more Southern Hemisphere marine thrills on New Zealand's South Island, also make time for sea kayaking around Akaroa's quiet bays.

Go overboard with Hector's dolphins from October to April; see Black Cat Cruises (www.blackcat.co.nz). If you're there in October, don't miss the biannual French Fest celebrating Akaroa's Gallic heritage.

754 EXPLORING THE DEEP BLUE WITH HUMPBACK WHALES, NIUE

Defiantly alone in the planet's biggest ocean, the Pacific island of Niue (population 1400) is the world's smallest self-governing nation. But despite the compact isle's remote and rocky isolation, humpback whales are regular return visitors from their nutrient-rich feeding grounds in the Southern Ocean. Dropping carefully into the waters above them is a humbling experience. Newly born calves nestle close to their leviathan mothers in shallow waters just fifty metres off Niue's cave-studded coastline. Diffuse Pacific sunlight refracts through crystalline waters to project whale-shaped shadows on the ocean floor, and languid flicks of their giant tails propel them slowly and silently through the sea.

Humpback whales calve in Niue's warm and clear waters from June to October. Book a snorkelling trip with Niue Dive (www.dive.nu).

JEFF ROTMAN/GETTY IMAGES ©

One shark you can swim alongside of with complete peace of mind. The whale shark is a gentle giant

755 SPLASH OUT WITH SEA LIONS, SOUTH AUSTRALIA

Say g'day – with a broad Aussie accent – to some of the most curious and playful creatures in the Great Australian Bight. Baird Bay Ocean Eco Experience has been visiting with sea lions since 1992; tours also include swimming with dolphins. The surrounding waters are shark territory but interactions with the sea lions take place in safe and shallow rock pools around the coast, making this an ideal experience for families. Wetsuits are provided but bring along an underwater camera for surprising sea lion portraits.

Exciting sea lion adventures can be undertaken year round in Baird Bay; see www.bairdbay.com. Visit in summer to see the stunning Eyre Peninsula at its best

756 HANGING OUT WITH WHALE SHARKS, WESTERN AUSTRALIA

If Western Australia were a separate country it would be the world's tenth-largest nation, so it's appropriate the ocean's largest fish chooses to drop by the World Heritage–listed Ningaloo Marine Park each year. These gentle giants of the sea – up to 10m long – return for seasonal feeding in the Indian Ocean's nutrient-rich waters. Snorkelling with the creatures, you quickly segue from anxious to blissful. The worryingly familiar profile of a shark, only much larger than expected, emerges from Ningaloo's sun-dappled depths but the huge creatures drift innocuously past, their expansive mouths hoovering up nutritious coral spawn.

Whale sharks return to Ningaloo Marine Park from April to July. From June to November manta rays and humpback whales also swing by.

269

Jumpin' jellyfish, Batman! Well no, quietly drifting jellyfish in Ongeim'l Tketau, Palau

757 PEACEFUL DRIFTING WITH JELLYFISH, PALAU

Palau's jellyfish lake – Ongeim'l Tketau in the local language – is less than six hectares (14 acres) in area but that's still enough to accommodate around 10 million jellyfish. The lake's population of endemic golden jellyfish actually waxes and wanes – 31 million were estimated to be in the forest-clad waters in 2005. Every day the jellyfish follow the sun to make a 1km migration across the lake and a lack of natural predators means they have evolved without being poisonous. Recommended form for swimmers is to drift languidly in the water, reducing the potential to damage the delicate creatures.

Get jiggy with jellyfish from December to April, avoiding Palau's rainy season from May to December and the possibility of typhoons from July to October.

758 'OH, THE HUGE MANATEES' IN FLORIDA

Even a manatee gets chilly in Florida, especially during winter. That's why the warm springs of the Crystal River National Wildlife Refuge are such an important habitat for the West Indian manatee. More than 30 natural springs create a consistent temperature of 22°C (72°F), comfortably tepid to support the survival of this endangered species. Manatees aren't too keen on the bubbles from scuba tanks so a leisurely snorkelling trip is the best option for interaction. A wetsuit is also recommended – the water's warm, but not *that* warm – and the manatees are surprisingly curious and social.

Visit from mid-October to mid-March when up to 400 manatees crowd around warmer underwater springs during winter cold snaps. See Birds Underwater Inc (www.birdsunderwater.com).

759 DIVING WITH FUR SEALS FAMILIES, NEW ZEALAND

Near the South Island coastal town of Kaikoura, a playground for New Zealand fur seals is concealed in the knotty tangle of kelp surrounding Barney's Rock. Adolescent seals spin, dive, and lay back amidst this labyrinthine marine forest but it's the younger seals that seem most interested in the wetsuited interlopers floating amongst them. Curious pups sweep recklessly towards swimmers, make underwater eye contact and then dart playfully away into an inky darkness broken by occasional beams of light. Older seals laze in the sun on the rocks above, throwing an occasional languid glance towards the energetic marine nursery below.

Book with Seal Swim Kaikoura (www. sealswimkaikoura.co.nz) from October to May. Kaikoura is also a good spot to tuck into local *kai moana* (seafood) including crayfish.

760 PADDLING WITH PENGUINS, GALAPAGOS ISLANDS

It's around Isla Bartoleme's crescent-shaped beach where the true diversity of the Galapagos Islands is brought home. Equipped only with snorkelling gear, you can encounter many species on their own terms in the water. Harmless reef sharks mingle with flightless cormorants and curious sea lions, and Humboldt penguins zip past in the crystalline depths, celebrating an equatorial environment that's only possible because of the cool waters of the Humboldt current. Awkward on land, they're entirely different creatures after sliding their plump but sleek bodies into the water, where clumsy Chaplin-esque shuffling is replaced with effortless underwater action.

Visit from June to November, when the cooler Humboldt Current flows north from Antarctica to enrich the ocean with nutrients and increase marine life.

BEST MARINE ENCOUNTERS

SENSATIONAL SNOWSHOE ESCAPADES

One of the most accessible ways to explore mountain terrain and amazing winter wilderness: discover the world of snowshoeing.

763 LAKE LADOGA, RUSSIA

Walk along the frozen surface of Lake Ladoga and you are tracing a unique piece of Russian history. The largest lake in Europe, Ladoga served during WWII as the lifeline to a besieged Leningrad (now Saint Petersburg), connecting it to the rest of the Soviet Union. A breathtaking collection of pine forests and high rocky ridges, it's the ideal backdrop for a snowshoeing expedition. Russia does pretty well for snow, with over 70 percent of the country permanently covered in the white stuff. Base yourself in Lumivaara not far from the Finnish border in an area that boasts over 60,000 lakes.

Snowshoeing is gaining popularity in Russia with more equipment available in outdoor stores and a growing number of clubs and races.

761 HARDANGERVIDDA PLATEAU, NORWAY

Snowmobile into a remote Norwegian cabin in the middle of Europe's largest mountain plateau and you're in the perfect terrain for a snowshoeing adventure. This is an extreme Arctic wilderness, home to the Telemark region, made famous by Norwegian resistance fighters in WWII. Taking your first steps on the white stuff, you're confronted by mountainous landscapes, frozen lakes and snow-laden forests. Sharpen your winter skills here, or to simply wander out to a lake and fish for your supper. Overnight trips can take you camping deep in the wilds with the chance of catching the Northern Lights.

With average temperatures of -20°C, warm clothing is obviously required but you'll find the drier cold relatively easy to manage.

762 WHITE MOUNTAINS, NEW HAMPSHIRE

Once the holder of the highest wind speed recorded on earth (231mph on the summit of Mt Washington), New Hampshire's White Mountains are famed for their unpredictable weather. Temperatures can plummet and storms quickly move in, so this is an area that doesn't favour the ill-prepared. But it's a magnet for outdoor enthusiasts because it holds snow longer than most US regions, and offers superb summit hikes and challenging trails. To enjoy them safely you need good winter navigation, sound avalanche assessment skills and to ensure you're carrying sufficient clothing, shelter and food.

Carry and know how to use a map and compass. Reception is patchy here so do not rely on mobile phones to get you out of trouble.

764 QUEENSTOWN, NEW ZEALAND

In Queenstown, the world of heli-snowshoeing can transport you a few thousand feet above the valley floor, onto high mountain terrain. In winter this is the kind of landscape that's only accessible to mountaineers, but with a chopper and snowshoes it could be yours. If your budget doesn't stretch to rotary uplift, you'll find deep snow and a profound sense of serenity crunching across pristine snow around the Southern Alps. You can use this as a launch pad to sample the world-famous 32km Routeburn Track, or a base to explore The Remarkables mountain range.

If you're tackling the Roteburn Track, you'll find a number of huts along the way. In winter the route is subject to weather and avalanche conditions.

765 DOLOMITES, NORTHERN ITALY

Not the tallest but quite possibly one of the most beautiful mountain ranges in the world is nestled in the northeast of Italy. The Dolomites are an awesomely sculpted collection of steep vertical walls, sheer cliffs, sharp ridges and towering spires, separated by narrow, deep valleys. Spend a day snowshoeing through this astonishing terrain and you'll see the pale limestone turn a rich pink as the sun starts to sink. Trekking from hut to hut is the best way to explore this region, hiking the sublime mountains during the day, then sharing stories in a traditional mountain refuge in the evening.

Come back in the summer to sample the world of *vie ferrate*, the fixed-protection climbing routes around the mountains.

766 NAHUEL HUAPI NATIONAL PARK, ARGENTINA

About as good as it gets in terms of snowshoeing locations, Nahuel Huapi National Park sits in the foothills of the Patagonian Andes. Start exploring from San Carlos de Bariloche, situated on the southern shore of Lake Nahuel Huapi, and you'll discover rich local wildlife and a huge variety of trails. This is a well-developed winter sports destination but you can escape the crowds easily around Mount Lopez, 30km northwest of Bariloche, or the richly forested slopes of Mount Challhuaco, with its high deciduous beeches.

The three distinct types of terrain, from the high snow-covered Andes to the Patagonian desert, make this an incredibly diverse area to explore.

767 BANFF NATIONAL PARK, CANADA

The summer hiking trails of Banff National Park could be the perfect terrain for your first snowshoeing adventure, taking you into a wilderness that delivers astonishing mountain views. Drive half an hour out of Banff to the Agnes Teahouse trail to discover the surreal blue of Lake Louise. Follow the Johnston Canyon trail with its waterfalls and deep canyons and explore the Ink Pots, a cluster of small mineral springs, each a different shade of blue. But finding your own trails really gives you a taste of the serenity of the Canadian Rockies and exploring with showshoes is the best way to get out there.

Certain trails in Banff are specifically for cross-country skiing so if you're exploring be careful to avoid these.

768 YATSUGATAKE MOUNTAINS, JAPAN

Rainfall from the Pacific and cold air from Siberia give Japan quality snow that's renowned amongst skiers and showshoers alike. Just a two-hour train ride from Tokyo, the Yatsugatake mountains are a 30km string of eight main volcanic summits that in winter offer trails to suit all abilities and tastes. With challenging terrain on offer you might want to hire a guide and there are plenty of huts here if you want to organise an overnight stay. One of the most popular routes is the Natsuzawa Pass that splits the vertiginous southern section from the more genteel north.

You need to be avalanche aware here: make sure everyone in your group is equipped with a beacon, probe and shovel.

769 SIERRA NEVADA, SPAIN

The Sierra Nevada mountains offer the most southerly snowshoeing in Europe, just a short drive away from the Mediterranean. With a number of peaks over 3000m, the highest of which is Mulhacén (3472m), there are trails for all levels of experience. So whether you're looking for a mixture of forests and open hillsides or high snow-bowls and silent valleys, there's plenty to explore. And unlike other ski destinations, it's easy to escape the resorts and get really dramatic terrain to yourself. A great experience is to combine your trip with an overnight stay at the Poqueira Mountain refuge (2500m).

Snowshoeing overnight in this terrain requires the right gear; don't be surprised if you're stopped on the drive in and asked to confirm you've got everything you need.

770 CAIRNGORMS, SCOTLAND

Scotland's mountains may not be the highest but they are home to some world-class mountaineering. Trek up into the Lairig Ghru pass and you are surrounded by five of Scotland's six highest mountains: on one side Cairn Gorm and Ben Macdui and on the other Cairn Toul, Sgòr an Lochain Uaine and the fearsomely sculpted Braeriach. The wildlife is some of Scotland's best, with snow buntings, ptarmigans, eagles and even snowy owls frequently spotted. Pack your snowshoes and overnight kit and plan your route around a bothy.

Bothies are free mountain huts so don't be surprised to find other walkers also using them. Carry out all your rubbish, and any other trash you can pack up.

SPORTIVES FOR SERIOUS CYCLISTS

Slip into some lycra, jump on your bike and join thousands of cyclists on these single-day mass rides on closed roads.

Cruising on cobblestones. Keen cyclists take up the challenge of the Paris–Roubaix Cyclosportive

771 LA MARMOTTE, FRANCE

A marmot is a small, cute, furry animal that makes its home in burrows on alpine mountain sides. Don't confuse it with La Marmotte, which is a big beast of a bike ride that drags its victims up the *hors categorie* (unclassified) climbs of the Col du Glandon, the Col de Telegraphe and the Col du Galibier in the Haute-Alpes before finishing them off at the summit of Alpe d'Huez. It's perhaps the toughest sportive in the calendar with 5000 vertical metres of climbing; this is where even cyclists who have ticked off l'Etape du Tour are likely to collapse by the wayside.

The ride starts from Bourg d'Oisans. Entries open in December for the July event and it's best to sign up for a package with a tour operator because the spaces fill up quickly. A medical certificate is mandatory.

772 THREE PEAKS CHALLENGE, AUSTRALIA

The Alpine National Park region is a beautiful corner of the state of Victoria, close to the handsome country towns of Beechworth and Bright. But halfway through the testing 235km course of the annual Three Peaks Challenge, as it climbs through forests of snow gums, you might well be gritting your teeth rather than enjoying the mountain views. The ride starts and finishes at Falls Creek Alpine Resort and the three peaks include the 1825m Mt Hotham, which is heralded by a relentless 30km drag uphill all the way from Harrietville. Luckily you'll have 13 hours to complete the distance.

The Three Peaks Challenge takes place in early March; details are at www.bicyclenetwork.com.au. Falls Creek (www.fallscreek.com.au) is around 350km from Melbourne.

773 L'EROICA, ITALY

White gravel crunches beneath your tyres. Tall, dark cypresses beside the road bend in the autumn breeze. Your fellow cyclists are a curious bunch, sporting large moustaches, goggles and woollen outfits. Yes, L'Eroica is a sportive with a difference: all bikes ridden on this excursion around the *strade bianche* (white gravel roads) of Tuscany must date from before 1987. Some are collectors' items from the 1950s and 1960s, with many riders taking the opportunity to dress accordingly. As with all vintage rallies, expect the extra camaraderie that roadside repairs breed. The ride began in 1997 with 92 cyclists – today around 5000 take part, covering 200km from Gaiole through Chianti, Montalcino and the Val d'Orcia on their elegant machines.

L'Eroica takes place in October (www.eroicafan.it). Gaiole lies between Siena and Florence.

774 PARIS–ROUBAIX CYCLOSPORTIVE, FRANCE

Paris–Roubaix is known as the Queen of the Classics, distilling the drama and triumph of bike racing down to 250km of blood, sweat and suffering over 18 cobbled sections of road (known as *pavé*). The Arenberg forest section is cited by competitors as one of the toughest experiences of any bike race; its cobbles are slippery whether they're dry and dusty or slick with water. The biennial Paris–Roubaix sportive, which starts from Compiègne, northeast of the French capital, follows the full route of the cobbled Classic but takes place in June rather than April so riders are spared the full force of northern France's wintry weather. Luckily, shorter options are available.

Book at www.vc-cyclo-roubaix.fr and plan your trip at www.picardietourisme.com.

775 L'ARDÉCHOISE, FRANCE

This four-day French festival of cycling (and therefore eating) spotlights the Ardéche, an often overlooked region of gorges, cave paintings and standing stones tucked between Lyon and Avignon. Every June up to 15,000 riders – making this the country's largest sportive – pedal through this corner of rural France on closed roads. It's up and down the whole way, with the 1244m Col de Rouvey delivering a sting in the tail. Off the bike, there's world-class kayaking and climbing in the Ardéche, which embraces part of the Cevennes National Park.

275

See www.ardechoise.com for details and book accommodation at www.ardeche-tourisme.com.

There be dragons! The hills and valleys of Wales attract keen cyclists – not all of them breathing fire – for Britain's premier sportive

776 MARATONA DLES DOLOMITES, ITALY

The Maratona dles Dolomites, Italy's greatest Gran Fondo ('big endurance' – it sounds better in Italian), reached its quarter century in 2012 with 30,000 applications from 45 nations for 9000 places. During this annual extravaganza the cyclists feast on wine, pasta and 300kg of cheese. They'll need the energy because the 138km route through the intimidating Italian Dolomites takes in seven gruelling ascents, the toughest being the Passo Giau at 2236m and Passo Valparola

at 2200m in the second half of the course. Few sportives can match the scenery of this Italian classic.

The Gran Fondo (www.maratona.it) takes place in late June or early July; book a package with a tour operator to guarantee a place. Verona is the closest city.

777 CAPE ARGUS CYCLE TOUR, SOUTH AFRICA

There can be no better way of seeing the Cape Town coastline than from a bicycle on a late summer morning. Except on the Cape Argus Cycle

Tour you won't be alone – there will be 34,999 other cyclists sharing the closed roads with you, making this the world's largest timed bike ride. The 110km route takes in the surf-smashed coast of Green Point, Camps Bay and Hout Bay, and crosses Table Mountain National Park. Winning riders can finish in less than 2½ hours but the rest of us have a time limit of seven hours in which to savour the scenery.

The ride is staged in March; reserve your place at www.cycletour.co.za. Accommodation in Cape Town fills up quickly; book at www.capetown.travel

GRAHAM M. LAWRENCE/ALAMY ©

779 THE DRAGON RIDE, WALES

Long before the bicycle was a glint in the eye of a Scottish/French inventor (a point of contention), the Welsh landscape of steep valleys and tight-packed hills had repelled all sorts of invaders. But since 2004 a new breed of weekend warrior has conquered Cymru with the help of 20 gears and a carbon-fibre frame. Clad in lycra, these men and women roam in packs up and down the closed roads of South Wales and the Brecon Beacons, covering up to 190km on Britain's premier sportive. But this dragon isn't especially difficult to slay; there are shorter route options of 40km and the climbing is not comparable to the Continental events.

Reserve your berth at www.verentidragonride.com. The route varies from year to year so book local accommodation at www.visitwales.com.

778 L'ETAPE DU TOUR, FRANCE

Imagine playing a game of tennis on Wimbledon's Centre Court. That's what L'Etape offers cyclists, the opportunity to measure themselves against their heroes on a mountain stage of the Tour de France just days before the Tour's circus of helicopters, team cars and svelte professional cyclists sweep through. L'Etape, like other sportives, takes place on closed roads with crowds and a split-second timing system adding to the excitement. The annual event covers up to 200km of breathtaking roads in the Alps or Pyrenees. If you're wondering, the winning pro typically finishes in half the time of an average amateur.

Application forms are published in *Vélo* magazine early in the year but applicants outside France are encouraged to sign up with one of the tour operators approved by the organisers, ASO. Details of the route are posted at www.letapedutour.com in late autumn.

780 EL TOUR DE TUCSON, ARIZONA

Give your legs a final workout before winter on America's largest mass bike ride, El Tour de Tucson. The sportive is staged on the Saturday before Thanksgiving, so it's also a chance to get some sunshine before the holiday season. Up to 9000 cyclists ride over a range of distances, with MAMILs (Middle-Aged Men In Lycra) riding the full 178km and families tackling shorter options of 67km, 96km and 136km, all raising thousands of dollars in the process.

Sign up at www.pbaa.com and plan your trip at www.visittucson.org.

SPORTIVES FOR SERIOUS CYCLISTS

BEST UNDISCOVERED US PARKS

Have the mountains, desert, swamplands and wolf packs all to yourself at these remote, rarely visited public lands.

781 CONGAREE, SOUTH CAROLINA

Maybe the crowds of tourists stay away from Congaree because they're spooked. Paddling past giant, moss-draped cypresses along sunless channels of murky water conjures a Southern Gothic novel. You'd be forgiven for thinking it a swamp, what with the slithering snakes, hooting owls and feral pigs snorting from the banks of the creek, but Congaree actually is in a flood plain (meaning it's not always

The locals may by oblivious to the stunning scenery in Katmai National Park, but visitors are certain to be spellbound

covered by water). Another oddity about this primordial setting: it's close enough to Columbia, the state capital, that you can get mobile phone reception as you canoe, angle for catfish and swat mosquitoes in the oozingly wet environs.

Congaree is 32km (20 miles) southeast of Columbia, in central South Carolina, and it's open year-round. Spring and autumn are the best seasons to visit. See www. nps.gov/cong.

MINT IMAGES · FRANS LANTING/GETTY IMAGES ©

782 NATIONAL PARK OF AMERICAN SAMOA

This park sits closer to Tahiti than it does the 50 states. The protected paradise spans three of American Samoa's volcanic-peaked islands, where blue sea laps palmy beaches in a guileless Polynesian idyll. Wade in to snorkel the coral reefs alongside jewel-toned parrotfish and flame angelfish. Mosey on day hikes that climb from seashore to cloud-cloaked rainforest. Salute the local flying foxes. At night, stay with a village family in their traditional *fale* (home). If they ask you to help with dinner – say, netting fish or shimmying up a tree to pluck coconuts – all the better.

The park headquarters is in the capital Pago Pago (on Tutuila). Contact npsa_ info@nps.gov for homestay info. Weather is driest from June to September. See www.nps.gov/npsa.

783 ISLE ROYALE, MICHIGAN

Morning fog wisps over the lake. You hear sloshing on the far shore and see a moose plop in for a drink. A loon calls. Or maybe it's a wolf howling? Either is probable in Isle Royale's unspoiled forest. The 72km-long, 15-km-wide (45 by 9 miles) island floats by its lonesome in Lake Superior between Michigan and Minnesota. Isolation and cruel winters keep mammals to a minimum, and that includes humans. This is the least-visited park in the continental US. There are no roads, so wolves and moose have room to roam, and visitors have boundless places to camp (or bunk at the lone lodge).

The park is open mid-May to October. Ferries sail from Houghton and Copper Harbor, Michigan, and Grand Portage, Minnesota. There's also floatplane service from Houghton. See www.nps.gov/isro.

784 KATMAI, ALASKA

You know those stock photos of hulking grizzly bears snagging salmon in mid-air as they splash through a crystal stream? At Katmai National Park you'll be the one capturing the moment, complete with growling sound effects. More than 2000 grizzlies prowl this mountain-stubbled preserve in southern Alaska. (For those who've seen Werner Herzog's film *Grizzly Man*, Katmai sets the scene.) Beyond bear gazing, you can hike to the Valley of Ten Thousand Smokes, a starkly beautiful landscape left behind after Novarupta Volcano blew its stack a century ago, or kayak the Savonoski Loop 138km (86 miles) through wind-whipped back country.

Katmai has no road access. Fly or boat in from Homer, King Salmon or Kodiak. Brooks Camp offers the best bear viewing (July and September especially). See www.nps.gov/katm.

785 BIG BEND, TEXAS

Tumbleweeds and ghost towns are the view out the window as you drive to Big Bend. The desert park seems like a huge expanse of nothing until your senses adjust, and then you notice the buttes shimmering with colour and birdsong drifting through the arroyos. Rafting the Rio Grande is the big to-do, a gentle glide through pink-hued cliffs along the Mexico border. Hiking and horse-riding in the Chisos Mountains, which erupt in Big Bend's midst, are cool alternatives under the shade of piñons and junipers. Outdoor hot springs add to the relaxed vibe.

The park is busiest November–April, when the weather cools and the river runs deep enough for rafting. Several outfitters are based in nearby Terlingua. See www.nps.gov/bibe.

786 VOYAGEURS, MINNESOTA

Voyageurs spatters a mosaic of forest, islands and lakes across a vast tract of Minnesota's North Woods. Roads are limited, so do like the locals and float a houseboat to get around. By day, beavers splash and eagles swoop along the interconnected waterways. By night, the green-glowing aurora borealis flickers in the sky. You'd think the fun stops in winter once the water freezes, but the change of season simply means swapping your boat for a snowmobile. The ghostly white landscape makes it easy to spot wolf tracks; several packs creep among the spruce trees.

High season is late May to late September, when most roads are usable. International Falls is the main access town. See www.nps.gov/voya.

787 BLACK CANYON OF THE GUNNISON, COLORADO

Little light penetrates the deep, narrow chasm – the sun's rays reach the floor just an hour a day – hence the dark name. The Gunnison River bashed through here two million years ago, leaving sheer 820m (2700ft) cliffs in its wake. That's good news for rock climbers, who set their ropes for Painted Wall to grunt and pull their way up a mineral-streaked precipice taller than the Empire State Building. Hikers huff and puff along the canyon rim's steep, sage-dotted trails. And anglers get weak-kneed casting into the icy Gunnison, which teems with plump trout.

Montrose, which has a small airport, is the jump-off town. Much of the park closes from November to mid-April. See www.nps.gov/blca.

788 GREAT BASIN, NEVADA

You feel the solitude coming when you veer off on Highway 50, aka 'the loneliest road in America' and the main route into Great Basin. Then you hike the trails up and around alpine lakes, groves of gnarled bristlecone pines and even a glacier. The vistas, especially from 3960m (13,000ft) Wheeler Peak, are sublime but you're the only one soaking them up. When night time falls, the isolation yields one of the nation's darkest skies. Look up to see sweeping view of stars, meteors and galaxies like the Milky Way. Or get your darkness fix underground by touring Lehman Caves' marble splendours.

Baker is the gateway town; the nearest airport is in Ely. The caves stay open year-round but many other sights close between November and April. See www.nps.gov/grba.

789 NORTH CASCADES, WASHINGTON STATE

This gem unfurls a vintage patch of Pacific Northwest wilderness that stretches right up to the Canadian border, snowy peaks providing the backdrop to turquoise lakes. More than 300 glaciers seep from the mountain cracks. Waterfalls tumble into wildflower-strewn valleys. The back country reigns supreme, prime for hiking or boating in and pitching a tent under the pines. Even the place names – Desolation Peak, Jagged Ridge, Mt Despair and Mt Terror – point to the park's awesomely forsaken nature. Many adventurers rank North Cascades as the most rugged terrain outside Alaska.

May to October is peak season. Winthrop, on the park's east side, makes a good base. Seattle has the closest airport. See www.nps.gov/noca.

BUD FORCE / AURORA OP/AGEFOTOSTOCK ©

The beauty and creative genius of Mother Nature on full display at Black Canyon of the Gunnison

790 DRY TORTUGAS, FLORIDA

The wee, seven-island park drifts deep in the Gulf of Mexico, near Cuba. After you gawk at red-brick Fort Jefferson, a massive, 19th-century military fortress, it's time to look deeper. Don a mask and flippers and behold the underwater world where sea fans wave, green turtles and loggerheads slowpoke through the waves, and schools of blue tangs and trumpetfish dart. Dive down further and you'll see shipwrecks from conquistador times. Back on land, the raucous squawks of 100,000 sooty terns (and 300 other bird species) remind you Dry Tortugas is smack in the midst of a major flyway.

The park is open year-round. Bird watching peaks in April. Access is by ferry or seaplane from Key West. See www.nps.gov/drto.

BEST UNDISCOVERED US PARKS

BEST ADVENTURES IN THE BUFF

Strip down to your birthday suit in the name of politics, to take part in an offbeat event or just to add a little spice to your next big adventure...

793 SKI AND BE FREE

No one celebrates the end of ski season quite like the locals of Nanshan in China. Their 'Naked Pig Festival' is actually a surprisingly coy cavalcade of fancy dress and swim wear but you've got to be impressed with the levels of bravado that bring skiers out onto the slopes wearing very little. The tradition actually originated in the Crested Butte Mountain Resort in Colorado, but since 2003 this Chinese ski resort has also been getting in on the action. Skiers have to descend a 200m-long beginner's slope and winners are judged on their costume, performance and overall creativity.

In recent years a decibel measure has been used to gauge the reaction of the crowd, so if you're looking to win, make sure you get spectators on your side.

791 ABSOLUTELY NO BULL

Stripping off is an increasingly popular way to get your political messages across and in Pamplona, Spain, an annual event is designed to campaign against bullfighting. The Running of the Nudes takes place just two days before the more famous Running of the Bulls, which kick starts the festival of San Fermin. Protestors wear just red scarves and plastic horns and follow the same 800m route from the Santo Domingo corrals to the town's Plaza de Toros. The event started in 2002 with some 25 participants and has grown to attract well over 1000 runners.

There have been 15 recorded human deaths in the Running of the Bulls since 1924, and presumably a 100 percent fatality rate for the bulls. Nudity feels like a far safer option in this instance.

792 ANTARCTICA 300 CLUB

Initiation to this exclusive club requires getting yourself to the Amundsen–Scott Research Station, at the geographic South Pole. That's no easy task on the world's least-visited continent; a round trip from Europe will set you back at least $40,000. The club gets its name from the 300°F (149°C) change in temperature that aspiring members have to endure. First you need to wait for winter conditions to drop to -100°F (-73°C). Then you warm up in a sauna heated to 200°F (93°C) before heading outside in the altogether to dash for the ceremonial South Pole and back inside to warm up once again.

Be careful as you run; freezing temperatures can damage your lungs and have a very adverse effect on your extremities.

794 WALK ON THE WILD SIDE

Between 2002 and 2004, wearing nothing but a pair of boots, socks and a rucksack, Britain's infamous Naked Rambler, Steve Gough, managed to walk over 870 miles (1400km) from Land's End to John O'Groats. He attempted the feat again in 2005 and was arrested twice in England and multiple times in Scotland, where he subsequently made a nude court appearance. Britain's high population density makes it a difficult place to navigate naked, but there are plenty of wilderness walks around the world where you walk for miles without bumping into anyone else. You decide which one's for you.

Keep yourself shielded from the elements with a good sun protection and have a sarong close at hand to cover up quickly in case you bump into clothed hikers.

795 SKYDIVE NAKED

Leaping out of a plane at 14,000 feet will buy you a heart-pumping 65 seconds of freefall. Not exciting enough? Then skydiving naked could add the required spice. If you're a first-timer, a tandem dive will fast-track your aspirations. Having a stranger strapped to your back could be a little unsettling, but that won't matter as you hit a terminal velocity of 220km per hour. The internet is awash with people who've done just that and skydive companies who seem pretty open to the idea, so if you want to add this to your bucket list find an instructor somewhere scenic… it probably won't be the first time they've been asked.

When you've made the jump, you qualify to join the Society for the Advancement of Naked Skydiving; head to www.thesans.org for your certificate and fridge magnet.

796 BE A WORK OF ART

American photographer Spencer Tunick has an uncanny ability to gather hordes of volunteer nude models to create his unique art installations. And what better reason to strip off than to create a piece of high art in the company of a few thousand strangers? Recent examples include mud-plastered models lying by Israel's Dead Sea, nudes in Ireland with roses gripped between their teeth and thousands of people covering the tarmac outside the Sydney Opera House. This might not involve dangling from a rope or climbing a mountain, but it's a great adventure in the name of art.

You can sign up for a future gathering at www.spencertunick.com. All participants get a free print of the final piece.

797 BUNGEE JUMP IN THE BUFF

If you're going to try bungee jumping just once, here are two things that will keep the memory sharp. Firstly, do it naked. Preparing to launch into the abyss can cause momentary hesitation. Doing it with your bits and pieces on show means there's an added incentive to leap, when you're being gawped at by the crowds. Secondly, make your jump in New Zealand, the home of the bungee. AJ Hackett, the bungee pioneer, runs his own jump company out of Queenstown on the South Island of NZ and there's at least one blogger out there who's leapt in the nude.

To record your big leap, and the reaction of any onlookers, consider getting a chest-mounted video camera.

798 CRITICAL ASS

Want to improve the lot of cyclists and challenge our reliance on the motorcar? Then World Naked Bike Ride could be for you. This 'clothing optional' event takes place in cities around the world, featuring a creative mix of body painting, costumes and customised bikes. Riders often use themselves as canvases, wearing slogans such as 'less crude, more nude', 'less gas, more ass' and 'burn fat, not oil'. Clearly, different countries have varying attitudes to nudity but tactical body art or a judicious thong can distract onlookers, add a bit of fun and help to avoid a run-in with the law, if you're concerned.

Events take place in June and July in the Northern Hemisphere and March in the Southern Hemisphere.

799 NIGHT SKINNY-DIP

If you can muster 413 of your broadest-minded friends and assemble them in the same body of water, you could be in line to break the world skinny-dipping record, set in Christchurch, New Zealand. And there are no shortage of wild swimmers who have this target in their sights, with attempts last year in Spain and the unappealingly chilly waters of Britain's North Sea. But if you only have a handful of people willing to join you, we suggest a night-time dip in a secluded lake or quiet beach, as close to the summer solstice as possible.

Not great with cold water? Take the plunge anyway, but stay close to the shore and always swim with a partner.

800 KAYAK COMMANDO

Naked kayaking could be a good starting point for the cautious exhibitionist. With a spraydeck keeping your nether regions under wraps and a life-jacket concealing your upper bits, you can skirt that fine line between technical nudity, safety requirements and the most stringent of public decency laws. As far as destinations go, you want to steer clear of the Arctic Circle and avoid the Equatorial sunshine. The Mediterranean could offer just the right conditions and touring the Greek Ionian islands means you can paddle between secluded beaches and relax in the sun without causing a commotion.

Sun protection is clearly an absolute must no matter what time of year you're out. Wear a good hat and sunscreen and reapply regularly.

SWEETEST SNORKEL SPOTS

Don your mask and fins, bite down on your snorkel and bravely join surreal underwater worlds.

801 MOOREA, FRENCH POLYNESIA

Snorkel right from the beach on this small French Polynesian island. Shallow, clear waters right off land offer views of tropical fish, while coral rings the island. White and black sand beaches beckon when you're ready for a rest, and when you emerge from the water, you'll be greeted with the stunning view of Moorea's green volcanic mountains and spires. Many snorkellers stick to the lagoon outside their resort or hotel, though the *motu* (reef islets) near Moorea are popular sites for boat excursions. Through your facemask you will see triggerfish munching on coral, as well as lionfish, angelfish and white- and black-tipped sharks.

Moorea is easily accessible from Tahiti, 14km (nine miles) across the Sea of the Moon. Visit between April and October for the dry season.

802 AMBERGRIS CAYE, BELIZE

Don't scream into your snorkel! Jaws-lookalikes and sting rays patrol Shark Ray Alley, a sandbar where ferocious-looking (but docile) nurse sharks might leave you quaking in your fins. This famous snorkelling spot near Caye Caulker is Hol Chan Marine Reserve, where a cut in the coral reef creates a channel 30 feet deep (*hol chin* means 'little channel' in Mayan). Here snorkellers will be face-to-mask with moray eels, black groupers and several types of coral adapted to the channel's strong currents. It also has a small Blue Hole that snorkellers can peer deep into. Shark Ray Alley and Hol Chan are on the southern tip of Ambergris Caye.

Ambergris Caye is just south of Caye Caulker; take a day trip or stay in nearby San Pedro. Check out www.holchanbelize.org.

803 CHAMPAGNE BEACH, DOMINICA

Tiny bubbles rush from geothermic fissures on the sea floor, cascades of them tickling you as you swim over. A float through these bubbles feels like you're bobbing in a bottle of champagne, which is how this beach got its name. The warm volcanic fizz, which starts just a few feet from shore, hosts an abundance of sea life including sea urchins, frogfish and seahorses. Inside the Soufrière–Scott's Head Marine Reserve, the waters of Champagne Beach are part of a sunken volcanic crater, the reason for the fumaroles. Adventurous swimmers can kick out past the bubbles to the reef for a more varied look at the area's marine life.

Champagne Beach is located on the south side of Dominica. There is a US$2 entry fee.

Enjoy some bubbly of a different kind at Champagne Beach

Take the plunge to snorkle in the startlingly clear waters of the Silfra fissure that lies between tectonic plates

804 ÞINGVELLIR NATIONAL PARK, ICELAND

Known for its inland beauty of fire and ice, Iceland may not be on your immediate list of hot snorkel destinations. But the volcanic and tectonic activity that makes this island country geographically stunning translates into some amazing freshwater snorkelling. In Þingvellir National Park you can drift in clear water of varying shades of blue in a thin canyon between tectonic plates. Called the Silfra fissure, this underwater rift valley is literally in between two continents. Not only that, but the water here is so clean, thanks to filtration by volcanic rock, that you can remove your snorkel and drink it.

Snorkelling trips are on offer year-round and depart from Reykjavik. Air- and watertight dry suits are provided. Visit www.extremeiceland.is for more information.

805 RED SEA, EGYPT

Head to Dahab, on the Sinai Peninsula and part of the 'Red Sea Riviera', and submerge into warm waters laced with coral. The flat-water conditions inside Dahab's sand spit are a snorkeller's dream and there is an abundance of reefs easily accessible from shore. Primary-coloured fish dart from coral that has adapted to the Red Sea's unique conditions: very little water exchange and plenty of dust. The water visibility is stunning thanks in part to little rainfall and snorkellers can take advantage of the Sea's supersalinity, which results in extra buoyancy.

Snorkel from the beach in Dahab or take a day trip to Ras Mohammed National Park, where world-class reefs await.

806 GALÁPAGOS ISLANDS, ECUADOR

If only Darwin had had a mask and fins. One of the most diverse spots in the world, the Galápagos Islands offer snorkellers the chance to swim with equatorial penguins, sea lions, marine iguanas and dolphins. Devil's Crown, a volcanic cone characterised by steep walls textured with coral, is a protected spot where swimmers might get eye-to-eye with sea turtles and is one of the most popular snorkelling spots in the Galápagos Marine Reserve (the second-largest marine reserve in the world). Varied underwater topography means you can snorkel for days and never get bored.

Visit from December to May for best conditions. Visitors to Devils Crown will have to go on live-aboards as day trippers are not allowed.

807 SIMILAN ISLANDS NATIONAL PARK, THAILAND

With blue water as clear as the sky above, the Similan Islands offer stunning scenery in and out of the sea. On the sea border with Myanmar (Burma), these remote islands in the Andaman Sea are characterised by smooth granite boulders and soft white sand, which continue into the water. Ko Bon and Ko Tachai were recently added to the marine park and offer some of the best coral in the archipelago. Sea turtles, whale sharks, manta rays and dolphins are on the buffet of sea life you will observe whilst bobbing in these warm waters.

Day trips depart from the mainland at Khao Lak from October to April, or you can also join live-aboard trips for longer and deeper excursions.

808 BRITISH COLUMBIA, CANADA

Experience snorkelling in an environment like no other: in the salmon-spawning currents of BC's Campbell River. Ogle massive Chinook (King) salmon as they hump their way upstream, spawning until they die. Intense habitat restoration in the past 50 years has ensured plentiful returning salmon, with all five species on display throughout the summer months. Snorkellers squeeze into wetsuits and, with the direction of a guide, join the salmon in clear pools as they take a breather for the next push upstream, or drift slowly on the current above the silvery homecoming.

Tours run from July to September; snorkellers are bussed from the start and picked up again downriver. Head to www.beaveraquatics.ca for information.

809 GREAT BARRIER REEF, AUSTRALIA

Grab your mates and head to the Great Barrier Reef – perhaps the world's best-known snorkel spot and for good reason. It is the world's largest coral reef system, stretching nearly 1900 miles along the Queensland Coast of Australia – so large it is visible from space. A World Heritage site, the Reef supports a number of endangered species including the dugong (sea cow), the blue whale and seven species of sea turtles. Snorkellers will float with many of the 1500 species of tropical fish, which can be seen through the gin-clear water expected of any top-notch snorkel site.

Day trips to the reef abound, particularly at the north end where the reef runs closer to the mainland. Cairns is the most popular gateway.

810 PERHENTIAN ISLANDS, MALAYSIA

The Perhentian Islands are tropical paradise stereotypes: warm, clear water and palm-fringed beaches define the half-dozen islands. Not surprisingly the underwater viewing isn't bad, either. Here you can gawk at black-tip sharks and float with giant green sea turtles. As a laid-back hippie haunt the Perhentians also enjoy a relaxed night-time scene, when you can compare aquatic sightings with other travellers over a curry and beer. Alternatively, you could camp out on one of the uninhabited islands, where it will be just you, the ocean and the stars.

The Perhentians are off the north-east coast of peninsular Malaysia. There are two inhabited islands: Besar is larger and family-oriented while Kecil is smaller and less expensive.

SWEETEST SNORKEL SPOTS

BEST HUT-TO-HUT TOURS

Go deep into the wilderness by foot, ski or bike thanks to perfectly placed huts that offer hot meals and shelter from storms.

811 HIKE THE HAUTE ROUTE, CHAMONIX, FRANCE TO ZERMATT, SWITZERLAND

If iconic Alpine peaks, rugged high-mountain passes and nights spent with a fun mix of international travellers sounds like your cup of tea, grab your backpack and your best hiking boots and head to the Haute Route, a 180km-long adventure-waiting-to-happen that spans two countries. While skiers may mock summertime hikers for missing out on the famous back-

Shelter at the end of a long day's trekking on the Via Alpina, huts such as this offer comfortably lodging, food and good company

country powder, hikers will enjoy the thaw as they take in the looming Matterhorn and Mont Blanc, the brilliantly green glacier-carved lakes and the lush valleys. That's not to say that you won't encounter snow. Choose between a high-altitude route that includes glacier crossings or a lower, less-arduous route; both make use of the string of established mountain huts.

The whole route takes about two weeks on foot, but it's easy to conquer sections instead.

JACQUES PIERRE/GETTY IMAGES ©

812 TREK THE GRAND RANDONNEE (GR) 20, CORSICA, FRANCE

On the mountainous Mediterranean island of Corsica, Europe's toughest trek dishes out all manner of highs and lows, from hard-earned 360-degree views from the top of spiked granite peaks to burning blisters and thoughts of quitting. But no matter where you've been mentally and physically, at the end of each day of this 16-stage 168km (104 mile) trek, you can recharge and refuel inside a range of *refugios* (huts) along the route. Some are simple stone huts with shared bunks, while others are more like minihotels with attached restaurants – hosts keep hikers happy with hearty pastas and carafes of table wine.

The entire route takes about 15 days, but you can walk smaller portions and hit just a few huts, which are staffed from June to September.

813 SKI THE 10TH MOUNTAIN DIVISION HUTS, COLORADO, USA

One of the world's largest hut systems has inspired thousands to explore the stunning beauty of a small wedge of Colorado's Rocky Mountains. The system's 30 huts are scattered between Vail, Leadville and Aspen and were first developed as training grounds for 10th Mountain Division of the US Army during WWII. You can explore the surrounding peaks, forests and valleys at any time of the year, but back-country skiing is superb in the winter. First-time visitors should consider staying a couple of nights in each hut, but ultimately it's up to you – the system encourages people to plan their own trips.

Consider forging your own path to one of the three huts with access to wood-burning saunas.

814 CONNECT THE COUNTRIES ON THE VIA ALPINA

Scrape Alpine skies and soak up some of Europe's most beautiful natural scenery while traversing ridgelines and summitting peaks as you make your way through the eight European countries that share this new network of hiking trails. Five colour-coded trails intersect and part ways like the best subway systems, and a range of huts run by local alpine clubs provide the most accessible lodging, food and company on the entire 4989km-long (3100-mile) route. At these huts you'll find hearty feasts featuring local specialities from fondue to spaetzle, as well as hot showers and new friends with tall tales.

Head to Slovenia's Julian Alps for a prime concentration of adventures, from kayaking to rock climbing.

Take in varied landscapes and stunning vistas by day, and cosy huts by night on the Appalachian Trail

815 HIKE THE APPALACHIAN TRAIL, WHITE MOUNTAIN NATIONAL FOREST, NEW HAMPSHIRE, USA

As one of the granddaddies of long-distance hiking, the Appalachian Trail is as spectacular as ever. Take this 196km (122-mile) stretch through the White Mountains, which skirts the treeline and plunges into leafy valleys. The Appalachian Mountain Club runs eight off-the-grid huts here, which are spaced about a day apart by foot. That makes the planning easy but not necessarily the hiking. Many parts of this stretch will test you, especially if you head to the Lakes of the Clouds hut on Mount Washington, the highest hut in the system, which offers jaw-dropping valley views and mist-shrouded mornings.

Say hello to the through-hikers you'll meet along the way. If they're headed north to south, they've just begun their journey.

816 SKI TOUR IN BARILOCHE, PATAGONIA, ARGENTINA

While the Northern Hemisphere sweats through summer then watches leaves fall, you can be carving turns on untouched snowfields sparkling in the sunshine of Patagonia's Lake District. A handful of back-country huts, best accessed from the town of Bariloche, provides perfect access to steep chutes, long lung-burning runs and endless powder framed by granite spires. The best-known hut is Refugio Frey, a stone cottage surrounded by spectacular peaks that are often illuminated with alpenglow at sunset. Back-country skiing here is at its best between August and November.

Create your own self-guided ski tour or leave the logistics to the numerous local guide services and tour companies.

818 SKI THE WAPTA TRAVERSE, BANFF AND YOHO NATIONAL PARKS, CANADA

Head out the door at first light from any one of the huts on this famous Western Canadian ski route across the Continental Divide, and conquer an array of summits before skiing over glacial ice fields and down powdery chutes. Then do it again tomorrow. You'll feel both small and powerful as you survey the endless wintery wonderland punctuated by peaks, crevasses and icefalls. The spectacular terrain and coveted snow rival Europe's greatest hut-to-hut ski routes. Trips can take anywhere from one to five days, depending on your level of ambition and skill.

Plan your trip for the spring, when days are longer and temperatures are a tad warmer.

820 MOUNTAIN BIKE THE SAN JUAN HUTS, DURANGO, COLORADO TO MOAB, UTAH, USA

In this stretch of the West, you can join the cowboys who ride the range by hopping in the saddle of a mountain bike, but pursue swooping singletrack and epic descents instead of cattle. The San Juan Huts are some of the most famous in the US and for good reason. Of the two established routes, Telluride–Moab has been around for longer and it's easier. Durango–Moab is more technical and demanding a ride – read: prime singletrack. The well-stocked huts have everything from energy drinks to bacon, making them perfect waypoints in a steady vista of vast desert skies, sorbet-hued sunsets, fragrant sage and red rock overlooks.

Huts are spaced about 56km (35 miles) apart to help keep ride days consistent.

817 TRAMPING THE MILFORD TRACK, NEW ZEALAND

New Zealanders excel at 'tramping' (hiking) and the Milford Track is the country's most famous place to do just that. The stunning route winds through Fiordland National Park for nearly 54km (33 miles), with hikers being required to walk one direction: south to north. The four-day adventure will take you past waterfalls roaring into pristine pools, sheer granite peaks, lush vegetation and light dustings of snow on mountain passes. Independent hikers can spend the night in three huts along the way from October to April. Permits and reservations are an absolute must.

Recover from or prepare for your walk in the town of Te Anau, where you can kayak on Lake Te Anau and visit a glowworm-filled cave.

819 RETREAT INTO RONDANE NATIONAL PARK, NORWAY

Retreat from civilisation into a barren land where brilliantly coloured lichen covers mountain basins carved out way back in the Ice Age. Rondane was Norway's first national park (formed in the 1960s) and it remains home to herds of wild reindeer. In the park, the small system of huts (hyttes) are run by the Norwegian Trekking Association. Trek between huts on foot or, if you feel like staying put, make a home base at Rondvassbu, a popular lodge perched on the corner of an alpine lake. It's a good starting point for summitting nearby peaks.

The majority of huts are staffed during the summer months, but some are self-serve during the winter.

BEST HUT-TO-HUT TOURS

ADVENTURE INSTITUTIONS

Be inspired by organisations that launched the most daring and intrepid of adventures.

823 ALPINE CLUB, UK

As you climb the final rock face of the highest mountain in the world, Mt Everest, you're following in the icy footsteps of Sir Edmund Hillary and Nepalese Sherpa Tenzing Norgay, who planted the first flag here on 29 May 1953. Hillary was sent by the Joint Himalayan Committee, which was made up of the elite of the even older Alpine Club, formed in 1857 in London to basically climb a lot of peaks. What nearly anybody can do today as a tour package in Nepal bears the snowy echoes of conversations between old-time gentlemen who dreamed of conquering the world's greatest mountains.

Visit the website of the world's first mountaineering club to meet, chat with and be inspired by other mountaineers in the forums: www.alpine-club.org.uk.

821 BRITISH ANTARCTIC SURVEY, UK

Some of Captain James Cook's trips may now be controversial (take the first European landing in the east of Australia) but his spirit for pushing into unknown territory is undeniable. In 1773 his crew was the first to circumnavigate the Antarctic continent (although pack ice prevented them from reaching the coastline). If you follow his route, you'll find not much has changed – the winds are still icy and breath-freezing and the harsh landscape is mile-thick and dotted with hardy penguins. Cook's journey prompted Britain's interest in this continent, leading to the formation of the British Antarctic Survey, which has evolved in its research purposes, from military to scientific.

The British Antarctica Survey website (www.antarctica.ac.uk) has fascinating articles on how researchers live in such harsh conditions.

822 CHINA EXPLORATION & RESEARCH SOCIETY (CERS), CHINA

You are standing by the Yangtze river. It's the longest river in Asia and a waterway that winds through the cultural history of China. Since the Han Dynasty, around two thousand years ago, the Yangtze has allowed communities to irrigate crops from its waters, while its path through misty mountains has inspired timeless Chinese ink art and poetry. But nobody knew where exactly this river began until Hong Kong-born Wong How Man led a team to discover the Yangtze's true source. He founded CERS in 1986 to continue the conservation and exploration of China's remote areas, a new concept in a land that still has ample undiscovered space.

More about how CERS protects nature, and preserves cultural sites including Tibetan monasteries, can be found on its website, www.cers.org.hk.

824 NASA, USA

OK, so it's pretty difficult for the average person to wrangle a flight into space, but NASA has done more than any other organisation to inspire explorers to land on the moon or ponder what is beyond our stars. You can still visit the Kennedy Space Center and meet astronauts who have left Earth's pull to float around in space, or even help look for patterns in the surface of Mars with online photos. NASA was created in 1958 to show us mere mortals how space science could be applied peacefully, allowing us to better appreciate our lonely unique planet.

Commercial space flights will soon start blasting out of our atmosphere. Track the progress on the NASA website, www.nasa.gov.

825 NATIONAL GEOGRAPHIC SOCIETY, USA

Travelling to new lands connects you to other cultures – it makes them personal – and that's the insight that the National Geographic Society seeks to replicate. Its motto is 'Inspiring people to care about the planet since 1888,' and the stunning travel photography and vivid articles in its magazines have inspired generations of adventurers. It has brought us stories of such pioneers as zoologist Jane Goodall, whose studies of Tanzanian chimps have enthralled the world since 1960. 'Only if we understand can we care,' says Goodall. You too can seek insight into the chimps today in the Gombe National Park and still have time for a snorkel in Lake Tanganyika.

Visit www.nationalgeographic.com for more stories about our planet, its creatures and its explorers.

826 SMITHSONIAN INSTITUTION, USA

The blue Hope Diamond has made more international journeys than the people who wore it. Its journey is said to have started in India, next falling into the hands of King Louis XIV in 1678 in France, then crossing the Channel to London in 1812, and finally landing in the USA's Smithsonian Institution in 1958. You can still see it in a museum there today and feel inspired by the people and places it has touched. That's just one of the incredible stories the institution, set up in 1846, has collected, inspiring visitors to its many museums to look beyond their own horizons.

The Smithsonian website (www.si.edu) has art, stories and history to inspire new and veteran travellers.

827 NORWEGIAN GEOGRAPHICAL SOCIETY, NORWAY

If you're going to try to be the first to make it to the North Pole, it helps to be a professional skier and ice skater like Fridtjof Nansen, a Nobel Peace Prize laureate. In 1895, Nansen managed to get further north than anyone had previously by using the natural drift of ice, dodging Arctic foxes and pack ice, and eating walrus and seals to survive. He first announced his daring expedition plans to the Norwegian Geographic Society a year after its formation in 1889. The Society continues to work to explore and conserve the North Pole and its surrounding Arctic regions.

The Norsk Geografisk Selskap publishes a peer-reviewed journal and website, in Norwegian only: www.geografisk.no.

828 RUSSIAN GEOGRAPHICAL SOCIETY, RUSSIA

If you manage to stare eye-to-piercing-eye with an Amur (or Siberian) tiger, you'll realise how magnificent and regal these big cats are. Many in the Russian Far East worship this tiger's majesty, but that hasn't stopped the huge drop in animal populations in the snowy taiga forests. That's where the Russian Geographical Society muscles in with studies and programs to protect the wild feline. This may be a modern campaign but the society dates back to 1845, bringing together scientists and nature enthusiasts who want to promote sustainable growth in the world's largest country by area.

More information on the Society's work in Russia can be found on their website: http://int.rgo.ru.

829 SIERRA CLUB, USA

Groves of giant sequoias, the granite monolith of Half Dome, mountain-climbing paradise El Capitan, the rushing waters of Yosemite Falls – who knows what would remain of these sights today without the Sierra Club? Thanks to its efforts, the land that became Yosemite National Park was saved from being put up for auction. Not bad for the club's first lobbying effort shortly after its creation in 1892. Today the club continues to push to keep the air clear, trees unchopped and water clean for future adventurers.

The Sierra Club website provides activities to get young people involved in its campaigns and the spirit of adventure: www.sierraclub.org.

830 THE ROYAL SOCIETY, UK

Talk about an adventurer – Charles Darwin's voyage on the *HMS Beagle* in 1831 took him to extraordinary places. He felt the tremors of an earthquake in Chile, rode with gauchos in Patagonia around Argentina, met Australian Aborigines, and made his famous observations about evolution and natural selection in the Galápagos Islands that would change science and challenge religion. No wonder the Royal Society of London honoured him as a fellow in 1839. Its founding charter from the 1660s states that the society promotes science for the benefit of humanity, and today it still supports adventurers to go out on a limb and explore our varied planet.

Be inspired by the biographies of Darwin and other science adventurers on www.royalsociety.org.

MOST VERTIGINOUS VENTURES

Climb up dodgy ladders, jump off bridges, teeter along narrow walkways, plummet alongside mountains – just don't look down!

Keeping an eye out for leaping tigers and taking in the breathtaking scenery of this almighty gorge

831 BLACKPOOL TOWER EYE, ENGLAND

It might be a tiddler in world tower terms – Blackpool's answer to the Tour Eiffel measures up at a relatively paltry 158.12m. But Lancashire's Victorian iron-and-steel steeple is both a listed building and a local icon and, since 2011, has offered a discombobulating view of the seaside town. Take the lift up to the top and you'll step out onto the Tower Eye Skywalk, a corridor of wall-to-ceiling-to-floor glass; walking along the transparent ground, the beach and tourist-bustle are fully visible below. It's like gliding on air! Or it's an acrophobe's nightmare, depending on your take on this dizzying perspective.

The Tower Eye (www.theblackpooltower. com) is open Monday to Friday 10am to 3.45pm, Saturday and Sunday 10am to 4.45pm; the Skywalk may close in bad weather conditions.

832 DAVE EVANS BICENTENNIAL TREE, WESTERN AUSTRALIA

WA's native karri trees are one of the world's tallest species, growing to around 90m. From the 1930s, rangers in the Pemberton area took advantage of this, hammering spikes up the trunks of a few fine specimens to provide lookouts for monitoring bushfires. Some of these flimsy spiralling 'staircases' are still climbable, with the 165 pegs nailed into the 68m Dave Evans karri being the highest. You get no harness or safety net, but it's alright, mate! According to the local tourist board, no one has ever *died* climbing Dave. Though, it adds, two people may have had heart attacks...

Dave Evans is in Warren National Park, 15 minutes' drive from Pemberton; climbing certificates are purchasable from Pemberton Visitor Centre. www. pembertonvisitor.com.au.

833 ACONCAGUA TREK, ARGENTINA

South America's tallest peak is arguably the highest nontechnical climb in the world – that is, the most breathtaking extreme reachable by someone physically fit but rope-and-crampon novice. Nontechnical doesn't mean no problem, though – just existing in the oxygen-starved air at Aconcagua's 6962m summit is a challenge. And before that there's the *penitentes* ice spikes to negotiate, the katabatic winds to withstand and the infamous Canaleta to battle – 300m of punishing, energy-sapping scree cruelly positioned at the 6500m mark. But, if you overcome all of these challenges, you can proudly claim to have stood atop the trekkers' world.

Permits are required to climb Aconcagua, available from the Aconcagua National Park Office in Mendoza. Treks take around 3 weeks.

834 TIGER LEAPING GORGE, YUNNAN, CHINA

Michael Palin's been about a bit. So when the esteemed Monty Python-turned-peregrinator confesses he's 'never experienced such vertiginous feelings as when sandwiched between this gorge's walls', it's worth noting. Indeed, Tiger Leaping Gorge is among of the deepest geological gashes in the world, measuring 3900m (12,795ft) from river-ribboned bottom to the tops of the Haba Mountains. At some points it's so narrow an agile feline could (allegedly) jump it – hence the name. A trek here is head spinning but special. Wend through hardwood forests and rice terraces, squeeze along skinny trails, gasp at goats perched right on rock edges. Don't look down...

Buses from Lijiang run via Qiaotou, the start-point for gorge treks. The best time to visit is May to June, when the hills are covered in flowers.

835 HOT-AIR BALLOONING, NAMIB DESERT, NAMIBIA

It's a lot of faith to put in a bit of wicker... Hot-air ballooning may not seem particularly high-adrenalin, but the fact is, once you're up, there's just a creaky basket and a roaring furnace keeping you from pitching to the land far below. But what land: the apricot undulations of the Namib, too vast to properly appreciate from ground-level, are one of the finest places for this kind of old-fashioned floating. Take off at dawn and watch as the sun slowly sets fire to the endless ochre sands, with only the odd blast of the burner breaking the peace.

295

Balloon trips take off from the Sesriem area of the Namib; precise departure location is dependent on wind conditions.

836 CANOPY WALKWAY, TAMAN NEGARA NATIONAL PARK, MALAYSIA

Tropical jungles are just plain annoying. Deep down you *know* they're the most biodiverse habitats on the planet; you can hear the squawking and sense the presence of a million critters. But, often, you see squat. The Canopy Walkway at Taman Negara – home to some of the very oldest tropical jungle anywhere – gives you a fighting chance. Teetering 45m up at treetop level and stretching for 510m, it's the longest such gantry in the world and offer's a bird's eye glimpse (think hornbill, bulbul or one of the other 348 species) into this dense, profuse if frustrating land.

The Walkway is open Saturday to Thursday, 11am to 2.45pm, and Friday, 9am to noon; tickets cost Rm5; see www.taman-negara.com.

837 HEAVEN'S GATE MOUNTAIN CABLECAR, CHINA

Cablecars always look a bit iffy – it just doesn't seem possible that those chunky metal boxes can dangle like that and not occasionally drop off their wires. Which makes the service running up Tianmen Chan – China's sacred Heaven's Gate Mountain – the scariest of all. Being the world's longest and soaring amid sheer-sided rocks, this cablecar covers 7.5km, gaining 1279m in elevation to reach the summit of the holy peak. Of course, many would rather take this giddying transportation, regardless of risk (real or imagined), than face the arduous alternative: a steep 'n' sweaty hike up no less than 999 steps.

Tianmen Chan is 8km south of Zhangjiajie; buses run to Midway Gate, from where the cablecar connects to the summit.

838 BLOUKRANS BRIDGE BUNGEE, TSITSIKAMMA, SOUTH AFRICA

If bungee jumping started at New Zealand's 43m Kawarau Bridge, you could say the South Africans have taken the concept and run with it. The petrifying plunge from Bloukrans Bridge is a whopping 216m, the highest commercial bridge-bungee in the world. Yes, 216m – that's several seconds of freefall in which to contemplate the ground you're hurtling towards, plus several more spent bouncing about a river gorge on a piece of elastic as you wait to be reeled back in. Thankfully, the safety record is exemplary – Prince Harry is just one of the thousands who have lived to tell the tale.

Bloukrans Bridge is on the Garden Route, around six hours' drive west of Cape Town. Jumps operate year-round. Visit www.faceadrenalin.com.

839 EVEREST SKYDIVE, NEPAL

If you don't have the skills to climb the world's highest peak, why not jump off it instead? Well, almost – the Everest Skydive kicks you out of a plane over the Himalaya at 29,500ft (8990m) so you can plummet down from the same height as the mountain, eyeballing it all the way. Equipment is checked rigorously and checked again, oxygen masks are provided, and an acclimatisation trek must be completed beforehand to prepare you for landing at 12,350ft (3765m),

Get another perspective on tropical jungles, 45m up at treetop level at Taman Negara

the world's highest dropzone. All that's left, then, is to take an almighty leap of faith and enjoy the vieeeeeeeeeew.

The 11-day trip costs $25,000 for solo skydivers or $35,000 for tandem skydivers, including prejump acclimatisation trek and equipment; see everest-skydive.com.

840 CN TOWER EDGEWALK, TORONTO, CANADA

First, the facts: it's 150m long, just 1.5m wide, oh, and 116 storeys up... The ledge encircling the main pod

of Toronto's CN Tower had long been fairly inconsequential – since the needly spire was completed in 1976 (then becoming the world's tallest free-standing structure), the ledge just sat there being ledge-y. Then, in 2011, some bright (and brave) spark decided it would be fun if punters could walk round this 356m-high protrusion: the EdgeWalk was born. Now you can join handfuls of other heights-lovers, be harnessed to the overhead safety rail and dare yourself to dangle over the city below.

The EdgeWalk experience (www.cntower. ca) lasts 90 minutes, with around 30 minutes on the ledge itself; trips may be cancelled in extreme weather.

MOST VERTIGINOUS VENTURES

BEST 'PHOENIX' DESTINATIONS

Get here before the tourists do. Once regarded as too dangerous for travellers, these places are now starting to come into their own.

841 NICARAGUA

Amid the subdued grace of Granada you stretch your neck, strolling upon cobblestone streets to view perfect rows of colonial relics. On the Corn Islands you gaze out to sea, registering palm-tree and white-sand overload. You head to the cloud-forest-clad volcanoes of the northeast, itching to knock off a peak or two. Shadowed by the lingering memory of the 1980s Contra Wars, then eclipsed by the tourism

Myanmar has re-emerged, presenting itself as the 'Asia that modernity forgot'

bandwagon of neighbouring Costa Rica, this nation of poets has long been overlooked. Shoe-stringers, travelling the breadth of Central America, have been singing Nicaragua's praises for years, but it's only now that people are starting to sit up and listen.

Both Managua and Granada have international airports but it's usually cheaper to fly into Costa Rica and then head north by bus from there.

842 RWANDA

Your heart is pumping. The silverback stares at you silently for what seems an eternity before dismissing your presence and sloping off into the trees. Rwanda is a wilderness adventure to satisfy anyone's wildest dreams. As home to some of Africa's most lush countryside and the iconic gorilla-tracking experience, you'd think it would be overrun with travellers, but the memory of the 1994 genocide, along with troubling reports of ongoing rebel activity in the areas bordering the Democratic Republic of Congo, mean that Rwanda's tourism resurgence hasn't really taken off just yet. If you do come you'll find an Africa of unparalleled beauty. Oh yeah...and those gorillas.

A limited number of gorilla-tracking permits are issued each day at Parc National des Volcans and cost US$500 per person.

843 HAITI

From tin-can tap-tap buses decorated with vividly coloured panache, to bustling fruit markets and down to the beach, the pulsating kompa beat follows you wherever you go. If you were anywhere else in the Caribbean, those beaches would be jam-packed with tourists and locals alike, but Haiti seems beset by tragedy. Corrupt leadership has led Haiti into a cycle of abject poverty and 2010's earthquake piled misery onto the already huge hill of misfortune Haitians have to battle. But tourism is helping this country rebuild, and the rugged red-earth countryside and fascinating local culture are primed for those seeking a less commercialised Caribbean experience.

Factor extra time into your itinerary if you're going to use public transport; poor infrastructure means travel between towns can take up the whole day.

844 MYANMAR/BURMA

It spent years languishing on the tourism blacklist but with Aung San Suu Kyi now urging people to visit, Myanmar is back on track and becoming one of Asia's most exciting places to see. The first thing you notice is its rawness. Stuck in a time-warp due to decades of harsh authoritarian rule, from the old-fashioned pace of Yangon to the glittering Bagan temples Myanmar is the Asia that modernity forgot. For those who miss the thrills of a dodgy bus ride and genuine welcome from locals, Myanmar really is the Asia of old.

By travelling independently, staying in small guesthouses and choosing to spend money in locally run businesses you'll be supporting the Burmese rather than the ruling government.

JANE SWEENEY/GETTY IMAGES ©

The 16th-century Stari Most (Old Bridge) in Mostar, Hercegovnia, rebuilt, phoenix-like, after the troubles of the '90s

845 BOSNIA AND HERZEGOVINA

Neighbouring Croatia has been pulling in the punters for years. Cross the border into tiny Bosnia and Herzegovina though and the crowds suddenly fall away. In Sarajevo, celebrate this city's vibrant revival from the brutal war of the 1990s. Get your hiking boots on to venture east into one of Europe's least trodden, and most rugged, wildernesses amid the peaks of Sutjeska National Park. Next, turn back the clocks as you enter the hilly Herzegovina region in the south, which seems unfazed by modern life's rush. This crossroads of cultures is a trip down memory lane to a Europe fast fading away.

Weather-wise, spring and summer are the best times to visit but if you're into winter sports there's excellent skiing from January to March.

846 CHERNOBYL, UKRAINE

In Pripyat you tread softly with museum-silent reverence into a world frozen in 1986. Weeds have crept up between the concrete cracks, slowly swamping the town. Soviet propaganda posters hang on walls. The Ferris wheel stands motionless, its top peeking out above unpruned trees. This ghost town is an eerie monument to the night in April 1986 when Reactor Four exploded at the Chernobyl nuclear plant, showering its toxic cloud of radiation down on the town. Today, tours of this eerie radiation 'dead zone' are a reminder of humanity's failings in the Cold War's era of secrecy.

Tours to the Chernobyl exclusion zone need to be arranged in advance; the easiest place to do this from is Kiev. SoloEast (www.tourkiev.com/chernobyltour) is a reliable operator.

847 IRAQI KURDISTAN

Face it. Any country where they serve you tea and let you lounge on comfy chairs while the border officials complete the visa formalities is going to get high marks for hospitality. Ever wanted to travel to a place without a guidebook? Welcome to the semi-autonomous region of Iraqi Kurdistan. Occupying the northern sliver of the country, this fascinating place is a far cry from the Iraq you see on the TV news. Official sights may be few, but the wild and mountainous terrain begs to be trekked and the open smiles and friendly curiosity of your hosts will resonate with you long after you've left.

To get you started see www.tourism kurdistan.com or Lonely Planet's *Middle East* guidebook.

848 SOUTH LEBANON

Sidon's labyrinthine *souq* (market) leads you down to the harbour, which is guarded by a storybook Crusader castle. An hour south, passing a haze of Mediterranean citrus orchards, you pause in front of Tyre's El Mina ruins where the marble columns roll down to the shore. South Lebanon has been labelled a no-go zone because of its association with Hezbollah but scaremongers forget to mention the miles of sandy beach, the Ottoman architecture and the ancient sites so empty that the site guardians invite you to sit down for a chat and cup of tea. Shush, let's keep it a secret a little longer.

Both Sidon and Tyre are easily reached as day trips from Beirut, or you can spend the night in Tyre at family-run Auberge Al-Fanar (www.alfanarresort.com).

849 ALGERIA

From Algiers' whitewashed casbah, which dips its way down to the sea, to the Sahara's endless never-never of sand that stretches out to a shimmer on the horizon, Algeria is North Africa's most surprising nation. Having wrapped itself in a bloody civil war for much of the 1990s, Algeria has yet to experience the tourist influx of neighbouring Morocco but for those prepared to rough it a little, the desert here is the big-sky stuff of explorer heaven. Vast lunarscapes of craggy rock, epic mountain vistas and ancient rock art are just some of the rewards for those who venture here.

Tourist visas need to be applied for in advance and, if travelling independently, proof of accommodation bookings within Algeria must be provided with your application.

850 COLOMBIA

It may be more famous for its drug cartels and reputation as a kidnapping capital, but curious travellers have been venturing here for years, coming back with stories of easy hammock-on-beach living, colonial cities and stunning hill-country hiking. This is South America in a nutshell and it's as easy on the wallet as it is on the eye. Once you've been wooed by Cartagena's pastel-hued beauty, partied with the locals in Cali and jungle-trekked to the mysterious ruins of Ciudad Perdida in the Sierra Nevada, you'll understand what all the fuss is about.

Some of Colombia's more rural areas are still considered unsafe for travellers. Check the latest government travel advisories for up-to-date warnings.

BEST 'PHOENIX' DESTINATIONS

TOP ADVENTURE SKILLS

The know-how you'll need to save your skin when you're adventuring. Here's how to...

853 TREAT A SNAKEBITE

When herpetologist Joe Slowinski was bitten by a krait in Myanmar, miles from medical assistance, he knew that the following hours would seal his fate. If he'd been able to survive for 48 hours, the venom's toxins would have expended themselves – but within 27 hours he was dead, unable to access treatment. If you're bitten by a venomous snake, whether it's a rattlesnake in the American southwest or an eastern brown snake in Australia, the clock is ticking. Immobilise the limb. Apply pressure by bandaging tightly with strips of clothing. And keep as still as possible while someone goes for help. Tourniquets are no longer recommended, and cutting and sucking the poison out only happens in Hollywood films. Prevention is better than the cure; watch where you're putting your hands and feet!

851 STAY WARM

The lowest recorded temperature of an adult who survived hypothermia is around 15.5°C (60.8°F), which doesn't seem excessively cold. Yet our bodies are designed to function from 36.5°C to 37.5°C (98°F to 100°F), which is a reminder of what delicate, tropical organisms we actually are. With a body temperature of 35°C (95°F), you'll start shivering. By 31°C (88°F), you've entered hypothermia so severe you'll no longer shiver. We lose heat through exposed skin; cold wind on a damp body will strip heat as effectively as snow. You need to get dry, find insulation and get out of the wind. Stuff your clothes with leaves and curl up to shield your extremities. If you have a large plastic bag handy, get into it. As survival guru Tony Nester says: think like a squirrel.

852 NAVIGATE BY STARS

When your smartphone has run out of juice and your map is so crumpled it's illegible, you'll need to use your powers of observation to navigate. In the 7th and 8th centuries, star maps were more comprehensive than maps of the world. But, keeping things simple, as long you can recognise the North Star in the Northern Hemisphere and the Southern Cross in the Southern Hemisphere, you should be able to orient yourself. The North Star – Polaris – is the last star in the handle of the Little Dipper; walk towards it and you are heading north. The bad news: it's a myth that the North Star is the brightest in the sky. In the Southern Hemisphere, find the Southern Cross (four stars in a tilted cross; check tattooed Australians for exact configuration); the longer axis points south.

854 FIND WATER

It can take up to five days to die of thirst, though when exercising it's possible to lose two percent of your body weight in moisture per hour, which speeds things up a bit. But you will have time to try to find water. Using containers to collect rainfall is a good idea. Watch to see where birds and insects congregate. Next, you could try digging for it, though without advice from locals this should be a last resort. A less laborious technique is to make a condensation trap, for which you will need as large a plastic bag or sheet as is available. Find a tree or bush and tie the bag around as much foliage as possible. Through transpiration, plants lose water vapour through their leaves, which will recondense in the plastic bag.

302

855 MAKE A FIRE

Nobody knows for sure when mankind first worked out how to light fire. The best guess? Around a million years ago. What we do know is that cooking meat helped us digest protein more efficiently, thus enabling our brains to grow, which meant we developed the smarts to invent magnesium fire starters. Make a nest of tinder – dry moss, grass, cotton fluff – with some kindling of dry leaves and small twigs. With a knife, shave some filings from the magnesium stick then run the back of the blade down the flint side of the stick. The sparks will make the magnesium flare up, lighting the tinder. Introduce kindling and you have the beginnings of a campfire. Don't have a magnesium fire starter? How about matches?

856 CROSS A RIVER

Crossing a fast-flowing river – with or without piranhas – is one of the riskiest things to do in the wild. Whether you're with others or not, you'll need to check out the best crossing spot. Currents usually flow more powerfully around bends, so pick a straight stretch of river. If there's a choice between wide or narrow, remember that wide might mean more shallow, whereas narrow channels can often be deep. Ripples might also be sign of shallow water. When you've picked your spot, undo your pack (you don't want it to drag you under if you slip), remove your boots and socks, and face upstream as you sidestep across the river. A stout stick adds stability. Link arms with others if possible.

857 SHELTER IN THE SNOW

Constructing an igloo could be an ambitious undertaking without a saw and Eskimo know-how. Let's start with a snow cave. Find a large bank or drift of snow. At right angles to the prevailing wind, tunnel into the snow. You want to dig slightly upward. To stop the ceiling collapsing, make it domed. With a stick, add a small ventilation hole in the roof. You can use your pack as a makeshift door. Insulate the floor of the cave with dry foliage if you can find any; Sweden's famous Ice Hotel uses animal furs but then they also have ice glasses for vodka so perhaps it's best not dwell on what your cave lacks.

858 SIGNAL FOR HELP

You followed back-country best practice and told someone where you were going and when you'd be back. Now that you're late in returning they have, hopefully, alerted a search-and-rescue party. How do you make their job easier? Stay with the vehicle if you have one. If not, get to somewhere in the open where you can be seen. This means leaving the cover of a jungle's canopy. If you spot a plane and you have a mirror, angle it at the sun until you can see the reflected light against an object, then flash the rescue party with the light three times. Or use the internationally recognised distress signal of jumping up and down and waving your arms. If you need to clarify whether help is required, hold both arms up for 'yes', or angle one arm up and the other down for 'no'.

859 CLIMB A CANYON

When you go past the point of no return, sometimes the only escape from a slot canyon is up. Use the chimney climbing technique (this also works when climbing cracks in rock faces). Wedge yourself with your back against one wall, your hands pressing back against the wall below your buttocks and both feet jammed against the facing wall. With your torso higher than your feet, bend one knee and move the foot beneath your buttocks and lever yourself upwards. Slide the foot against the facing wall up. Repeat as required.

860 BUILD A SHELTER

Whether you're lost in the Appalachian woods or the African savannah, you'll need a shelter for the night. The first rule of making a shelter is to sleep off the ground (this is where squirrels have an advantage over people). First, find the lee of a rock or build a windbreak with branches. If you have a lightweight tarp (an essential piece of kit for backwoods adventures), string it between two trees, weighting the lower edge with rocks. Collect branches, leaves, pine needles – whatever is around you – and build a platform. It won't be comfortable but it will help you retain warmth. If you have the energy, dig a trench in which to build a fire parallel to the awning.

BEST BEGINNERS' CLIMBS

Lace up your boots and slip on a harness as we bring you 10 beginners' climbs to blow your mind.

CHRISTIAN KOBER/GETTY IMAGES ©

Imja Tse (Island Peak) has a reputation for being the 'easiest' of the 6000m peaks, but don't let that lull you into a false sense of security

861 YELLOW CIRCUIT, ROCHER AUX SABOT, FONTAINEBLEAU, FRANCE

Fontainebleau is a climber's paradise – perfect sandstone boulders above flat, sandy landings, set amidst a beautiful forest only an hour from Paris. Climb in the steps of the bleausards who marked the bouldering circuits with small arrows that you can still follow today, safe in the knowledge you are never too far from a *boulangerie*. If we had to pick one of the many great circuits, it would be the yellow at Rocher Aux Sabot. It lacks the cold and misery of mountaineering, the terrifying falls of rock climbing, but never fear if you like it spicy, things can go wrong in Font – someone could kick sand in your baguette.

You can climb all year round in Fontainebleau; the warmer months are more pleasant, although purists might prefer winter when friction is best.

863 GOUTER ROUTE, MT BLANC, FRANCE

Mountaineering is all about the objective dangers – rockfall, avalanches, cold, altitude – but on the Gouter Route you can add one more: other climbers. Being the easiest route up Mt Blanc, it's as popular as an ice-cream shop in summer. Thus the idiot quotient is high. So get up early, one, because you want to cross the Grand Couloir before it turns into a bowling alley of rock-fall, and two, because you might beat some of the crowds. It isn't all bad though; the route gets easier as you get higher, the Bosses Ridge right before the summit is supremely beautiful and the summit...well, you are at the highest point in the Alps and western Europe – need we say more?

The Gouter Route is best attempted by novices in summer with a guide; allowing four days to summit helps with acclimatisation.

862 IMJA TSE (ISLAND PEAK), NEPAL

Crunching up the summit ridge of Imja Tse in your crampons, a mighty drop either side, its reputation as the easiest 6000m (19,685ft) peak in the world may seem a distant memory as you gasp for breath in the thin air, feeling the 1000 vertical metres of ascent deep in your leg muscles. But all that falls away at the summit, the massive bulk of Lhotse towering 2km (1.25 miles) higher to the north, and you see why the peak was dubbed Island Peak by the explorer Eric Shipton – because it sits proud and solitary amidst an ocean of ice.

Imja Tse is usually climbed from Base Camp at 5087m (16,690ft); it is mostly a nontechnical, steep snow plod, with the last section to the summit involving some ice climbing.

864 TOWER RIDGE, BEN NEVIS, SCOTLAND

You've been climbing all day, mostly easy scrambling up what seems like a never-ending ridge, but now it's all getting serious as the sun drops low in the sky and you come to Tower Gap, a narrow spine of rock with a massive drop either side. If you were braver you'd walk across, but instead you shuffle over on your bum, before nervously abseiling into the gap. Now relax – it's just a few easy pitches to the top. Not only will you have climbed Tower Ridge, the best alpine route in Scotland, but it's also only a short journey to tag the summit of Britain's highest peak (1344m/4409ft) before descending to the warmth of a hut and dinner.

Tower Ridge is best attempted in summer – it is also climbed in winter but this is a much more serious proposition.

865 SNAKE DIKE, HALF DOME, YOSEMITE, USA

Wiping sweat from your brow, you dump your pack at the base of the wall and look up: 300m of vertigo-inducing granite looms above, its curving back to the sky. Four hours of hiking has brought you below the rump of Half Dome, rising 1400m (4593ft) from the Yosemite Valley floor. Starting up Snake Dike, a sinuous, pink-granite intrusion that's the easiest technical route, you climb the slabby wall for hours, basking in the sun. Finally you reach an incredible view...and the million tourists who took the easy route – a tourist track with cables and queues.

305

Snake Dike is best attempted with an experienced leader as it has a long approach and many run-outs. May and September are the prime climbing months in Yosemite.

866 THE BARD, MT ARAPILES, AUSTRALIA

Rising from the wheat fields of western Victoria like an ancient, crumbling fortress is Mt Arapiles, the best beginner's crag in the universe. And for any beginner there's one rite of passage that cannot be missed: the 120m (394ft) Bard. Winding its way up the proudest part of Arapiles, the second pitch is the one everyone fears – a short, awkward traverse below a roof, the world dropping away beneath – but once overcome, three more brilliant pitches are followed by an adventurous descent through a cave and a long abseil. Does it get any better?

The best time to climb at Arapiles is March to November; summer is very hot.

867 STANDARD EAST FACE, FLATIRONS, COLORADO, USA

Rising behind the outdoor paradise of Boulder like a set of ragged shark's teeth are the Flatirons. Like fingers there are five, and the third – an immaculate, massive slab of sandstone, conglomerate and shale – holds what many, including legendary climber Yvon Chouinard, call the finest beginner's route in the US: the east face. It romps up the easy, low-angled face to the pointy summit, where three exciting abseils take you back to the ground. And if the 'standard' route is not challenging enough for you, consider some past ascents – it's been climbed naked, speed soloed (in 5.59 minutes) and, in 1953, ascended in rollerskates.

The Flatirons are closed from February to July for the raptor breeding season, but can be climbed at all other times if conditions are suitable.

868 VIA FERRATA DI MARMOLADA, DOLOMITES, ITALY

Some climbers may look down on *vie ferrate* (iron roads) with their cables and steel rungs as not being 'real' climbing, but for history, convenience and pure fun they are hard to beat. And what better one to choose than that which climbs the west ridge of the 'Queen of the Dolomites', the Marmolada. Ascending a thousand vertical metres, it is one of the most difficult *vie ferrate*, which means you still have to exercise common sense, particularly regarding the weather – iron, lightning and high places ring any bells? Don't forget to bring your crampons for the icy sections. This route was established before WWI, making it the oldest *via ferrata* in Europe.

Conditions are king here, and best between June and September; beginners should hire a local guide.

869 NORTH-WEST RIDGE, MT ASPIRING, NEW ZEALAND

While Aspiring may not be the highest peak in New Zealand it's definitely the most handsome – an aesthetic pyramid towering over surrounding peaks. Called Tititea (Glittering Peak) by the Māori, the north-west ridge is considered a classic first summit for an aspiring mountaineer. You'll have to be ready to down your morning porridge at an ungodly hour ahead of a long, long day traversing an epic ridge, but if you survive the South Island's notorious weather, terrible rock, avalanches and crevasses, you'll have climbed New Zealand's second-highest summit (or at least

Mt Arapiles provides climbers with a gravity-defying traverse and an unforgettable descent

come close, as the Māori consider it disrespectful to stand on the very highest point).

Mt Aspiring is best climbed in summer with an experienced partner or guide. You will need to have solid basic mountaineering skills.

870 KAIN ROUTE, BUGABOO SPIRE, BUGABOOS, BRITISH COLUMBIA, CANADA

If you like climbs with an alpine flavour, a good helping of wilderness, perhaps a side garnish of glacier travel and a dollop of commitment, the Kain Route will be to your taste. Following a ridge up the mighty granite monolith of Bugaboo Spire, it's the easiest way up (and back down) one of the finest summits in North America. Climbing here also has a unique flavour; aside from all the usual alpine hazards (weather, crevasses, rockfall) it has as a few others – bears and, worse still, rubber-eating porcupines. Laugh as you may, there's almost nothing worse than returning from an epic ascent to find a porcupine's eaten half your car.

June to September is the Bugaboos' climbing season, although the area is subject to extreme weather at any time. Ice-axes and crampons are mandatory, and roping up on glaciers is recommended.

BEST BEGINNERS' CLIMBS

GET YOUR THRILLS INDOORS

Take a thrill-ride indoors on these adventures – you don't have to be out in the elements to get the adrenalin pumping.

871 CHAKAZOOLU INDOOR THEME PARK, BAHRAIN

Dust storms ride the winds from Iraq and Saudi Arabia each summer and blanket Bahrain with grit. Up the deathly stakes with temperatures reaching 50°C and you'll be panting to get to the indoor theme park of this island kingdom. Savour the calm of cool air, because soon your hair will be standing on end as you take the first ridiculously steep ascent on the roller coaster… and then drop into an Africa-themed tunnel. The heat isn't going anywhere soon, so there's time for the ghost train and indoor hot-air balloon ride – yes, really.

The theme park is nestled in the Dana Mall, which is in the Seef district of Bahrain.

872 INDOOR SKIING AND SNOWBOARDING, DUBAI

Only this sweltering Middle East city, flowing with oil wealth, could turn a 40°C day into a below-zero wonderland. Inside this mall, you can feel the cold air rush by you as you soar down one of five runs on your snowboard. You can see your breath and if you fall, real snow will cushion your faceplant – though not your dignity. Head back up to the top on the chairlift and drop in again from the 85m 'peak'. The giddy view to the bottom is nerve-rattling and the workout on your legs very real. Get ready for the surreal heat blast as you step back outside.

Ski Dubai is in the Mall of the Emirates. All equipment and clothing rental is included in the ticket price.

873 INDOOR ROCK-CLIMBING IN TOKYO, JAPAN

In the space-squeezed Japanese capital even indoor sports are looking skywards to make the most of limited real estate. All around this metropolis people are discovering that, after the day's work is done, stretching out your fingers for the next colourful plasticine-like lump is more than a good bicep booster, it's a way to meet and strategise with other

MAREMAGNUM/GETTY IMAGES ©

people – forget lonely gyms. In rock climbing, the music is beat-heavy to get you moving, so that when you reach the top and take a peek at the faces of onlookers below your breathing and heartbeat will be racing along with the soundtrack.

Indoor rock-climbing has become more popular than its outdoor cliff-face cousin. In Tokyo, try J&S Vertical Climbing Zone; see http://js-ebisu.jimdo.com (Japanese) or http://whereintokyo.com/venues/25214.html (English).

874 INDOOR SKATEBOARDING, COPENHAGEN, DENMARK

Danes, known for the finest designer chairs, can also get their wheels grubby at Copenhagen's indoor skate park. Alis Wonderland Skate Pool wears its cred on its graf-covered walls, fitting decor for this one-time ramp which was turned full-blown skate bowl with support from hip-hop music labels, and it's made a happy home in the rebellious Christiania area, where street stalls are filled with piercing jewellery and smoking paraphernalia. The wooden skatebowl is surrounded by benches of onlookers, so when you drop in over the edge of the coping, you'd better be sure you can make that vert (that's a vertical ramp in skate speak).

Alis Wonderland Skate Pool doesn't have fixed opening or closing times – nor an entrance fee – and is in the autonomous community of Christiania, which has its own special laws about soft drugs.

Sweltering in Dubai? Go skiing indoors. Problem solved

875 ZERO GRAVITY WITHOUT THE HASSLE, CAPE CANAVERAL, FLORIDA, USA

Want to experience that outer-space feeling where everything is floating about you but don't have the grades to get into NASA? Grab some air hang-time (upside down) in a flight from Cape Canaveral, lift-off point for the Apollo moon missions. Your plane soars towards the horizon and in half an hour starts to fly in parabolas – basically flying up and down to make you feel weightless. Now unbuckle and float in the air in a slow-motion high. You'll feel one-sixth your weight, as if you were on the Moon. Don't lose your lunch!

The Zero Gravity Corporation conducts the flights; NASA itself has used them for training. Visit http://www.gozerog.com.

Turn yourself upside down at Cape Canaveral

876 INDOOR BUNGEE JUMPING, SHEFFIELD, ENGLAND

If leaping into the air from a great height tied to nothing more than elastic isn't enough to make you sweat, this chamber of thrills makes your heart thump even faster by plunging you into semidarkness, obscuring a deep drop with smoke machines and projecting video of other screaming jumpers. The industrial setting of this former steelworks adds an extra edge to the atmosphere. And that's all before you've made the head-first leap of faith. After you come down from the adrenalin high, grab some quiet time in one of Sheffield's many parks, perhaps the aptly named Peace Park.

Indoor bungee jumping is available at Magna Science Adventure Centre in Rotherham. From the Sheffield Interchange coach station the 69 bus takes you right there.

877 INDOOR SKYDIVING, LAS VEGAS, USA

Las Vegas is the logical place for a simulated skydiving experience – it's the perfect fit amongst replica Eiffel Towers, pyramids of Egypt and Venice canals. A vertical wind tunnel padded like a bouncy castle creates the illusion of a skydive without the vertigo-inducing heights – plus here you've got a net to catch you at the bottom. Stretched out on the net, your body thrills as the high-powered fan underneath suddenly shoots you into the air. When it ends you itch for your next turn, planning a jump against the fan blast for that plane-leap feeling.

You'll be kitted out with the necessary jumpsuit, helmet and gloves after your short training session on how to land. See www.vegasindoorskydiving.com.

878 INDOOR BULL-RIDING, TEXAS, USA

How long you can stay seated on an irate bull in Texas, where the minimum riding qualifier is a life-flashing-before-your-eyes eight seconds? The bucking animal tries to thrash you off as you fight with one hand to keep hold of the attached rope. Every kick and spin brings you closer to being tossed into the air and closer to the ground of the rodeo or the bull's horns. Hmm...maybe not. Less lethal and less exploitative (for the bovine), go animal-free on a mechanical bull in a bar, where the shouts of moustached drunks are as beastly as it gets.

Bars with mechanical bulls in Austin often feature bar girls in bikinis and live bands – love 'em or hate 'em. Try http://rebelshonkytonkaustin.com.

879 INDOOR LASER TAG, MELBOURNE, AUSTRALIA

Shooting friends is a good way to lose them, unless it's with a harmless laser light. But don't be fooled, laser tag can get competitive, especially if the first person down is buying the post-combat drinks. Your eyes flit and your ears are alert in the darkness; you step quietly so your prey won't hear you. And then – zap! – your laser hits your friend's chest, their vest light changing colour as they suffer a pain-free 'death'. Drinks are on them! Melbourne has often been voted most liveable city in the world but woolly scarves come out in winter so it's handy to take adventure sports indoors.

Melbourne has indoor laser-tag venues all over the city and its suburbs. Melbourne is Australia's second-largest city after Sydney, a one-hour flight away.

880 INDOOR SURFING IN YORKSHIRE, ENGLAND

Let's face it, Yorkshire weather is unpredictable; the region can dish up lush green hills on land and some mighty barrels on the coast (if you can find them) but equally it can pound you with wind and rain. Head indoors, then, for some gentle machine-generated waves perfect for body boarding before leaping to your feet for some serious surfing when the instructors flip the FlowRider switch and make some powerful waves. It's controlled and safe yet thrashing enough that the organisers advise you bring close-fitting swimwear – you don't want any wardrobe malfunctions.

The pool is limited to groups of twelve. Optional wetsuits are provided to keep you warm between rides. Visit www.flowhouse.co.uk.

GET YOUR THRILLS INDOORS

ROUSING READS FOR ARMCHAIR ADVENTURERS

Find inspiration for your next adventure in these tales of amazing people and incredible places.

881 THE WILDER SHORES OF LOVE, LESLEY BLANCH (1954)

The decision taken by the Royal Geographic Society in 1913 to admit women fellows was a little overdue: female adventurers had been every bit as bold as their moustached and pith-helmeted counterparts over the 18th and 19th centuries. Lesley Blanch profiles four such women. There's Isabel Burton, wife of explorer Richard Francis Burton (of *Arabian Nights* fame), who explored Africa and lived in Damascus and Trieste. And most remarkable of all, Aimée Du Buc de Rivéry, a steely French woman who was captured by pirates while a teenager and allegedly sold into a harem in Turkey, where she became Sultan Selim III's confidante and the mother of his heir. Blanch herself, a features editor for *Vogue* magazine in the 1930s and 1940s, travelled widely in Central Asia, hitchhiking through Afghanistan and riding the Trans-Siberian Railway.

882 MOUNTAINS OF THE MIND, ROBERT MACFARLANE (2003)

Robert Macfarlane's award-winning exploration of humanity's fascination with high places will almost certainly kindle your desire to head for the hills. An academic at Cambridge University, Macfarlane punctuates his stories of the geology, art, literature and philosophy of the mountains with his own adventures in Scotland's Cairngorms and the European Alps. Most mountain ranges were mapped, if not conquered entirely, in the 19th century and this work concludes with George Mallory's death on Mt Everest in 1922. 'Mountains seem to answer an increasing imaginative need in the West,' Macfarlane writes. 'But for most of these millions of people, myself included, the attraction of mountains has more to do with beauty and strangeness than with risk and loss.'

883 KING OF THE CLOUD FOREST, MICHAEL MORPURGO (1988)

From Hogwarts to the Himalaya, as children we're inspired by books that conjure unknown worlds. Michael Morpurgo's 1980s novel tells the story of Ashley, the son of missionaries living in western China in the late 1930s when the Japanese invade. Ashley and Uncle Sung flee towards the safety of India, a journey that means crossing the Himalayan mountains. Separated from Uncle Sung in a storm, Ashley encounters far more mysterious protectors in the cloud forests of Shangri-La. He stays in this enchanted land until an incident makes him wonder whether his hairy friends might be better off without him.

884 BRUCE CHATWIN, NICHOLAS SHAKESPEARE (1999)

Bruce Chatwin's books – *In Patagonia, The Songlines* and *What Am I Doing Here?* (his collected journalism), among others – should be on every traveller's bookshelf. But Nicholas Shakespeare's biography of this enigmatic, omnivorous writer is just as much a joy to read, as he explores the complexities of a writer who loved people (his vast circle of friends ranged from Salman Rushdie to Werner Herzog) but sought solitude off the beaten track. Chatwin's travel writing weaves together truth and fiction, and Shakespeare spent seven years tracking his footprints around the world to unpick his embellished anecdotes. Later, Shakespeare settled in Tasmania where he wrote – yes, you guessed it – *In Tasmania*.

885 WATERLOG, ROGER DEAKIN (1999)

There's something particularly thrilling about the caress of wild water. It's a thrill that drives Roger Deakin to take 'a long swim through Britain' over the course of a year. He dives, or steps gingerly, into rivers and streams, ponds and lakes to rediscover a natural world many long thought lost. But for all the free-floating, frog's-eye view of the Scilly Isles and Jura's lochs in Scotland's Hebrides islands, some of Deakin's most illuminating dips take place at his moated farmhouse in Suffolk. It's a reminder that rewarding adventures can be had on your doorstep. Early on, Deakin quotes Australian poet Les Murray – 'I am only interested in everything' – and the remainder of the book proves it true.

886 A SHORT WALK IN THE HINDU KUSH, ERIC NEWBY (1958)

In *A Short Walk in the Hindu Kush*, Eric Newby fashions the wry, self-deprecating blueprint for the comic jaunts of travel writers Bill Bryson and Tim Cahill through the tale of an amateurish adventure across the Afghan mountains. Aware that a degree of preparation for the peaks of Nuristan would be sensible, Newby and companion Hugh Carless scramble about in Wales for a weekend. Then it's off to the Hindu Kush via Istanbul, Armenia and Tehran. Newby and Carless meet Wilfred Thesiger near the Panjshir River. On spotting the two men blowing up air beds for the night, Thesiger declares: 'you must be a couple of pansies.'

887 THE RIGHT STUFF, TOM WOLFE (1979)

What greater adventure is there than to break free of Earth's bonds and reach the heavens? It would have been difficult for any writer to stuff up the story of the race to send the first person into space. But Tom Wolfe, with his propulsive turn of phrase, skill and a wealth of technical detail, has created an extraordinarily engaging account that focuses on the lives and personalities of the very first astronauts, such as John Glenn. The book is as much about ambition, a familiar Wolfe theme, as it is about rockets. It opens with hotshot test pilot Chuck Yeager taking the rocket-powered X-1 aircraft beyond the sound barrier with a couple of broken ribs – the result of a half-cut, moonlit horse race two days before his flight. Yeager, clearly, had the right stuff.

888 A RIVER RUNS THROUGH IT, NORMAN MACLEAN (1976)

Moby Dick, A Perfect Storm, The Old Man and the Sea: there's a shoal of must-read books about fishing. They're mostly from the flinty-eyed-man-against-the-elements school of adventure writing. Norman Maclean's short story, set in the 1930s, is different. It's about family and love and art and the passage of time itself. The cold, fast-flowing Blackfoot River in western Montana is the backdrop for this soulful American classic and Maclean's sentences move with the rhythm and grace of a fly-fisherman's cast, building to a final paragraph that lives on long after the book is closed.

889 THE SNOW LEOPARD, PETER MATTHIESSEN (1978)

The Snow Leopard isn't really about snow leopards. Or the blue sheep that Peter Matthiessen's companion, zoologist George Schaller, is studying in the Himalaya. Rather, in Dolpo, a remote corner of the Tibetan plateau northwest of Dhaulagiri, Matthiessen seeks to come to terms with nothing less than life and death. Hiking the sheep tracks of these ridges and ravines, he reflects on the death of his wife the previous year and the cycles of life in Zen Buddhism. It's a journey that perhaps could only be undertaken in these mystic mountains: 'I am not here to seek the "crazy wisdom"; if I am, I shall never find it. I am here to be here, like these rocks and sky and snow, like this hail that is falling down out of the sun.'

890 JOHN KRAKAUER, INTO THIN AIR (1997)

John Krakauer's authoritative account of the disaster of May 10, 1996, when eight climbers died in a snowstorm high up on Mt Everest, will put most readers off joining the ever-growing number of commercial expeditions up the world's tallest mountain. But as a cautionary tale of how minor errors can snowball into major problems at high altitude, it can't be bettered (though its lessons haven't necessarily sunk in – in May 2006, 11 people died on the mountain). For a response to Krakauer's allegations, read *The Climb* by G Weston DeWalt and Anatoli Boukreev, one of the guides on the mountain that day.

THE TWO OF US: ADVENTURES IN TANDEM

Share the most buddy-friendly adventures in the world and be all smiles through the sublime and ridiculous.

Come fly with me.... OK, we'll glide, then.... Views of Rio don't come any better than this

891 HASH HOUSE HARRIERS, ACCRA, GHANA

Adventure sports aren't all competitive. Hash House Harriers are social clubs that work like one large hide-and-seek game with a booze-up at the end. It makes for a regular Amazing Race with 'hounds' walking and running to find the 'hare', who lays down clues such as chalk or flour marks. This isn't a sprint for elite athletes though; as a 1950s Hashing registration card reflects, the aim is to persuade the older members that they are not as old as they feel. Most clubs or 'chapters' describe themselves as a drinking club with a running problem.

There are nearly two thousand Hasher chapters worldwide, from Ghana to Antarctica. For Accra Hashers events, check out http://www.accrahash.com.

892 HORSEBACK RIDING, MONGOLIA

The Mongolian horse is embedded in its country's culture – before they can walk, Mongolians are taught to ride this pony-like horse. The horses that the nomads ride across the endless Mongolian steppes today are the same as those ridden by Genghis Khan, who quipped, 'It is easy to conquer the world from the back of a horse.' Maybe it is conquering the humdrum of the everyday that's more doable these days! So take a friend along to discover diverse Mongolian ecosystems of forest, desert and lakes and visit culturally vibrant ethnic groups. At the end of the trek, toast your journey with an *airag*, a drink made from fermented mare's milk.

Riding tours can last up to eight hours a day. Visit www.hiddentrails.com for details.

893 TANDEM BICYCLE, AMSTERDAM

Nothing feels more team-like than two buddies riding the same bicycle. It's handy for riding with vision-impaired people but also great as a way to share an adventure, bickering aside: hey, no slacking off back there! Heads will turn as the two of you ride single-file through the towns and colourful tulips. Later, guide your bike back to a barge for a relaxing dinner and float to your next Netherlands destination, recharged for the next day's ride.

A Bike and Barge tour is available from the Bicycle Adventure Club and costs from US$1699 for a double, bike not included. See http://www. bicycleadventureclub.org/.

RENE FREDERIC/AGEFOTOSTOCK ©

894 HANG GLIDING, RIO DE JANEIRO

You're half-a-kilometre above the green mountains of Rio's Tijuca Forest National Park when your buddy, gliding with you in the sky, gives you a thumbs-up and points below to a golden ribbon of sand, nuzzled against the endless blue ocean. But these aren't just any beaches, they're drenched in sunshine and song. Over there is Ipanema, long and lovely...ahh. And far off is Copacabana, where music is always in fashion. You're both all smiles. It's like flying in dreams, with the rush of air and a soft-as-a-cloud landing on Pepino beach.

Flights are with a professional instructor. The best time for good wind conditions is between 9am and 2pm. See www.riohanggliding.com.

315

JAN WLODARCZYK/ALAMY ©

Drifting on the Mae Taeng River can be cruisey, but hang on to your buddy when the water gets swirly

895 BAMBOO AND WHITE-WATER RAFTING IN CHIANG MAI, THAILAND

A gentle float on a bamboo raft down the Mae Taeng River is pleasant enough and standing on the bamboo raft is a challenge you should take – you have to balance yourself as if on a surfboard or you'll drop into that frothing water. But it's more fun white-water rafting upstream where the river starts life thrashing about, grabbing at unsuspecting rafters, and proceeds through a series of rapids (some grade IV and V). It's the perfect opportunity to cement a friendship as you hang on for dear life, swirling, getting mighty wet and screaming with the excitement of it all.

Rides on the Mae Taeng River leave with guides from nearby Chiang Mai in north Thailand. Conditions can be treacherous so ask outfitters about their safety standards and training. See http://www.queenbeetours.com/

896 TOBOGGAN DOWN A SNOW SLOPE IN QUEBEC, CANADA

The indigenous Innu and Cree people of North Canada used a basic sled as transport across the icy landscape. Nowadays, two (or more) of you can take a toboggan down powder slopes for full-speed, high-on-snow laughs in and around Quebec. Choose a toboggan made from wood if you want a more culturally authentic descent. Grab that rope to steer, stretch out your legs and get your passenger to hold onto you tight as you take the plunge. It's about as cosy as you can get travelling at speed over icy terrain.

For safety it is advisable to wear a helmet on steeper slopes. A full list of nearly 50 Quebec tobogganing can be found on the city's official site: www. bonjourquebec.com/qc-en/attractions-directory/tobogganing-winter-sliding/.

897 ABSEIL IN THE BLUE MOUNTAINS, AUSTRALIA

Like most tandem adventures, abseiling (rappelling) in the Australian bush necessitates trust. Dropping over the edge of a cliff with a buddy on the other side to secure ropes and to balance your speed is the ultimate bonding experience. It's as if you were a Venetian blind being lowered and raised to face the dark green carpet of treetops below. Share the thrill of peering over the edge of a seeming abyss as cockatoos fly overhead, and share the excitement of pushing off from the summit in a rush of adrenalin and sweaty hands.

A combined train-and-bus ticket is available from major train stations in Sydney to take you to the Blue Mountains in under two hours. Numerous abseiling operators run day courses and can arrange pick-ups from Sydney.

898 UNDERWATER HOCKEY, EGER, HUNGARY

Some hardcore types in 1954 decided that weighing down a puck and smacking it at the bottom of a pool with a banana-sized stick would make hockey more challengingly fun. Well, it did – so learn to hold your breath and kick quickly to the top of the pool because you only have a snorkel to gasp through. Beautiful Eger hosted the World Championship 2013. Without the cameras, underwater hockey isn't so spectator-friendly so you'd better put on some fins and dive in yourself. After all that underwater exertion, you may need to rest your muscles in this baroque city's famous thermal spas.

Also called Octopush because of the two teams of eight, underwater hockey is governed by CMAS which collates upcoming competitions on its site: see http://www.cmas.org/hockey.

899 YACHTING IN CROATIA

Once the domain of Venetian traders and salt-encrusted Uskok pirates, the Dalmatian coast now sees plenty of bling as the glitterati cruise its azure waters. But there's still a seafarer's adventure awaiting you here – aboard a yacht charter. You can literally learn the ropes as you negotiate winds and tides amid the Kornati archipelago, a cluster of rugged, uninhabited islands. Along the Dalmatian coast, from Zadar to the Montenegrin border, are countless beaches, bays and islands where you can pursue a tandem nautical adventure – with no need to watch out for pirates!

Skippered yachts are available to rent from Dubrovnik to Zadar if you and your friends would prefer a less taxing Croatian Islands experience. See http://www. croatica-charter.com.

900 ROPES COURSE IN THE WEASENHAM WOODS, NORFOLK, ENGLAND

It's amazing how hardship can bring people together as a team. Combine some rope tied to trees, logs and poles and some friendly competition – heightened by the adrenalin born of vertigo – and soon you'll be a tight unit. In a rope course you climb up rope ladders, swing out monkey-bars style or race to the top of a pyramid made of logs. Don't worry, you're harnessed in with safety wires to catch you should you fall. Rope courses can be hardcore ('jungle') or 'low' courses – the latter are closer to the ground and focus on team problem-solving, building trust and defeating inhibitions and fears.

The Weasenham Woods are 8 miles north of Swaffham and offer some of Eastern England's tallest trees. The course is only open April to early November. See http://www. extreemeadventure.co.uk.

THE TWO OF US: ADVENTURES IN TANDEM

GREAT MOUNTAIN CYCLES

Put the mountain into biking with these epic routes over some of the world's most mountainous roads and trails.

901 ALPE D'HUEZ, FRANCE

Of all the pass climbs spread through the 100-year-plus history of the Tour de France, Alpe d'Huez is arguably the most illustrious. Since its first inclusion in the Tour in 1952, it's been the gruelling high point of 28 stages, turning it into a virtual cycling pilgrimage for those wanting to emulate the pros. The climb to the 1860m pass begins in the town of Le Bourg-d'Oisans and for 13.8km it snakes through 21 hairpin bends (all numbered just to torture you), with an average gradient of 8.1%. If you're setting your sights high, Marco Pantini once cycled it in 37 minutes, 35 seconds.

From Grenoble, Transisere (www.transisere.fr) buses run to Le Bourg d'Oisans, and will carry bikes.

902 ANNAPURNA CIRCUIT, NEPAL

As roads have been carved up the valleys surrounding the Annapurna massif, trekkers have seen the once-heaving Annapurna Circuit lose its appeal, but for adventure cyclists it's emerged as a tempting new mountain-bike tour. From Besi Sahar to Beni, it's a 300km circuit. You won't be cycling it all – the route is technical, and more than 20% of it might be unrideable, including the entire climb from Thorung Phedi to the high point of 5416m Thorung La – but it's good mountain scenery in which to push a bike. And who's to sneer at the opportunity to cycle through the Kali Gandaki, the deepest gorge in the world?

Nepa Maps publishes a dedicated cycling map – *Biking Around Annapurna* – available in Kathmandu map shops.

903 KARAKORAM HIGHWAY, PAKISTAN/CHINA

Once a Holy Grail of cycling routes, political ructions in Pakistan have dampened enthusiasm for this epic ride, but the mountains and the road remain. Cut through the Karakoram mountains in the 1960s and '70s, and opened to travellers in 1986, the 1300km road connects Rawalpindi (Pakistan) with Kashgar (China), passing through the semimythical Hunza Valley and crossing 4730m

Khunjerab Pass. The Karakoram Range has the greatest concentration of peaks and long glaciers on the planet, and some are virtually at the edge of the highway, so you won't lack for scenery. Most cyclists choose to begin in Gilgit rather than Rawalpindi.

Red Spokes (www.redspokes.co.uk) runs cycling trips along the Karakoram Highway. If cycling independently, check ahead on permit situations in China.

904 ICEFIELDS PARKWAY, CANADA

This mountain road is often touted as the most beautiful drive in the world, but it's even better on a bike. Stretching 230km from Lake Louise to Jasper, the Icefields Parkway threads through the Rocky Mountains, following valleys past mineral-blue lakes, sharp-tipped peaks and glaciers that leak down from North America's largest icefield. Though it's a mountain

setting, and one of the finest imaginable, the road itself is not especially mountainous, with only two significant pass climbs, each one ascending around 500m. For the full experience, extend the ride to Banff, 60km from Lake Louise, cycling along the Bow Parkway, which is often said to be Canada's finest road for spotting wildlife.

Full information on the Icefields Parkway can be found at www.icefieldsparkway.ca.

319

Putting a new spin on it: taking on the Annapurna Circuit by bicycle

The lonely roads of the Pyrenees make for some challenging riding through stunning scenery

905 RAID PYRÉNÉEN, FRANCE

The Pyrenees' Col du Tourmalet was the Tour de France's first big mountain climb, added to the race in 1910, but if one high pass isn't enough, the Raid Pyrénéen may be just your thing. Traversing the Pyrenees from Cerbère to Hendaye, it involves cycling 800km over 28 cols (a total of 18,000m of climbing) inside 10 days. Still not challenging enough? Then try the randonneur version, cycling 720km across 18 cols (11,000m of climbing) in less than 100 hours. Cyclists taking the challenge can apply for a *brevet* (route card) and have it stamped at nominated checkpoints to earn the Raid Pyrénéen medallion.

Apply to the Cyclo Club Béarnais (www.ccb-cyclo.fr) for your *brevet*.

906 QUEEN VICTORIA RIDE, AUSTRALIA

In the pantheon of world mountains, Australia might only have hills, but you wouldn't know it as you grind up the slopes of Mt Hotham or Falls Creek. The 230km Queen Victoria Ride is a touring route that loops out from the town of Mount Beauty, crossing two of the highest mountain roads in Victoria. Throw in a smaller climb over Tawonga Gap and it adds up to around 4000m of climbing, including the brutal Back o' Falls road, which ascends 700m in just 9km. The gentler of mind (and thighs) will stretch the ride across three or four days, while a hardy few attack it in a single day in the Alpine Classic (January) and 3 Peaks Challenge (March).

For more information, see www.queenvictoriaride.com.au.

907 STELVIO, ITALY

Alpine Italy's own megapass, 2758m Passo dello Stelvio marks the top of the highest road pass in Italy, and the third highest in the Alps. From Prato allo Stelvio, it's a 25km climb, ascending around 1800m with an average gradient of 7.4 percent. It's revered by road cyclists, and is a regular stage in the Giro d'Italia. It has 48 numbered hairpin bends, and rises high above the tree line, treating you to remarkable views over mountains, glaciers and the road itself. At the pass, look for the stone monument to Fausto Coppi, Italy's most famous cyclist. What took you hours to climb should take less than an hour to descend.

Spondigna, 3km north of Prato, is the most convenient transport point – buses run to Bolzano via Merano.

908 MANALI TO LEH, INDIA

As mountain rides go, few cycling journeys reach the heights – literally – of this remote Indian highway. Beginning in the Himachal Pradesh city of Manali, it crosses five high Himalayan passes, including 5300m Taglung La (said to be the second-highest road pass in the world), as it heads north to the Ladakhi city of Leh. Each pass brings something new, from the inevitable muddy crossing of 3900m Rohtang La to the high desert of the Indus Valley. None of the climbs are especially steep, though they are sustained – from Manali it's 50km of pure climbing to Rohtang La. Note that the highway is usually open and free of snow for only three months of the year (July to September).

Exodus (www.exodus.co.uk) operates guided cycling trips from Manali to Leh.

909 GREAT DIVIDE MOUNTAIN BIKE ROUTE, USA

Said to be the world's longest off-road cycling route, the GDMBR is an unbroken 4400km (2734 mile) trail between Banff (Canada) and Antelope Wells, on the US–Mexico border in New Mexico. It crosses the Great Divide (the ridge line that sheds water east to the Atlantic Ocean and west to the Pacific) 30 times, rising as high as 3630m (11,909ft) at Indiana Pass in Colorado, and in total climbing more than 60,000m (196,850ft). It's a committing ride; you'll need to be self-sufficient and equipped to camp, although it's not a technical test, following mostly unsealed roads and trails. Expect to be in the saddle for three months.

Find full details about the route at www.adventurecycling.org/routes/greatdivide.cfm.

910 CARRETERA AUSTRAL, CHILE

If you've ever wondered where exactly the end of the world is, and whether you could cycle there, meet the Carretera Austral. Beginning in Puerto Montt, the little-used, mostly unsealed road journeys south for 1200km to Villa O'Higgins and has become a sleeper favourite with touring cyclists. It travels along the edge of the Andes, with sublime mountains views as the range nears its southern oblivion. The scenery is wild and so is the weather – if you think you've experienced tough headwinds and crosswinds on other trips, wait until you get a blast of Patagonian wind. The route is remote, with Coyhaique being the only town of any real size, and the road is all but impassable outside of summer.

LAN Chile flies to Puerto Montt from Santiago.

GREAT MOUNTAIN CYCLES

BOY'S (AND GIRL'S) OWN ADVENTURES

The classic books of your youth are bursting with travel inspiration for adventures accessible enough for kids of all ages.

911 LOOK FOR MOBY DICK'S DESCENDANTS IN THE ATLANTIC OCEAN

It was revenge that sent Captain Ahab's ship the *Pequod* sailing out of Nantucket and down past the southern tip of Africa on a three-year hunt for the white whale Moby Dick. You're likely to encounter your first whale much sooner in Hermanus, which is considered the best land-based whale watching site in the world. Annually southern right whales migrate from the krill-rich feeding grounds of Antarctica and head for warmer waters to mate and rear their young from June until November. You can sight them from the shore, callous-encrusted leviathans whose graceful breaching and tail fluking aquabatics defy logic.

Pack a copy of Melville's book, published in 1851, for a visceral taste of life on whaling ships and a surprising slice of cetology.

912 DOG-SLED UNDER THE NORTHERN LIGHTS, ALASKA

The Alaskan town of Fairbanks prides itself on being the dog-mushing capital of the world. It's some 600km west of Dawson City, where a 21-year-old Jack London turned his gold rush experiences into the classic *Call of the Wild*, but it's a fine place to try dog sledging. Come in February to cheer on competitors and their dog teams in the Yukon Quest, a 1000-mile route over four mountains, following early routes used by trappers, miners and the postal service. Experience dog sledding for yourself with an overnight trip away from the city glow and you'll discover why Fairbanks is even more famous for its amazing Northern Lights displays.

These solar-wind-powered lights are often visible for hours in winter, turning the night sky a haunting milky-green.

913 TREK TO A LOST WORLD IN SOUTH AMERICA

Tales of the great table-top mountains of Venezuela (known as *tepuis*) inspired Arthur Conan Doyle's *The Lost World*, in which a high, isolated plateau bristles with prehistoric creatures. Of all the *tepuis*, Mt Roraima is possibly the most accessible and while there are no confirmed sightings of iguanodons, keep your eyes peeled for the endemic black frog, carnivorous plants and other flora unique to the plateau. On the summit you'll find haunting, improbable rock formations that make you feel like you've stumbled upon another world.

The ascent from the Venezuelan side is the only nontechnical route to the top, while the approach from the Brazilian or Guyanan sides requires serious rock-climbing skills.

914 DISCOVER ABORIGINAL ART IN AUSTRALIA

It was a plane crash that dropped two children into the Outback in James Vance Marshall's book *Walkabout*. They were helped to safety by a young Aboriginal man, and if you head to Kakadu National Park, you're guaranteed a cultural connection in far less arid surroundings. With at least 23,000 years of Aboriginal history, this is one of Australia's richest treasure troves of rock art, also offering up amazing wildlife from rainbow bee-eaters and endemic black wallaroos to more lethal saltwater crocodiles. Walks will take you from bird-filled billabongs to spectacular lookouts, with the option to camp in the bush.

For overnight walks in Kakadu you'll need permits that take at least seven days to process, so plan well in advance.

915 SAIL AND CAMP WILD IN THE LAKES, UK

The outdoor adventures of *Swallows and Amazons* are set against the backdrop of a fictionalised Lake District. Hire a sailing boat on Coniston Water and discover Arthur Ransome's inspiration for Wild Cat Island while exploring the 8km (5-mile) length of this astonishingly serene lake. Once back on land, you can climb 'Kanchenjunga', the book's name for the Old Man of Coniston. One side of this 803m mountain is ravaged with slate mines, while the other drops to Goat's Water under the impossibly complex Dow Crag, a hub for climbing in summer and winter.

Pitch a tent high in the fells or book into the Coniston Copper Mines Youth Hostel to enjoy one of the wildest cheap sleeps in the Lakes.

916 WASH UP ON YOUR OWN DESERT ISLAND

The inspiration for *Robinson Crusoe* was Scotsman Alexander Selkirk, who spent four years marooned on an island 570km off the coast of Chile, surviving on shellfish and goats' meat, and domesticating cats to keep rats at bay. The largest island of the Juan Fernandez Archipelago, it was formerly known as Más a Tierra but renamed Robinson Crusoe Island in 1966. With a bit of effort you can still find the solitude that plagued Selkirk, as well as the remains of his hut and the lookout where he would have scanned the horizon for the rescue vessel that finally arrived in 1709.

In high season, regular flights operate from Santiago de Chile to Robinson Crusoe Island. Monthly sea crossings take just under two days.

917 TRACK DOWN A YETI IN NEPAL

Tintin headed to Tibet to see one, but we recommend the route in to Everest from Nepal if you want to track down a yeti. We can't guarantee a sighting of the real thing, but stop in at Khumjung Monastery en route to Everest Base Camp to see a 'yeti scalp' (actually made from the skin of a serow, a goat-like antelope). If you find footsteps in the snow, you're in good mountaineering company; Eric Shipton photographed a yeti print, Sir Edmund Hillary, Sir Chris Bonington and Bruce Chatwin have all gone in search of the creature, and Reinhold Messner claimed to have seen one, publishing an account of the experience.

Local accounts of the creature describe red fur, a conical head, a high-pitched cry and a slight whiff of garlic.

918 LEARN HOW TO TIME TRAVEL

Jules Verne knew the International Date Line would figure in *Around the World in Eighty Days* before he wrote it. Heading east, Phileas Fogg returns to London thinking he's lost his challenge, before realising that crossing the date line has bought him an extra day. While the official line now zigzags through the Pacific, it used to pass through Taveuni, Fiji, on the 180th meridian. Just out of Waiyevo you'll find a wooden board marking the divide, where kids enjoy leaping from yesterday into today. Walk, dive and kayak round the island to see amazing bird life and stunning corals.

Set yourself a botanical quest to track down Fiji's national flower, the *tagimaucia*, in highland rainforest where it grows above 600m.

919 TAKE A DAY TREK THROUGH MORDOR, NEW ZEALAND

When Peter Jackson was looking for a landscape savage enough to do justice to JRR Tolkien's Middle Earth, this volcanic hub was the obvious candidate. Tongariro is New Zealand's oldest national park and its three volcanic peaks of Ruapehu, Tongariro and Ngauruhoe (Mount Doom in the films) are best discovered on the 20km Tongariro Alpine Crossing. You'll be treated to raw, dramatic terrain, emerald lakes, active steam vents and the evidence of recent eruptions. Mount Ngauruhoe can be climbed as a side trip, a quest that's made easier with a night at the Mangatepopo or Ketetahi huts.

To make this one-way trip across Mordor easier, there's a host of regular shuttle bus services that'll pick you up at the end and bring you back to the start.

920 EYEBALL A LATTER-DAY SHERE KHAN

In *The Jungle Book*, it is tiger Shere Khan who hunts Mowgli, the boy raised by wolves, but the reality in India is a big-cat population threatened by human development. One of your best chances of spotting a Royal Bengal Tiger in the wild is in Madhya Pradesh, where Kipling based his series of tales. Famous Kanha National Park delivers an immersive jungle experience of sal forests and vast meadows that are home to more than 200 tigers as well as leopards, jackals, swamp deer, pythons, cobras and honey badgers.

Travelling alone? Team up with other travellers to share safari costs as charges are per jeep load, not per person.

LEGENDARY ODYSSEYS

Gutted it was Odysseus with so many excuses not to head home? Envying Eiríksson? Saddle up and trace their pioneering paths.

921 ODYSSEUS' JOURNEY HOME, MEDITERRANEAN, ITALY/GREECE

Never was more tourism generated from an epic adventure than in Ithaki, that elusive Greek isle Odysseus kept attempting to get back home to. But most of his misadventures could have happened off the Italian coast. It is thought to have been Sicily where he evaded the Cyclops, and Sardinia where he had to recover his men after their binge on lotus flowers. But you can create your own Mediterranean itinerary following in his wake between Troy, Messina and modern Ithaki, where you can trek through stark landscapes with phenomenal azure sea views.

The most fabled Odysseus locale on Ithaki itself is the Fountain of Arethusa, where swineherd Eumaeus took his pigs to drink.

922 HANUMAN THE MONKEY GOD, INDIA/SRI LANKA

Hanuman is the embodiment of Hindu strength and perseverance, and there's good reason why. In Indian epic *Ramayana*, Hanuman heroically aids avatar-protagonist Rama in finding his wife Sita, who has been captured by Ravana, king of Lanka. Having taken on sea monsters, transformed shape several times and hiked the Himalayas in search of a curative herb, Hanuman reaches Lanka and helps free Rama's wife. Before you embark on your Sri Lanka voyage, check the lofties of a series of Hanuman statues in Himachal Pradesh's Shimla, before forging down to Seetha Amman temple in Sri Lanka, where Ravana hid Sita.

You can now reach Sri Lanka via ferry and thus travel the sea where Hanuman's endeavours unfolded.

923 LABOURS OF HERCULES, PELOPONNESE, GREECE

A whopping seven of the Greco-Roman strongman's labours occurred in what the Greeks call Pelopónnisos. Slaying the Nemean lion, battling the many-headed hydra, rerouting rivers to wash out the Augean stables and the final capturing of the underworld's canine guardian, Cerberus – it all happened on this peninsula in southern Greece.

Of all the labours' localities, Cape Tainaron is perhaps most poignant – a lonely headland below which lie the caverns where Hercules dragged Cerberus up from Hades.

Destino Tours (www.destinotours.gr) embark on a number of novel trips around Greece, including one in Hercules' heroic footsteps.

924 LEIFR EIRÍKSSON'S DISCOVERIES, NEWFOUNDLAND AND LABRADOR, CANADA

Old Norse adventurer Leifr Eiríksson was all set to introduce Christianity to Greenland when he got blown off course quite significantly and

Mt Ararat arises from the Turkish plateau beckoning to ark-seeking adventurers and mountain climbers alike

landed off the coast of what he called 'Vinland', today's Newfoundland. At L'Anse aux Meadows, the Americas' most important Viking settlement at Newfoundland's northern tip, you can stare out at the merciless Atlantic and ponder the long sea voyage to Greenland. There's no wilder spot to feel that Viking vibe of first-human-in-the-wilderness than Torngat Mountains National Park, where mountains rear up from lonely flower-filled meadows in rippling red-brown hues and polar bears sometimes prowl the shores of the fjords.

Norse sagas suggest two areas likely to have featured in Leifr's discoveries: 'Helluland', a bleak rocky place likely to be Baffin Island, and Markland, a forest wilderness most probably Labrador.

925 RESTING PLACE OF NOAH'S ARK, TURKEY

Contention rages as wildly as the flood that originally cast Noah adrift; where did his ark end up? Well, probably Turkey. Mount Ararat, in the east near the Iranian and Armenian borders, should of course grace the itinerary for those reliving this favourite Biblical boat trip. But other locations have been touted as the true spot, including Durupınar, a prominent topographical bump near the Mt Tendürek volcano which entered the fray of the ark debate in the 1970s. Well, the site looks a bit ship-like...

A good launch point for visiting either location is Doğubeyazıt, where fabulous Ottoman architecture will delight anyone alighting from a long-haul voyage.

325

926 SEARCH FOR EL DORADO, NAPO RIVER, ECUADOR/PERU

Cruise this river that rises in the stark Ecuadorian Andes then descends into the Amazon Basin and follow in the wake of treasure-seekers of yore. In this most-celebrated of quests, conquistadors Francisco de Orellana and Gonzalo Pizarro sailed this tributary with the ambitious mission of discovering El Dorado, legendary land of gold. Pizarro survived mutiny and aggressive tribespeople, going on to become the first-ever European to navigate the Amazon in its entirety. You too can brave the waters downriver to Iquitos in Peru, past hidden villages on stilts, and on down the Amazon to the Atlantic Ocean.

One of the only cruise ships operating on Ecuador's Napo River is the *Manatee* (www.rainforestcruises.com).

TTL/PHOTOSHOT ©

927 CHRISTOPHER COLUMBUS' VOYAGES, CARIBBEAN

When Rodrigo de Triana, a sailor aboard Columbus' ship *La Pinta*, spied land in October 1492, the Old World collided with the New; Europeans were, for the first time, seeing the Caribbean. But it's unclear precisely what land that was. It's been whittled down to somewhere in the Turks and Caicos or the Bahamas, so you should probably anchor up at Grand Turk Island, along with the Bahamas' San Salvador and Samana Cay (the archipelago's largest uninhabited island) at the least. Finish up with a reconnoitre of the Dominican Republic's coast, which Columbus visited on all four of his voyages.

Faro a Colón (Columbus' Lighthouse) was erected in Santo Domingo to commemorate the 500th anniversary of the explorer's discovery of the Americas, and contains what are purportedly his remains.

928 MARCO POLO'S TRAVELS, KAZAKHSTAN/ TURKMENISTAN/UZBEKISTAN/ TAJIKISTAN/CHINA

Marco's father and uncle were in Bukhara (modern-day Uzbekistan) establishing trading posts when Kublai Khan, being unacquainted with Europeans, invited them to his HQ in Dadu (modern-day Beijing). After cursory cultural exchanges, the Khan requested that the Polos bring back a mere 100 countrymen well-versed in arts and sciences, a request the Polos embarked on fulfilling in 1271 – now with young Marco in tow. Follow their epic route along the Silk Road through the 'Stans, taking in extremes like the desolate Taklamakan Desert, before hitting Shang-du (popularly Xanadu) where the Mongol Emperor hosted the Polos at his summertime palace in 1275.

Xanadu (a Unesco-listed site) is in China's Inner Mongolia Autonomous Region, near the town of Dolon Nor.

929 CAPTAIN COOK'S ENDEAVOURS, TAHITI/ EASTERN AUSTRALIA/NEW ZEALAND

For centuries they speculated: did *Terra Australis Incognita*, unknown land of the south, really exist? British explorer James Cook settled the debate in 1770, stopping in at Tahiti to make observations of Venus before opening sealed orders to track down *Terra Australis*. Cruise around and take in the small Pacific islands – as well as the entire coastline of New Zealand – that were mapped by Cook, before sailing up Australia's east coast, new territory for Europeans when the *Endeavour* dropped anchor. Cook

Following the Napo may lead to a legendary land of gold, or other riverside delights

brought home never-before glimpsed plant specimens and tales of wild aborigines, but you can stick to smaller souvenirs.

The captain has many museums devoted to him, including the Cook Collection in Sydney's Australian Museum (www. australianmuseum.net.au).

930 LIVINGSTONE AND STANLEY, LAKE TANGANYIKA, BURUNDI/TANZANIA/ZAMBIA

Dr Livingstone, I presume. The most renowned phrase in travel history, uttered by Henry Morgan Stanley above this lakeshore upon finally finding fellow explorer David Livingstone, then AWOL in Africa's interior. But where exactly? Burundi folk erected a monument on their side marking the spot but Livingstone's accounts suggest the encounter was at Ujiji, on the Tanzanian shore. By then, Livingstone had completed the first European transcontinental crossing of Africa, explored the Zambezi as a commerce route into Central Africa and sought the source of the Nile. The poor chap probably just needed some time out.

Even intrepid Livingstone would have welcomed a sleep-over at Zambia's Royal Livingstone (www.royal-livingstone-hotel.com) by Victoria Falls, which he named after his queen.

LEGENDARY ODYSSEYS

BEST SURF BREAKS FOR BEGINNERS

Surf the most chilled-out waves in the world before making your big break.

931 **MUIZENBERG BEACH, SOUTH AFRICA**

The barrels that roll towards the end of the beach known as Surfers Corner are regular and gentle. It's a perfect mix for beginners and you needn't worry about getting chomped by aquatic beasties either: the shark spotters maintain a constant lookout. Any sign of danger and you can head back to the cafes to enjoy the mellow,

Beach magnet: Byron Bay has regular breaks and great atmosphere to attract beginner surfers and died-in-the-wool hippies

learner-friendly surf culture. It's a photogenic spot for learners with colourful beach changing boxes all around. When you're ready to dip into heavier waves, you can walk over to Kalk Bay or aptly named Danger Reef.

Visit when lifeguards are on duty in Blue Flag Season from December to March, when the weather is also warmest. Lessons are available from www.garysurf.com.

BECK ROCCHI/GETTY IMAGES ©

932 BANANA BEACH, TAGHAZOUT, MOROCCO

The waves here can get pretty big but always break on the beach, meaning that even if things get challenging you'll be carried safely to shore, not left stuck out in the depths. It's perfect conditions for keeping beginners safe. If you're fleeing the cold of Europe, you'll relish tumbling into these warm waters. Nearby Banana Village (Aourir), nicknamed by Jimi Hendrix in the '60s for its banana plantations, offers an authentic Moroccan experience, especially when the Wednesday *souq* (market) fills the town with spices and the calls of fabric traders.

The best time to visit is in winter (November to March) when the swell is constant and the weather still warm. For lessons and more information visit www. bananabeach.biz.

933 WHITE PLAINS BEACH, O'AHU, HAWAII, USA

The birthplace of surfing and towering waves may not sound much like a mecca for surfers who are just learning the ropes but Hawaii does have some gentle spots where beginners can ease their pinkies into the blue water. Being secluded makes White Plains Beach on O'ahu a nice surfer's kindergarten and means there are few other learners to crash into. The glossy waves roll in endlessly and are easy to catch, carrying you onto a white ribbon of sand without huge crowds watching you wipeout if you fall. Lessons are conducted by local firefighters, who are trained paramedics, so jump up on that board without fear and earn your luau later that night.

Lessons are conducted by the Hawaiian Fire Surf School (www.hawaiianfire.com).

934 BYRON BAY, NEW SOUTH WALES, AUSTRALIA

If you're a beginner surfer you'll need frequent breaks from the breaks, and since Byron Bay has been a haven for hippies and seachangers for decades, taking a breather to the sound of guitars and the scent of incense is what Byron knows best. The bay itself is the best spot to find waves lazing their way to shore on a sunny day. One section, the Wreck, may sound ominous but it's actually named after a shipwreck that creates consistent hollow waves off the sandbank. The surf spots are near enough to the town centre that you can wander up for a time-out if the waters become rough.

Byron Bay is a nine-hour drive from Sydney or a two-hour drive from Brisbane. See www.byronbaysurfschool.com.

Kuta's not all about rabble-rousing nightlife. There's a gentle surf break as well

935 KUTA BEACH, BALI, INDONESIA

The breaks at Kuta foam over in a satisfying, creamy white beneath your board but the waves are never gargantuan. You know you're in a tropical paradise because schools of fish flash by like silver arrows in the water, and later you'll be sipping from a coconut as you chat about how to get aboard a six-footer tomorrow and ride it all the way to the shallows. Surfing lessons are a good introduction to understanding this blue beast and there are plenty of friendly locals to help you out. Lifeguards are on constant watch in case the rips get feisty.

Bali is generally safe but check travel advice for up-to-date information. Odyssey Surf School (www.odysseysurfschool.com) guarantees you'll stand on your board in the first few lessons.

936 HIKKADUWA BEACH, SRI LANKA

If you're only learning to stay on that slippery board, the last thing you want to deal with is icy cold waters so the balmy waves of Hikkaduwa make things so much more bearable for beginners. The reef breaks have really mellow sections, the clear expanse dotted with snorkellers where the Indian Ocean rolls over the yellow sand. The 2004 tsunami hit hard here but all is calm now and the sewing machines donated to affected families have helped make it a tailoring hot-spot – grab some respectable new threads before visiting the temples.

Hikkaduwa is on the southwestern coast of Sri Lanka, near Galle. Visit from November to April for the best surfing.

PETER PTSCHELINZEW/GETTY IMAGES ©

938 PLAYA JOBOS, PUERTO RICO

Most of the waves in Puerto Rico come crashing down over a reef, but at Playa Jobos they are born inside a sandbar and break softly within a blue lagoon that perfume ads are made of – it's a perfect practice area for beginners. It's even gentle enough to snorkel in. When you need a rest, grab a meat or crab-filled *pastellilo* pastry right on the golden beach. Then when your legs are no longer wobbly, step it up a notch and head for the grown-up waves outside of the lagoon.

Mid-December to mid-April is the most popular time to escape the Northern Hemisphere winter and learn to surf in the warm waters. For lessons visit www.purelifesurfschool.com.

940 NEWQUAY, CORNWALL, UK

So you may have to brave England's infamously icy weather but with such a vibrant beach and surf scene in Newquay, you can just zip yourself into some neoprene and enjoy learner-friendly breaks while keeping the chills at bay. Great Western Beach is a cliff-sheltered sandy beach with smaller surf that won't be so harsh on those finding their balance. At high tide the sea covers the beach, but this is the perfect excuse for refuelling on some fish and chips or comforting bangers and mash.

Lifeguards patrol this beach from late May to the end of September. For beginner lessons visit www. escapesurfschool.co.uk.

939 HOSSEGOR, AQUITAINE, FRANCE

You're bound to find a chilled-out place to learn to surf on the longest continuous expanse of sandy beach in Europe, where you'll be free to fall off that board time and time again without losing too much cred. Dropping into a glassy barrel after a full day of surfing will put a smile on your face as you gaze out into the endless expanse of ocean. Just make sure you stay within view of the lifeguards. There's also a naturist section of beach known as Bare Bottoms, if you feel like a different kind of adventure.

May to September is warm and best for beginners. For lessons visit www. unitedsurfcamps.com. Stay till October if you want to see how the pros do it at the ASP World Tour.

937 PLAYA SANTA TERESA, COSTA RICA

This is the postcarded beach you've been seeing in your dreams. White sand, sunbathed Pacific Ocean, extremely gentle and consistent waves, plus a beach surrounded by a tropical jungle full of toucans, monkeys and richly green trees. You'll soon understand the rush that gets surfers hooked, but it's the relaxing moments sipping a drink in a beach shack or riding a horse with the lap of crystal water below you that really make Santa Teresa such an addictive destination.

The best time to rent a board and get some lessons are the warm, dry months from December to April. Visit www. mambosurf.com.

BEST SURF BREAKS FOR BEGINNERS

CLASSIC SOLO SORTIES

More lone wolf than pack animal? These inspiring solo feats should get your tail wagging, though be aware that these are all of the attempt-at-your-own-peril variety.

941 DIY SOLO BALLOONING

The idea had been gnawing away at Larry Walters for 20 years. Finally, in 1982, he relented and purchased a lawn chair and more than 40 helium balloons. Walters, a veteran of the Vietnam War and a first-time balloonist, attached the balloons to the chair, tethered in his Los Angeles garden. Then, clutching the pellet gun with which he planned to pop balloons one by one (see, those 20 years of dreaming weren't wasted), he cut the chair free. Anticipating a gentle ascent to about 100m, he was surprised to find himself whoosh up to 5000m, where the pilots of two jetliners spotted him on their approach to LAX. Understandably now hesitant to shoot the balloons, he finally came down on Long Beach, cold and frightened. He was later fined $4000 by the Federal Aviation Administration.

Walters christened his contraption 'Inspiration 1'; he has indeed inspired several people to copy him – most died.

942 CYCLING AROUND THE WORLD

There's a well-worn trail of tyre tracks around the world, with cyclists such as Vin Cox and Mike Hall knocking days off each other's times for a solo circumnavigation. Adhere to the latest rules and you'll take around 105 days, blogging as you go. But rewind to 2001 when one of the pioneering round-the-world cyclists, Alastair Humphreys, took a different tack. He rode across Europe, through the Middle East, down Africa, up the Americas and then homeward via Russia, China and Central Asia, seeing 60 countries and five continents in four years. As he wrote: 'Life is too brief and too rich to tiptoe through half-heartedly…'

A solo circumnavigation by bicycle is achievable by anybody with six to 12 months free, a sense of direction and a credit card. See www.alastairhumphreys.com for ideas.

943 SOLO MOUNTAINEERING IN THE ALPS

The great unclaimed prize in solo mountaineering is K2, the world's second-highest mountain. But it's a prize with a potentially high price: one in four ascents of the Himalayan giant ends in death. Better to shift your focus to the Alps where the light-and-fast style of peak-bagging was pioneered. The Matterhorn is the iconic summit of the Alps and to climb it takes a minimum of six to 12 hours, depending on the route and the weather. If you want to be back in time for lunch, ask Swiss alpinist Ueli Steck for tips; he has made spectacular solo ascents of the Matterhorn in less than two hours.

For any climbing on the Matterhorn or hiking in the region, base yourself in Zermatt (www.myswitzerland.com).

944 SOLO CLIMB EL CAP, USA

One summer's day in California in June 2012, 'rock star' Alex Honnold solo-climbed Yosemite's three largest walls – Mt Watkins, El Capitan and Half Dome – nonstop in 19 hours. And he climbed all but 500ft of the 7000 vertical feet without a rope. To put that in perspective, an average climber takes five days… just to climb El Capitan. Indeed, the first solo ascent of El Capitan, in 1968, took 10 days. There are several routes up the rock buttress, with the Nose ranking as one of the world's classic climbs, taking more than 30 stages ('pitches') to complete. You'll need to be a highly skilled and experienced climber at the peak of your fitness to attempt it. An easier option for nonclimbing soloists might be to hike around the back of El Cap…

945 PARAGLIDE IN COLOMBIA

You're alone in the sky. Around you soar birds, sharing the thermal updrafts. And below you lies the one-time capital of Colombia's cocaine trade, Medellín. Over the last decade, fortunately, the city has changed. Drug barons have been replaced by those dealing in another type of high: paragliding instructors and white-water rafting guides. Medellín has become Colombia's adventure-sport hotspot and paragliding is its ace attraction thanks to the surrounding hills and those spiralling plumes of air.

Sign up with a local operator such as Zona de Vuelo (www.zonadevuelo.com) in the Aburrá Valley. Solo pilots require a minimum of six years' experience.

946 ROWING THE ATLANTIC

The first man to row solo across the Atlantic was Briton John Fairfax, who died at the age of 74 in 2012. In 1969, he rowed the 8000km from the Canary Islands to Florida in six months. According to his wife, he also spent time as a pirate, was a frequent baccarat player in Las Vegas and lost a chunk of his arm to a shark. Clearly, it's a character-building journey. Another Brit, Andrew Brown, set the record for the fastest crossing in 2012, racing 4800km in 40 days, nine hours and 44 minutes from the Canary Islands to Barbados as part of the Atlantic Challenge, a biannual race first held in 1997.

If you can cope with massive waves, sleep deprivation and severe chafing, sign up for the race at www.taliskerwhiskyatlanticchallenge.com.

947 HIKE THE JOHN MUIR TRAIL, USA

The John Muir Trail in California, one of the most spectacular treks in the world, pays homage to the Scottish naturalist who fought to protect Yosemite in the 19th and 20th centuries. John Muir was never happier than when wandering alone in the wilderness of the Sierra Nevada, and no wonder – this might just be heaven for solo hikers. The 340km trail that bears his name starts in Yosemite Valley and passes through King's Canyon and Sequoia National Parks before ending at Mt Whitney.

It's possible to through-hike the entire trail but you will need to prearrange food drops. Bring good walking boots, a tent, stove and a bear canister in which to store supplies; see www.johnmuirtrail.org.

948 RACE AROUND THE WORLD BY BOAT

Single-handed, round-the-world yachting might seem like a niche interest but there are two famous events to choose between if you fancy a go at it. The Ocean Race is sailed in stages and the Vendée Globe is raced nonstop; in 2012 Frenchman Francois Gabart broke the Vendée Globe's record when he finished in 78 days. In comparison, Sir Francis Chichester, the first person to make a full solo circumnavigation by sail, took his time in the 54ft yacht *Gypsy Moth IV*. He started his 226-day journey from Plymouth in 1966 and stopped only once, in Sydney.

Follow the sailors' progress at www.vendeeglobe.org.

949 KAYAKING THE AMAZON

Children's TV presenters are known for being multitaskers but kayaking the world's second-longest river isn't in the job description. The BBC's Helen Skelton didn't let the fact that she had never kayaked before prevent her from paddling all 3200km of the Amazon from Nauta, Peru to Almeirim, Brazil in 2010. It took her six weeks, millions of paddle strokes and hundreds of insect bites but it made her the first woman to paddle the river's length. There's no more enthralling way to experience a country than from its waterways. Any river will offer a challenge but watch out for local wildlife: South African kayaker Hendrik Coetzee was killed by a crocodile in Uganda, paddling his way to the source of the White Nile.

950 SKI ACROSS ANTARCTICA

There's a wind blowing that freezes you to the bone. Straining to pull your supplies over the ice, you shuffle your skis forward again, one after another. Congratulations! You've just completed the first kilometre in your Antarctic adventure. Only another 1744km to go! By skiing across the Antarctic alone and unsupported you'll be joining a very exclusive club; if you're female it is a club of one. In 2012 Felicity Aston became the first woman to complete the feat, taking 59 days, while dragging 85kg of supplies in temperatures as low as -30°C (-22°F). But the mental challenge was just as tough. 'Being alone sounds such a simple thing,' she said, 'but when was the last time you went a whole day without seeing any person?'

FAMILY-FRIENDLY ADVENTURES

The best adventures to keep kids and grown-ups smiling while exploring the world.

Once upon a time there was a magnificent castle on a hill where the kings of Bohemia lived, travelling through the cobbled streets and over a bridge where a wild river ran underneath. Eight centuries later and Prague Castle still stands as the largest castle in the world, looking like something from a bedtime story. Its awe-inspiring cathedral will have

Spotting a striped resident of the savannah on safari in South Africa

even the most world-weary kids standing with their mouths open. Ride the funicular up Petrin Hill to a miniature replica of the Eiffel Tower. From there, your panoramic view over Prague captures glimpses of Cinderella-like horse-drawn carriages below that your family can ride back down in the city.

Visit in April and May for colourful spring blooms, or December and January for a snowy winter wonderland and Christmas markets.

952 HAVE YOUR BEACH AND TEMPEH TOO IN BALI, INDONESIA

Families on a budget, you can still have a tropical adventure! Bali is affordable and has sunshine, white-sand beaches, palm trees and clean waters where kids can snorkel and dive to see colourful fish and coral. Locals are friendly and can help keep the little tackers well fuelled on *gado gado* veggies for sunrise surfing. If you're a land lover, bicycle to the pinecone-like temples at festival times and discover that they aren't solemn and serious, but places of music filled with Balinese dancers waving shimmering finger jewellery. Kick back, eat your fragrant coconut curries topped with crunchy fried onion and enjoy!

Bali is best in the dry season between April and October, but the rainy season still offers warm weather and turns everything a lush green.

953 KEEP BODY AND SOUL ACTIVE AT A RANCH IN SANTA FE, NEW MEXICO, USA

City-slicker kids may go a little wild with all the play space they'll find on this ranch, but let them loose – that's the beauty of being in the mountains of New Mexico with acres of lawn and forest. Horse ride or bike ride together through fields of wildflowers and rocky creeks, or let the children learn how to make their own wooden racing carts while you sneak off to a yoga session. There are also more spiritual adventures, such as the 'drum and journey circle' to promote healing and self-expression. After all, Santa Fe is a haven for artists and explorers alike.

Santa Fe is sunny all year round, so pack some sunscreen. Check with the Bishop's Lodge (www.bishopslodge.com) for accommodation prices and availability.

JOHN WARBURTON-LEE/GETTY IMAGES ©

954 COME FACE TO FACE WITH WILDLIFE ON AN AFRICAN SAFARI, SOUTH AFRICA

Children's storybooks of lions, hippos, zebras and giraffes come to life on the open plains of a wildlife park in South Africa. You can really feel part of the action in an open-top safari vehicle, gaping in awe at the mighty elephant just metres away from you. Waking up in a lodge to see the sunrise over the arid grassy savannah, seeing huge flocks of ibis swirling overhead, gaining a true sense of untamed nature... these are experiences your family will remember long after you've returned home.

This adventure is best for children over 12. To avoid annoying pill-taking, seek out one of South Africa's malaria-free wildlife parks.

The best way to get a feel for Costa Rica is to immerse yourself in the jungle

955 FEEL THE LIVING JUNGLE IN COSTA RICA

That steam rising from the volcano in the distance isn't dangerous, but its breath does make it seem like everything is alive in Costa Rica, where parrots call, monkeys howl and the Sarapiquí River speaks in whooshes as you raft down its white-water back. Your kids can meet the locals in their village and make ceramics or get more active with a zip-line through the forest canopy, hyped up on raw chocolate from the local cacao plantation. You can even get up close to the volcano crater's rim but this ain't no school science project – it's real.

Visiting in the dry season (December to April) makes it easier to avoid rain; May to November brings fewer tourists but soaking afternoon showers.

956 MAKE A SPLASH AT MARMORE FALLS, UMBRIA, ITALY

When Ancient Romans decided to divert the river Velino to the cliffs at Marmore, sending it crashing into the world, pouring over treetops, it's unlikely they knew they were creating the world's tallest human-made waterfall. Today you can take the kids up close and feel the clean spray on your face as you make your way along the paths to the gardens above. Alternatively, take a raft to the waterfall's base on the Nera River. Once you're ready to dry off, take a donkey ride around the town, exploring archaeological sites that date back to the Bronze Age.

Check the official Marmore Falls website (www.marmorefalls.it/indexen_GB.php) for opening times.

957 CRUISE DOWN THE NILE, EGYPT

Egypt is a bustling world of bazaars filled with exotic bargains and iconic pyramids but it offers a gentler side too. That side is best experienced on a relaxing ride down the Nile on the cushions of a *felucca*, a motorless sailboat that has caught the breeze since ancient times. The ruins of Karnak and Luxor present an incredible open-air educational adventure for children and adults alike. If you take a horse-drawn carriage, you can avoid tiring out the little ones and spend more time looking into the faces of centuries-old statues towering above you.

If you want to avoid the one-hour flight between Cairo (home of the pyramids) and Luxor, take a sleeper train, or spend a day and night travelling down the Nile via *felucca*.

958 SLEIGH RIDE IN A WINTER WONDERLAND, WYOMING, USA

Kids (and grown-up kids) love playing in Wyoming's snow. Here, elk roam among the snow-heavy trees, mountains turn into ski slopes and alpine lakes become the dark ice of 'wild' ice-skating rinks. For extra Christmas-style magic, take your children on a horse-drawn sleigh ride around town to Teton Village, a fairy-tale setting with its rugged mountains and twinkling stars looking over you at night. The sleighs resemble massive apple crates on skis pulled by powerful horses; get your family aboard, sit back and enjoy the vast spaces of Wyoming.

Visit Wyoming in the coldest months (December to February) for a snow-filled adventure; see www.elkadventures.com.

959 BIKE THROUGH HISTORY IN ANDALUCIA, SPAIN

So your family likes things sporty and spiced? Steer clear of tourist crowds by biking the ancient route of Los Pueblos Blancos. Stop off in the whitewashed villages set in the hills to taste Andalusian tapas, rich in local olive oil and sunshine. The cathedrals and Moorish buildings make a living history lesson for the children – no laptops necessary – as you follow your guide along the river to Granada. Passing glowing groves of sun-drenched citrus trees will whet your thirst for some fresh orange juice en route.

Setting aside a week allows for an easy ride from Sevilla to Granada – people don't rush here. See www. andaluciancyclingexperience.com.

960 ANCIENT AND MODERN MEET IN TOKYO, JAPAN

It's the details that make a family holiday stress free. Japan has excellent transport and a safe, child-friendly culture where climate-controlled bullet trains and ubiquitous vending machines keep kids excited and adults at ease. The adventure may be nature focused – a whispering forest of towering bamboo. Or a step into a fascinating culture that dazzles children with samurai, sumo and video games, where spiky-haired teenagers on the street dress like manga characters. Keep everyone active with a bike ride around peaceful Yoyogi Park, where Elvis impersonators and other interesting characters abound.

Despite the radiation scare of 2011, Tokyo is very safe for travel.

FAMILY-FRIENDLY ADVENTURES

TOP DIVING ADVENTURES

Check your reg and neoprene up to delve into a magical submarine world of sea dragons, stalactites, wrecks and ruins.

Swim with a little ray of sunshine – some of them not so little – in the Cayman Islands

961 DRIFT BETWEEN CONTINENTS, ICELAND

What does plate tectonics mean to you? Snooze-worthy school geography lessons? Well, forget dusty textbooks and dull teachers: in Iceland's Þingvellir Lake (aka Thingvellir), you can experience continental drift firsthand and it's mind-blowing. Silfra is the rift between the American and European continents, a fissure fed by glacial water so crystal clear that visibility runs to tens of metres, or even 100. Sure, it's nippy down there – dry suits de rigueur – but with spectacular canyons and swim-throughs, and the surreal mirror effect of reflections off the surface, a dive here is unlike any other. Don't expect fish; do expect visual wonders.

Silfra is in Þingvellir National Park, site of the first Icelandic parliament, and can be reached on an easy day trip from Reykjavík.

962 PLUNGE INTO A SACRED WELL, MEXICO

Humans worked wonders with limestone in the Yucatán – check out the Maya's jungle-set step pyramids. But nature always goes one better. Witness the cenotes – caves accessed through portals breaching the surface – that riddle the peninsula, created when soft limestone was dissolved by subterranean water. Most are now adorned with spectacular stalactites and stalagmites, shimmering with otherworldly light play. No wonder the Maya considered some to be sacred wells. A few stretch for tens of kilometres, but many, including Gran Cenote, much of it just 10m deep, allow relatively inexperienced divers to admire the amazing formations.

Gran Cenote is just 4km north of Tulum on the road to Cobá. Take care not to damage the delicate stalactites while underwater.

963 JOIN A CORAL ORGY, GREAT BARRIER REEF

The world's longest reef isn't just about size. Sure, you can swim with plenty of big stuff – 150kg potato cod and Maori wrasse at Cod Hole, century-old giant clams off Lizard Island, and manta rays, sharks and whales at various spots along the 2300km-long reef. But for a night to remember, time your plunge for the swingers' party to end them all. On just a few dates each year, the corals all spawn in a synchronised sex act – millions of eggs and sperm are jettisoned into the ocean, drifting upwards like a kaleidoscopic snowstorm. It's bizarre and unforgettable.

Spawning usually occurs a few days after a full moon in late spring, generally around November. Check with local dive operators for likely dates.

964 CATCH SOME RAYS OFF THE CAYMAN ISLANDS

Watching a dozen metre-wide sea monsters, each armed with a venomous barbed sting, gliding menacingly towards you is one of the most electrifying experiences you can enjoy in just 3m of water. The submarine dinner party held daily at Stingray City in Grand Cayman's North Sound is, legend has it, the legacy of local fisherfolk who cleaned their catch in these calm waters, attracting peckish stingrays. Today the fishermen have gone but the rays still shimmy in for snacks. Kit up (no fins) and prepare the feel the elasmobranchs' sucking kiss. Just don't touch, to avoid disrupting the rays' protective mucus.

The driest, coolest season is from December to April. Stingray City is best dived in the afternoon, after cruise-ship passengers have left.

965 CHECK COUSTEAU'S CHOICE, PULAU SIPADAN, BORNEO

Jacques Cousteau knew a thing or two about the deep blue – so any spot described by him as 'an untouched piece of art' must be pretty special. What an understatement. Pulau Sipadan is a limestone pinnacle soaring 600m from the seabed off the east coast of Sabah, Malaysian Borneo. It's the sole oceanic island in the area and, as the only show in town, it attracts a dizzying array of sea life. It's renowned for turtles (alive and dead – pay your respects at the 'turtle tomb', resting place for scores of chelonians) plus plunging drop-offs and more than 3000 fish species.

Dive permits are strictly limited to 120 per day, and overnight stays on Sipadan are prohibited. Book with an experienced operator who can obtain your permit.

339

The gargantuan underwater museum of the Ghost Fleet of Chuuk

966 EXPLORE THE CORAL TRIANGLE

The waters between the Philippines and Australia, stretching east of Papua New Guinea, encompass some of the planet's most diverse ecosystems – and possibly the world's finest diving, among some 605 species of coral. The bommies of Raja Ampat, alive with constellations of reef fish, are justly famous, but for giant gorgonians (fan corals) and sea whips in dazzling hues, blue sea stars and reef sharks, caves and overhangs, head to the sharp volcanic pinnacles of remote Kimbe Bay, West New Britain, off Papua New Guinea.

Some experts have even speculated that this could have been where the world's first corals originated.

Diving at Kimbe Bay is best February to June and mid-August to late December.

967 DISCOVER THE MYSTERIOUS RUINS OF YONAGUNI, JAPAN

Whether it's a submarine pyramid built by the ancient civilisation of Mu, an alien artefact or just a bizarrely regular natural rock formation (doubtful), the huge structure beneath the waves off Yonaguni,

Japan's westernmost island, is jaw-dropping. Discovered as recently as 1986, this weirdly geometrical, seemingly carved chunk of stone 100m long and rising up to 25m from the sea floor has been estimated by some to be 8000 years old. Strong currents mean this isn't the easiest spot to dive, but the mystery – and the thrilling added possibility of seeing schooling hammerheads – makes it well worth the effort.

Hammerheads are most commonly seen in the cool winter season, from December to February. Yonaguni is served by twice-daily flights from Ishigaki, which also boasts exceptional diving.

JOE DOVALA/GETTY IMAGES ©

969 NAVIGATE AMONG THE GHOST FLEET OF CHUUK, MICRONESIA

In February 1944, American forces bombarded the Japanese fleet anchoring in the natural harbour offered by Chuuk Lagoon, a 225km-long near-circular reef. Some 60 ships were sent to the bottom, where they still lie, comprising probably the most impressive wreck-dive zone in the world. Traversing the glassy-clear waters is like a visit to an underwater military museum, with dozens of exhibits including fighter planes, tanks, cars, weapons and other martial paraphernalia. The ghost fleet is now manned only by platoons of gorgonian corals, anemones, dense shoals of reef fish and bigger species, including turtles, manta rays and sharks.

Dry season in Chuuk is December to April, though at other times rain is only intermittent and visibility usually good.

968 GO WITH THE FLOW IN RANGIROA, FRENCH POLYNESIA

A drift dive at Rangiroa is about the closest you'll get to feeling like you're being sucked through a plughole as a washbasin empties. As the tide in the Pacific rises, the ocean swells through the twin Avatoru and Tiputa Passes (channels) in this 80km-long atoll – time it right and you can hitch a ride, along with a morass of marine life. Gaze up to watch bottlenose dolphins frolic, and gawp at schools of tuna, barracuda, trevally and eagle rays riding the currents alongside you. Sharks are a given. Reef sharks are ever present, joined periodically by schooling hammerheads and huge manta rays.

Hammerheads are most commonly seen in January and February, and manta ray sightings most concentrated in September and October, but diving is fabulous year-round.

970 PAY RESPECTS TO THE POOR KNIGHTS, NEW ZEALAND

It's cold, but it's hot – that's the secret behind the fantastic biodiversity in the waters surrounding the Poor Knights Islands (allegedly named by Captain Cook after a favourite breakfast pudding). Warm currents streaming south from the tropics mix with the cooler, nutrient-rich waters welling up alongside the continental shelf, tempting marine life as diverse as stingrays, several wrasse species, groupers, orca, moray eels, schools of kingfish, vividly coloured nudibranchs and coral shrimps. Among waving kelp forests, gorgonian corals and sponges, caves and cliffs. Visibility is great here too. It's one for every diver's bucket list...at least, according to Cousteau.

The Poor Knights Islands have been separated from the mainland for at least 18,000 years and host many rare terrestrial species. Landing is not permitted without a permit.

TOP DIVING ADVENTURES

IN THE FOOTSTEPS OF FILM HEROES

Saw the movie? Step through the screen and live the adventure like the stars in these set-to-impress destinations.

973 İSTANBUL, TURKEY

What's not to love about İstanbul as a chase-scene setting? An invigorating blend of east-meets-west culture (how many other cities straddle two continents?), a mosque-studded skyline, and all those bunched-together bazaars and rooftops… stunts in the making, sure, and ones Bond movie *Skyfall* (2012) evocatively captured in its opener. But Ian Fleming's favourite city was already a famous cinematic backdrop and it was lesser-known heist flick *Topkapi* that really put it on the adventure film map, way back in 1964.

Steel yourself for Daniel Craig whizzing by on a motorbike in Eminönü Square, the Grand Bazaar and the New Mosque.

971 MURCHISON FALLS NATIONAL PARK, UGANDA

Hollywood didn't really do ambitious film locations in the 1950s and following in movie-makers' footsteps was unheard of. Filming of the *African Queen*, therefore, hasn't inspired too many devotees to trip out to Uganda and present-day Congo, where many scenes were shot. But perhaps they should. This tremendous forest-flanked grassland bisected by a nascent River Nile is known for its stunning wildlife (lions, giraffes, buffalo, and more besides). It's near Murchison Falls itself – just off Lake Albert – where Bogie and Hepburn make contact with German boat Louisa in the film's famous final moments.

Seek up-to-date advice when planning a visit: although the park is generally safe, it's quite close to the Democratic Republic of Congo, which has security threats.

972 NORTHERN AMAZON, PERU

'Reality itself' is what Werner Herzog set out to film with his two Peruvian jungle-based masterpieces, *Aguirre, the Wrath of God* and *Fitzcarraldo*. Several locations on the Nanay and Huallaga rivers were used for locations in *Aguirre* – in which conquistadors undertake a river quest to find El Dorado – with the crew navigating large sections on rafts. *Fitzcarraldo's* filming a decade later generated some legendary stories – disease, amputations, quarrels with tribespeople and, most notably, the on-set tension between Herzog and his lead in both films, Klaus Kinski. Amidst this Amazon region's waterways there are rafts to float on, jungle forays galore and people still living in Iquitos with first-hand stories of *Fitzcarraldo's* filming.

Base yourself at La Casa Fitzcarraldo (www.casafitzcarraldo.com), a colonial house in Iquitos in which *Fitzcarraldo's* film crew stayed.

974 LORD OF THE RINGS LOCATIONS, NEW ZEALAND

Never before did an adventure movie showcase a place as well as Peter Jackson's landmark trilogy did his native New Zealand. Fancy skipping the hardships of the hobbits' journey in the films? Head straight for Mordor, known to mortals of this earth as Tongariro National Park. In the bowels of its massif lies Mt Ngauruhoe, the Mount Doom of the movies. The Mavora Lakes area northwest of Te Anau became Fangorn Forest, while seekers of hobbit homeland the Shire should focus their quest on the undulating pea-green farmland around Matamata near Hamilton.

Climbing Mt Ngauruhoe requires several hours and is akin to scaling a large sand dune, the mountain basically being a vast pile of ash.

975 PETRA, JORDAN

You won't have to pass the tests Harrison Ford did in *Indiana Jones and the Last Crusade* (repent or be beheaded, for example) so you can relax and savour the majesty of this world-famous desert city hewn into the sandstone cliffs. The classic approach is via the Siq, a narrow rust-red gorge, that ushers you up to Al Khazneh (the Treasury), poster boy of Petra's many ruins – it's just like the movie, minus the Nazis. But there's enough archaeology here to occupy you for several days and no lives hang in the balance, so take your time.

If Indy wasn't classic enough for you, gallop out to another rock-gouged valley, Wadi Rum in southern Jordan, where *Lawrence of Arabia* was filmed.

976 PIRATES OF THE CARIBBEAN LOCATIONS, DOMINICA

Avast! No wonder Captain Jack Sparrow (of *Pirates of the Caribbean*) felt so in his element here that he returned for the sequel. Of all the swashbuckling sights, movie-lovers' principal ports of call should be the north coast's rugged forested cliffs (remember the water-wheel duel?), and Titou Gorge (where the crew is pursued by a dart-blowing tribe). Float through cerulean waters here in between fern-fringed cliffs and spy some filming paraphernalia left in place. Dominica is renowned for its diving, but just because Johnny Depp did it in a pirate outfit doesn't mean you should.

Incorporate Titou Gorge into a sublime hike to Boiling Lake on the other side of Morne Trois Pitons National Park.

977 MT RUSHMORE, USA

OK, so in the climactic scene of *North by Northwest*, Cary Grant and Eva Marie Saint didn't really need to stray near the edge of this monument, right? But it made for a truly classic movie moment. Travelling to the South Dakota landmark today, you'll get far closer than Cary and Eva ever did to those four enormous presidential personages, carved out of the natural cliffs by Gutzon Borglum and helpers between 1927 and 1941. Don't be imagining you can abseil down from Lincoln's eyebrow though – climbing has been prohibited here since the carvings were completed.

Mt Rushmore should merely kick-start your adventure in South Dakota's Black Hills and Badlands, a huge swath of mountains, prairies and weird lunar-like rock desert.

978 FORMER ROUTE 66, USA

Latch onto the wheels of Dennis Hopper and Peter Fonda and hit the road *Easy Rider*-style at such Arizona locales as Sunset Crater Monument (where a hitchhiking Jack Nicholson is picked up) and the Painted Desert (scene of memorable on-the-road moments). Tracing much of this classic road movie's action involves cruising the sadly declassified Route 66, but while the highway never passed through Louisiana, *Easy Rider* sure did. Hit New Orleans – where the film took in Mardi Gras – and Krotz Springs – where the heroes' journey abruptly ends.

Stop by Roadhouse Bar & Grill in Bellemont, Arizona, fuel up on tales from *Easy Rider* lookalikes passing through, and catch that notorious 'No Vacancy' sign.

979 ANJI GRAND NATIONAL BAMBOO FOREST, CHINA

Crouching Tiger, Hidden Dragon put the cinematic art back in martial arts films. Though partly due to the flowing *wudang chuan* kung-fu style favoured by director Ang Lee, the film's epic visuals were completed by this awe-inspiring forest, one of China's last sizeable tracts of bamboo. Stand among the whispering stalks and remember Zhang Ziyi and Chow Yun Fat swinging through here in what must surely figure in any list of the greatest-ever film fight scenes. Within the forest, there's a roller coaster that zooms you through the trees at breakneck speeds that even the film's characters would marvel at.

Bus connections from Shanghai are notoriously complex: change in Anji city for one of the frequent taxis/tuk-tuks to the forest.

980 SAHARA DESERT, TUNISIA

Luke Skywalker's home planet, Tatooine, isn't really far, far away but in Tunisia's southern desert. Four *Star Wars* films used this area as a shoot location and the planet's name derives from a Tunisian town, Tataouine. For true *Star Wars* immersion, you can stay in Luke's house (OK, foster home), modern-day Hotel Sidi Driss (and dine in the Lars dining room). Obi-Wan Kenobi's abode is an abandoned hermitage on the island of Djerba. Of the film sets, that of Mos Espa – one of Tatooine's corrupt spaceports – remains impeccably intact, as bizarre looking today as when it graced the screen.

The pick of Tunisia's *Star Wars* sights could be the *ksour* (grain stores) in and around Medenine.

MOST SPECTACULAR HONEYMOON ADVENTURES

Getting loved up doesn't mean going slow.
Keep exploring together and finding new exhilaration
to get your hearts racing. Romance haters, look away now.

981 SKYDIVE WEDDING, IN LAS VEGAS, USA

Start your commitment off with an I doooo. OK, you can't actually get married midair, but you can tie the knot on the plane and then take a literal plunge. Or you can glide in gracefully (ish) on a parachute to give your vows on the ground amongst family and friends in the Nevada desert outside Las Vegas. Either way, all that pre-ceremony anxiety and edginess can be relieved with a joyous scream as you embark on the next stage of your adventure side by side, flying through the air.

For safety reasons, you and your betrothed leap into the atmosphere each strapped to an instructor, not to each other. For more details visit www. vegasextremeskydiving.com.

982 HOT-AIR BALLOONING IN BURGUNDY, FRANCE

For a more gentle adventure to share together, climb into a giant basket with your other half and soar over the forests and vineyards of France's Burgundy region. A glass of wine from the region is a must-have accessory while you take in a fairy-tale landscape of villages and rivers. It may feel exhilarating, but the ride is smooth and won't bring on motion sickness because the basket is stable. Instead there is a sense of freedom as you tickle the tops of trees and watch the sun rise or set.

Wear layers: warm clothing for landing and taking off but cooler clothing in the air to account for the burners. Rides tend to cost around $250 per person and last a few hours. See www.franceballoons.com.

983 HORSERIDING IN THE ATLAS MOUNTAINS IN MARRAKECH, MOROCCO

The arid harshness of the terrain around this massive range makes for a real challenge. The rocky plains and solemn mountains of Marrakech may seem unforgiving but there are great rewards: the living beauty of waterfalls, fresh-water springs and encounters with camels, monkeys and birds. As you travel on horseback from ancient Fez to a Berber village of clay huts, then on to a mountain lake, get some friendly competition going with your partner over who's the better rider.

Trips such as this can take from one to 10 days and involve up to eight hours of riding a day. See www.trekmorocco.com.

984 FLOAT IN THE DEAD SEA, JORDAN & ISRAEL

Sink or swim...you can't do either in the Dead Sea. The high salt content forces you to float on your back or fly like a superhero on its milky-blue surface. You'll feel romantically serene. People have been coming here for thousands of years for the health benefits (King David of Biblical fame was a regular) and reduced risk of UV skin damage, due to its location at the lowest point on Earth. The black mud gives your skin a reborn softness, but don't get it in your eyes or the sting is likely to make you sob in an unheroic way.

The best time to visit the Dead Sea is in the cooler months of October to April. For more information and operators, visit www.goisrael.com.

Relaxation and romance: naturally occurring in Iceland's Blue lagoon

985 SWIM THE BLUE LAGOON, ICELAND

This misty outdoor spa nestled in a lava field has the power to clean away past baggage. Well, it won't remove relationship ghosts but the mineral-rich waters will leave your skin feeling smooth and pure. Some even claim that the 37–39°C water cures skin complaints. The Blue Lagoon people know how lovey-dovey some partners can get when they're whisked off to this magical place and encourage it with tailored Romance for Couples packages that include an intimate dinner and a dip in the waters.

You must shower before and after bathing. The Blue Lagoon (www.bluelagoon.com) is a 40-minute drive from the Iceland's capital, Reykjavik, or 20 minutes from the main airport.

Guatemalan grandeur: celebrate your honeymoon by seeking out the 'Lost World' of the Mayans

986 DISCOVER THE LOST WORLD OF THE TIKAL PYRAMIDS, GUATEMALA

The Mayan temple ruins of Tikal are beautiful and mysterious – and a sure-fire romantic experience. You can't help but feel like an Old World explorer here as you find yourself in the depths of the jungle amongst howler monkeys, parrots, toucans and myriad other animals you've never seen before. Clamber up the steps of a pyramid with your partner – careful, they are very steep – for a view of the 'Lost World' of a Mayan epicentre that once thrived with prosperous trade over 1000 years ago.

The best time to visit Tikal is December to February, avoiding the heat of April to May and the rain of May to September.

987 CAVE-TUBING, BELIZE

Belize's utterly blue skies and swaying palms may be a recipe for an idyllic honeymoon, but for more thrills take the cave-tubing challenge at Nohoch Che'en Caves Branch. The water of this underground cave system may be chilly, but the sights are breathtaking. Illuminated by your headlamps are jagged stalactites and glittering crystalline formations, eyeless cavefish and artefacts from the Mayans. For a romantic edge, a sunset cave-tubing adventure is perfect, entering the caves at dusk, plunging through the darkness, then emerging to drift downriver under a panoply of stars and serenaded by the nocturnal choruses of the jungle.

Nohoch Che'en Caves Branch Archaeological Reserve is near Belmopan, an easy drive from Belize City. For more information, see www.cavetubing.bz.

988 IZUMO-TAISHA SHRINE, IZUMO, JAPAN

Clap your hands four times while praying at Japan's oldest Shinto shrine, twice for yourself and twice for the one whose heart you desire (even if you've already tied the knot with them). With luck, and a coin in the offering box, the god of marriage and happiness will bring joy and keep you two together in bliss and health. At the very least the sprawling, beautiful buildings of this temple will awaken your love for Japanese culture. Visit at festival times for extra happiness points.

The shrine is open every day and admission is free. You can walk there from the Izumo Taisha-mae train station. See www.jnto.go.jp/eng/location/spot/shritemp/izumotaisha

989 SWIM AT A NUDIST BEACH, SYDNEY

Australia's beaches have their best features on show in Sydney, where golden sand meets blue sky, clean surf and a relaxed culture. Lady Bay Beach is a secluded nudist beach and the perfect place to shed taboos and enjoy the warmth of the Aussie sun. Remember to slap extra sunblock on seldom-exposed skin. Cuddling is OK but anything more amorous is best kept for your hotel suite. Afterwards there is great outdoor dining within easy reach, or enjoy a post-nuptial champagne right on the beach with a classic sunset.

The best time to visit is from December to February when the sun is warmest.

990 CRUISE THE ARCTIC OF GREENLAND

The Arctic Circle is a wild land. It's a sight that most travellers don't get to experience in their lifetime but that's what keeps it so pristine. The icy landscape is mostly untainted by humans and their buildings, pollution or politics. Despite its name Greenland is a snow-white world in winter, dotted with polar bears, caribou and musk ox. You can take it all in while safe, snug and well-fed aboard your ship, ready for a glimpse of a humpback whale breaking through the water in the distance.

This indulgent luxury adventure can cost in the thousands of dollars. Tours run in the 'summer' (June to September). See www.arcticodysseys.com.

MOST SPECTACULAR HONEYMOON ADVENTURES

ADVENTURE OFF THE PAGE

Be inspired to great adventures that follow in the tracks of remarkable travellers or, failing that, settle down on the sofa with the book.

993 CYCLE INTO HIMACHAL PRADESH

The appalling winter of 1963 was the backdrop to a solo bike ride from Ireland to India undertaken by travel legend Dervla Murphy and recorded in her book *Full Tilt*. She had to contend with frozen mountain passes, thieves and attempted assault on her way to India. From Delhi, she cycled up to Dharamsala – home of the exiled Dalai Lama – where she volunteered for Save the Children. The ride from there into the Kullu Valley is an astonishing route for cycle tourists, leading to an ascent of the 3978m Rohtang Pass.

Fly into Delhi with your bike and then it's a five-day ride up to Kullu, but allow plenty of time to contend with the heat out of Delhi, the ascent past Chandigarh and then the altitude.

990 CLIMB IN THE FOOTSTEPS OF HILLARY AND TENZING

How is a corner of Britain connected to the first ascent of the world's highest peak? Snowdon, Wales's loftiest summit, played host to Hillary, Tenzing and other members of the 1953 Everest expedition (led by Sir John Hunt) as they trained for their epic climb. You can follow in their footsteps by tackling the classic Snowdon Horseshoe, which takes you over the knife-edge ridge of Crib Goch, onto the summit and down over neighbouring peak Y Lliwedd. If you're itching for more, the team also tested out their hiking boots on the Jungfraujoch and the Mönch in Switzerland...seems like a good excuse for a side-trip to the Alps.

Read about the 1953 expedition in Hunt's book *The Ascent of Everest*; when at Snowdon, visit the Pen-Y-Gwryd for a post-walk pint to see artefacts from the climb.

991 DISCOVER YOUR MOTORCYCLING ZEN

As an adventure *Zen and the Art of Motorcycle Maintenance* may not rate highly – it's the philosophical rather than adrenalin-fuelled content that made this such an influential book. But the route itself takes in an awesome slice of America, flowing from Minneapolis through the mountains of Montana and down through Idaho and Oregon onto the famous Pacific Coast Highway. Whether via car or motorbike, whether you've read the book or not, following in author Robert Pirsig's tyre tracks will serve up a USA that most do not experience. The original trip took Pirsig and his son 17 days back in 1968, so allow at least this much time to complete it.

Head online to find a number of Google maps of the full route annotated with pictures, route descriptions and even excerpts from the book.

994 GET THE BEST VIEW OF THE MATTERHORN

The Matterhorn looms over Zermatt but the tale of its first ascent casts a longer shadow. Edward Whymper was in the party that first made the summit in 1865, striking disaster on the way down when an inexperienced climber slipped, taking three others to their deaths. The route that Whymper wrote about in his book *Scrambles in the Alps* has now become the 'normal' line to the top and it's a classic Alpine ascent for experienced mountaineers. If you want to tackle your first Alpine climb, head to neighbouring peak the Breithorn for amazing views of the Matterhorn and a taste of altitude over 4000m.

Good acclimatisation, the right gear and mountaineering skills, including the ability to use ice axes and crampons, are essential to tackling the Breithorn.

995 CYCLE ACROSS SPAIN

In 1934, with only one phrase in Spanish and a violin, Laurie Lee set sail for Vigo then hiked across Spain into the arms of the Civil War. His book *As I Walked Out One Midsummer Morning* tells how he busked across the country, sleeping rough and discovering the generosity of its people. Ferries now operate from the UK to Santander or Bilbao, and from there a cycle tour over the Picos de Europa and then via cities like Salamanca, Madrid, Cordoba and Granada will give you a taste for Spain and its people while challenging your expectations.

Spain is surprisingly mountainous but an excellent place to explore by bike. Allow at least three weeks and book your return journey from Malaga airport.

996 TREK ACROSS SOUTH GEORGIA ISLAND

It is a contender for the greatest survival story of all time. Ernest Shackleton's expedition to cross the Antarctic ended when his ship *Endurance* was trapped in pack ice. His men were forced to survive on the frozen terrain for months before making two daring open-water voyages and the first recorded mountain crossing of South Georgia. It is a testament to his leadership that not one life was lost. You can follow in Shackleton's footsteps on an organised trek across South Georgia to whaling station Stromness. Shackleton returned to the island in 1922 where he suffered a heart attack and his grave lies there, in Grytviken.

Aurora Expeditions (www.aurora expeditions.com.au) offers the South Georgia trek. Pack a copy of *South*, Shackleton's own account of the *Endurance* expedition.

997 GO ON A VOYAGE OF DISCOVERY

Stuffy scientist or hardcore traveller? Charles Darwin spent five years on the HMS Beagle, but it's his five-week visit to the Galapagos and its association with his theory of natural selection that have given these islands near-mythical status. Exploring the 13 major islands that make up this group will bring you face to face with marine iguanas, rays, sharks and turtles and possibly even a giant tortoise. Or if you're looking for some high-adrenalin bird watching action, track down the tool-wielding woodpecker finch, flightless cormorant or Galapagos hawk.

Don't fancy a sea voyage to the Galapagos? You're in good company. In *The Voyage of the Beagle*, Darwin wrote: 'I loathe, I abhor the sea and all ships which sail on it'.

998 WALK THE ANNAPURNA CIRCUIT

The first team to climb an 8000m peak made the summit with poor mapping, no oxygen and bad weather, then on the descent lost gloves, were avalanched and hit by frostbite. Maurice Herzog lost his fingers in the incident and had to dictate, rather than type, his book *Annapurna*. If all that puts you off attempting your first 8000m peak, then try the Annapurna circuit. It will take you up to 5416m over roughly three weeks of walking through spectacular Himalayan terrain and deliver a sense of journey like no other. Considered Nepal's finest trek, you'll discover picturesque villages, spectacular mountain views and get access to excellent trekking lodges.

Side trips to places like Manang, Muktinath and Jomsom add time but are some of the highlights of the route.

999 DISCOVER A SILENT WORLD

Jacques Cousteau introduced millions to the wonders of the sea during his prolific career. His first book, *The Silent World*, documents his development of the aqualung that liberated modern divers and describes underwater wildlife and discovery in lyrical detail. You can experience this sense of adventure for yourself on courses around the world. Thailand's Koh Tao is a popular place to start and boasts some superb diving. Expect to see turtles, manta rays and clown fish, while gently gliding above colourful reefs and learning the art of neutral buoyancy.

Easy to get to and inexpensive to stay in, Koh Tao is a hugely popular location for divers. You can avoid the crowds off-season from April to October.

1000 DISCOVER PERU'S FINEST ALPINE TREK

A disastrous descent off the summit of Siula Grande (6344m) left climber Joe Simpson dangling in midair with a broken leg, and his climbing partner with no choice but to cut the rope. The story of how Simpson clambered out of a crevasse and crawled across the glacier to safety became part of mountaineering legend with the publication of his *Touching the Void*. The mountain is a serious undertaking, but this area is home to some of the best alpine trekking in the world, offering serrated snowy summits, crystal-blue lakes, knife-edge ridges and opportunities to connect with local communities.

May to September is the best time to trek here; find a knowledgeable guide in the local villages.

INDEX

A

Afghanistan **40**
Algeria **259, 301**
American Samoa **279**
Antarctica **11, 21, 31, 113, 145, 205, 282, 333**
Argentina **27, 42, 53, 79, 82, 93, 95, 104, 111, 171, 188, 214, 236, 249, 273, 291**
Australia **10, 21, 25, 47, 48, 51, 56-7, 61, 68, 75, 83, 93, 101, 102, 115, 118, 123, 126, 134, 146, 151, 155, 168, 173, 178, 186, 193, 196, 208, 229, 238, 243, 247, 251, 252, 264, 267, 268, 269, 275, 287, 295, 306, 317, 321, 322, 326**
   Great Barrier Reef 339
   Kakadu National Park 237
   Melbourne 175, 311
   Sydney 131, 160, 347
   Uluru 112
Austria **28, 77, 92, 256**

B

Bahamas **89**
Bahrain **308**
Bangladesh **231**
Belize **38, 284, 347**
Bhutan **73**
Bolivia **120, 135, 142, 197**
Borneo **165, 339**
Bosnia and Hercegovina **213, 300**
Botswana **47, 63, 79, 231, 249, 259, 267**
Brazil **53, 79, 121, 197, 211, 232, 249**
   Rio de Janeiro 40, 129, 160, 315
British Virgin Islands **77, 195**
Burma **197, 299**
Burundi **327**

C

Cambodia **115, 232**
Canada **28, 37, 44, 48, 49, 53, 63, 74, 83, 96, 101, 106, 122, 139, 141, 153, 157, 179, 188, 197, 198, 199, 206, 208, 232, 239, 240, 242, 249, 252, 256, 267, 273, 287, 291, 307, 317**
   Calgary 223
   Toronto 174, 297
   Vancouver 163
Central African Republic **117**
Chechnya **41**
Chile **53, 68, 73, 104, 142, 156, 182, 243, 249, 256, 321**
   Easter Island 235
   Tierra del Fuego 236
China **50, 65, 101, 112, 150, 151, 164, 165, 248, 249, 282, 292, 295, 296, 318, 343**
   Bogota 175

Corsica **57**
Costa Rica **47, 57, 69, 71, 117, 136, 149, 188, 223, 245, 266, 331, 336**
Croatia **153, 317**
Cuba **96, 195**
Czech Republic **82, 334**

D

Democratic Republic of Congo **40, 164**
Denmark **177**
   Copenhagen 309
Dominica **59, 284, 343**

E

Ecuador **37, 85, 92, 95, 117, 137, 214, 287, 326**
Egypt **21, 166, 173, 213, 225, 226, 260, 286, 337**
England **25, 69, 77, 80, 92, 103, 111, 121, 122, 126, 130, 149, 150, 177, 199, 209, 232, 239, 247, 292, 295, 311, 317**
   London 103, 160, 175, 228
Ethiopia **37, 145, 229**

F

Fiji **153, 267, 268**
Finland **42, 229**
France **16, 29, 44, 68, 75, 83, 93, 121, 126, 130, 141, 173, 178, 179, 189, 200, 203, 209, 229, 239, 256, 267, 275, 277, 289, 305, 318, 320, 331**
   Chamonix 201
   Paris 103
French Polynesia **284, 341**

G

Germany **73, 82, 178, 207**
   Berlin 130, 162, 175
   Munich 203
Ghana **261**
   Accra 315
Greece **53, 87**
   Athens 113
   Kalymnos 50
Greenland **42, 145, 155, 207, 347**
Guatemala **117, 347**
Guinea **116**

H

Haiti **299**
Honduras **41**
Hong Kong **130, 163**
Hungary **317**

I

Iceland **72-3, 85, 286, 339, 345**
India **27, 38, 43, 49, 76, 79, 99, 135, 164, 172, 180-1, 211, 216, 267, 321, 324, 348**
Indonesia **67, 86, 116, 165, 264, 330**
   Bali 67, 335
Iran **226**
Iraq **41, 248**
Iraqi Kurdistan **301**

Ireland **16, 63, 213, 245**
Isle of Man **183**
Israel **18, 225, 344**
Italy **29, 121, 123, 125, 129, 141, 183, 200, 221, 243, 246, 251, 273, 275, 276, 306, 321**
   Venice 80

J

Jamaica **113, 137**
Japan **22-3, 27, 55, 93, 106, 136, 157, 193, 213, 255, 273, 337, 340, 347**
   Tokyo 308
Jordan **34, 227, 343, 344**

K

Kenya **113, 136, 151, 260**
Kiribati **264**
Kyrgyzstan **248**

L

Laos **66, 146**
Lebanon **225, 301**
Lesotho **118, 135**

M

Macau **67**
Madagascar **260**
Malaysia **25, 39, 287, 296**
   Kuala Lumpur 89, 174
Maldives **31**
Mali **37, 70**
   Timbuktu 235
Mexico **15, 17, 98, 107, 110, 150, 208, 339**
   Acapulco 90
Micronesia **341**
Mongolia **18, 62, 164, 196, 315**
Montserrat **85**
Morocco **100, 137, 159, 261, 329, 344**
Myanmar **299**

N

Namibia **19, 39, 63, 120, 209, 259, 295**
Nepal **13, 25, 31, 32, 59, 67, 72, 116, 140, 165, 188, 209, 214, 216, 240, 250, 296-7, 305, 318, 323**
Netherlands **203**
   Amsterdam 315
New Zealand **32, 44, 53, 73, 86, 92, 93, 104, 111, 118, 138, 147, 151, 154, 165, 173, 177, 187, 199, 209, 220-1, 236, 245, 252, 268, 271, 283, 291, 306, 323**
   Auckland 163
   Queenstown 272
   Wellington 143
Nicaragua **85, 239, 298-9**
Niue **268**
North Korea **249**
Norway **103, 122, 135, 155, 181, 187, 203, 233, 247, 272, 291**
   Tromsø 112, 158

O

Oman **107, 110, 158**

P

Pakistan **40, 52, 132, 137, 217, 249, 318**
Palau **271**
Palestinian Territories **225**
Panama **41**
Papua New Guinea **39, 115**
Peru **19, 95, 101, 243, 249, 326, 342, 349**
Philippines **108, 164, 169**
Portugal **16, 81**
Puerto Rico **331**

Q

Qatar **226**

R

Réunion **59**
Russia **35, 44, 45, 79, 85, 100, 132, 156, 182, 217, 248, 272, 293**
Rwanda **156, 299**

S

Saudi Arabia **21**
   Mecca 212
Scotland **25, 30, 42, 68, 70, 83, 90, 93, 98, 106, 112, 123, 128, 136, 138, 195, 239, 246, 273, 305**
   Edinburgh 163
Seychelles **168**
Singapore **101**
Slovakia **111**
Slovenia **69, 188**
South Africa **15, 46, 49, 77, 106, 108, 127, 187, 223, 276, 296, 328**
   Cape Town 130, 162
South Korea **249**
   Seoul 102
Spain **58, 83, 202, 211, 239, 273, 282, 337, 349**
Sri Lanka **90-1, 170, 178, 213, 324, 330**
St Maarten **30**
Sweden **151, 152, 170**
Switzerland **29, 34, 44, 75, 89, 113, 122, 137, 200, 202, 288-9**

T

Tahiti **15, 59, 326**
Taiwan
   Taipei 174, 228
Tanzania **35, 87, 137, 150, 215, 259, 327**
   Zanzibar 236
Thailand **65, 69, 101, 151, 221, 287, 316, 349**
Tibet **30, 101, 212, 235**
Tunisia **343**
Turkey **58-9, 227, 248, 325**
   Cappadocia 32
   İstanbul 105, 342
   Ölüdeniz 35

Colombia **41, 221, 249, 301, 333**
   Bogota 175

U

Uganda 49, 342
Ukraine 301
  Chernobyl 301
United Arab Emirates
  Abu Dhabi 18, 121
  Dubai 191, 308
United States of America 18, 23,
24, 26, 28, 52, 57, 63, 69, 77, 79,
82, 83, 89, 91, 96, 106, 109, 113,
124, 140, 141, 147, 149, 158, 173,
176, 183, 191, 197, 198, 199, 208,
209, 216, 228, 229, 231, 238, 242,
246, 249, 252, 254, 256, 271, 272,
277, 278, 279, 280, 281, 289, 290,
291, 292, 305, 306, 310, 311, 321,
332, 333, 337
  Alaska 12, 133, 172, 180, 206,
    231, 279, 322
  Albuquerque 123
  Chicago 174
  Grand Canyon 35, 71, 97
  Hawaii 15, 31, 80, 86, 95, 159,
    191, 222, 329
  Las Vegas 223, 311, 344
  Los Angeles 102, 103
  New York City 103, 129, 175
  Phoenix 163
  Santa Fe 335
Uzbekistan 235

V

Vanuatu 90, 223
Vatican City 145
Vietnam 37, 66, 67, 126, 183
  Ho Chi Minh City 175

W

Wales 25, 200, 229, 277

Y

Yemen 226

Z

Zambia 35, 107, 231, 241, 249,
327
Zimbabwe 231, 241

SIGHTS & ACTIVITIES

SUBINDEX

abseiling 118, 187, 305, 306, 317
birdwatching 30, 37, 79, 80, 126, 153, 165, 264-7, 281
boat trips 10, 49, 166-9, 219, 232, 235, 284, 323, 333, 337
bodyboarding 191
bouldering 53, 74-7, 189, 305
bungee jumping 67, 90, 118, 202, 283, 296, 311
camel rides 151, 172, 173, 225, 261
canoeing 147, 199, 231, 246
canyoning 18, 56-9, 89, 226
caving 55, 108-11, 347
climbing 50-3, 65, 90, 128-31, 200, 238, 304-7
cycling 82-3, 96, 124-7, 176-9, 239, 274-7, 315, 318-21, 332
diving 89, 95, 226, 338-41
festivals 122-3, 229
flights 30-1
heli-skiing 207, 239, 254, 255, 256
horse riding 60-3, 171, 238, 245, 260, 315
hot-air ballooning 32, 34, 295, 332, 344
indoor adventures 308-11
jungles 67, 114-17
kayaking 66, 152-5, 238, 260, 333
marine encounters 268-71
motorcycle journeys 180-3
mountain biking 120, 138-41
mountains 22-5, 136-7

movies 184-5
nocturnal adventures 54-5
nude adventures 282-3
paragliding 32, 333
parks 278-81
pilgrimages 210-13
racing 68-9
rafting 97, 117, 227, 240-3, 316
road trips 132-5
running 112-13, 208-9, 246, 315
sandboarding 120
skateboarding 191, 309
skiing 11, 26-9, 44-5, 54, 93, 96, 103, 122, 198, 203, 247, 254-7, 289, 291, 308, 333
skydiving 35, 118, 283, 296-7, 311, 344
skysurfing 89
snorkelling 49, 95, 110, 164, 195, 269, 271, 279, 284-7, 330, 335
solo adventures 332-3
surfing 14-17, 67, 95, 116, 198, 239, 328-31
swimming 104-7
train rides 98-101
treasure hunting 194-7
trekking 70-3, 82-3, 250-1
tribal encounters 36-9
volcanoes 31, 84-7
walking 32, 65, 160-3, 199, 214-17, 288-91
waterfalls 35, 113, 136, 181, 187, 188, 249, 337
wildlife spotting 46-9, 95, 104, 146-9, 150-1, 164-5, 230-3, 258
windsurfing 193
zip-lining 115, 146, 149, 188, 220-3, 336
zorbing 121, 187

1000 ULTIMATE ADVENTURES

SEPTEMBER 2013

PUBLISHED BY

Lonely Planet Publications Pty Ltd
ABN 36 005 607 983
90 Maribyrnong St, Footscray,
Victoria, 3011, Australia
www.lonelyplanet.com

10 9 8 7 6 5 4 3 2 1
Printed in China.
ISBN 978 1 74321 719 1
© Lonely Planet 2013
© Photographers as indicated 2013

LONELY PLANET OFFICES

AUSTRALIA Locked Bag 1, Footscray, Victoria, 3011
Phone 03 8379 8000 Fax 03 8379 8111
Email talk2us@lonelyplanet.com.au

USA 150 Linden St, Oakland, CA 94607
Phone 510 250 6400 Toll free 800 275 8555 Fax 510 893 8572
Email info@lonelyplanet.com

UK Media Centre, 201 Wood Lane, London,
W12 7TQ
Phone 020 8433 1333 Fax 020 8702 0112
Email go@lonelyplanet.co.uk

IMAGES

Front cover images (from left to right)
Antony Spencer | Getty Images: Aurora borealis, the Arctic;
Predrag Vuckovic | Getty Images: snorkelling; Klaus
Brandstaetter | Getty Images: sandboarding, Namibia;
Jean-Luc Armand | Getty Images: paragliding, Chamonix

ACKNOWLEDGEMENTS

Publishing Director Piers Pickard
Publisher Ben Handicott
Commissioning Editor Will Gourlay
Designer Mik Ruff
Coordinating Layout Designer Frank Deim
Assisting Layout Designers Wibowo Rusli,
Joseph Spanti, Wendy Wright
Coordinating Editor Elizabeth Jones
Editors Catherine Naghten, Justin Flynn
Image Researchers Aude Vauconsant, Gerard Walker
Pre-Press Production Ryan Evans
Print Production Larissa Frost

WRITTEN BY

Brett Atkinson
Kate Armstrong
Andrew Bain
Robin Barton
Sarah Baxter
Greg Benchwick
Joe Bindloss
Paul Bloomfield
Catherine Bodry
Lucy Burningham
Jean-Bernard Carillet
Ethan Gelber
Sam Haddad
Virginia Jealous
Pat Kinsella
Jessica Lee
Kate Rew
Caroline Sieg
Matt Swaine
Phillip Tang
Ross Taylor
Jonathan Thompson
Steve Waters
Luke Waterson
Jasper Winn
Karla Zimmerman

THANKS TO

Liz Abbott, Sasha Baskett, Robin Barton, Helvi Cranfield,
Chris Girdler, Jane Hart, Darren O'Connell, Rebecca Skinner